BARING BROTHERS AND THE
BIRTH OF MODERN FINANCE

BARING BROTHERS AND THE BIRTH OF MODERN FINANCE

BY

Peter E. Austin

Routledge
Taylor & Francis Group

LONDON AND NEW YORK

First published 2007 by Pickering & Chatto (Publishers) Limited

Published 2016 by Routledge
2 Park Square, Milton Park, Abingdon, Oxfordshire OX14 4RN
711 Third Avenue, New York, NY 10017, USA

First issued in paperback 2015

Routledge is an imprint of the Taylor & Francis Group, an informa business

BRITISH LIBRARY CATALOGUING IN PUBLICATION DATA
Austin, Peter E.
Baring Brothers and the birth of modern finance
1. Baring Brothers & Co. Ltd – History 2. Merchant banks – Great Britain – History 3. Banks and banking, International – Great Britain – History
I. Title
332.6'6'0941

ISBN-13: 978-1-138-66356-5 (pbk)
ISBN-13: 978-1-8519-6922-7 (hbk)
Typeset by Pickering & Chatto (Publishers) Limited

CONTENTS

LIST OF CHARTS, TABLES AND FIGURES

NOMENCLATURE

Capitalized 'House' refers to Baring Brothers and to other financial institutions.

'American Houses' refers to specific British merchant banks having large interests in the United States. Though global, Baring Brothers was an 'American House' for the period of this book.

Capitalized 'Bank' refers to the Bank of the United States or the Bank of England.

Threadneedle Street refers to the Bank of England, and reflects an address.

CHRONOLOGY

1763	Baring Brothers & Company established at Exeter and London. Peace of Paris ends Seven Years War.
1777	Francis Baring assumes management of the firm.
1796–1803	Alexander Baring (later Lord Ashburton) tours the United States.
1798	House of Rothschild establishes a presence in England.
1803	Louisiana Purchase.
1810	Alexander Baring assumes leadership of the House.
1814	Barings acquires Hope & Company. Treaty of Ghent (Belgium) ends British-American war (December).
1815	Congress of Vienna ends war in Europe.
1816	Argentina declares independence from Spain. Second Bank of the United States chartered.
1817–19	French reconstruction loans.
1821	Mexico becomes an independent state.
1823	President James Monroe appoints Nicholas Biddle president of Second Bank; closes American continent to colonial settlements by European powers (Monroe Doctrine).
1824	Erie Canal completed in the United States.
1825	American gross national product tops $1 billion for first time.
1825–6	Financial panic; Rothschild assists Bank of England.
1827	Alexander Baring hires Joshua Bates.
1828	Second Baring partnership formed; Thomas Baring tours United States. Andrew Jackson ('Old Hickory') elected seventh United States president. Business cycle trough.
1829	Jonathan Goodhue recommends Thomas Wren Ward for Baring agency.
1830	Belgian difficulties. France captures Algiers. Year of revolutions across Europe.
1831	Belgium crisis. Polish rebellion. Ward remarks to Bates that severe problems develop every '5–7 years'.
1832	English Reform Bill. Liverpool to Manchester Railroad opens. Jackson vetoes Bank of the United States charter. South Carolina nullification; 'compromise tariff' (Daniel Webster's 'pretty little bill').

Barings' Liverpool office opens, booms; Bates calls '3Ws' envious.
Barings' agreement with Russell & Company in Canton (Houqua).
Biddle arranges for Barings to lead Union Bank of Louisiana floatation.
House of Representatives reports Bank of the United States more solvent than Bank of England.

1833   French indemnity problems.
Calcutta indigo 'Great Houses' fail.
Belgium festers.
Bank of England rechartered.
Deposits moved from Bank of the United States to 'pet banks' (Kendall).
Unusual rise in the American cotton price: Rothschilds corner?
Ward restless with Baring rules.
Barings' first American trimming.

1834   Financial pressure; Biddle clamps down.
Webster describes United States economy 'Like a strong man chained'.
Gold Coinage Act (August).
East India Company monopoly abolished.

1835   Transatlantic boom; American demand unleashed.
United States government switches account agency to N. M. Rothschild.
United States federal debt extinguished.
Ward concerned about American import surge ('imbalances correct themselves').
Barings' China relationships yield results; purchases/builds ships.
Ward explores Canadian business opportunities.
Union Bank warning: Bates apprehensive; Baring syndicates state loans.
Barings sells Maine lands acquired by Ashburton in 1796.
Bates detects psychology shift; lower prices.
Barings' second American trimming (Ward: 'top of a wave, takes care in descending').
New York fire (December).

1836   French indemnity problem solved; war averted.
Hezekiah Niles becomes bullish.
Surplus Distribution Act (June).
Urban real estate boom; public land boom; railroad share floatation boom.
'3Ws' reported to be accommodating freely.
Bates and legacy.
Specie Circular (July) – 'specie moving about the country like bills of exchange!'.
Bank of England detects over-discounting among American houses; raises bank rate (August).
Bank of England indiscreet letter to Liverpool (September).
British joint-stock bank failures (November).
The Times warns of very fragile American situation: cotton fall?
Bates advises Bank of England; Biddle strengthens ties to Barings.
Jackson's eighth State of the Union address.

1837   British prices break in the first quarter; American in the second quarter.
Continental banks tighten in response to Bank of England.
Herman & Briggs fails in New Orleans; Josephs in New York (March).

Bank of England assist '3Ws' and Brown Brothers (March).

Martin Van Buren inaugurated eighth president of the United States.

Biddle and New York banks look for liquidity (substitute credit of the Bank of the United States for private credit); Barings as underwriter of London offering (April).

Liverpool and London waits for remittances.

Van Buren refuses accommodation on Specie Circular (May).

New York banks suspend (May).

Loco-Foco backlash against 'Barings and Biddle Bank'.

Bank of England refuses further aid to American Houses (June).

Victoria becomes Queen of England (June).

Biddle attempts to corner cotton market; improve American balance of payments.

1838	American states aggressively market debt in London; *The Times* sceptical.

Barings cuts ties to Biddle.

New York Herald is first United States newspaper to employ European correspondents.

Barings guarantees gold to United States in effort to reinflate American economy.

1839–42	First Opium War.
1839–43	Depression in the United States (debt defaults by states).

Ward coordinates campaign to effect state debt repayment (1839–40).

Barings syndicates loans to Bank of the United States on European bourses (1839).

Barings manages Bank of France loan (1839).

1842	Webster-Ashburton Treaty defines Canadian frontier.
1846	Repeal of British Corn Laws.

Mexican War in the United States begins.

1848	Year of revolutions in Europe.
1856–60	Second Opium War.
1858	First transatlantic telegraph communications.
1861–5	American Civil War.
1867	Confederation of Canada.
1873	Edward Baring (later Lord Revelstoke) assumes leadership of the House.
1886	Baring Brothers floats Guinness & Company shares.
1888	Revelstoke takes Buenos Aires Drainage & Waterworks shares.
1890	Baring Crisis; Bank of England assists (Lidderdale).
1965	Singapore becomes an independent republic.
1996	'Big Bang' deregulates London Stock Exchange.
1989	Peter Baring appointed Chairman of Baring Group; Barings hires Nicholas Leeson ('a clerk').
1992	Leeson sent to Singapore to manage floor operations and back office of SIMEX.
1993	Christopher Heath fired; Barings Brothers Bank & Baring Securities combine.
1994	Leeson wins 'Trader of the Year' award.
1995	Leeson flies to Thailand (22 February).

Barings collapses under £869 million liability; sold to ING (27 February).

1999	Leeson released from Singapore jail; returns to England (3 July).

There is a mystery about Barings
that time alone must unravel.

James Morrison (London) to Richard Alsop (Philadelphia), 5 May 1837,
Morrison Cryder Papers, Guildhall Library, London, MS 11,720, folder 1

INTRODUCTION

The Republic has Degenerated into a Democracy!

'Richmond Whig'[1]

Nobody cares a damn for the House of Lords. The House of Commons is everything in England, and the House of Lords is nothing.

The Duke of Wellington[2]

This is the story of the financial panic of 1837 and its remarkable outcome for the British merchant bank Baring Brothers & Company. It is the story of a bank's response to unusual events during the transformation of American life in the 1830s, and the effect of this transformation on Barings and global finance long term.

Events of the 1830s took place amidst changes that began before the French Revolution, and accelerated in England, Continental Europe, the United States and elsewhere around the world with the end of the Napoleonic Wars.

The years 1770–1815 put in place that clutch of marvels of the Industrial Revolution involving textiles, steam, patent protection, coal, machines and factories that made Great Britain the first nation in history to achieve sustained economic growth. The French Revolution started the process in France to sweep away privilege that would give that country a politics sufficiently liberal to follow a growth path similar to England's. When the long eighteenth century came to peace in 1815, the energy and talents of so many – distracted by war for so long – were freed, and the world could pursue in full measure those aspects of industry, technology and trade that peace allowed.

Free from war in Europe, the western powers scrambled for land worldwide, and human activity spread to all quarters of the globe. Russia expanded to the south and east. Canadians and Americans went west. Britain committed itself to India and the subcontinent, fortified its wartime base at Singapore and thrust inland from coastal enclaves in South Africa and Australia to create in rough form the nations we see today. The Dutch continued their turbulent presence in Indonesia after the war, and established a small commercial settlement at Nagasaki in the 1820s. France captured Algiers in 1830 to begin its African empire, and

1

considered expansion of its settlements in south-east Asia. Even the north and south poles saw a string of explorations in the immediate post-Napoleonic years. Advances in ship design and engineering, railroads, and the telegraph made geographical expansion more possible than ever before, and helped overcome what the Australian historian Geoffrey Blainey called 'the tyranny of distance'.[3]

Changes were palpable. But they paled against the coming of the greatest theme of the age: democracy. In the first half of the nineteenth century, agitation for political reform stirred monarchies and parliaments across almost all Europe. Newspapers multiplied as an outward and visible sign of a widening freedom of expression. In 1830, Paris alone supported six dailies; London nine. The slave trade in the Atlantic and Indian oceans was stopped by law and by the vigilance of the British fleet. With the coming of peace, reform spread to economics. The case for free trade which Adam Smith made famous in 1776 could now be turned into policies which, by the 1840s, unlocked new commercial opportunities throughout Asia and the Atlantic world.[4]

While Europe bubbled, the greatest theatre of democracy was the Americas. Independence movements throughout the Latin world set back the imperial states Portugal and Spain after 1815, and stood out as examples of decolonization in an age of empire-building. But in the first decades of the nineteenth century, most eyes focused on the large and restless United States developing north of Mexico which, until 1815, had been moulded largely by forces from Europe, and would now set its own course.

Few were more interested in the progress of the United States than Baring Brothers & Company. First a merchant house, then a bank, Barings had built a high reputation since its founding in 1763. Its aspirations were as global as the British Empire, and this included the growing market of the United States – colony or not. Its involvement was at first professional, then familial with the marriage of two partners into Philadelphia society in 1798 and 1802. When it was an emerging market at the start of the nineteenth century – as China, India or Brazil are today – the American Union was a slapdash mix of risk and reward. And Barings experienced both in a relationship that lasted for a remarkable 200 years.

The House did not cause or directly prompt the industrial, political and economic forces unleashed after 1815. Instead, Barings was an unusually successful example of a new breed of merchant-turned-banker who quietly provided the credit instruments that turned the wheels of investment, commerce and innovation. Barings epitomized British confidence after 1815 and many viewed Britain itself as the model of what a successful nation might be. After Napoleon, Britain stood alone, possessed of a financial and industrial paramountcy that, for a time, was unique; and in the nineteenth century most of world trade and finance went through London in one form or another.

Barings committed formally to the American market in the form of a new partnership in 1828. By this time, the United States had transformed itself from a struggling ex-colony to a nation on the move – curious to Europeans and the world for its vigour and style, and for its experiment in republican government. By 1828 the United States was well into an industrial revolution of its own which would match and later exceed Britain's in scope and scale; and it made sense in the nineteenth century that Barings would ride – indeed facilitate by finance – the wave of progress and change wherever it might lead.

To match the economic exuberance of the young nation, the late 1820s saw the rise of a new kind of American to political power. In the four years after 1824 vast numbers of voters, many with little or no property, were added to the electoral roles in the United States, and these new participants in the political process elected General Andrew Jackson their president by a large margin in 1828. Not only did this end the elite Virginia-Massachusetts line of presidents since Washington, it swept Jackson into office with a mandate for reform unprecedented in the history of the American republic to that time. The kind of man that an Adams or a Jefferson or a Baring called unlettered and ill-suited to rule, was the same man that President Jackson – this 'Napoleon from the Woods', this 'Old Hickory' – called honest, virtuous and wise. Out were the genteel politics comfortable to European sensibilities. In was a more abrupt, ordinary, levelling, boisterous and practical pattern. Moreover, this democracy of the common man was coupled with a muscular American assertion of rights on the world stage that would grow ever more confident as the nineteenth century progressed.

In the main, the United States turned from the trappings of aristocratic leadership in 1828 just as Barings increased its commitment. Welcome or alarming, democracy at this time became the permanent engine of American expansion and growth at home and abroad. It became the unmistakable fact of the American scene and – to the extent the United States set a sort of 'rough and tumble' standard and style in economics, politics or finance outside its borders – it became an unmistakable fact on the world scene as well.

This study of the Panic of 1837 illustrates part of the tidal wave of change after 1815. It is also a contribution to the Jackson literature with a much-needed foreign view of America in the 1830s, and a look at the financial aspects of these years in a global context. It is a work of history relevant to international business and management as an example of a superb business institution adjusting – or not adjusting – its approach to changing events, information and norms.

But it all began with a question: how the pre-eminent British bank of the time, Baring Brothers, managed to avoid significant harm from the terrible troubles of 1837 – indeed to emerge with increased prestige and influence – when others did not. Specifically, it seeks to find when and for what reasons the bank decided to pull back from its commitments in the United States. Importantly, this book also contrasts the success of the House during the 1830s with that of the House in later years, when Barings encountered great difficulties and finally collapsed from mismanagement, hubris, ignorance and nonchalance.[5] By a close-up view of what happened in the 1830s it hopes to illustrate larger themes.

Economic events, that is to say, 'what' happened in the 1830s in the United States, are not at issue historically. An inflation developed in the early part of the decade, after two decades of falling prices. Prices rose moderately from roughly the first quarter of 1830 to the fourth quarter of 1833, then backed off in a mild contraction in 1834. American commodity prices then rose sharply for two years, as did urban real estate, exchange-traded securities, the number of state-authorized bond issues, slaves and, in the last stages, money itself.

The years 1835–6 were characterized in the United States by what may be called a boom psychology – for example in public land sales. The psychology followed a common panic pattern, generically described as follows: after a period of some restraint (1833–4), new profit opportunities are perceived (1835–6), and people move to take advantage of them. This stimulates business, and various forms of credit come into play (e.g. bank notes, bills of exchange, hypothecated bank deposits) to enable people desiring to borrow to do so. At a certain point, some kind of shock or 'displacement' occurs that changes expectations as to a given set of investments.[6] Business euphoria, credit expansion and speculation falter (gradually or all at once) because it becomes clear to a few, then later to many, that credit positions are extended beyond what are sustainable in the long run. The objective becomes to preserve any gains one has to this point, and usually involves getting out of whatever assets one owns before others do. The end of 'overtrading', in Adam Smith's word, was followed by what Smith called 'convulsion', or in current finance parlance, 'distress'. In this study, the latter occurred with a vengeance, as the financial events of 1837 (panic) became the deflationary economic events of the years 1839–43 (depression).[7]

In the 1830s the troubles were transatlantic, indeed international, though the focus of the present study is Great Britain and the United States. The British displacement occurred when the Bank of England discovered that four merchant banks, nominally under its supervision, had extended themselves a bit too far in the American trade. The Bank moved to restrain credit in the summer of 1836, having a great effect on the fortunes of the firms to which the British Houses were connected in the United States. Though made nervous by the Bank of England's action, Americans did not move to topple the United States boom right away. The American displacement came later from the failure of several New Orleans cotton commission Houses in March 1837.

The problem of 'what' happened as to the panic is settled. The actual etiology of the panic – the 'why' – is less so. The years of the Jackson presidency (1829–37) were ones of bitter political partisanship, and years indeed went by before a dispassionate historical account was penned. Most twentieth-century studies stress one or more internal American factors as the panic's cause – the veto of the recharter bill, the deposits removal, the proliferation of banks, the 'Specie Circular', the Distribution Act to allocate the federal surplus – in general, the policies of the Jackson administration.[8] More recent studies claim these political problems are overemphasized in explaining the inflation of the 1830s, and look rather at the Anglo-American trade system within the larger world economy, including supplies of specie, and conditions in the international capital market.

Contributions by economists and economic historians Walter Buckingham Smith, Peter Temin and Hugh Rockoff emphasized global influence and balanced the explanations that focused mainly on the domestic side.[9] Added to the rocky domestic scene of Jacksonian politics and banking reform initiatives in England, these later accounts detail the evolution of new patterns of capital flows in the early 1830s that involved trade credits between the United States and Great Britain, and changes in specie flow patterns to and from China and Mexico. The combination of so-called 'real factors' (Jacksonian politics) and monetary ones (specie and money flows) caused a destabilized situation in the late 1830s.

The questions of what happened, and why, are provided here for historiographical context. The present study, however, is concerned with these considerations only as they affected what contemporaries thought, and what made them act the way they did. In these terms, Baring Brothers certainly paid close attention to the 'real factors' such as Jackson administration policies, but as a bank of international scope and commitments, the 'monetary factors' of flows of money, specie and credit were givens as well. The prime consideration was always survival in a business that Barings' American agent considered 'inherently hazardous'.

Though not literally hazardous of course, unravelling past events in business history is nonetheless difficult – financial history particularly so. In contrast to those of other fields, personalities attracted to commerce and money tend not to be as expressive, impressionistic or prone to lengthy description in the sense they tend to see value in action rather than thinking. There are exceptions of course, but there is a reason why a favourite aphorism of the notoriously terse Pierpont Morgan was the Provençal phrase: *pense moult, parle peu, écris rien* ('think a lot, say little, write nothing'). The high-stakes business of merchant banking required strict confidentiality and discretion.

Nevertheless, the historian intent on getting at answers is sometimes left only with the third item of Morgan's triplet. Certainly this is the case with Barings, in whose correspondence there tend to be many actions but few explanations; many orders, but little theory or elaborated reasons of actions. The present author has, therefore, taken what he has described as an 'aspirin approach'. That is to say, like drug action, one may see a striking effect or outcome, perhaps repeatedly, but not know the reasons for such results. Therefore, in the 1830s, while six other British merchant banks required assistance from the Bank of England, Barings did not. We know this is true, but are not sure why. Indeed, we know Barings was healthy

enough to coordinate a rescue of ailing banks. But the evidence for Barings' moti-
vation is circumstantial and fragmentary, and must be pieced together.

This investigative approach is very different from other historical studies of
Baring Brothers, of which there are three of note. Ralph Hidy's *The House of
Baring in American Trade and Finance* (1949) is a meticulous account of Barings
in the United States to 1861. Philip Ziegler's *The Sixth Great Power* (1988) is
Barings' official history, and an elegant survey of the House from its founding to
1929. John Orbell's *Baring Brothers and Co. Limited. A History to 1939* (1985)
is a slim but highly-informed volume by the current archivist of ING Barings in
London. All provide masterful descriptive overviews of the House, but few provide reasons for partner decision-making. This is what the present study attempts
to do. It magnifies one episode within the House's long history – albeit a pressurized one – and seeks to explain in detail what the partners believed and why
they behaved as they did.

In this regard, this book will argue four reasons for Barings' pull-back from
the United States before the 1837 downturn. These weave as themes through
the chronological text. First, Barings was uneasy about the democratic administration of Andrew Jackson, and what they considered to be a disruptive lack of
propriety developing in the United States – different in spirit from earlier days
of doing business in America. Second, the firm had an instinctual sense of caution and conservatism about it. The London partner most in charge of American
affairs, Joshua Bates, appears to have possessed the personal quality of 'changing
before he had to'. This resulted in acting too early at times, but allowed the firm
to maintain initiative and control. Others, more propelled by circumstances, were
surprised by the suddenness of events. They lost control or transferred control
to someone else – in our case, the Bank of England. Historical caution and conservatism kept the firm in good stead in the 1830s but, as we shall see, doomed
their ultimate leadership in the rough-and-tumble American market, and indeed
the world, longer term.

Third, this study posits that the firm pulled back from the United States simply because they were able to do so. Barings' operations had terrific geographical
spread. The United States, though important, was not its only venue. In this
regard, the House of Rothschild was similar. It was fabulously successful yet did
not commit to the United States until relatively late. Though chary about Latin
America in this period, Barings' diversification efforts into South Asia, Canada
and the Far East are clear.

The fourth reason for Barings' American pull-back had to do with the issue of
maintaining continuity from one generation of partners to another. Continuity
translated into a sense of legacy, and a created a gentle pressure to perform hon-
ourably. Throughout our period, Barings maintained a posture of self-conscious
leadership, as if watched; as if somehow a different set of standards applied to
a firm of such pedigree. This may have been one source of Barings' caution, of

'changing before one had to', of arranging its affairs in a way that precluded cavalier behaviour and gross failure. Once again, an organization can take this inclination too far so as to stifle innovation and daring, but in the 1830s, it served Barings well.

Elements of the story of Barings in the nineteenth century will strike readers as familiar, though nearly two centuries old. Some of these include the ongoing importance of the Atlantic economy in the history of the United States, and the connection of London and New York; the rise of Liverpool and the development of the American south and west; issues of moral hazard and lender of last resort; overseas trade versus domestic economic development; tariffs; bank regulation; balanced government budgets and budget surpluses; the participation of China and Mexico in the world economy; international trade and investment flows; the role of central bankers; politics' effect on markets; fixed exchange rates; the importance of people in decision-making in an age of machines and technology; and, finally, the ability of smart people close to the best information to make mistakes.

Chapter 1 provides an overview of Barings' early history, prestige derived from the French Wars, the avoidance of disaster in the excesses of 1825, and the bank's connections to the United States before 1828. Chapter 2 describes the members of a new Baring partnership formed in 1828, its rules and standard procedures, and provides macro-economic data on the Anglo-American trade economy. Chapter 3 describes the new business connections which the partnership established in the United States, highlights the House as a 'value' player that committed when markets were at low points, describes Barings' increasing options worldwide, and the House's relationship to the influential Second Bank of the United States.

Chapter 4 describes a bundle of economic and political problems between 1832 and 1834 that created tension in the financial community. In these years, Barings was unnerved by what it learned about the Andrew Jackson administration. Chapter 5 sees the 'problems' of Chapter 4 swept away, the American economy boom in 1835 and 1836, the pressure of competition on Barings in the United States, and the decision of the Baring partners to reduce their American position based on what it considered unsustainable values in real estate and commodity prices. In the autumn of 1836, the Bank of England discovered excesses among several merchant banks doing large business in the United States. The Bank raised its borrowing rates and, with the counsel of Barings, curbed these merchant banks' activities – taming, at the same time, certain speculative excesses in the British economy. Chapter 6 recounts the ripple effect of the British moves on the American economy which continued its boom into the early spring of 1837, but which had become vulnerable by this time to unexpected shocks. An American downturn began in March 1837. Healthy for its early exit, Barings assisted where it could, but the Panic of 1837 began an extended period of American economic distress lasting until 1843.

In closing, this study discusses Barings' triumph in the 1830s in terms of the serious lapse of the House in 1890 and the mortal difficulties in Singapore in 1995. It argues that Barings' impulse to reject the American democratic style of the 1830s saved the partnership by causing its timely pullback from the United States. It argues also that – ironically – the very values and behaviour that enabled the House to triumph in the 1830s foretold Barings' inability to compete long-term with more flexible financial institutions in later years, and led to its destruction in the late twentieth century.

The years covered in these pages to approximately 1840 constitute what the author has come to consider Baring Brothers' 'American moment'. The House continued its contribution to American development for several decades after this time, but never again would it be so preoccupied with the United States or have a 'lock' on its business. Competitors in the emerging United States took Barings' place as American financial institutions matured. With the possible exception of the Panic of 1873, never again would foreign credits and business play so large a part in an economic disturbance as they did in the events that triggered the Panic of 1837.

In 1830 the Duke of Wellington noted the winds of change blowing through the English Parliament. Five years later, an American newspaper in Richmond, Virginia, also commented on big changes in American politics. On both sides of the Atlantic, men once thought inappropriate for positions of influence or leadership were coming to power amidst the relentless forces creating a modern world. Companies, however distinguished their pedigree, ignored these forces at their peril.

1 GROWTH OF CONFIDENCE (1763–1828)

> Strong, sensible, self-reliant men, with a profound belief in themselves, in
> their family and in their country – eminently just and fair; no trace of hypoc-
> risy or cant; not only solid and square but giving the impression both of
> solidity and squareness ... not subtle or agile, but endowed with that curious
> combination of character which lends authority even to doubtful decisions,
> and makes those who possess it respected in counsel and obeyed as rulers.
> Viscount D'Abernon on Barings[10]

The early history of Barings reflects the early history of merchant banking in general, and the foundations the banker must lay if he is to garner trust and a good
reputation among traders, manufacturers, correspondents and, on occasion, governments. Before the turbulence of the 1830s, Barings had been in business for
nearly seventy years. These years involved finance in war and peace, European
reconstruction loans in 1815, and a widespread financial panic in the middle of
the 1820s. The Barings, particularly Sir Francis and his second son, Alexander,
were also among the first British merchant bankers to realize that westward across
the Atlantic, in America, lay a land of very large possibilities. Barings forged its
American connection almost before the United States was a nation.

This chapter will show, in outline, the characteristics of Barings' early experience and operations, which provided continuity with later years, and likely
benefited the firm. In sequence, the narrative includes the establishment of the
firm, the anchoring of the firm's reputation in Great Britain and Europe, contact
with America, the 1825 downturn, and formation of the third Baring partnership
that navigated the events leading to the troubles of 1836–7. From the start, the
firm was not local or regional in orientation, but international. It made influential financial and political contacts, including those by marriage. It exhibited
caution, made mistakes, and incited fear and envy among peers and those outside
the banking community. Above all, the illustrious position which it established
firmly in its early years allowed Barings to play a coveted role of objective helpfulness in questions of high finance in both the United States and Great Britain in
the first important decades of the nineteenth century.

Establishment and Early Reputation-Building

The House of Baring is a classic example of an international merchant and trading firm which, over time, changed into an organization almost wholly devoted to finance. It began modestly as a manufacturer and dyer of serge cloth under Johann Baring (1697–1748), who emigrated from Bremen to Exeter, Devon, in 1717.[11] After Johann's death in 1748, business continued under his wife and three sons, John, Francis and Charles. The end of the Seven Years War in 1763 promised increased commercial opportunities, and the firm reorganized into Exeter and London offices. The Exeter firm continued the emphasis of the original cloth business, whereas the London House was an import and export commission operation from its inception, albeit having as its most important client its Exeter complement. Through its London partner, Exeter bought raw materials from the Continent for its own and other Exeter manufacturing enterprises. It also secured wider markets for its merchandise, and an effective agency for negotiating bills of exchange on the major money market in London.[12] In its earliest years the firm forged ties to the Low Countries and northern Germany in the textile trade, and made contacts in Spain, Portugal and the Canary Islands for imports of spirits.

John Baring's grandson, Francis (1740–1810), de-emphasized the merchant aspects of business when he took over from his older brother John in 1777, and established Barings as a world banking force. Francis steered the London operations, which soon eclipsed Exeter in importance and influence. Francis started from meager resources, sharing perhaps £4,200 with Exeter, but he established the contacts for the firm which opened doors and provided diversification, safety and options in future decades.[13] He made connections with commercial Houses throughout the Mediterranean, northern Europe, the Baltic and West Indies. Among these was the well-known Dutch banking and trading House, Hope & Company of Amsterdam, whose relationship provided an important fulcrum into Continental commerce, countering the growing influence of Rothschilds. The London branch of the House had always bought and sold commodities on commission for correspondents and for its own account. Now it did a growing business in exchange as well, with Continental Houses and with its longstanding Exeter correspondents.[14] Only later, after years of mercantile service and an enhanced reputation in the wake of the Napoleonic indemnity, would Francis fully establish the acceptance business that proved so lucrative to the House.

From 1777 until the outbreak of the French Wars in 1793, capital of the House grew threefold to £61,177, and rose as high as £75,891 in 1792. Profits from trade fluctuated wildly – from as low as £352 in 1784 to as high as £13,268 in 1792. On the other hand, commission income increased steadily from £4,248 to £10,448, and the direction of business becomes clear from the dramatic expansion in acceptances. Liabilities on acceptances rose from £41,608 at the close of 1777 to a staggering £121,202 in 1793.[15]

Increases in business complemented the House's expanding political contacts and associations. Not long after arriving in London, Francis Baring was appointed a director of the Royal Exchange Assurance, the leading insurance company in the City. Baring investments in the East India Company began in 1776, were followed by a directorship for Francis in 1779, and the chairmanship in 1792. Francis's developing international knowledge and experience interested a growing list of politicians and organizations which enlisted his advice on matters of money and politics. His circle of associates in politics included William Pitt the Younger, the Duke of Rockingham, Edmund Burke, Henry Dundas and Jeremy Bentham. During the American War, the Earl of Shelburne chose Francis as an adviser on American commercial and financial matters.

Government wartime contracts led to Barings' heightened reputation by the 1820s. The House had secured its first significant assignment as contractor for public loan subscriptions to finance the rebellion in Britain's American colonies, placing stock among the public and its private client list. This was new ground for the House, but turned out to be a lucrative revenue stream that complemented more volatile income from trade. Between 1780 and 1784, loan contracting yielded Barings £19,000 and accounted for over half of overall profits. Throughout the American war, commission and acceptance income from trade grew 90 per cent.[16]

Barings distanced itself from its merchant banking peers most of all, however, by its participation in Britain's financing of the coalition wars against France and funding the French indemnity loans thereafter. France declared war on England in February 1793, and the commercial crisis, brought on the previous autumn by poor harvests and growing anxieties over developments in revolutionary France, intensified. A run on the Bank of England met with restricted note issue and a raising of the discount rate. London and country banks refused to undertake discounting in an attempt to maintain cash solvency, and British industry slowed almost to a standstill in 1794. Leaders of the City, including the newly-knighted Sir Francis Baring, met Prime Minister William Pitt at Mansion House in April, and issued 'exchequer bills' for immediate discount in order to relieve the commercial pressure and restore confidence. Gold continued to flow out of the country, however, and the Bank ceased convertibility of its notes in 1797, and did not resume again completely until 1821.

Between 1793 and 1816 the British national debt swelled from £243 million to £778 million.[17] This colossal increase in government obligations offered London financiers great opportunities, which the House of Baring seized through its earlier experience with government finance, connections in government circles, and high standing in the eyes of the investing public. The House headed the group of contractors for twelve public loans marketed for the wars against France. It took the majority share of the £28 million British loan in 1813 at 60, which went to a 3 per cent premium on the day of offer. The British government tapped

Barings (Smith, Payne and Smiths) again to handle a £30 million issue of 3 per cent bonds that coalition forces used to defeat Napoleon at Waterloo.[18] Barings profited handsomely from British wartime borrowing and public loan contracting. For example, the House made £21,000 in 1799 and £18,646 in 1801, which represented 47 per cent and 34 per cent of total profits respectively.[19] The war provided other business opportunities. In the 1790s the House shared in contracts for the supply and finance of provisions for Jamaica, for example, as well as for the British expedition to Hispaniola. Francis also offered the services of the East India Company in Asia to Pitt.

However significant the opportunities of the war itself, it was the management of the loans for the rebuilding of Europe that gave Barings its greatest triumph since Johann founded the House, and indeed cemented Barings' prestige in the banking community in the postwar years. In 1815, the second Peace of Paris imposed an indemnity on the restored monarchy of France to pay England, Prussia, Austria and Russia 700 million francs in war reparations, and 150 million in occupation costs per year for five years.[20] To pay these sums, the French government had to overcome major difficulties. In 1816 the government ran a deficit serviceable only by drawing down cash advances made by British loan contractors against French *rentes* sold on exchanges or through mercantile and banking firms. French public credit was at low ebb, and investors and financiers recalled the insolvency of former Bourbon regimes. The French capital market was also weak, and bonds could be issued only at deeply discounted prices. France and the Allies alike were anxious to come to some sort of terms – France so the occupation of its country might end; the Allies so they could secure badly-needed funds to stabilize their war-torn economies.

A foreign loan seemed the solution, and Messrs Baring and Hope visited Paris in January 1817 to explore possibilities. Shortly after the French defeat, Barings had arranged provision contracts for the armies of occupation through the agency of Gabriel-Julien Ouvrard, Paris banker and financial advisor to Napoleon. This relationship was taken up again now and, by February, Baring Brothers, together with Hope & Company, agreed to buy enough *rentes* at 52.5 francs, less a commission of 2.5 francs, to provide the French government with an initial 100 million francs. The contractors paid all expenses for marketing the loan and transferring the funds to foreign states.

The February *rentes* sold promptly and prices rose. In April, Barings took a second 100 million franc *tranche* at 55 francs and, amidst market enthusiasm, took still a third at 61.50. The latter furnished 115 million francs to the French treasury. These 1817 transactions cemented Barings' reputation as a lead underwriter of government debt. The loans were so successful that Paris bankers and the French public overcame their caution, and three years after Waterloo – in May 1818 – the French treasury itself sold *rentes* with a face value of 290 million francs. The loan was oversubscribed ten times, with much of the bidding coming from the provinces. Despite French public enthusiasm, however, the victors in the war were chary of the safety of French internal flotations, and the bulk of loans remained in the hands of major Allied financiers who managed their affairs from London.[21]

Banking syndicates took up several subsequent French loans, but most profit and risk of the French transactions remained in the hands of the Baring-Hope partnership. Considerable friction developed between Barings and the firm of Rothschild & Sons over loan apportionment, but since the French firm wished not to be too unpopular in London, it agreed to take only junior interests in the last major French securities offerings which were placed in March and September 1818 for issue in the first nine months of 1819. Rothschilds desired participation in the indemnity loan business, but had lost much of its influence when many of its contacts inside the French government resigned or were discredited in 1815. Hence Barings secured management of the second and enormous 480 million franc loan series in May 1818. Barings parcelled out a total of just 11 per cent between Rothschilds, the Anglo-German banker David Parish and the Paris banks Hottinguer & Company and Jacques Laffitte. The large remainder Barings took at optimistic prices of 74–6 francs.[22]

The loan did not go well. Deteriorating economic conditions caused by poor harvests in England and Holland made 1819 a trough year in the postwar adjustment period to such an extent that the Bank of England had to postpone resumption because of a drain of specie. Prices had already peaked by the time the loans were consummated, and 1819 turned out to be a year of severe economic dislocation. Falling prices, high unemployment and severe labour strife – all adjustments to peace after twenty-five years of war – caused Sir John Clapham to designate 1819 as 'one of the most wretched, difficult, and dangerous in modern English history'.[23]

Francis Baring's son, Alexander (1774–1848), sued for a rescheduling of loans in light of exchange bids dropping to 60 francs. Rescheduling took place and by 1821 the loan issues had risen to over 87 francs, by 1823 to nearly 90.[24] But Barings' timing had been poor in terms of what is now known economically; its judgement as financial professionals precipitate. Their high government loan bid was based on earlier successes of 1817 as well as the illusory prosperity of the year 1818. Rescheduling took place easily because participants at the Allied indemnity negotiations at Aix-la-Chapelle had themselves taken shares, and wished to preserve their positions. In the years 1818–25 Barings shared Russian, Austrian and Danish loans with several firms, such as Parish, Rothschilds, Thomas Wilson & Company and Bethmann Brothers of Frankfurt. It was the French reparation loans, however, which transformed Barings from a prominent British merchant bank to a major international financial force.

Profits were considerable from these loan operations, though difficult to assess. Estimates from some sources cite profits from loan operations as high as

£1,500,000 but were most probably lower. Swinton Holland, Baring partner and manager of the counting house at 8 Bishopsgate from 1809 to 1827, wrote that business related to the French loans produced a profit of £720,000, a titanic sum for a mercantile House from a single operation.[25]

In the winter of 1818 the Duke of Wellington told Lord Liverpool that he thought that, with Barings in control of French securities and French securities all the rage in London, the House was beginning to control the money market of the world. Even in 1817 James Rothschild in Paris had commented that Barings had grown so dominant in the area of postwar finance that, if they handled the loans exclusively, this in itself would make the business world uneasy.[26] Power was perhaps more apparent than real. Despite postwar loans, overall profits to the firm were actually a bit lower in this period. From 1813 until 1817 the annual average acceptance and commission income had been slightly over £50,000 but between 1818 and 1822 it fell off to £35,304 and still farther to £26,463 between 1823 and 1827.[27] Still, Barings' reputation – the fragile bedrock of the banker – stood high in the postwar years and its financial influence was considerable.

Just prior to Waterloo, Barings had taken another step to strengthen its European operations which assisted the workings of its postwar indemnity loan contracts: it took over the Dutch House of Hope & Company. By 1808, almost all the Hope partners lived in wartime England, and were either unwilling or unable to continue active management of their House in occupied Holland. In 1814 Alexander Baring bought the assets of Hope & Company for £250,521 and gave the House a new partnership structure. He had managed Baring Brothers & Company since the death of his father, Sir Francis, in 1810.[28] Alexander – the future Lord Ashburton – retained a one-third interest himself, and divided the rest between his brother-in-law, P. C. Labouchere, and his nephew, Thomas. Alexander's creation of a Hope & Company subsidiary expanded the access of Barings to the competitive loan activities of Continental Europe and served as a financial beachhead during the indemnity loan period.[29]

Barings and America

Barings' meaningful connections to the United States began shortly after Francis began managing the House in London in 1777. Earlier, the House had developed cloth export operations to the American colonies by way of commercial Houses in the West Indies. Francis's first recorded business relations with North America were in 1783 with Willing, Morris & Company, which proved a valuable conduit to securing American business. The Willings were an established Philadelphia mercantile family. Thomas Willing himself (1731–1821) was an associate of Alexander Hamilton and first president of the United States' first commercial banking institution, the Bank of North America, founded in 1782. Willing's partner, Robert Morris (1734–1806), served as superintendent of finances during the American War for Independence, had interests in the China trade, and was the most respected financier of the Confederation period.

Francis's connections in the United States complemented a developing relationship with Hope & Company in Holland so that Barings was beginning to acquire knowledge of men and markets on both sides of the Atlantic. With the return of peace to Great Britain in 1783 Hopes and Baring Brothers provided a venue for many American businesses to re-enter the Atlantic economy, and soon after the war Anglo-American trade resumed its former vigour and volume.

Whether colony or independent nation, Francis sensed that America and Great Britain would maintain ties of some kind after the war, and that any commercial House with global ambitions would have to include the young United States in its planning. Alexander Baring noted his father's broad interests, observing that 'he was of all men the one who most happily combined a capacity for distant and large views and for the detail of business'.[30] Cosmopolitan and active, Francis had indeed forged connections of great geographical spread by the 1780s – underwriting at Lloyd's as part of the insurance House's 'list' in the City and piloting the most international of British business institutions, the East India Company. As early as February 1784, Francis had expressed what he believed should be a proper British-American commercial relationship. He was convinced that Americans must continue to buy British manufactures particularly if British financial Houses offered credit. As Baring told William Pitt: 'it would be utterly impossible, not withstanding any absurdity or folly on our part, to deprive Britain of a considerable share of American trade'.[31] From the late 1780s to roughly 1812, Barings laid the foundation that served as its platform for American business ventures in future years.

The House found a dynamic commercial environment in the United States. The French Revolutionary Wars after 1792 enhanced the price of American wheat and flour, encouraged American trade with the West Indies, channelled much East Indies trade to America's neutral shipping and spurred investment in American land stocks as a refuge for European capital. As business boomed in Britain's former American colonies, and even wider war seemed likely in Europe, Francis sent his second son, Alexander, to the young United States in December 1795 to seek opportunities for investment and to shelter from the approaching European storm.

The twenty-one-year-old Alexander Baring moved easily among the business elite of the United States, and secured contacts and relationships for his father's House of importance, variety and depth.[32] One month after arriving in Boston, Alexander took Barings' first significant land stake in the United States when he bought over one million acres in Maine for $401,000 from Pennsylvania senator William Bingham (1752–1804) and General Henry Knox (1750–1806), close friend and advisor to George Washington. At the same time, Baring made several loans to General Knox based on land collateral and he speculated in foreign exchange throughout the winter of 1796.

American contacts multiplied – and not just in business. Alexander and his brother, Henry, married two of William Bingham's daughters in 1798 and 1802; and for Alexander, Philadelphia would be the birthplace of his first two sons, William (1799–1864) and Francis (1800–68) – both future peers.[33] The London firm established correspondence relationships with American trading Houses in New England and mid-Atlantic states: in Boston with the Codmans, in Philadelphia with Willing & Francis, in Baltimore with Robert Gilmor & Company, and Robert Oliver & Brothers.[34] On the political front, Alexander made the acquaintance for the first time of the financier and statesman Albert Gallatin (1761–1849), an encounter that started a life-long friendship between the two men. He also met the future speaker of the American House of Representatives, Henry Clay (1777–1852). Baring, Gallatin and Clay would meet in Ghent, Belgium, to negotiate the peace that ended the 1812 war, and the accompanying commercial side agreements.[35]

For seven years to 1802 Alexander transmitted a steady stream of business intelligence from North America, as future Barings agents in the United States would do. He investigated the merits of American stocks, judged several suitable for investment, and noted many with higher yields offering as much security as anything in Europe. The number of American trading accounts in the House's books also grew as the House solicited consignments either for sale in London or for forwarding to Europe. Proceeds from these sales were collected, cargoes of British manufactures purchased and dispatched to North America, and British manufacturers' drafts on 'American Houses' paid. Alexander also formed an opinion of the American businessman that he expressed to Henry Hope of Hope & Company, writing:

> The merchants in this country are generally speaking a low Class of Man ... the best at this place [Philadelphia] and New York are travelling Clerks to English manufacturing Houses ... The Northern States are always some degrees above their Neighbours in everything and the scale sinks lower as you go South ... To the south of Baltimore I understand there is nobody worth trusting.

Then he discussed methods of interaction with the Americans, whom he said had a 'rage for speculations'.

> The proper mode of business with this Country to most advantage is certainly to give a large Credit to very few, selecting only one or two Houses you can depend on in each place, and then give liberal assistance on proper security.[36]

Mr David Parish took over from Alexander as Barings' agent in the United States and served until 1820, but Alexander's opinion established the principled tone for policy regarding accounts maintained by the firm in the years ahead.

The House realigned its business geographically so that the six years 1808–13 saw between 70 and 80 per cent of commission income derived from 'American and Colonial Account'.[37] Whether Barings' interest in the United States followed or simply mirrored a wider British interest in her former colony is unclear. In any case, at the beginning of the nineteenth century, British investment in American stocks rose rapidly. By 1803 almost half the total of $32 million held by foreigners was domiciled in Britain, and Barings was at the heart of that business.[38]

Barings' relationship with the United States government began informally in a spirit of service in the 1780s and evolved gradually into an exclusive contract. Thomas Willing was influential in securing Barings the account of the First Bank of the United States in 1792. With the Bank's assistance, the London partners soon raised $800,000 for military and naval ordnance that facilitated negotiations with the Barbary powers of Algiers, Tunis and Tripoli in 1795 and 1796. The firm delivered similar services for the administration of John Adams in 1798 when it bought armaments through contacts in Hamburg and from the British government in preparation for what seemed to be imminent war with France. After 1799, Barings acted also with London merchants C. T. Cazenove & Batard on behalf of the Bank of the United States in paying dividends to British stockholders. Several years later, in 1802, Barings assisted the American government in paying its debt to the Bank of the United States by buying the government's shares in the Bank at a premium of 45 per cent.[39] This decade-long sequence led to a formal offer to Barings to act as financial agents in London for the United States when the government's former agents, Bird, Savage & Bird – a pioneer at marketing American securities in Europe – failed in February of 1803.[40]

Barings won the agency of the American government in the same year France offered to sell Louisiana to the United States. Subsequent arrangements in November 1803 to buy Louisiana tested the House greatly, but cemented the American relationship with Barings still further. Alexander Baring and Albert Gallatin worked side by side at the Louisiana negotiations in Paris. According to his father, Alexander was responsible for lowering the price France was willing to accept for its prized North American territory. Despite some bargaining downwards, the transaction remained large and risky, especially in view of the financial disruptions caused by resumption of the European war in 1804. 'We all tremble about the magnitude of the American commitment', Francis wrote to his son-in-law at Hope & Company. The American risk, he thought, was justified if it reaped future rewards. 'I am satisfied', wrote Francis, 'that if we manage this business well, we shall have frequent occurrence to us in circumstances or events that must arise and keep the Ball at our feet for many years to come.'[41] Barings split the risk of marketing the $15 million in bonds issued by the United States with Hope &

Company and also enlisted Willing & Francis of Philadelphia to be the American agent through which $2 million would be paid to France monthly. Interest on the Louisiana fifteen-year securities was payable at 6 per cent in London, Amsterdam and Paris.[42]

A few years before the 1812 war, Barings established correspondent relationships with private New York banking firms Prime, Ward & Sands and John Jacob Astor, as well as the Philadelphia House of Stephen Girard. The latter two possessed networks to the Far East. The link to powerful Prime, Ward & Sands proved most useful as partner Samuel Ward (1786–1839) became a close colleague, and the firm itself remained one of the most intimate financial contacts and reliable sources of information for the House in the United States until the 1860s.[43]

War with the United States in 1812 complicated Barings' American relationships, as the ongoing war in Europe also complicated the House's relationship with France over the payments from the Louisiana bond contracts. Barings retained the agency of the United States government but did not take new Federal debt issues, though it continued to pay interest to holders of American securities issued before 1812.

Immediately after 1815, high finance concerned itself with the reconstruction of Europe, and some time elapsed before Barings could focus its energies on the United States as it once had done. American finance had been rudderless throughout the war with the failure to recharter the Bank of the United States. Raising money at home either by direct taxes, the excise or bond offerings was difficult, and attempts to float loans in Europe possible only on the most concessionary terms. The revival of trade supplied Europe with materials for postwar reconstruction. The charter of a second Bank of the United States in 1816 stabilized American finances and contributed to postwar confidence. Budget surpluses reduced the Treasury's outstanding debt accumulated by the issue of fiat currency during the war.[44]

Despite its postwar focus on Europe, Barings continued its duties as financial agent to the United States. In July 1815, the House offered to advance at an interest rate of 5 per cent any sums necessary to cover interest payments due on American government debt offered during the war, or to assist in the flotation of further United States loans in Europe. Barings cleared all accounts current of American legations and consulates in Europe, and offered its good offices to uphold the credit of the American government. The American commissioners at Ghent counted on Barings, for example, to honour their bills when another House refused, and out of this action Barings secured the business of making payments for the account of the United States Navy in the Mediterranean after 1816.[45]

But the ongoing management of the Louisiana bonds from 1803 afforded the largest single block of business to Barings for the account of the United States. Payments to British bondholders in London continued until 1822 when the firm successfully carried through the last repurchases of the so-called 'Louisiana 6s' (bonds paying 6 per cent) in the London marketplace at the behest of the American government. The buy-back of the bonds that had connected the United States to European investors for over a decade represented a considerable retrenchment of capital and reduction of British investment in American funds. Baring partner S. C. Holland figured the 1818 total to be approximately one-fifth the 1805 amount of £5,747,000.[46]

Barings was obliged to curtail its operations in debt finance with the United States because of a steady drop in American long-term government debt levels after the war. Liabilities decreased by over half in the first fifteen years of peace, and the Bank of the United States managed those issued. Debt issues could easily be absorbed by American domestic institutions and financiers, such as the Manhattan Company, without the assistance of foreign merchant bankers.[47] American investors in the early 1820s actually had surplus capital to deploy in domestic projects that resulted from the early payoff of their Federal securities.

Despite the apparent health of American federal finances, Barings edged only cautiously into the debt business of individual states. The first American state securities quoted in London were New York 6 per cent Erie Canal certificates in 1817. Listings of city and state bonds gradually accelerated through the 1820s, but did not bloom fully until early 1830 when American state financial offerings began to flood European markets, totalling nearly $27 million. The amount was hugely more six years later. Barings stood generally aloof from individual state finance, with the exception of Louisiana, which greatly interested the firm because of the spectacular trade potential of New Orleans. Barings had helped to finance the paving of the Rue Royale in 1822, for example, and in 1824 took a small portion of Louisiana bonds offered in favour of the newly-established Bank of Louisiana. Until the 1830s, however, the state securities market, and Barings' stake in it, remained quite modest.[48]

Association with the Bank of the United States in the years before 1828–9 enhanced Barings' public reputation, and agency relations continued through the Bank's transformation into a Pennsylvania corporation in 1836. Bullion sales on very favourable terms from Barings to the Bank took place from 1817 onwards, with United States government bonds deposited as collateral. The Second Bank remained indebted to Barings and Hope & Company for the first eight years of its operations, including the depression years of 1819–20, at a level of approximately $2 million.[49] After 1825, the Bank entered actively into highly-lucrative foreign exchange operations under the presidency of Nicholas Biddle (1786–1844), which Barings' open credit to the Bank made possible. Through London's accommodation, Biddle dominated the United States foreign exchange market, and ably supplied the mercantile community with sound bills to remit payments to England in their transatlantic trade. As we shall see, Barings provided the Bank with generous lines of credit, enabling greater flexibility for the American central bank than ever before.

Apart from government accounts and Bank of the United States contracts, all merchant bankers who touched trade in the United States touched cotton. For Barings, though, their first attempt to establish cotton connections was unsuccessful. Barings' initial contact with the cotton market was a family connection through a friend of Francis from his college days at Exeter – a merchant trader of German lineage named Vincent Nolte. Alexander underwrote Nolte to the sum of £6,000 to establish an operation in 1812 at New Orleans, but the effort was interrupted by war. Revived in 1815, Nolte claimed to have built the operation into the largest single cotton purchaser and exporter in the southern United States. Nolte failed in 1825, however, and Barings lost its direct link to the American cotton market until it was re-established a few years later.

Troubles of 1825 and Reorganization of the Partnership

Before British capital flowed in great volume to the United States, Latin America caught the fancy of European investors, and in the 1820s excited a frenzy of investment and trade involving the states born from the defunct Spanish and Portuguese empires. Mexico, Buenos Aires (now Argentina) and Brazil beckoned for investment. From the years 1822 to 1825, roughly £40 million of stock in twenty foreign states – including Greece – entered the London money market.[50] These securities presented an appealing picture for inquiring British investors. They came from new states with, as yet, little foreign debt, seemingly limitless natural resources, flourishing export trades in hides and tallow, and an established mercantile community.

The pursuit of profit in distant places, such as Latin America, was one effect of the general recovery of British and European economies after the economic downturn in 1819. Barings' sponsorship of postwar loans brought the name of the House before the public, but served a broader economic venue for foreign securities to reach Amsterdam, Paris and London. The success of Baring loans to France and Rothschilds' reconstruction loans to Russia, Austria and the German states provided regular interest payments to the Continent, and thereby increased liquidity throughout Europe. From the postwar trough of 1819, Britain experienced a mild recovery in 1820–1 which developed into a boom with a steady increase of domestic commodity prices, sharply rising export volume, large increases in private investment and capital exports, and levels of domestic investment not matched for twenty years.[51]

In the 1820s, British capital became an export item, reversing what had been a net flow of capital into the City for most of the eighteenth century.[52] Sterling now developed into the world's currency, and in the nineteenth century would be universally accepted as a means of payment and exchange. With the elevation of sterling came the maturation of London as a financial centre which some referred to, even in the 1820s, as the 'great money-meter of the world'.[53]

The exuberance and liquidity of 1822–4 turned to mania in 1825. Besides loans to foreign governments of unprecedented number, investment promotions of joint-stock companies of all sorts floated on the thinnest pretence. The number of companies that went through the preliminary stages of organization in 1824–5 was enormous at over six hundred in Britain alone.[54] A proliferation of banks on both sides of the Atlantic brought a monetary expansion that sparked speculation in mining stocks in Great Britain, and cotton in the United States. The American minister in London, Richard Rush, recorded in a letter home in January 1825 that all London was active:

> Nothing was ever like it before, not even the South Sea scheme ... Shares in some of the companies have advanced to seventeen hundred per cent within a few months, and are bought with avidity at this price. I hear it said that noblemen of great estates, even directors of the Bank of England, participate and press forward to obtain shares.[55]

Companies and foreign loans were bought on margin – often for 20 per cent or less down – and banks accommodated on the collateral of these same securities pledged. The British company frenzy and capacity for popular delusion reached such a pitch in the middle 1820s that it was even possible to issue bonds for an imaginary country called Poyais, promoted as somewhere in Central America.

At the speculative peak in March 1825, Alexander Baring declared in the House of Commons that the Royal Exchange had become 'a gaming-House' and warned that mining companies, domestic and foreign, which had proliferated so rapidly in past years, 'would turn out to be delusions'.[56] The prime minister, Lord Liverpool, stated there would be no relief from government quarters for those who engaged in rash company investments. Rumours about the spurious nature of some of the companies circulated in London that spring and summer; and even worthwhile long-term projects, such as canals and roads, were said to be very unlikely to turn a profit for several years.

In autumn, American cotton prices dropped by a third, and reports of failures from Liverpool 'of Houses in the American trade' began a scarcity of money in the London money market. The trigger for general panic came in December with the suspension of payments by the large Liverpool cotton House of Sir Peter Pole & Company. Five London banks suspended in sympathy. Blind reliance on continued and expanding banking facilities – a major cause of inflated asset prices over the past year – was over; the financial expansion ended.[57]

Though Alexander Baring's warning came nine months too soon, the caution now seemed warranted. In winter 1825, Britain entered into one of its worst financial crises of the century. Share prices and exports weakened substantially in

December. A bullion drain of alarming proportions hit the Bank of England so that specie resources in January 1826 stood four-fifths below year-earlier levels. Agricultural commodity prices such as sugar, cotton and wheat declined, as well as non-agricultural articles such as coal, iron and tin. Between 1821 and 1824 one commentator had stated that the 'trade and manufactures of the country had never been in a more regular, sound, and satisfactory state'.[58] By February 1826, however, the wife of the British joint secretary of the Treasury described in her diary a very different scene:

> The state of the country at this moment is extraordinary; there is no circulating medium, no means of getting money or of paying for any thing ... The manufacturers are almost entirely at a stand, credit is totally destroyed, the funds are today at 76, having this time last year been at 97, & every person in the City is in despair.[59]

Eventually 73 out of 770 English country and city banks failed; trade was disrupted, bank paper discredited and hoarding of gold and silver became widespread.

British troubles and excesses extended to the United States – indeed occurred there first – but were not of the broad spectrum of those occurring in Britain. An expansion of credit, flotation of companies of all sorts and speculation in shares had taken place. These were connected in large part to the lucrative cultivation, sale and speculations in cotton. The price of cotton had advanced considerably in the spring and summer because of Britain's rising markets.

As early as July 1825, a New York newspaper had noted the sudden 'scarcity of money' in Wall Street, as well as the international scope of problems:

> New companies were chartered [by the last legislature], and great demand was created for these stocks: a spirit of speculation was engendered, and men of all descriptions and degrees were seen striving to get shares in this or that bubble; not with a view to permanent investment ... Persons without means or knowledge in such matters became subscribers; borrowing, on the pledge of their shares, the money to pay for them ...
>
> All of a sudden in the natural course of trade, that capital deemed so superabundant, is called for – the purchaser of cotton has to pay for it – the importer of goods has to remit, the projector of distant voyages has to prepare his funds ...
>
> Receipts from foreign shipments have fallen short of expectation. The adventures round Cape Horn and to the Brazils, in flour, &c., have brought back few or no returns; the markets are glutted – the shipments to the Spanish Main, of dry goods, have been overdone. The pause in cotton abroad has interrupted sales. From all these combined causes, the merchant is thrown upon his resources at home, and the money that has been lent is recalled to its natural and proper vocation. Another cause of the scarcity of money is the disproportion between specie in the bank and the paper in circulation

is inexcusably great. Failures are daily occurring, and numerous; some to a considerable amount.

In November, a Boston paper followed up:

> We have seen many private letters from New York which mention that several failures growing out of the late cotton speculations were daily occurring in the city; the Bank [of the United States] had stopped discounting. A general gloom prevailed in the mercantile community. Debts of five mercantile Houses which have recently failed in New York were estimated at 2,500,000 dollars and the available funds would not exceed 75,000 dollars.[60]

It was hardly surprising to have such trouble amid the pyramiding 'puff and paper' schemes that have proliferated over the past year, wrote *Niles' Weekly Register* in December 1825. 'The wild speculations in cotton, superadded to the gambling projects of the stock-jobbers, are all built on various moneyed institutions without any money at all. No wonder so many of them [banks] fail. Instead of being in the hands of persons who have money to lend, they are under the direction of those who want to borrow'! The challenge was to keep problems in the financial community from spilling over into the lives of people in the broader economy, wrote Niles, who reported that the Bank of the United States under Nicholas Biddle was actually increasing its discounts throughout the country aggressively – thereby containing the contagion of panic.[61] The basic health of American finances made possible a robust response to the price declines. With very low debt, government securities had the status of gilt-edged investments.

In Great Britain, the financial picture was more serious. Seventy-three bank failures had brought the country, in William Huskisson's phrase, 'to within twenty four hours of barter'. Moreover, Bank of England reserves were low due to a drain of gold for imports, and it appeared close to being another 1797 (the year when the Bank had last suspended cash payments). At this time there was no explicit British lender of last resort. It would take nearly a century to resolve this question definitively. The Treasury made it clear it would not assist. Fortunately, arrangements with the Bank of France, the delivery of £400,000 in gold to the Bank by Rothschilds, and the discovery of a large block of £1 and £2 notes in the Bank's vault prevented suspension.[62]

Alexander Baring favoured the Bank's role as financial steward and, if need be, the country's lender of last resort. In this he agreed with his father, the late Sir Francis, who had called the Bank 'le dernier resort' in 1797.[63] In 1826, Alexander expressed the belief in Parliament that the Bank was at least partially responsible for failing to restrict credit in 1824. In this respect, he considered that the institution contributed to the instability and to the crisis that followed.[64]

The function of the central banker in the economies of nations was far from clear in this period. The assertive and confident president of the Bank of the United States, Nicholas Biddle, was exceptional. The Bank of England on Threadneedle Street considered his interventionist inclinations generally untoward and inappropriate for a banker. So too at times (as we shall see) thought Baring Brothers. *Niles' Weekly Register* gave the opinion that the 1825 speculations and subsequent downturn came not only from rash investments in England and the United States, but because those in positions of influence did not know how to employ the financial resources they already had.[65]

Financial mechanisms at this time were 'delicate plants', one historian wrote recently, and in many ways the nineteenth century was a story of the strengthening of these 'plants' in the aftermath of each business cycle trough.[66] In Great Britain, the year 1825 was a key date for reform of the banking structure and financial markets. It involved the beginnings of joint-stock banking as well as Bank of England branches, and began a quasi-regulatory role for the Bank of England in the form of the first stages of a note issuing monopoly.[67] Similarly, the United States saw ongoing efforts at financial reform and, some would say, 'experimentation' in the 1830s and beyond.

The House of Baring – through public pronouncements of its managing partners, Francis and Alexander – had progressive views on the role of the Bank of England as a possible regulator of the British economy. Barings had also done quite well in weathering the worst of the 1825 downturn. Partners' capital decreased only slightly in the 1825–6 period, from £452,654 to £445,126. In 1826, the firm experienced its first loss in thirty-six years, of £65,000, but returned to profitability in 1827.[68]

Barings remained cautious in its approach to the South American republics and avoided the worst excesses of the 1820s mania. The House had not involved itself with joint-stock companies, but touched activities centred on trade and foreign government loan finance. In 1824 British shipping helped support over £1 million of exports to the River Plate area alone, and London investors had committed an equal amount to bonds of the Province of Buenos Aires. British trade to Latin America climbed steadily in the 1820s, doubling what it had been as a percentage of total British exports in 1815.

Barings was first publicly associated with Latin American securities when it underwrote a £1 million ($5 million) loan for a waterworks infrastructure project in Buenos Aires at 6 per cent in July 1824. A consortium originally purchased the loan at 70 which, in turn, convinced Barings to market it to London investors at 85 for a 3 per cent commission. This was the biggest capital investment in any Latin American republic since independence as well as the single largest commitment to the area by a foreign interest.[69] Barings' timing was poor, however, and not even the prestige of the House could induce the investing public to take a large-scale interest. War with Brazil over La Banda Oriental (Uruguay) and a contraction of the British economy in 1825–6 decreased international trade through the port of Buenos Aires and made it impossible for the Argentine government

Figure 1.1: A View of the Bank of England, Threadneedle Street, London. Engraving (1797), Emmet Collection, New York Public Library.

to pay its sterling creditors. Buying in by Barings failed to stem the fall of prices against London speculators who unloaded the Buenos Aires issue. The stock went to a discount, leaving the House with much of the offering on its hands unsold. Buenos Aires would not resume payments on a regular basis to foreign bondholders until 1859.

Argentina was not Barings' only skirmish with Latin American finance. At the start of 1825 Alexander Baring sent his second son and recently admitted partner, Francis, to Mexico to report on opportunities for business. While in Mexico, Francis committed the House to a number of investments in real estate, mining and government stocks without first obtaining approval of his London partners. He did not know how violently London investors had turned against Latin American securities in the spring of 1825, but his lack of judgement horrified his father. 'We are a House of trade', Alexander reminded his son, 'and have no business with any adventures of this kind, to say nothing of one out of all proportion to the extent of our capital. I must insist that if you have made any landed or mining adventure for us [that] you do not leave the country until you have placed it in good hands.'[70] The 'good hands' turned out to be Barings itself, for the House took on the time-consuming business of being Mexico's financial agent in September 1826. Only with substantial advances from Barings could Mexico meet its interest obligations, and the greater part of the advance was repaid by 1830.[71]

British foreign trade and investment would not surpass 1824–5 levels until 1833.[72] Indeed, the sullied reputation of Latin American governments in London shifted general investor interest to regions north of the Rio Grande in the late 1820s. For Barings, the malaise following the 1825–6 panic corresponded with the revitalization of its historical link to the United States. It corresponded with the firm's reorganization, and the taking on of additional personnel.

In 1828, Alexander Baring was fifty-four years old. He was ready to retire from active business management, and devote more time to politics. Early in the decade he had been away in Europe for as much as eleven months on leisure travels. In September 1826 he had confided to Vincent Nolte in New Orleans that he was 'everyday more and more retiring from active life', perhaps meaning business activity, and likely alluding to the effect of recent severe economic and financial shocks to international trade and business.[73]

The man whom Benjamin Disraeli would eulogize in 1848 as 'the greatest merchant England ever had' was ready to retire, but Alexander had reason not to rest altogether easily with the House in the hands of its current six partners.[74] His brother Henry (1776–1848) was never deeply committed to the business and left it in June 1823. Alexander's second son, Francis (1800–68; later third Lord Ashburton), was admitted to the firm the year of Henry's retirement but his adventures in Mexico soon lost him the confidence of his fellow partners and, although he was nominally senior partner from 1830–64, was never permitted to play an active role in the business. Francis's first cousin, John (1801–88), did not become a very active partner and retired to the country after ten years' service in 1837 with £180,000.[75] Of the four familial partners, only Thomas distinguished himself as part of Baring Brothers & Company and became a leading figure in the City.

In the late 1820s Alexander reached beyond the immediate Baring family for banking talent, and assembled what was, in the estimation of one writer, the greatest partnership the firm would ever know.[76] Beside his nephew, Thomas, Alexander chose as managing partners his son-in-law, Humphrey St John Mildmay, and Joshua Bates, an American businessman who had established a business in London in 1818. These were the men who navigated the vagaries of the Atlantic economy for the House after 1828, and created the world's top ranking Anglo-American firm to mid-century. They added their experience and judgement to a banking institution of already high repute built upon the French reconstruction loans, general prudence, good contacts and service.

The reorganization of the House came none too late. The return of prosperity in the late 1820s brought increased competition to Barings from established Houses and attracted newcomers to the field of merchant banking eager to thrive in the expanding world economy. It also brought new methods to transatlantic business, at the centre of which stood the United States as a magnet of opportunity.

The aftermath of the panic of 1825–6 saw a need for an adjustment in financing the import and export trades of the United States. During Great Britain's important early period of industrialization after 1780, many manufacturers integrated forward into merchandising partly because the profits in this pioneering period offered such strong incentives to do so. The existing mercantile community had neither the knowledge nor the capacity to deal with new or improved products and rapidly extending markets.

After the French Wars, and most especially after the 1823–5 boom, increasing competition and bankruptcies among manufacturer-merchants reduced the interest of the group as a whole in trade and finance, and they drew back in significant numbers from overseas markets. By the middle 1820s British trade had increased to such scale and scope that it was now quite difficult to conduct and finance a diversified trade on a small capital.

In place of the manufacturer-merchants, there emerged a new breed of specialists called commission agents who became resident in foreign commercial centres. There also emerged a handful of wealthy merchants who had graduated to pure finance since 1815, and who formed 'acceptance Houses' which provided the credit to manufacturers to send their goods to these agents abroad. In the decade after 1825, a particular set of firms assumed the financing leadership as 'merchant bankers' in the transatlantic trade. These included the House of Baring, Brown, Shipley & Company, Thomas Wilson & Company, George

Wildes & Company, Timothy Wiggin & Company, Lizardi & Company, and Morrison Cryder & Company. At the end of this decade, the continental Houses of Rothschild & Company, and Frederick Huth & Company committed themselves to the American trade as well.[77]

Between 1820 and 1830, over a third of American exports went to Britain, and more than 40 per cent of American imports were British. Of cottin in Lancashire, 80 per cent came from the southern United States.[78] By 1837 the *Circular to Bankers* estimated that British-domiciled merchant bankers provided as much as 80 per cent of the finance required for exporting to Britain's biggest customer, the United States.[79] Of this trade, the House of Baring held a significant share.

In 1815 the firm stood at the head of British merchant banking organizations. It was the leading marketer of British government debt; its connections with mercantile firms in the ports and capitals of Europe were solid. In trade and financing services for the United States, particularly, it yielded primacy to no other British House. Conceived by Francis and built largely by Alexander, no British firm was better known or respected in the United States than Barings. For the last quarter of the eighteenth century, the House had been associated with the best American merchants, and had enabled these merchants' commercial relations with Great Britain and the Continent.

But the road was not always smooth. The firm had been humbled by its own bad judgement over a major French reconstruction loan. It was not badly damaged by the 1825–6 downturn, but had experienced mixed results in Latin America. Its managing partner, the eminent Alexander Baring, devoted less time to business as he gave more energy to politics.

The new partners had to work hard to maintain existing business and attract new accounts. No doubt, Barings was a force to be reckoned with internationally, but the House by no means dominated the banking community by financial muscle. The combined resources of the four Rothschilds Houses had grown to ten times that of Barings; its position in the area of international loans by far the strongest in Europe. Rothschilds capital stood at a formidable £4,330,433 against £409,803 for Barings.[80] In the second half of the 1820s, also, capital at one of Barings' competitors in the Anglo-American trade – Brown, Shipley & Company – had surged by 200 per cent to stand just under the resources of the English House.[81]

Barings' reputation was its best currency, and its judgement would prove equally fine. It would meet competition on its own terms and on its own course, confident that its past experience would provide keys to the future.

2 OPPORTUNITY AND SYSTEM (1828–30)

It seems that the long years of experience in the international trade of the United States is yielding something of worth. Perhaps this new opportunity as partner in the House of Baring Brothers and Co. will grant me the means and respectability to use some of what I have gathered over the past years.

Joshua Bates[82]

Credits are the great steam power, the great railroads of commerce. The difficulty is to make them safe.

Thomas Wren Ward[83]

When the new partnership decided to recommit the House to the United States trade, it did so after a period of sluggish profits and little growth in its capital base. In 1828, commission and acceptance income were half the levels of 1825. The profit and loss account – including expenses from all parts of the business – remained positive but erratic, with firm-wide profits failing to increase year over year until the early 1830s.[84]

Barings' expansion in the United States was not unusual. The other six so-called 'American Houses' were also doing so aggressively. In 1828 in fact, Joshua Bates reported during a brief trip to the United States that he had counted thirty-five agents from different parts of Europe in New York City alone.[85] The United States was attractive for many reasons to British businessmen. It could serve as a haven from the problems of Europe, or as a diversifier for a firm looking to add another market to an existing portfolio.

Alexander was a cautious man who hired carefully for the firm his father had all but founded. Barings headed back to the United States amidst great changes in the Anglo-American trade and investment environment. The new men in management felt compelled to develop rules in the late 1820s so they would not incur injury – always remembering the irregularities the firm had encountered before they came on board. As with much enterprise, the firms' success or failure depended on the decisions and talents of individual personnel.

Foreign Investor Interest in the United States

Foreign interest and investment in the United States was not new, as the early history of Barings shows, but, by the late 1820s, interest in American affairs had increased for new and specific reasons. In 1828, New York's quickly-profitable Erie Canal had operated for three years, and its well-publicized success drew attention to the canal as a symbol of the United States' fast-developing economy. The canal was a precursor of many internal improvement projects of the separate American states in the antebellum decades, and of the outside capital required to fund them.[86]

According to Professor Leland Jenks, the first state to issue securities quoted in London was New York in 1817. Pennsylvania, Virginia and Louisiana debt offerings debuted in London in 1824, followed by Ohio in 1828, Maryland in 1830, Mississippi in 1831, and Indiana and Alabama in 1833. In addition to state offerings, loans by Washington DC in 1830, and Philadelphia and Baltimore in 1832, provided European investors avenues by which to participate in American municipal finance.[87] Foreign investors, mostly British, held 33 per cent of the total national debt of $67.5 million in 1828.[88] By January seven years later, Congress and the administration of Andrew Jackson had paid off all debts of the national government, domestic and foreign.[89] In the middle 1830s, investments in states and municipalities replaced the long-standing foreign component in American federal debt. By 1838, state and municipal debt totaled $172 million – six times what it was in 1830; and an amount greater than the federal government had ever owed to that time.[90] The end of the decade saw the bond issues of twenty-five American banks and railroads of various states and municipalities listed on the London stock exchange.[91]

Additional cause for foreign interest in the United States for business and investment was the stability brought to American finance by the Bank of the United States, rechartered in April 1816. The Bank had a somewhat ignomini-ous start under its first two presidents, William Jones and Langdon Cheves, but appeared to have restored order to the American banking and currency systems by a return to a disciplined specie standard under Nicholas Biddle's leadership after 1823. In the twenty years after 1811, the number of banks in the United States grew from fewer than 90 to more than 500.[92] Most of these issued their own currencies. The Bank of the United States did not possess the monopoly on note issue of the modern central bank. Through a programme of vigorous note state redemption Biddle sought to regulate, and thereby stabilize, the nation's cur-rency, as well as prevent the over-expansion of loans and bills by individual state banks. Moreover, its large capital base, exercised through its exclusive privilege of branching, enabled the Bank to create a national market for its notes, which tended to be interchangeable at par in the major money markets of Boston, Philadelphia or New York.

Notes circulated at full value because of market confidence of redemption on demand. To a great extent this confidence came from Biddle's insistence that the Bank rest the bulk of its operations on short-term commercial paper – credit extended for thirty to ninety days on the basis of real or mercantile ('in-transit') assets. With a tight rein on commercial credit, Biddle aimed to smooth large geographical and seasonal movements in domestic exchange rates between eastern, western, and southern regions of the United States. Particularly in connection with the cotton trade, the bank became a large player in exchange after 1828 and created a very liquid domestic exchange market. It bought exchange in the south throughout the autumn and winter cotton export season, and sold exchange in the large Atlantic cities to meet the needs of importers in the spring and summer. The Bank's scale of operations in sterling bills tended to keep down transaction costs, and crowded out competitors like Alexander Brown & Sons. Biddle's conservative policies and deft handling of the 1825 pressure attracted the backing of Barings, which in 1829 extended the Bank a credit line of £100,000; later increased to £250,000. This support not only insured Biddle greater capital flexibility in domestic markets. It made the finance of American trade in the 1830s truly international in scope and character.

The efforts of the Bank of the United States to provide liquidity, credit and financial stability to markets on a national scale accompanied several similar initiatives on a regional level. The so-called 'Suffolk Bank System' allowed for the everyday buying and selling of goods throughout antebellum New England without the worry of what kind of currency a customer intended to use. Most currencies in circulation in New England after 1824 were part of a cooperative arrangement agreed upon by private Boston banks, whereby all notes would be channelled through a central clearing bank with substantial reserves and redeemed at par. In New York, attempts to protect the circulating currency of the banks and deposits of bank customers against bank failures led legislators to enact the so-called New York Safety Fund in 1829. All chartered banks paid a small percentage of their capital into a pool that would compensate noteholders and depositors in the event of bank failures. Limits on note issuance, requirements on paid-up capital, and a state regulating commission also were features of the Act.[93]

Finally, though the Bank of the United States operated twelve of its twenty-four branches below the Mason-Dixon line, a series of land or property banks sprang up in new states after 1816 to service the needs of the south. Planters relied increasingly on cotton as a source of income, as a basis of credit and as the foundation of their banking system.[94] Whether privately financed or capitalized by the states, property banks as a rule sold bonds to farmer-planters, who paid for their stock by mortgages on their estates for up to two-thirds of their market value. The states then issued bonds based on this mortgage pool and typically sold them for working capital in the money markets of the eastern United States or London.

Subscribing planters could borrow from the fund thus created, pledging their crops as security.[95] So long as commodity prices held reasonably steady – and this was key – the land bank system in the south provided capital and credit to a region chronically short of both.[96]

Foreign investor interest in the United States increased throughout the nineteenth century, but trade was by far the primary driver that connected British merchant banks such as Baring Brothers, Morrison Cryder or Alexander Brown & Company to the fortunes of the American economy. Overseas commerce had been central to American life since the nation's founding; the importation and distribution of foreign goods crucial.[97] After several wartime breaks, 1776–83 and 1807–15, American merchants quickly renewed commercial intercourse, particularly with Great Britain. With the gradual settlement of the American interior, coastal cities extended and deepened their function as intermediaries for trade begun many decades before.[98] Boston, Philadelphia, New York and Baltimore looked eastwards and processed British, European and Asian imports. At the same time, these seacoast cities were oriented increasingly to the southern and newly-settled western states, receiving the growing number of agricultural goods for export such as wheat, corn and cotton that earned the United States valuable credits in its balance of payments account.

General Domestic and Foreign Trade Profile

Demand in the United States for trade credit had much to do with the shape of trade routes and the direction of commerce. Before extensive canals and certainly before railroads, trade in the United States was a slave to the natural course of rivers. Goods travelled in a roughly triangular pattern among the three sections of the country – north-east, north-west and south – that in the antebellum years would become increasingly distinct in political and economic character. From the north-west, farmers shipped crops down the Ohio River and its tributaries to the Mississippi and New Orleans, where they sold the goods for cash, which they took home. From the south, cotton and other agricultural staples travelled along the coast around the peninsula of Florida and up to various north-eastern ports such as Baltimore, Philadelphia or New York. In return, these eastern cities shipped imported manufactured goods southwards, often to New Orleans.

Likewise, western states bought foreign goods in the east by sending coin obtained from crop sales in New Orleans. In the 1830s, the shape of the east-west-south triangle changed with innovations in transportation such as canal networks, steamboats and most particularly railroads. No longer in thrall to river currents, merchants and farmers in western states could more cost-effectively earn currency by shipping products east without first going to New Orleans. Additionally, any manufactures that westerners received from the east could be sent south. Eastern goods could more expeditiously go south. North-south shipments were always larger than those going south to north because cotton, the largest southern product, most often went directly to Europe from a southern port.

A large theme of nineteenth-century United States economic history is the expansion and maturing of its interior economy. As this occurred, the country became ever less dependent on the foreign trade which had been the backbone of American economic life since colonial times. Foreign trade, though, remained integral and vital until the 1840s.

Trade with the United Kingdom was particularly substantial. Indeed, British exports to the United States averaged 17 per cent of the declared value of the kingdom's entire worldwide exports and re-exports in the sixteen years after 1820 and, though volatile, peaked in the years 1835 and 1836 at a robust 23 per cent (see Table 2.1).[99] British goods made up approximately one third of American imports in these same years.[100]

Table 2.1: United Kingdom Exports to the United States as a Percentage of United Kingdom Exports Worldwide, 1820–36 (in thousands of pounds). Sources: Imlah, *Economic Elements of the Pax Britannica*, p. 37; Mitchell and Deane, *Abstract of British Historical Statistics*, pp. 313–14.

Year	Exports Worldwide (Declared Value)	Exports to US (Declared Value)	%
1820	36,400	3,875	11
1821	36,700	6,215	17
1822	37,000	6,865	19
1823	35,400	5,465	15
1824	38,400	6,090	16
1825	38,900	7,019	18
1826	31,500	4,659	15
1827	37,200	7,018	19
1828	36,800	5,810	16
1829	35,800	4,823	13
1830	38,300	6,132	15
1831	37,200	9,054	24
1832	36,500	5,468	15
1833	39,700	7,580	19
1834	41,600	6,845	16
1835	47,400	10,568	22
1836	53,300	12,426	23

Britain supplied the United States but, at the same time, exceeded all other countries in taking American products in the antebellum period. The United Kingdom took an average of 40 per cent of United States exports by value between 1821 and 1840, and nearly half by the middle 1850s.[101] American southern states supplied 80 per cent of Lancashire cotton.[102] Only France approached Britain as an export market for American goods, but even at their peak in the 1830s and 1840s, American exports to France reached but half the British totals.[103]

American foreign trade in the antebellum years increased, but not as quickly as its gross national product. Moreover, the composition of its foreign trade remained stable, with primary products making up most of American exports. According to one estimate, finished and semi-finished goods never formed even one-quarter of exports by value during the period, although they did begin to grow relative to exports during the 1840s.[104] American manufacturing exports hardly increased beyond the category of low-quality textiles. No general increase in manufacturing took place before the 1850s, and even then, value-added products did not become statistically significant for another two decades.[105]

The United States had an unfavourable balance of trade worldwide for most antebellum years. In the years 1828–37, for example, only 1829 and 1830 produced surpluses. However unbalanced, United States trade increased enormously in dollar value through four periods of alternating business peaks and troughs. After a wartime peak in 1816, trade declined steadily by over half to reach a bottom in 1821. A four-year upswing to 1825 ended with a sharp correction in 1826 followed by glacial slippage for four years to 1829. After a two-year standstill period, an explosive upswing began in 1831 that pushed American foreign trade to more than double its 1829–30 volume by 1836, and to levels not touched again until 1850. In the upswing periods, imports exceeded exports in percentage gain, but in downswing periods, imports exceeded exports in percentage loss.[106]

British foreign and colonial trade mirrored the American general trade pattern in rough outline (Chart 2.1).[107] From 1821, overall British total commerce increased steadily to a peak in the middle of 1825, then abruptly halted and reversed. By 1827 foreign trade had recovered almost fully, then vacillated in a band of 5 per cent until 1832. That year, a five-year upswing began which lifted aggregate British worldwide trade more than 35 per cent beyond the highs of 1825, with imports increasing more quickly than exports.[108] Bilateral British trade volume with the United States was less regular and prone to quick reversals than its trade with the world overall, of course, but it did track the ebbs and flows of the American total trade pattern generally. This is not surprising given the large amount of commercial intercourse between the two countries as outlined above.

In the first half of the nineteenth century, Great Britain was a net importing nation in its foreign and colonial merchandise trade.[109] With the United States, however, Great Britain maintained a nearly continuous trade surplus in the years 1816–36, with exports averaging 18 per cent over imports by value. Aggregate Anglo-American trade levels of 1836 would not be matched again for ten years but, by then, the internals of the trade had changed. The two decades of surpluses to 1836 formed both a peak and a climacteric because, in subsequent years, favourable British trade balances with the United States were the exceptions, not the rule. British imports fell off in the face of surging American cotton exports and increasing American manufacturing capabilities.[110]

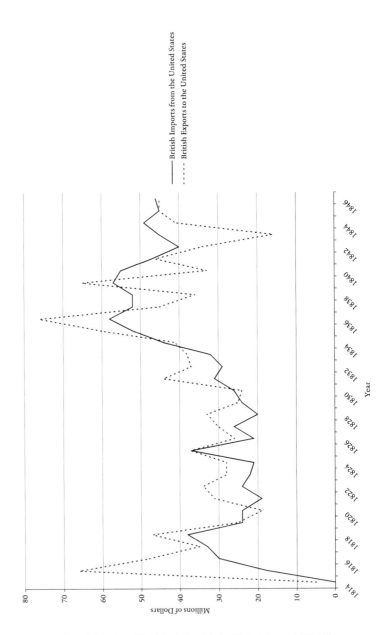

Chart 2.1: Value of British Trade with the United States, 1814–46.

Credit Arrangements and Trade Mechanics

Ever-growing commerce between Great Britain and the United States required credit arrangements. To the late 1830s, the balance of trade remained soundly in favour of Great Britain. Until more competitive American manufactures redressed the import–export imbalance, financing of Anglo-American trade generally originated in Britain. The British surplus was due in part to the structural changes that transformed Britain into an industrial country from the 1780s to the 1830s. The typical unit of the new economy became the factory, which housed the new technology and machines of the industrial revolution. Whether in glass, iron, ceramics, non-ferrous metals, paper or textiles, larger capacity and technology-led productivity increases allowed lower prices and greater output which sought wider markets. The improving production prowess of British industry combined with a ferocious pent-up demand for consumer goods in the United States after 1815 created a favourable British trade picture.

Manufactures stored in Liverpool, Halifax and Bermuda since 1808 streamed from the United Kingdom to the United States in great quantities with peace and the restoration of regular trade relations.[111] Most exports arrived on British account; mainly on consignment to American agents, who sold them at auction to traders ('jobbers') who, in turn, bundled the various goods they bought for sale to American retail merchants doing business throughout the United States. Huge numbers of goods were consigned to overseas destinations. A representative of Barings' competitor, Thomas Wilson & Company, testified about the reasoning behind such a practice:

> The manufacturers in England are obliged to operate on a very large scale; they have a regular demand [at home] for two-thirds or three-fourths of what they make, and the rest they ship; and their reason for shipping is that they do not choose to depreciate their own articles, and they do not choose to compete with their customers; they can only sell at a fit price a certain quantity, and the excess they export.[112]

Prices of goods which manufacturers consigned to American port cities were lower than the same goods in the British domestic market. Until the 1830s, this British export 'dumping' thwarted American importers' usual practice of buying goods in the British market for shipment home. The relatively high prices American importers paid in Britain made profits nearly impossible. In 1825 *Niles' Weekly Register* reported resentment from many quarters in the American mercantile community that an estimated 'three-fourths of all dry goods of cotton, wool, linen, and silk, etc. received at New York were on foreign account.'[113]

Some British manufacturers shipped surplus output directly to their own resident agents abroad. More likely, however, they consigned goods to a commission merchant in their home city who had experience with shipping and insurance, as well as knowledge of particular markets where the manufactured goods would sell best. Besides commercial know-how, the manufacturer preferred to consign his surplus to the commission merchant because the merchant would likely advance the manufacturer two-thirds to three-quarters of the value of the goods consigned. This advance commonly took the form of the manufacturer drawing a bill on the merchant, which the manufacturer could convert to cash in the evolving discount market in order to pay wages and suppliers. The merchant then reconsigned goods to his own agent – for example in the United States – and settled with the manufacturer when he received the proceeds of the goods' sale in the American market. Price competition made the British industrialists unable to afford the expenses and risks of exporting and marketing surplus goods abroad. As a result, they put such services into the hands of merchant banking specialists.[114]

While the merchant extended credit to the manufacturer, the merchant depended on bankers and note brokers such as Baring Brothers & Company, who, financially, formed the coordinating hub of the Anglo-American trade system from the early 1820s.[115] The banking and credit facilities available to the British merchant and manufacturer were of broad value since, through them, accommodations extended along the transatlantic credit chain to the American jobber, retail merchant and consumer to connect United States commerce to the British money market. Comparable commercial credit facilities, such as foreign exchange, were not available on the American side so conveniently or in such variety.[116]

American agricultural exports after 1815 balanced British manufacturing imports, but only until Europe rekindled farm production, which occurred approximately in the years 1819–20. The United States economy experienced a general downturn during these years, with a concomitant drop-off in foreign exchange earnings. These trends opened American auction markets ever more widely to the products of already-competitive British industry. Additionally, instability in financial markets because of the dissolution of the First Bank of the United States left American merchants and businessmen looking to British capital for credit resources.

American suspicions of British designs to overwhelm the United States by dumping manufactures were not unfounded. As early as 1817 Lord Henry Brougham had stated boldly in Parliament that 'it is worth while to incur a loss upon the first exportations in order, by the glut, to stifle in the cradle those rising manufactures in the United States which the war had forced into existence contrary to the natural course of things'.[117] Sixteen years later, a leading merchant banker testified to Parliament that British industry would readily sell below cost 'if this would do mischief to competitors'. As for the United States, this banker said the British exporter was glad 'to ruin the American manufacturer with a surplus of goods'.[118]

British exports by volume remained on a slow uptrend after 1814, and certainly must have appeared formidable to American consumers and businessmen in their variety and low price. But the Anglo-American trade picture was deceptive and shifting. Heavy British export volumes to the United States were not matched by export values, which actually fell off steadily between 1815 and the mid-1820s.[119] Fierce price competition among British manufacturers at home caused a contraction of margins. American tariff increases in 1816, 1818, 1824 and 1828 weakened the position of British goods within the consignment and auction systems that Great Britain had controlled utterly since 1815. [120] In the years 1826–30, American exports to Great Britain increased 24 per cent by value, while British exports to the United States were flat. In 1830, trade approximately balanced between the two partners.[121] As we shall see, the trade picture changed somewhat in the British favour with American tariff reform in 1832.

By the early 1830s, the American importer reappeared as a buyer of goods on the spot in England. This indicated that postwar dumping of British merchandise in the United States had likely moderated and prices in the American market had risen to levels which made the American importers' purchases in England worthwhile. In 1837, *The Edinburgh Review* commented on the reconfiguration of trade in past decades:

> The increase in trade gradually reintroduced, and ultimately established, a more convenient and cheaper mode of carrying on the trade. This was brought about by the importing houses in America establishing agents in the manufacturing districts of this country, and also on the Continent, China, etc., for the purpose and shipment of products for the United States.[122]

British merchant bankers also noted the change in trade pattern in the form of numerous American importing merchants in England seeking credits to purchase British manufactures. In 1833, a Baring managing partner reported the large number and growing sophistication of Americans abroad. At a given time, one hundred Americans might be in London with an introduction to the House, he said, and these merchants of the United States were 'generally more wealthy and systematic in their business than in former times'.[123]

Americans crossed to London in the decade after 1825 and sought credits from mercantile Houses for goods purchased overseas, but these same Houses now crossed to the United States to establish or expand operations. Their commitment stemmed in large part from an interest in the consignment trade in American cotton, but more generally had to do with the enormous long-term potential they considered the United States to possess as a stable market for British exports, as well as for portfolio and direct investment. The British credit system that had supported the American trade from the eighteenth century came to the United States in the late 1820s in the form of agents in major east coast

Figure 2.1: View of London by Patten. Hand-coloured aquatint
(n.d.). Emmet Collection, New York Public Library.

cities for the more direct coordination and financing of the American import-
export business.

The Anglo-American credit system in the 1830s generally included a banker
in London or Liverpool, together with an agent in a large American east coast
city who coordinated the financing of merchandise shipments. In the case of the
American importing merchant in the United States, the first step was to apply
to the British banker's agent for a letter of credit (an advance in the case of an
exporter). If granted after investigation by the agent, the London banking House
entered into its ledgers the specific amount of the credit which the agent passed
along to it. A British manufacturer from whom the American merchant purchased goods then drew on his London banker, who accepted the bill of exchange
the manufacturer received back from the importer for goods forwarded to the
United States. The London banker generally sent the shipping documents to the
importer's bank in the United States, with which the London bank had a correspondent relationship. The American bank then held the shipping documents as
security for the importer's payment. Thus, the introduction of banking intermediaries greatly streamlined a formerly cumbersome and time-consuming process
of bill payment across great distances. Without merchant bankers, traders had to
go into the marketplace and seek out bills from other traders that fit the specifications of their debts in amount and destination.

In the case of an American exporter of cotton, the operation would likely be coordinated out of a major American eastern city as follows. The exporting merchant maintained a correspondent in a major southern city, say Charleston or New Orleans, who he would order to purchase a cargo of cotton. The merchant would direct the southern correspondent to draw a bill of exchange on him for the amount of the cotton, which he would do while, at the same time, shipping the cotton to, for example, Liverpool. The eastern merchant would meet the southern drafts on him by bills on Liverpool drawn upon his agent there, who would pay them out of the proceeds of the cotton when it was sold. The merchant banker followed this pattern of credit within the thriving American trade environment, the enormous potential of which the new Baring organization hoped to tap by various means after 1828.[124]

The New Partnership

Of the three managing partners, Joshua Bates (1788–1864) dominated day-to-day operations at 8 Bishopsgate. At just forty, Bates was several years senior in age and experience to his colleagues. He was an American from Boston, where he had trained before coming to London in 1816 as agent for several United States shipowners specializing in the Russian and Indian trades. Bates became a close friend of Hope & Company partner P.C. Labouchere, from whom he borrowed capital in 1826 to set himself up in business with John Baring. Bates's entry into Baring Brothers two years later gave him, in his own words, 'the means and respectability' to exploit his sound judgement which was founded upon a rigourous understanding of the mechanics of international trade.[125]

Besides a great knowledge of American commercial affairs, Bates brought to Baring Brothers a connection to the China House of Bryant & Sturgis of Boston. He had married the first cousin of the head of the firm, William Sturgis, in 1813, whose House Barings took over in 1828 in the wake of the difficulties of 1825–6. By bringing the 'colonial' Bates into the firm, Alexander Baring also captured the valuable American client list which Bates and John Baring had assembled as business partners. The list included nearly three dozen firms, most with trade in the East Indies and Far East. Bates & Baring's operation was generating revenue of some £14,000 a year when absorbed into Baring Brothers & Company. Of the firms retained, fourteen were American, and this provided an enlarged platform from which Barings would expand its United States business.[126]

Bates replaced Swinton C. Holland as American specialist for the firm after Holland died in 1827. Meticulous, cautious and slow to form a judgement, Bates also replaced Holland as manager of routine operations of the counting house. 'While I am in business, I like and wish to play the game well', wrote Bates in 1846. 'It is for this reason that you find me, watching and trying to take advantage of every circumstance calculated to benefit the House'.[127] In the words of Samuel Ward, American agent of Barings after 1853, Bates was the 'balance wheel of the firm'. Just half a dozen years after his appointment as partner, informed opinion recognized Bates as 'the most extensive, and certainly one of the best informed merchants in England'.[128] It was a hauntingly similar evaluation to the public praise Sir Francis and Alexander had received in their lifetimes.

Thomas Baring (1799–1873) carried on the lustre of the Baring name as a grandson of Sir Francis, and was the eponymous member of the firm from 1828 until his death. Besides being a noted banker, Thomas served as a member of Parliament, as his uncle, Alexander, had done, and was a confidant of Disraeli. He was twice offered Cabinet posts, and quite possibly the Chancellorship, but declined. His expertise tended towards affairs of the Continent, which he had gained in Amsterdam as a partner of Hope & Company for almost ten years. He worked intimately with Bates to spearhead the drive for business in the United States, and when Baring Brothers decided to try its hand at railroad finance in the 1850s, Thomas represented the House on several corporate boards including the Russian Railroad Company and the Grand Trunk Railway Company in Canada. For nearly twenty years to 1868, Thomas was chairman of Lloyd's at the time Barings began to manage and finance sailing (and later steam) ships extensively. He never retired from business to leisurely estates, and in this respect matched Bates in laborious dedication to the firm. To Bates, Thomas Baring appeared the firm's most public figure, ill-suited to the tedious exactitude of a counting house. Thomas, Bates recorded, 'has a very clever head and is just fitted for loan operations which require great effort for a short time and not a steady attention to business as commission and banking business requires'.[129]

Humphrey St John Mildmay (1794–1853) joined the partnership and the Baring family as Alexander's son-in-law in 1824. Though Mildmay's background was as an officer in the Coldstream Guards and he possessed little mercantile experience, he connected Barings to the Bank of England, where he held a directorship.[130] He seemed to play a middle-man role between Thomas Baring and Joshua Bates and, like the other two men, shared the task of dictating the enormous Barings daily correspondence worldwide. Mildmay likely had considerable responsibility for Far Eastern affairs since, upon retirement in 1847, his replacement was the prominent American China trader Russell Sturgis.[131]

The anchor of Barings operations in the United States was Thomas Wren Ward (1786–1853), who served as agent for the London house from 1828 until shortly before his death. Ward came from a well-established, though not prominent, banking family. He briefly did business with fellow Bostonian Jonathan Goodhue in New York under the partnership of Goodhue & Ward, but Ward moved back to Boston in 1817 to found an import-export house with William Ropes.

Ward dissolved the Ropes & Ward partnership in late 1826 and in 1828 visited his close friend in England, Joshua Bates, who had recently been admitted as a Baring partner. Ward and Bates were once colleagues at the counting house of William Gray many years earlier. When they met in London, Bates asked Ward to be American agent for the firm. Ward delayed his decision until the autumn of the following year, when Thomas Baring visited him on the last part of a United States tour.

Thomas Baring confirmed Ward as representative for the firm in October of 1829, commencing duties on the first day of 1830.[132] At first, London retained control of exchange accounts, security operations and consignments from the southern United States. Ward's authority was limited to granting commercial credits and gathering reliable correspondents for the London House. In 1833 Barings handed Ward full responsibility to coordinate all of the House's American business – including transfer of shipping documents, collecting debts, negotiating loans and the general marketing of Barings services in the increasingly competitive United States. Above all, Ward supplied Baring with a continuous flow of intelligence on the United States: political trends, state bond offerings, correspondent status reports, infrastructure projects, weather, shipping schedules and routes, credit information and commodity prices.

The position of Ward was so respectable, and the market of the United States so important, that Barings assured Ward that he was a de facto fourth managing partner of the firm and should feel at liberty to act freely in the name of the House. From 1829, the firm provided Ward with a yearly base salary of £1,000 – about $4,800 – which he could augment by joint financial and commercial ventures as opportunities presented themselves.[133] At the beginning of 1832, Ward's salary doubled,[134] and his personal status and the value of the American market to Barings may be indicated by comparing the salary of the bank's wool agent in Europe, M. Sussman, whose annual salary in 1832 stood at only £300.[135] For someone already financially self-sufficient and retired because of earlier success in business, Barings' American agent appeared to have a good salary. The mayor of Boston, for example, received only $2,500.[136]

Ward addressed most news of American matters to the general 'Baring Brothers & Co., London' heading, but he also wrote a separate and voluminous correspondence to his fellow Bostonian Joshua Bates. Bates and Ward were exceptionally well-informed and practical men of business; well versed in global issues, economics, monetary questions, banking, property rights and the law.[137] But they also shared a common unadorned lifestyle and personal code. It was perhaps on this basis that the two men worked so well together for over thirty years and created a strong British-American business axis.

Ward was conscientious in his role as Barings' guide and agent from his post at Boston – at times, strenuously so. His diary reveals an introspective personality, meticulous and cautious; dedicated to all things moderate and simple. In later years, qualities of a self-consciously devout and self-sacrificing Christian, merely hinted at in the 1820s, come to dominate diary entries as Ward worried increasingly about the quality of the tasks he performed for his London employer, Barings. 'I must work. I must not smoke, drink wine. I must resist extravagance', he admonished himself. 'By having no concerns and my own mind clear, I am free for Barings'.[138] And he wrote to Bates:

> If I could shake off the feeling of responsibility, or rather of anxiety, from my mind and be willing to do the best I can and leave the result, I should do well enough, but I am always, while awake, looking after possible causes of loss to you, and often even while I sleep. And I suppose this will continue so long as I hold the agency ... If I could have my own way I think I could keep you safe, but while I have agents around me ready to do what I decline, and who urge facilities upon your correspondents, it is difficult to place things on the most secure basis. I am no doubt more rigid than others and I shall bring others with me and shall gradually make things into a more perfect system.[139]

The exertions of the agency were many. From his home in Boston, Ward travelled throughout the United States, but most often to Baltimore, Philadelphia and New York. His correspondence was voluminous, averaging four detailed letters weekly to Barings alone. On occasion, Ward could dispatch as many as six letters per day on various topics to London or Liverpool for the partners' review – written by himself or an amanuensis; all under pressure of packet ship departures from Boston or New York.

Perhaps his great conscientiousness was fuelled by the fact that he carried the burden of Barings' operations in the United States alone. One recent writer found that Ward's innate conservatism would have prevented his making a fortune trading on his own account.[140] This was not Ward's usefulness to Barings, which was, rather, as effective executor of policy, reporter of news and judge of character for extensions of the House's credit. He aspired to devote himself to Barings, and did so unsparingly. In fact, his very idiosyncratic seriousness, honesty and piety appear to have made Ward invaluable to Barings as a man able to deliver independent and crisp business assessments and thoughts. He was at once a cheerleader and optimist for America's long-run prospects, and a Cassandra of imminent short-term dangers.[141] A prominent New York merchant vouched for Ward:

> He thinks the organization of your house very perfect and he will be your devoted friend. You are well aware that his opinions have great weight in Boston, as he is known to be cool in judgement and thorough in his observations. No one of our Countrymen is a greater admirer of England.[142]

In time, Ward requested that Barings furnish him a partner to share his formidable agency duties. In 1838 this wish was at last fulfilled when Ward's eldest son, Samuel, began to assist his father, and, after close Barings scrutiny, Samuel finally took over full agency duties in 1853.[143]

Like Ward, Joshua Bates was a tightly focused man, a diligent organizer and manager. He matched Ward's conscientiousness, but lacked the Christian duty that overlaid so many of Ward's introspections and motivations. For Bates, it seemed that joy was work, and he was likely pleased when his American colleague Thomas Ward told him by letter that he was 'the most uniformly laborious man' he knew, marvelling at how Bates wrote so many letters apparently with so much ease and leisure.[144] 'I have some thoughts of petitioning the House of Commons for extending the 10 hours labour bill to commission merchants and bankers. If we cannot get this we are entitled to some relief under the Slavery Emancipation Bill', wrote the hard-working Bates.[145]

Bates was acknowledged publicly as a master of commercial affairs, but he was never fully accepted into the patrician Baring line. It was, for example, several years before he was invited to Alexander Baring's estate, The Grange. For this reason, he may have felt he had to prove himself beyond the normal extent of a Baring partner. He worked six days a week and sometimes lamented that he could not keep the counting house active on Sundays.[146]

Some writers have portrayed Bates as a less attractive character than he might have been. For sure, there is no second-guessing in Bates's letters – especially to Ward. He was a man in tight possession of himself with a sharp confidence regarding business affairs that must have been off-putting to some of more delicate temperament. For example, he wrote:

> Having been generally successful in business, we have become too free and open in our conduct and have incurred risks that it will not be wise to repeat. A system of secrecy should be encouraged in our office and none but clever persons admitted into the office. A rigid economy should be enforced as much as in less prosperous times, avoid all pride & ostentation & unnecessary show.[147]

Despite – or perhaps due to – Bates's austere personality, the firm flourished in the first decade of his partnership and beyond. By the mid-1830s, some forty clerks at Bishopsgate kept up a voluminous correspondence with firms all over the world as well as with the Liverpool branch after 1832.

Bates reorganized the firm's financial and correspondence record-keeping upon his arrival in the late 1820s. Henceforth, transactions of clients were entered into oversized lockable green ledgers from which the firm tallied year-end balances. Copies of the partners' most important out-letters were now kept in a series of letter books. On packet-arrival days, usually Tuesdays and Fridays, Mildmay typically perused and answered over 200 letters of inquiry to the firm.[148] A 'numberless' stream of American visitors came to London with introductions to Bates, who resolved to increase business with the United States. Average accepting and commission income increased 118 per cent over the previous ten-year period,

1819–28. Partner capital increased by the even larger amount of 123 per cent to £776,768 by the end of 1837.[149]

Rules and Principles

Banking, particularly in the early nineteenth century, had a very personal aspect, yet in the early 1830s Barings attempted to systematize operations in order to manage its great financial ambitions and far-flung commitments. In the autumn of 1831 Thomas Ward remarked in a letter to Bates that he had noted from his years in business that 'there usually comes round every five or seven years a period of failing & distress which may produce loss'.[150] The last general business contraction in England and America had been 1825–6.[151] If Ward was right, the United States seemed due for some kind of financial or economic shock in the medium term. Bates took Ward's admonition seriously and the firm set about to establish rules and principles of business which would not change substantially for three decades.

Under the 1828 partnership, Barings' business had several aspects. The firm bought and sold merchandise, including bullion, specie and bills of exchange for clients throughout the world. Barings was also an acceptance House – extending short-term credits on commission to facilitate the movement of raw materials and finished goods in trade. Some clients utilized Barings to keep personal funds on deposit; others as an exchange account – which meant that, for a fee, Barings made collections and payments. Like other bankers whose business was trade, Barings entered the field of cargo shipping, albeit briefly, in the middle 1830s, and continued with the concomitant service of providing insurance to trade clients.[152] Finally, Barings became involved with the business of investment banking that brought the House some public notoriety, but remained a relatively small part of the partners' overall activity before the American Civil War.

Multiplicity of talents and activities was characteristic of busy merchant bankers but, even among these, Barings was diversified. The partners seemed interested in everything and, unlike other Houses which specialized in narrow lines of business or merchandise, Barings remained general merchants until well into the nineteenth century. The House extended credits on virtually all major staples, including tallow, coffee, indigo, wool, rice, wheat, iron, sugar, tobacco, cotton and hemp.

The principle operations of Barings in the United States involved letters of credit for American importers and credit advances to American exporters for consignments. After 1832, Thomas Ward managed both. In moving merchandise over a given distance, a cardinal decision involved the part of a given shipment's cost the bank was willing to finance, and the amount and type of collateral the bank required to back up the shipment. For advances on consigned exports from the United States, London left final judgements to Ward, but they preferred he operate within general guidelines for three categories of American customers. To men of 'unquestioned' means and trust, Barings required no invoice, and no lading documents or proof of insurance. To men of slightly more modest account and reputation, the partners asked for shipping documentation made out to the order of Barings, including insurance, and delivered to Ward in Boston. For safe, respectable business enterprises of smaller scale, the partners asked for full shipping documentation to be sent to the London office.[153]

From these three classes, Ward developed methods of reporting to Barings on his fast-growing list of American clients. He numbered each firm with which he did business, for brevity in writing as well as for confidentiality, and used these numbers when communicating with the London house about particular firms. He also classified clients according to their character, repayment reliability and prospects for future business. Under such headings as 'No trust', 'Houses having various connexions', 'Failed', 'Do not know', 'Dissolved' and 'Dead', as well as the three main categories of credit outlined above in Barings' instructions, Ward reported to London on United States business. According to Ward's lists, the number of American clients for the House (of all above classifications) was 917, 1,030 and 1,295 respectively for the years 1832, 1835 and 1837.[154] Impressions of particular American clients were logged into 'private remarks books' collected in London at the request of the American agent, a copy of which Ward kept for his own reference.[155]

For an importer's letter of credit, Ward outlined varied specifications. Generally, he issued a letter to the American petitioner for credit, then forwarded a copy to London. The letters varied according to where the applicant planned to do business. This determined the time the merchant had to exercise his credit. The most common credits involved transatlantic transactions, and typically had a maturity of sixty to ninety days. South American credits were usually confined to Atlantic ports, and issued for periods up to three months. Barings intended the longest credits of up to eighteen months for use in the Calcutta and Far Eastern trades – the latter of which the United States had played a major part in since independence.[156]

The ready acceptance of Barings' drafts by merchants in distant trade centres indicates the reputation enjoyed by London and Barings in the international mercantile community of the 1830s.[157] Ward's home in the city of Boston happened to be the centre of the China trade in the United States. To accommodate the large American demand for means of payment in this trade, the Bank of the United States under Biddle developed and popularized a long-dated bill on London in the late 1820s for use by merchants sailing to the Orient or remote destinations in the southern hemisphere. The large 'open credit' Barings extended to the Bank of the United States, in turn, gave Biddle latitude to extend bills to Americans in the China trade. Barings' creditor status to the Bank of the United States provided

Ward a certain proprietary window on the eastern long-distance trade. Moreover, these bills amounted to a business of almost $1 million a year for Biddle by the middle of 1831.[158]

Not only time-limited, letters of credit could be restrictive or non-restrictive as to the type of commodity shipped, at what price, the percentage of each cargo Barings would accept drafts upon, shipping documentation requirements, and whether the letter was transferable to a second party. Some letters specified regularly renewable credits as the House received remittances – an increasingly common and potentially abused device in the 1830s called an 'open credit'.

An example of Ward's rules of business may be seen in the list he sent to a new institutional client who had applied to him for credit in the autumn of 1835. He had the honour 'on behalf of Messrs. Baring Brothers & Co. of London' to inform the president of the Consolidated Association of the Planters of Louisiana that the House extended credit under the following conditions:

> 1. Remittances shall be made to Messrs. Baring Brothers & Co. to cover said credit so that said remittances be always received by them previous to the maturity of the Bills drawn on them.
> 2. The Credit when so covered to be in force to its full extent.
> 3. A commission of one half of one per cent to be charged both for paying & receiving in London.
> 4. Interest to be at the rate of five percent per annum when the balance is in favour of Messrs. Barings Brothers & Co. and at the rate of 4 percent per annum when the balance is against them.
> 5. The association is to have the privilege of drawing at 60 or 90 days sight at its option.
> 6. The Credit to be in full force for 12 months from the 1st day of September next.

Ward wrote that the Association was granted a fixed uncovered credit of 'twenty five thousand pounds thirty, the Bills to be drawn at the usual sight of sixty days'.[159]

Barings employed two general types of foreign bills of exchange for trade transactions. The first was the documentary bill of exchange. Sometimes called a 'secured credit', this instrument required that bills of lading accompany any exported cargo, and that these ownership-conferring documents be made out to the merchant banker who extended the credit. Alternatively, 'unsecured credits' (sometimes called 'uncovered' or 'open' credits by Ward) required no bills of lading or other documents attached. On occasion, Joshua Bates granted American credits in London.[160] As of the beginning of 1833, however, Barings granted Ward full power to authorize all trade arrangements with American merchants and tradesmen. By 1835, Ward reported that he was so well associated with Barings in the United States that it had become 'a matter of course' that American Houses who wished credits with Bishopsgate should inquire about them through him.[161]

Indeed, Ward requested numerous times that London refer inquiries about American credits specifically to him so that he could better know the complete client business in the United States.[162]

The objective of all operations of the Bank was profit, but only if achieved by a course of plodding moderation. Frequently, for the sake of safety, Ward passed up business offered to the House.[163] In the long term, preservation of capital and assets predominated over profit considerations, for the partners realized that the road to long-run growth lay in the direction of safety. 'What we do must be safe, and *may* be profitable', wrote Ward to London.[164] Many firms wanted credits and advances through Barings since this association added to their own prestige and their ability to attract business. The temptation of overextension was ever-present and resisted continuously by the partners, and was the ruin of other firms with less restraint.

To Bates, caution was close to obsession; with Ward, caution was part of a conviction that the best approach in most human affairs was moderation, girded by a high moral standard. Avoidable missteps were close to sin; a betrayal of trust to one's employer. 'Your position is a commanding one', wrote Ward, 'and only requires the business to be well managed on both sides of the water to increase indefinitely. But the great object of us both is safety to you. As this is attained, your end will be answered. To secure this, and to keep secure against evil days, must be my main object.'[165] One student of the House of Baring has written that 'an overwhelming proportion of the credits granted by Ward to American businessmen belonged in the 'uncovered' category'.[166] In order for this to occur, there required rigourous intelligence about the persons to whom the House extended credit, and under what conditions. With an eye to protection, the House followed certain concrete measures.

The mechanical safeguards by which Barings extended credit to American importers and exporters were several.[167] First, Ward's granting of uncovered credits was rendered less risky by Barings' policy of operating as merely a financial *enhancer* to firms, rather than as an actual financial *enabler* of firms and of their trade undertakings. That is, credits could not exceed a firm's total capital. Paradoxically, a firm received credit from Barings only if it had the resources and public standing to purchase goods in its own good name to the amount it was requesting from Barings.

Second, advances on exports would be accompanied by automatic liens against any sales on commodities in the event of delinquent payments. This understanding would be in a written agreement between Ward and the borrower. Barings insured all shipments at the borrower's expense; if the shipment was lost, the insurance went to Barings.

For added security, Ward incorporated a receipt into his letter of credit agreements by 1831, which stated explicitly that the borrower would provide Barings with 'sufficient funds' to meet any obligations contracted in trade.[168] This device has been called a 'banker's trust receipt' and allowed, for example, an importer to sell merchandise shipped to him in order to generate funds to pay back creditors such as Barings. When the merchandise arrived, however, legal title to it lay with the creditor, not the trader; and before merchandise could be released, a copy of the receipt went to the banker for documentation of the trader's obligations.[169] For many years, receipts were Ward's innovation – unique to Barings – and in the middle 1840s became standard trade practice.

Whatever safeguards for credit extensions, Barings insisted on exclusive arrangements with its trading clients – a rule from which Ward and the firm rarely deviated. Ward specified, for example, that a trader who desired financing should first wrap up any projects pending before receiving Barings' funding. In American client lists, Ward separated for the partners' easy reference what he referred to as 'Houses having other connections'. These were firms Ward numbered and tracked which had links to Houses other than Barings. Ward was strict with these 'double accounts' and there are numerous examples of offending firms dismissed crisply from Barings for doing business with other merchant banks.[170] 'The general complications of business cannot but be complicated further by our merchants having commitments we know nothing about', wrote Bates to Ward in 1831. 'If we are bound to a single man, and he to us, it will give a better guaranty against loss.'[171] Exclusivity also applied to groups, such as long-distance traders engaged in the Far East or East Indian trades who frequently combined resources in what were called 'combination voyages'. Barings preferred the several participants to assume joint responsibility in the form of a single umbrella credit consolidating the entire mission.

Transparency with customers ensured better information and, with information, safety. With Barings, credits were irrevocable agreements, and the firm in general did not write revocation clauses, unlike other firms such as Brown Brothers. The Barings system was honour-based and somewhat rigid; and applied to all clients – even those whom Barings knew well through experience and investigation and for whom regulations were a mere formality.

While strict adherence to rules remained a general objective for London in terms of their distant agent in the United States, the partners intended that instructions serve merely as an outline for the firm's American operations. Joshua Bates had known Ward since 1817, and had identified him as a man little prone to recklessness or speculation. He trusted Ward to take Barings' general statements of procedure seriously, yet apply them in a way suited to the particular commercial and financial circumstances Ward faced in the United States. 'You must guide the House from your side within the instructions we have issued', wrote Bates to Ward in 1833. 'But at times you must judge the exceptions for us'. Ward responded confidently. 'Under your principles and my practice', he wrote, 'there will be no difficulty keeping everyone prompt and the whole business without too much restriction'.[172]

However stoutly the partners stood by rules set out in advance, and however well they broadcast them throughout the House and to related associates, the less tangible, non-mechanical side of doing business was likely equally crucial. The long-term tenure and energy of Bates and Thomas Baring in England, and Ward and others in the United States, will be described below. They provided the good judgement by which rules and devices were carried out. As the 1830s unfolded in the United States, the good fortunes of the House were the result of myriad individual decisions and judgements. The effectiveness of Barings' judgements, so far as they bore fruit in successful American operations, contrasted starkly with the struggles of their competitors.

3 GOOD TIMING (1830−2)

It is a great thing to have got along for two years and a half without making any serious mistakes.

In the present state of things, I find no overstocks, but rather British and American industry in vigorous action, and the world at peace. Things are in the main in a sound state, and it would not be possible to have again in the near future such a crisis such as that of 1825−6. Time will be needed to create overstocks, to raise prices, to induce price pressure.

Thomas Wren Ward[173]

The new partnership and Thomas Wren Ward established relationships with American commission merchants and bankers at New York and New Orleans that acted as additional anchors of operation to the main agency in Boston. The timing of the firm's renewed commitment to the United States was excellent. The recovery of depressed commodity prices, real estate and foreign trade was underway in the Atlantic economy.

On the eve of an economic uptick, the bank established an office in Liverpool for the receipt of American news and cotton, and for integration of its new operations in India and China. In the years 1830−2, Barings was quite confident of its ability to compete with more recently-arrived British firms in the United States. It was perhaps even more sure-footed in this market because of its American partner, Joshua Bates, who largely determined American policy. At this time, the firm was highly successful at attracting accounts, and profits were large. The firm experienced some difficulties with the Bank of the United States in the slight downturn of 1830, but resolved these to mutual advantage. Barings' timing in terms of politics was less good. As the House committed to the business of the United States in 1828−9, Americans elected a president less friendly to financial institutions than his predecessor, though the firm was unaware of this at the time. Barings had to determine if turbulence was a normal growing pain of a restless young nation, or a sign of more serious things to come.

Cornerstone Connections

Whatever extensive experience the partners had in the American trade, they nevertheless remained domiciled in London. The partners needed direct connections to the United States, arrangements whereby they could be supplied with a continuous stream of reliable and useful information from personnel on the spot. The mechanisms of the American trade on the western side of the Atlantic needed securing and, in the spring of 1828, Thomas Baring sailed to the United States to do just that.

Bates and Thomas Baring had visited the United States earlier in the late 1820s. It was Thomas's more lengthy travels, however, that introduced American businessmen to a new generation of Barings. In turn, the tour showed Barings for the first time a new, and more demonstrably democratic, generation of Americans. Thomas travelled from New England to New Orleans looking for opportunities to expand the services of the London firm. He re-established the steady, influential and exclusive connections with the United States that proved crucial to the House in the challenging decade ahead.

In a renewed effort to increase cotton consignments and other agricultural shipments to Barings, Thomas spent considerable time in New Orleans. Most surplus produce of the Ohio and Mississippi valleys came down-river to New Orleans in the years before the building of America's east-west transportation lines. At New Orleans, commodities of the American interior – pork, corn, tobacco, sugar and cotton – found their way into local markets or were transferred to coastal and ocean-going vessels for shipment to east coast and European ports. Manufactured goods from Europe passed through New Orleans as well, for distribution over a wide area of the lower south and Mexico. The War of 1812 had interrupted trade, but after the Treaty of Ghent, new mercantile Houses appeared. Indeed, from Latin America came coffee and cocoa which, after the 1820s, travelled upstream in ever-more powerful paddle steamers to the shelves of storekeepers throughout America's great central valley.[174] New Orleans merchants especially prized the Mexican trade, since Mexico had little produce to export, but paid for the bulk of its imports in silver bullion.[175]

Many mercantile firms appearing in New Orleans after 1815 flourished in the 1820s. Thomas Baring established relationships with William Nott & Company, and Yeatman Woods & Company, by agreeing to take shares in cotton cargoes and other commodities shipped to the order of Barings, opening credits on major New York banks so that these New Orleans Houses might issue drafts in advance of sales.

Nott and Yeatman remained two of Barings' trading contacts at New Orleans for several decades. Foremost, however, among Thomas's contacts established in 1828 was Edmond Jean Forstall (1794–1873), who enmeshed Baring Brothers & Company in American banking and southern commerce by providing the firm

with an important node for lucrative operations and information on market conditions in the United States in general.

Forstall was perhaps the most famous of the American polymath merchant
bankers in the antebellum American south, with major interests in sugar plant-
ing, finance and merchandising.[176] In 1824 he was managing partner at New
Orleans in the firm of Gordon, Forstall & Company, with his associate, Alexander
Gordon, in Liverpool. The firm had a branch in Tampico, Mexico, which sold
goods of all kinds on consignment from European Houses, sometimes bypassing
New Orleans. The firm sent specie to England from Tampico or New Orleans,
wherever the exchange spread was greatest. By the time Thomas Baring arrived in
1828, Gordon, Forstall & Company was doing a $250,000 cotton-consignment
business to Liverpool, representing approximately 8,000 bales of cotton per buying season. Forstall already did foreign business in the late 1820s and 1830s with
the Lizardi brothers – merchant bankers of Paris, London and Liverpool, but he
forged the important link to Barings through a landmark funding arrangement
involving a newly-established property bank, the Consolidated Association of
the Planters of Louisiana.[177]

Thomas Baring's interest in the southern United States was unusual for the
firm. After all, most of Barings' commercial relationships until the 1860s extended
from Baltimore northwards. But New Orleans was not usual. By the 1830s, it
stood as the American south's most important city, processing the most valuable
commodities in the country's domestic and foreign trade.

For trade finance, however, Thomas turned north-easterly to Boston,
Philadelphia and, most importantly, New York. Until the 1850s, the private
banking firm of Prime, Ward & King was the premier financial connection of the
Baring Brothers & Company in New York. As New Orleans held paramountcy
in the American cotton and commodity trades, so by 1830 New York held paramountcy in American finance. Nathaniel Prime (1768–1840), founder of the
firm and pioneer in the American securities and loan-contracting businesses,
built the House to such prominence that until 1839 it yielded first place for influence only to the Bank of the United States.[178] Its importance may be indicated
by the premium its bills often commanded in the New York money market. Like
Barings and Rothschilds, Prime maintained a large bill brokering business. They
bought up good bills on Paris and London, and remitted to their bankers. Such
was their reputation and credit that on packet days they were large sellers of their
own sterling and French bills at a huge 1 per cent spread over what they paid
for the best private bills. The firm supplied American securities to London, and
resold those returned as unattractive to European investors.[179]

From an agreement reached in 1830, Barings and Prime established a special relationship referred to in the official inter-House correspondence as 'joint
account E'. By this arrangement, the New York House enjoyed a revolving credit
of £50,000 for its exchange operations. This meant that Prime could draw up to

Figure 3.1: View of New York from Brooklyn by Carl Fredrik (after Axel Klinkowstrom).
Aquatint (1824). I. N. Phelps Stokes Collection, New York Public Library.

£50,000 on Barings before remitting bills, securities or bullion to cover. By the
time of the 1830 agreement, Barings' linkage to Prime was eighteen years old.
Barings showed the exceptional esteem in which it held the New York House by
allowing it to do business with other merchant bankers in the city – a measure
called a 'double account' that Barings accorded few other American firms.[180]

Prime, Ward & King served as the most direct financial conduit for Baring
Brothers to American state securities, and for general investment banking oppor-
tunities throughout the United States. It was with Prime, for example, that
Barings in 1832 took Louisiana state bonds issued in favour of the Union Bank
when Edmond Forstall was a state bank commissioner. Prime received the lot and
Barings sold them in England on commission.

In addition to Prime, Ward & King, Barings maintained correspondent relations with the firm of Goodhue & Company, founded in New York in 1809
by Jonathan Goodhue. An international commission House of long standing, Goodhue acted as agent for commercial firms throughout the world. The
firm dispatched clerks to form commercial Houses in Canton, Calcutta, St
Petersburg, London and throughout Mexico and South America. Contacts with
Barings appear to have started in April 1826, when Joshua Bates chose Goodhue
& Company as its confidential correspondents in New York for Bates and Baring.
Goodhue & Company served Barings as a financial intermediary in cotton opera-
tions, and as a deposit agency for funds collected from debtors throughout the
United States.[181]

Trough Opportunities and British Malaise

In the first years of Ward's agency, American trade contacts for Barings mush-roomed quickly, as Ward established a global correspondence from the United States that reflected Barings already great worldwide reach. Ward extended credit facilities to American merchants buying goods in Europe, Latin America and the Far East, and both he and the London partners worked to increase consign-ments to the House overall. Barings granted import credits to over three dozen American firms for various dry goods, bar iron, wool, small fabricated iron prod-ucts, hemp and sheet copper. In turn, London urged Ward to arrange to receive consignments through key American firms of piece goods through Barings from Swedish, French and Russian firms. Goodhue & Company (New York), Oelrichs & Lurman (Baltimore) and Samuel Comly (Philadelphia) all became cornerstone firms in the Barings consignment network.

In Asia, Barings' experience gave Ward confidence to extend liberal credits to traders doing business in so-called ports 'beyond the Cape of Good Hope'. The final abolition of the East India Company monopoly in 1834 allowed Barings to expand its mercantile business in the Far East. Trade liberalization directly affected trade patterns. The East India Company's monopoly in India was abol-ished in 1813, and for the China market in 1834. It made sense that the Barings partners reported that credits granted for use in Calcutta and other ports of India exceeded those for use in Canton in 1832, and they anticipated a surge in China business.[182] The partners commented to Ward that the credits he granted were obviating the need for specie as a form of payment in its eastern operations almost completely.[183]

Barings moved cautiously in its South American business, though its geograph-ical proximity to London and the United States seemed to make it a most natural arena for activity. Experiences in Mexico and Brazil, and the 1828 defaults in Argentina, caused the partners misgivings about the reliability of Latin American firms and governments. The only major venture into Latin American finance during this period was the assumption of the financial agency for the Chilean government in 1844.[184]

There was activity enough in the United States to take up any slack in the markets of Latin America or Asia. 'We have business coming from everywhere', Ward wrote to Bates from Boston in 1833.[185] Indeed, the United States was grow-ing rapidly. Population surged 30 per cent between 1816 and 1826, and galloped ahead again by a third the following decade.[186] The growing population was also mobile, mostly in a westerly direction; and in its movement, it changed the shape of the country. In the twenty years after 1816, Indiana, Illinois, Missouri and Michigan entered the Union as new states, and President Andrew Jackson recog-nized the Lone Star Republic of Texas.

The surge and spread of population matched increases in national production. The leading sectors of American economic growth and largest providers of private income were the staple crops of corn, wheat and, above all, cotton. The price of cotton firmed in the 1831–2 season from the dismal levels reached in 1827–31, and this firming paced a general quickening of American economic activity that so differentiated the 1830s from the middle 1820s. Increased cotton prices led to a sweeping demand for acreage throughout the south-western states of Alabama, Mississippi, Louisiana and Arkansas. Prices and profitability of basic staples affected western expansion. By 1830 cereals commanded the high pre-1825 prices.

In addition to price inducements, huge capital investment in canals encouraged east-west migration, led to an improved transportation net, and increased urbanization. In the 1830s, western cities looked to the eastern cities of Baltimore, Philadelphia and New York, as east-west trade became as vital an axis for business as the older western-southern route. Wheeling, Pittsburgh and Cincinnati symbolized the developing west, fuelled by immigrants and surging demand from the east, as well as new markets in the new southern states.[187]

By the early 1830s, a convergence of monthly prices in New York, New Orleans and Cincinnati suggested the integration of regional markets.[188] Geographical variations remained in the 1830s in the form of price lags in east, west and south – but these had diminished since the 1820s, and would largely disappear by the late 1850s. Based on wholesale commodity prices, apparently the United States was becoming more closely tied together economically, and price changes in one region tended to be reflected quickly in others.[189] The telegraph would hurry the process along.

While inter-regional activity increased, other measures of economic activity revived as well. American foreign trade, which so interested Barings and other merchant banks, troughed between 1828 and 1830 to levels not seen but once in three decades, and formed a base from which to advance. Prices had dropped for over a decade since 1819, and the particularly sharp decreases of 1822–5 were part of a larger declining price pattern. In the middle of 1830, however, commodity prices began to firm from low levels. As rising cotton prices caused the speculation in land sales in 1816–18, so it would do the same in the advance about to take place in the 1830s. Cotton exports increased significantly for ten years after 1828, and helped the United States to extremely favourable terms of trade for the balance of the decade.[190]

Indeed by 1836, cotton represented nearly 8 per cent of American gross national product, and likely exceeded this figure as a total contributor to economic growth due to the industry's backwards and forwards linkages. The centrality of cotton in the American economy of the 1830s was expressed by *Niles' Weekly Register* when it wrote: 'Cotton has passed from the condition of a mere article of commerce to the performance of the mighty function of being in a great degree, the regulator of exchanges and the standard of values of our country'.[191] What is striking is that Barings committed to the United States in 1828 at what appeared to be a lull in American trade and in the Anglo-American economy. If an advance came, the firm would be there to participate and profit (see Table 3.1).

At the time, conditions in Britain were less immediately promising than in the younger United States, and may have had something to do with the partners' decision to act. The late 1820s found Britain recovering from what Thomas Tooke modestly described as the 'memorable speculations of 1825'.[192] Falling profits, chronic unemployment and relatively high food prices followed in speculation's wake and, though there were attempts at recovery in 1827–8 and 1830, each lacked conviction.

By 1827, official foreign trade volumes nearly matched 1825 levels, but the real values of British foreign trade did not match 1825 figures until 1833. In the six-year period to 1832, security prices declined. Industrial prices remained anaemic, with the possible exception of textiles, and several sectors such as iron and coal had suffered depression since 1826. Evidence before the Parliamentary Select Committee on Commerce and Manufactures in 1833 revealed the years from 1826 as ones of profitless growth. British business was active but difficult, with margins slight amidst fierce domestic competition in such industries as shipping, woollens, silk and cotton spinning. Installation of labour-saving machinery increased unemployment in the short run. It also enhanced productivity in British industry with, in Tooke's phrase, a resulting 'increased power of supply', which put further downward pressure on prices and wages.[193]

The several alternations between economic recovery and distress in the years between 1825 and 1832 created a vague discomforting malaise that contrasted with the speculative exuberance of the early 1820s. The expected growing pains of an industrializing economy, such as labour problems and transitions to new technologies, together with a general cautiousness after the 1826 downturn, made these difficult years for British business. Apprehension for the future led one commentator to write of 'a want of confidence in every class', and of 'buyers paralysed'. The *British Farmer's Magazine* reported in 1828 that such flux might occur over the course of just weeks in the grain markets; that 'one can scarcely say what the prices are for a few days together'.[194] The supply side in 1830 was skittish also, as a knowledgeable observer of the British economic scene wrote:

> There had, at different times during the fall, been a rally of markets from the influence of opinion that they had seen their lowest. Under the influence of this opinion, the importers and manufacturers were occasionally induced to extend their stocks; but fresh supplies, at a reduced cost, repeatedly disappointed their expectations, and entailed losses upon their previous purchases. The repetition of disappointments naturally abated confidence in the maintenance of markets, and the usual buyers became discouraged from embarking freely, even at the reduced prices, by a feeling of disgust, for hav-

Table 3.1: Trough Indicators. Both American and British prices are yearly averages of monthly data. Sources: Rostow, *The World Economy*, pp.132–3; Taylor, *The Transportation Revolution*, pp. 444–6; Smith and Cole, *Fluctuations in American Business*, p. 158; Gayer et al., *The Growth and Fluctuation*, p. 468.

Year	US Cotton Production (1,000 bales)	US Cotton Price (cents/lb)	US Land Sales Receipts (unit=$1000)	Price of Slaves in Virginia (US$)	Total Foreign Trade: US ($millions)	Total Foreign Trade: UK ($millions)	Wholesale Prices: US (Base: 1834–42)	Wholesale Prices: UK (Base: 1821–5)
1825	892	18.6	1292	425	181	659	108	113
1826	1121	12.2	1130	400	151	517	95	100
1827	957	9.3	1405	400	145	627	92	99
1828	721	10.3	1219	400	145	599	89	92
1829	870	9.9	2163	400	135	601	88	96
1830	876	10	2409	425	134	638	85	95
1831	1038	9.7	3366	450	168	673	89	96
1832	987	9.4	2803	500	177	637	91	92
1833	1070	12.3	4173	525	189	653	94	89
1834	1205	12.9	6064	600	211	722	91	87
1835	1254	17.5	16165	650	252	749	108	85
1836	1361	16.5	24934	800	301	865	122	95
1837	1424	13.3	6941	1,100	242	783	110	94

ing been before mistaken as to the probable sources of supply, and the lowest possible cost of production.[195]

Even the securities of the South American Republics contracted for earlier in the decade were yet to unwind, and continued at their lowest quotations, with no prospect of recovery expected or dividends forthcoming.[196] The years 1826–32 were part of a large secular cycle of falling prices in Great Britain, lasting perhaps into the middle 1840s, during which supply significantly exceeded demand.[197]

By contrast to Britain, the 1825 speculations in the United States had been less serious; their aftermath less severe. Commodity prices declined but the strong commodity trade preceding the downturn had steeled the United States' economy, and it suffered comparatively few business failures and little unemployment. The cotton crop in 1824, most notably, was the largest produced to date; and the price, averaging 18 cents per lb., was still high. For the fiscal year 1824–5, the value of cotton exports alone amounted to about $36.8 million in contrast with $21.9 million the previous year. The American terms of trade turned from negative in 1820–3 to strongly positive at the peak of British speculations of 1824–5, and the American import-export equation with Great Britain was balanced in 1825.[198]

In addition to the commodity picture, American finances were in good order as well. Redemption of the federal debt began in 1817, when obligations stood at slightly more than 12 per cent of gross national product. Year over year, 1824–5 retired more than 7 per cent of total public debt, and obligations as a percentage of gross national product stood at 8.25 per cent. Public debt dropped to zero over the next decade, while gross national product increased roughly 80 per cent to nearly $2 billion.[199]

The fiscal agent for the Treasury was, of course, the Bank of the United States and, under the presidency of Nicholas Biddle (1823–36), it bought, repackaged and resold government debt obligations in the open market domestically and to customers abroad. The Bank was obliged to pay off the principal of federal debt when the government called upon it to do so, all the while carrying out its currency, exchange and depository functions. The Bank had sustained some silver drain as a result of a healthy China trade, but entered 1825 with ample specie reserves of $6.7 million. This figure represented an increase of 16 per cent from the previous year, and came from a firm money policy by the Bank and large silver imports from Mexico due to its political instability.[200] The Bank's liquidity was enhanced not only by its sale of government stock, but by its paying off debt to European bankers in May 1825 as well. With the spike in commodity prices in 1823–5, the supply of bills coming to market resulting from commodity sales provided the Bank with even more funding latitude.

Barings realized Biddle's central role in the financial steerage of the United States' economy. The Bank president understood the relationship between

currency and exchange and, thus, the importance of trade and international connections to a young economy. He also saw the importance of using the resources
of the Bank to avert problems in the financial system, as he did in 1825 with a
highly interventionist policy of discounting in major American cities to maintain
confidence and liquidity.[201]

Barings was aware of the Bank's effectiveness under Biddle because it had
maintained ties to American finance by its relationship with the United States
government and with the government's fiscal agent, the Bank of the United
States. As agent, Barings continued dividend payments to the Bank's numerous
foreign shareholders. The Bank agreed to remit dividends to overseas holders free
of charge as a perk to make its stock attractive to European investors. This was an
important consideration because Bank stock could be remitted for the settlement
of foreign debts, which were large for some time in the case of the developing
American market.[202] Settlement of foreign debts also affected the ability of the
Bank to maintain sufficient levels of specie for domestic convertibility which, of
course, had implications for its relations with the numerous state banks.

To temper one of the principal venues of specie outflows from the United
States – the China trade – Biddle introduced the '180 day sight bill' drawn on
Barings for use by merchants trading east of the Cape of Good Hope. The use of
such bills began in 1825 just before the pressure in the money markets appeared.
For a decade, drafts from Canton under letters of credit issued by London merchant bankers had increased in volume among eastern traders. These bills formed
part of a channel for exchange of New England manufactures for Chinese tea, as
well as the financing to ship British goods from America that competed directly
with the British East India Company. British merchant banks, such as Barings,
were much better known than American banks in the east, and so they acted as
intermediaries for traders from the United States.

After years of American silver payments to China, bills on London substituted
for physical specie shipments, which kept silver in the United States to serve as a
basis for note issues by American banks.[203] Biddle used the long-usance bills as a way
to keep specie at home deliberately, in order to finance growing demand for bills
drawn from the east. For American merchants, bills were generally cheaper to buy
than shipping specie, and more secure. As for Barings, the growing consumption of
Indian opium created a demand at Canton for bills on London which American
China merchants began to supply in place of Spanish dollars about 1827.

Acting as an intermediary in the China trade was a way to play the American
market in the latter 1820s as other areas of American business were winding
down. The conservative fiscal policies of American governments were not particularly conducive to expanding Barings' brokerage operations in Federal securities.
Barings knew first hand that opportunities in the federal debt business were
drying up since the House was responsible for the liquidation of the Louisiana
Purchase bonds. Ever since Francis and Alexander established the American link-

age, Barings had managed the United States' debt through flotations to European investors. Barings continued to clear all accounts of American legations and consulates in Europe, as well as accounts of the American navy. The House's open credit stood at £50,000 sterling to the Bank, through which the government made its remittances to London.[204] With the American debt elimination, it made sense that Barings work aggressively to build up another way to participate and profit from the growth of the United States. This additional venue was trade; and the additional 'cornerstone connection' in 1829 was Thomas Wren Ward.

Ward began his duties as agent at the same time the newly-elected Andrew Jackson entered the White House, and one of his ongoing duties was to pay attention to Jackson administration policies as they affected his British employer in the American market. Baring Brothers & Company viewed the United States as a very credible field and, by his tour, Thomas Baring built a system for American business operations with hubs at Boston, New York and New Orleans. Ward was to coordinate these operations as a man-on-the-spot on the American side and, as it turns out, was hired at a low point in the economic cycle before a long ascent in several markets. But if Barings wanted to become a contender in the cotton consignment arena, it had to add a crucial piece to its business platform that was missing up to this time. It had to set up an operation in Liverpool, and, in the 1830s, this is what Barings decided to do.

The growth of Liverpool was part of the rush to take advantage of the sense that a revival of trade was on the way and that commodity prices were firming. It was also part of a larger pattern in the Atlantic economy: England's economic power in textile manufacturing and the growth of the United States as a raw cotton supplier.

To meet this demand, Joshua Bates decided to establish an office of the firm in Liverpool as a processing hub for commodity consignments received from the United States and around the world. The Bank of England had made a point of establishing branches after the Country Bankers Act of 1826.[205] In 1827, branches opened in Liverpool, Birmingham, Bristol and Leeds. One historian of business enterprise has asserted that the most outstanding feature of British mercantile enterprise in the first half of the nineteenth century was the rise of the port of Liverpool as a close and scrappy rival to London. Statistics on ship traffic to Liverpool and to northern British ports tend to bear this out (Table 3.2).

Table 3.2: Number of Vessels and Amount of Tonnage of the Principal British Ports in 1816 and 1850. Source: Baines, *History of the Commerce and Town of Liverpool*, p. 825.

Port	1816		1850	
	Ships	Million Tons	Ships	Million Tons
London	6,198	1.25	16,437	3.29
Liverpool	2,946	0.64	9,338	3.62
Hull	1,185	0.18	4,249	0.84
Newcastle	1,127	0.16	7,206	1.16
Glasgow	89	0.01	1,470	0.3

All accepting Houses specializing in the finance of the transatlantic trade had important operations at Liverpool, including several 'American' Houses. Most based themselves in London, but most also had offices or partners in Liverpool. Alexander Brown & Company, which offered the broadest array of services of any single House in Liverpool, had maintained its headquarters there since 1804, and remarkably resisted a London commitment until 1863.[206]

Interestingly, Barings was relatively late among merchant banks to establish offices in the north of England. The impulse finally to expand the firm to Liverpool appears to have come from Joshua Bates, after he overcame fears that such a move would lack a banker's discretion. As early as 1830, he worried the House might seem 'so grasping that people will be set against us'.[207] Grasping or not, the export of American cotton to north English ports increased immensely between 1828 and 1832 from newly-settled and cultivated United States acreage across the American south, and merchant bankers geared up for this opportunity in cotton and other staples.

So long as Barings lacked direct facilities and personnel to receive consigned American staples, the firm would depend on others, would be a provider of credits to American importers only, and would not collect the 2.5 per cent commission from actually purchasing dry goods at the ports of entry in northern England.

'We must find the right man', wrote Bates in his diary early in 1831, but the search took over a year. Personnel in such a key centre of the American trade had to be at least as knowledgeable of markets as the London partners and Ward, and be known to the partners as reliable and steady. Bates was confident that, with proper facilities and Barings' financials, clients would flock to the House from competitors for American consignment business. 'The Yankees will soon discover', he said, 'that there is a difference in the rate of discount of nearly 3/8th per cent between theirs and ours on a 3 months bill. We have nothing to do but attend to our business and all will come entirely to us in the end.'[208]

After consulting with Ward, the House chose not one man for Liverpool, but two: Samuel Gair and Charles Baring Young. Gair was an American, and former partner of the Liverpool commission House of Latham & Gair. Charles Young was a grandson of Charles Baring of Exeter and, though family, he remained the junior side of the Liverpool pairing due to poor health.[209] As confirmed by Ward, Gair was experienced in the area of dry goods, cotton and iron products. Importantly, both men were acceptable to American shippers.[210] Young and Gair conducted a commission business in goods and services, negotiated insurance and arranged for the forwarding of passengers and freight.

In crucial cotton operations, Ward selected the commission Houses and supervised the buying and consigning on the United States side, while Liverpool handled selling. As for financial matters, only the home office in London could accept and pay bills of exchange, and for cotton operations these derived from strict limits on Ward as far as advances made to shippers and prices paid for cotton shipments. Functional divisions existed between offices but, despite this, the new men on the spot in the international port of Liverpool provided crucial information on world markets and on developments in the Midlands and northern England. Added to Ward's stream of intelligence from the United States, London had a more complete world picture than ever before.

Barings opened its Liverpool affiliate when business was good, the firm's financial position strong, and after the firm had confirmed a demand for such an office through observation of the traffic volumes through the port. To be sure, there existed an element of 'catch up' to draw even with other firms, but Barings acted to establish a separate Liverpool branch neither from weakness nor for lack of other options. In 1832, Bates wrote to Ward that the House was on solid ground, that they were in a condition to 'take losses' on the launch of its Liverpool operations, and that they were operating on such a scale and with large margins that 'we have capital enough for double the amount of regular business'.[211] And so business boomed.

Numbers of acceptances greatly increased to 1833 and suggest that, for the most part, Liverpool cotton operations contributed measurably to Barings' business. Acceptances increased from a mere £295,000 in 1828 to a staggering £1.4 million in 1833.[212] Profit for 1833 jumped nearly 19 per cent from the 1832 level of £96,000, and Bates reported to Ward that Liverpool commissions were already fully one fourth of total House revenues in 1833, and increasing rapidly.[213] Barings seems to have abandoned discretion in regard to an aggressive pursuit of American cotton consignments, at least as reflects the in-House correspondence of 1833, which states:

> One cannot be successful without exciting envy. As 617, 619, and 999 do not increase their businesses, rest assured they will have the bad taste to do all in their power to insinuate things against us – and in a manner that indicates a want of tact that gives to their ill will an exactly opposite effect from that intended.[214]

Bates told Ward that he believed the American House Thomas Wiggin & Company (no. 999), was upset at Barings' success. To Bates's mind, Wiggin had 'a rogue and bankrupt' for an agent in Liverpool, and they were full of hollow bluster. Likewise, Thomas Wilson & Company (no. 617) was complained of 'for some cause or other' by everyone. As to the firm of George Wildes & Company (no. 619), it was desirous of business but would remain 'small fry'.[215] Barings intended always to retain the moral high ground, shun appearances and 'fix the public mind strongly on the high character and honorable mode of the House, whatever others are disposed to say'.[216]

But the House would grow its business at Liverpool. 'The trade of this place [Liverpool] is increasing rapidly', wrote Bates, 'while that of London is stationary. Our establishment here is decidedly popular, except with Croppers and Browns.

We are No. 5 in the list of receivers of cotton but will be No. 2 before the year is out.'[217] Barings caught the cotton volume and price wave on the way up, and believed it could be good for several profitable years.

A Worldwide System

Foreign bankers, traders and merchants saw large opportunities in the emerging United States on the western side of the Atlantic economy, but also looked eastwards to Asia. Indeed, in the early 1830s, the mercantile community anticipated the final reform of the East India Company, and the cessation of its China monopoly. Half of British trade with China was already in private hands before reform took effect in April 1834.

Some writers have downplayed the economic importance of reform for this reason, but the consequences for prices in the most important Chinese export commodity, tea, were dramatic and immediate – declining by approximately half in the four years following reform.[218] Certainly, reform corresponded to an influx of new British firms to China, and the British trading community increased from 66 in 1833 to 156 in 1837.[219]

Like Britain, the United States had long traded with China. By the 1820s, American merchants had done business with major hong merchants for three decades, and had established factories at Canton said to be splendid – second only to Britain. By the time Barings recommitted to the American market in 1828–9, four large firms dominated purchases at Canton: T. H. Smith & Company, Olyphant & Company, Wetmore & Company and Russell & Company.

Financing trade to China was a perennial problem for American merchants. Chinese tea and silks were extremely popular in the United States, but the United States possessed few items that China really wanted to buy, apart from perhaps furs and ginseng. American traders therefore exported specie to Canton by way of a triangular pattern to make up for trade deficits.

Americans shipped produce to Europe or South America, from which they secured specie (often in the form of Spanish dollars), with which Americans bought Chinese goods. Tea shipped from Canton to the United States completed the third leg of the triangle. This pattern of Europe or South America as an intermediary to China made sense in the first decades of the nineteenth century because the United States lacked gold and silver sources, such as its own mines, or the mines of Mexico. According to Table 3.3, the average value of specie was a staggering 75 per cent of total American exports from 1816 to 1827. Between 1828 and 1837, the average value of specie as a percentage of exports fell to 32 per cent, followed by a rebound to 42 per cent from 1838 to 1844.

Why the reduction in specie? From the middle 1820s, the United States-China trade turned gradually away from the cumbersome triangular route to more sophisticated payment and credit arrangements. At the heart of the new mechanism were safe and convenient bills on London, which reduced the need for actual shipment of bullion to a given destination – in this case, China. London banking Houses such as Baring Brothers, the '3Ws' (Wildes, Wilson and Wiggin), Brown Brothers and Morrison Cryder issued credits and advances to American merchants first from London, then through trusted agents in the United States. Thomas Wren Ward for Barings or Richard Alsop for Morrison Cryder, for example, advanced clients a portion of what they needed for their purchases, and drew bills for their clients on terms that allowed enough time to sell the goods in question, remit proceeds and pay interest. The shift of payment method had a dramatic effect on specie deployment in the China trade, as Table 3.3 shows.

Table 3.3: Bullion and Specie in American Exports to China, 1816–44 (in thousands of dollars). Source: Y. Hao, 'Chinese Teas in America', p. 23.

Year Ending 30 September	Total Value	Merchandise Value	%	Bullion and Specie Value	%
1816	4,220	2,298	54	1,922	46
1817	5,703	1,158	20	4,545	80
1818	6,777	1,176	17	5,601	83
1819	9,057	1,643	18	7,414	82
1820	8,173	1,876	23	6,297	77
1821	4,291	900	21	3,391	79
1822	5,935	860	14	5,075	86
1823	4,636	1,052	23	3,584	77
1824	5,301	837	16	4,464	84
1825	5,570	1,047	19	4,523	81
1826	2,567	915	36	1,652	64
1827	3,864	1,339	35	2,525	65
1828	4,481	4,025	90	456	10
1829	1,355	753	56	602	44
1830	742	662	89	80	11
1831	1,291	924	72	367	28
1832	1,261	809	64	452	36
1833	1,434	1,144	80	290	20
1834	1,010	631	62	379	38
1835	1,869	477	26	1,392	74
1836	1,194	780	65	414	35
1837	631	476	75	155	25
1838	1,517	788	52	729	48
1839	1,534	541	35	993	65
1840	1,010	533	53	477	47
1841	1,201	774	64	427	36
1842	1,444	837	58	607	42
1843	2,419	1,847	76	572	24
1844	1,757	1,190	68	567	32
Average	3,181	1,114	48	2,067	52

Barings lay at the center of these changes through its influence as a banker within London and its contacts without. Bates himself joined the firm in 1828 with great Far Eastern experience from the American side under William Gray of Boston.

Like other American merchants, Bates had been free of East India Company regulations and discipline. Like all Americans, though, he had been excluded from
buying at the Company's sales in India and from the direct India-China trade. In
this business Americans could participate only through British subjects. When
Bates joined Barings and became British, in a sense, he kept continuity with his
China trade days by hiring Bostonian Thomas Ward. This seaport long stood at
the centre of America's activity in regard to China, with close family ties among
firms and businessmen, and the city's agents issued the bulk of bill financing for
the eastern trade. Philadelphia, home of the agent Richard Alsop of Morrison
Cryder, also active in China, was a distant second.[220]

With Bates, the London partners added a large American element to what was
already an active business in the Far East. From the early 1820s, Barings worked
at Singapore through A. L. Johnstone and at Canton through Dent & Company.
Even before Bates (or Ward) joined the firm, Barings extended commitments
through letters of credit to Americans for as much as £60,000 on a Canton-
bound ship out of Boston.[221]

In spring 1832, Thomas Ward made a new and important Far Eastern arrangement for the House. He concluded an agreement with Russell & Company – the
largest, oldest and most prestigious American commission House in China. The
agreement gave Russell the right to draw on Barings. A drawing account added
a quantitative advantage to the American firm in a part of the world where
financial resources were relatively scarce. It also added a qualitative element by
bullet-proofing Russell's bills throughout the Far East. In return, Russell provided
Barings with access to its thriving businesses in Manila and South Asia; and to the
Turkish opium concession Russell acquired from Perkins & Company in 1830, a
firm with which Barings had long done business.[222]

By its agreement with Russell & Company, Barings likely benefited also from
the firm's working relationship with Houqua – the most powerful hong merchant
in Canton and long-time friend of the Americans.[223] Arrangements with Russell
& Company occurred simultaneously with the reorganization in July of Magniac
& Company into the trading colossus of Jardine, Matheson & Company in
preparation for the end of East India Company dominance the following year.
Russell and Magniac already had a close association from which Barings could
profit as financial intermediary. If all this were not ample for a huge advantage
in the east on the cusp of East India reform, Bates's cousin by marriage, Russell
Sturgis, added to Barings' clout when he established a branch of the family firm,
long based in Manila, at Canton on 1 May 1834.[224]

Free traders hailed reform in the eastern trades – an area, after all, larger and
more populous than Europe and the United States combined. Like Alexander
Baring, Bates favoured complete repeal of the Corn Laws and was delighted with
East India reform. He hailed reform publicly as an 'impetus to general trade', and
privately as an opportunity for the firm to increase its revenue in the east.[225]

Figure 3.2: Wu Ping Chien (1769–1843), 'Houqua', by George Chinnery (1774–1852). Oil on canvas (*c.* 1830). The Metropolitan Museum of Art, New York. 'Houqua' was the Chinese agent to British and American trading firms in Canton, said to be the richest man on earth by the 1840s.

Competition in the China trade widened at the same time as six large British commission Houses in Calcutta collapsed between 1830–3 from bad loans to indigo planters. These 'Great Houses' were started originally by former civil servants, agents and military men of the East India Company who became private agents and bankers in the trade with India. The American publisher Hezekiah Niles cited the failures as over-extensions by relative newcomers trying to dislodge more established firms in a notoriously volatile commodity. Indigo prices declined 30 per cent in 1829. They never recovered from the highs of 1822–8 that originally lured new firms into the business.

Niles cited losses totalling £15 million. Other sources published even higher figures.[226] Here was an opening for Barings in a dangerous business at prices washed out to reasonable levels. 'In consequence of the recent failures, prospects present themselves on this side for India and China', Bates wrote to Ward. 'Business is tumbling into our hands … We now have contracts out for £90,000 for China – for American account.' Bates reported an uptick in wool and cotton processing at Liverpool with the addition of tea and indigo. Each man rarely mentioned opium.[227]

Ward and Bates concurred that England and Barings must attempt to supply all India with cottons.[228] And they were putting in place the financial machinery to do so. Ward wrote exuberantly that American cotton crops would increase as the country grew, and the export trade would match this growth. In turn, Bates had strong anecdotal evidence that Barings' bills would command the highest prices in the Calcutta market.[229] After the indigo disasters in Calcutta, Bates believed that 'we cannot fail to become receivers of a large proportion of the goods of that country'. Barings' agent in Calcutta, Gisbourne & Company – retained on Ward's good judgement – survived unaffected by the failures of the indigo Houses, and received financial reinforcement in 1833. Hope & Company was Barings' western European beachhead, as Gisbourne was the firm's beachhead in Calcutta, Bengal. Advancing funds to them on shipments of indigo became an integral part of Barings' eastern operations.[230]

The expansion of the India and China trades – with a hub at Liverpool to service the huge American cotton trade – put a potent worldwide network within reach. Barings already financed international trade and organized transport and insurance. It was a short step to lash the pieces together into a network by taking a direct interest in the ships that carried goods around the world. This the firm began to do in the middle of 1833.

The chief impetus to shipbuilding and ownership was scarcity caused by increased demand for more goods around the world as populations grew and standards of living rose, especially in England and the United States. Commodity prices advanced in the 1828–30 period – whether sugar, coffee, indigo, tea, lumber, cotton or silk. These advances revived prospects for business just as the sun set on the East India Company's trade monopoly, and just as prospects improved for general commerce. With this trend, and stimulated by the East India Company's gradual loss of its trade monopoly, Barings decided to enter shipping.

With the addition of transportation to its worldwide system, Barings continued to consider its transatlantic relationship with the Americans a lynchpin one, and cotton as an important growth driver. Bates wrote:

> The available Tonnage of the world is not sufficient. Taking into view the probable increase in the Cotton trade, the certainty of constant Emmigration [sic] from this country west and a chance that the Corn Laws will be altered,

it strikes me that the best trade to embark on now in America is that of ship owning, for you can now beat the world.[231]

Bates believed that the days of the Corn Laws were numbered as Great Britain lost its capacity to feed itself without imports. It seemed reasonable to Bates and Ward that, as the United States increased its role as a commodity producer and England its manufacturing capacity, the two countries could combine to 'beat the world' by specializing in what each did best. As Bates wrote to Ward in Boston in 1833:

> The enormous increase in the production of Cotton in the U.S. leads to the reflection how important this staple is to the welfare of Great Britain. It has become almost as necessary as bread and there can be no doubt but our United States Cotton is eventually to enable Great Britain to manufacture for all India. We shall drive the East India and other short staple Cotton out of the market.[232]

Bates favoured freer trade on commodities so the United States could generate more export earnings for itself and afford to buy British manufactures. Barings would supply financing and ships as intermediary to this highly cooperative and mutually-beneficial American-British trade.[233]

Despite the popular grievances that spawned the watershed British Reform Bill of 1832, Thomas Ward agreed with Bates that England's population was in the main prosperous in the early 1830s. For its part, he said, the less mature United States was presently assuming the characteristics of England's success – 'each day more temperate, industrious, and enlightened by common sense'. Ward even mused that, at some distant date, the United States might exercise greater influence in the world than England.[234]

But such grand projections embroidered the more mundane mechanics of Barings' business. In the middle of 1832, Bates forecast correctly that trade would likely be fine for three or four years. Bates boasted to Ward, in fact, that 'Business comes from all quarters and in all languages', including over three hundred European accounts, and the Canton and Calcutta trades. 'Our commissions this year will be between 60 and 70/m pounds – and from what I see it will be a third more next year'.[235] In turn, Ward's day-to-day balancing of operational responsibilities for the House in the United States are well illustrated by a letter to Mildmay typical of the start of the busy autumn export season. Ward wrote:

> I do not think the depression in coffee with you permanent. It is likely to be higher next year and with us the scarcity is now raising the price. Coffee in New York is ½ to 1 cent higher within a month. There is little now in the United States. Our merchants are again looking towards South America and Batavia and I shall furnish the credits for several Cargoes within a few weeks.

The general opinion here is also firmness in sugar –

> The prospects for cotton are favorable so far as can now be ascertained. Exchange continues dull – at 8 perCent. – I shall go to NwYork & Philadelphia soon & see what is best to be done in regard to the payments for the Bonds.[236]

Events in the United States soon made things uncertain. Most financial historians judge the years of Nicholas Biddle's presidency at the Bank of the United States as successful to 1829. In that year, however, Andrew Jackson and others questioned the Bank's constitutionality and even the expediency of its operations. Jackson's first annual address to Congress in 1829 asserted that 'private interests' ran the Bank, and that the Bank had failed anyway to provide the country with a uniform and sound currency.[237]

To Jackson's assertions, Biddle and his supporters claimed the Bank was governed by banking considerations only, and found the difficulties of the early 1830s to be the fault of government action. The general Bank controversy accompanied causes of concern in the United States by 1832, including reform of the tariff on manufactures in 1828, the mildly speculative craze for internal improvements, and ongoing debt retirements that threatened to constrain money from 1826 onwards.

Barings apparently found these varied risks in the United States tolerable for the time being, and expanded operations in marketing and exchange for a few years after 1830. They had watched Biddle and the Bank brilliantly pre-empt two potentially adverse financial situations: one in 1825 requiring expansion; the other in 1828 requiring contraction. By 1829 the Bank enjoyed its highest prestige, and its stock valued highly.

Nicholas Biddle built the Second Bank of the United States into more than the largest banking institution in the country after its recharter in 1819. The Bank acted as the fiscal agent of the national government; attempted to provide a uniform currency of national circulation; established the soundness of state bank notes, and held the ultimate specie and foreign reserves of the country. Increasingly, Biddle sought to counteract seasonal turbulence in agriculture as well as those normal disturbances of business which periodically occurred in the course of economic growth. More than his counterparts at the Bank of England, he considered the Second Bank of the United States as a central bank in the near-modern sense of the term, and his steerage of it as a public trust. It was his responsibility to anticipate and manage financial events for the good of business and, by extension, the nation.[238]

Biddle crafted the Second Bank into an emphatically commercial instrument after 1826. He managed the equalization of domestic exchange in the course of trade between the northern, southern and western regions of the United States, and importantly assigned foreign exchange a crucial role in the overall health of the American economy. Domestic exchange operations evolved naturally from the Bank's responsibility as the government's transfer agent, and involved Biddle's oversight of state banks. But achieving a sound and uniform domestic currency payable in various and distant parts of the United States involved more.

Biddle ascribed to the view that a nation best controlled and coordinated its currency and note issue by the course of the foreign exchange markets; indeed, Biddle believed that foreign exchange was the 'infallible barometer to indicate soundness or unsoundness of currency'.[239] In the United States, domestic and foreign exchanges very much intertwined by the late 1820s and 1830s, since America's chief export, cotton, made the nation's economy an international one. According to banking historian Fritz Redlich, Biddle used cotton to achieve his general objective: to widen the metallic basis within the United States and provide the country with the maximum possible flexibility in foreign trade, while maintaining a stable internal medium of exchange – paper currency – that was not liable to be drained away. A general increase in specie was important to the general expansion of the nation's banking system, and Biddle insisted the Bank husband and hold the bulk of American specie, since it was this metallic mechanism by which the Bank ultimately supported and managed the various paper

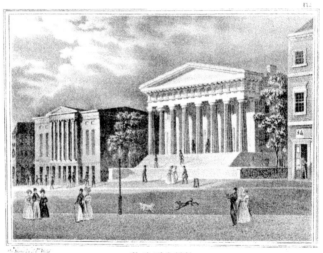

U.S. BANK
PHILADELPHIA.

Figure 3.3: Second Bank of the United States, Chestnut Street, Philadelphia, by John Caspar Wild (1804–46). Lithograph (1838). American Philosophical Society.

notes the state banks happened to issue. Specie retention, after all, was the basis for Biddle's issuance of 180-day bills in the India-China trade. Biddle explained the idea of a 'mixed currency':

> A mixed currency is eminently useful in prudent hands but a tremendous hazard when not controlled; and the practical wisdom in managing it lies in seizing the proper moment to expand and contract it – taking care, in working with explosive materials, whenever there is doubt to incline to the side of safety ... At all times and under all circumstances the currency and exchanges are objects of its [the Bank's] constant solicitude.[240]

Here was the kind of institution that resonated with Barings three ways: the importance it assigned to foreign trade, its business orientation, and its apparently conservative management.

The Deferred Threes

At first, Bates and Ward viewed President Jackson's criticism of the Bank as part of the common wranglings of American democracy. At least Barings' relations with the Bank were quite good in 1830, as Biddle had amassed an unused credit balance with the firm of $3.8 million by July of that year.[241] Moreover, general prosperity and peace marked 1830 and 1831 in the United States and promised a bright future. Cotton production boomed, canal construction continued vigorous, urban real estate values increased steadily, and investors oversubscribed hot railroad issues.[242] In major seaboard cities, demand for bills on London increased as Anglo-American merchant bankers extended credit facilities to finance increasing American trade volumes.

Interestingly, general prosperity from 1830 to 1832 coincided with some business pressures for Barings and the Bank of the United States. In England, events incident to the Reform Bill and political disturbances in Europe caused the Bank of England to curtail loans on stock and exchequer bills in the spring of 1831, and contributed to general skittishness in the London money market.[243]

British wheat harvests were erratic: one year, lean, with a price of 74*s.* per quarter (1831); one year, robust, with a price of 53*s.* (1832). Price weakness came also in non-agricultural commodities, such as lead, tin and linseed oil, which fell in November to levels not seen since the trough of 1825.[244] By contrast, American prices held up well, but tightening by the Bank of England threatened to curb foreign credits to American commodity importers, which would depress the American commodity trade.[245]

Amid this pricing backdrop, Barings manoeuvered around two other developments in the years 1830–2. Political turbulence in Europe brought the House a rush of deposits seeking safe haven. Some of the funds were liquidated positions in Russian, Austrian and French securities, the proceeds of which the House reinvested in securities of those individual American states, such as Pennsylvania and New York, for which Barings was currently the selling agent.[246] With augmented working capital also, the partners speculated in several commodities, including tallow, coffee and wheat – some, according to Bates, to great profit.

Contrasted with their flush cash position from Continental depositors, Barings experienced financial trials with the Bank of the United States so marked that the partners reconsidered their single most important American account. Throughout the 1820s, the Philadelphia bank did not use Barings' open credit of £250,000 on which Biddle paid 3 per cent. The events of the thirty months from 1830 to the middle of 1832 changed this pattern.

Loans, discounts, and extensions on personal security from Biddle's Bank increased smartly over the period and matched the modest business expansion that had begun in the second quarter of 1830. To spur business – for example in Boston – the Bank granted several branches the prerogative to lower their rates of discount from 5 per cent to 4.5 per cent in the second half of 1830. An expansion by way of business paper satisfied Biddle as both safe and profitable, and provided assets to replace the United States government bonds the Bank redeemed in 1830 and 1831.

It seemed that self-liquidating bills of exchange were neutral – neither adding nor subtracting from circulating currency – since their existence represented tangible goods traded, and their number increased or decreased with the ebb and flow of business. After all, the Bank had expanded its circulation before without difficulty from about $4.5 million in 1823 to $15 million in 1830 – during a time some have called the Bank's 'golden age'.[247] In 1831, however, the Bank's balances with European financiers began to drop, and stood at $2,383,000, fully 37 per cent below the 1830 peak. By July, the Bank's balance had almost vanished to $144,000.[248]

Unusual events disturbed Biddle's expansion. The merchandise trade balance turned negative in the United States for 1831 as imports surged, cotton exports fell and the United States exported specie in large amounts. Rates of exchange increased 1.5 percentage points in eight months, and by September stood at 7 per cent.[249] British exchange rates rose also, crimping American merchants engaged in Atlantic trade. Though Bank rate remained unchanged, heavy Continental bullion demand caused by political difficulties in France, Belgium and Poland was such that the Bank of England under Governor Horsley Palmer refused accommodation to country banks, and indeed obliged them 'to fend for themselves'.[250] Yields on first-class commercial paper (Overend Gurney three-month bills) spiked upwards from the previous year's average monthly rate.

Just as the trade began running against Biddle and the bankers who financed it, the Jackson administration announced immediate redemption of its outstanding 4.5 per cent (of 1824) and 5 per cent (of 1825) obligations – the funds for which would come from the deposits the government held at the Bank. Biddle began contracting Bank operations in October 1831, advising particularly the inland branch offices to settle their debts with the parent bank, to discount bills only on Atlantic cities, to cease lending on so-called accommodation paper, and to continue business only with 'habitual customers'.[251]

The New York *Journal of Commerce* attributed the 'scarcity of money' in the financial and trading communities at the start of 1832 to Biddle's being forced to tighten credit in the face of the government's effort to pay off the national debt. Niles's *Register* found 'overtrading' to be more at fault, and suggested that the last two years of favourable trade balances had produced in the country such a surfeit of gold specie, that some suggested 'American streets should be paved with it – to render it useful'. Niles continued:

> Banks were all overflowing with means to accommodate the people, and all wished to loan large sums of money, and at long dates – the longer the better, on approved security. Hence business transactions to the amount of very many millions, which had required from six to nine months for their consummation, were turned into active capital in the course of as many days, by discounts at the banks; and persons, having the means at command naturally desired to use them, in increasing their business – the interest paid being disregarded; and among other things, excessive importations of foreign goods were made.[252]

The *Journal of Commerce* cited problematic 'investments in railroads [particularly in Baltimore], investments in new manufacturing establishments in the eastern states supposed to amount to ten millions in the last two years'. In Philadelphia, 'money pressures were brought on by the lock-up of funds from the liquidation of the Girard Bank ... With seven to eight millions of coin withdrawn from circulation in six months, and currencies of various types vanishing at four or five times this amount', wrote Niles, 'it is wonderful and a testimony to the solid prosperity that had prevailed, that things are not worse than they are'.[253]

Since 1828, Biddle had shifted large funds from eastern cities to the southwest and west, and had engaged them in so-called accommodation loans, partly in the domestic exchange business. The contraction of 1832 represented a temporary retrenchment of a policy Biddle described four years before, as he attempted to create a seamless national market with a reliable currency. The Bank aimed for a triangular exchange policy involving branches in New Orleans, New York and western offices such as Cincinnati, whereby 'the funds of the Bank would naturally seek employment in those sections of the Union where there is less banking capital, and where the production of the great staples of the country seem to require most assistance in bringing them into the commercial market'.[254]

The deployment of funds to where they were most needed and efficiently used raises the issue of the distinct seasonality of different regions of the United States in the antebellum years. The sectional shifting of credit instruments – for example, bank notes – was a normal and usually automatic feature of the period, and did not connote a national expansion or contraction of circulation per se, though in any given region this might be the effect. The Bank of the United States might provide funds to the north-east in the summer for buying wool, to the west in the autumn for buying various provisions, and to the south in the winter for buying cotton.

The Bank went to the west and south-west because business was most robust there, demand for credit and loans greatest, and the competition least fierce. The Ohio River Valley and the south-west after 1823 experienced phenomenal growth in trade, industry and internal improvements. All required financing, and this was a reason why the New Orleans and Cincinnati branch offices ranked second and fourth by dollar value of bills issued on personal security at the end of 1831.[255] In January 1823, only $46,000 worth of western notes circulated. Nine years later there were an astounding $5,445,000. Matching the region's torrid growth and development, note issue of the bank increased a hundredfold in the west compared to just fivefold for the country at large.[256]

In 1832, the Bank's financial bias towards the west was acute. It bought 60 per cent of its bills in the west and south-west, and over the space of three years had increased its commitments in the west in dollar value by a factor of three. Apart from plain numbers, it appears that what Biddle had intended to be temporary and self-liquidating extensions of credit became permanent and accommodative in nature, with branch officers influenced to authorize loans of doubtful term and security. As one student of the Bank expressed the issue: 'By discounting too willingly the bills of planters on factors who were apt to loan too high a percentage on the crops, these discounts were liable to degrade into accommodation loans, as in fact they did'.[257]

Not only due to less than rigourous decisions by Bank branches, more 'natural' causes disrupted the Bank's operations in the west and south – the basis of most were tied to farm staples. The banker, of course, advanced money to grow a crop, and the loan was paid when the crop came to market. Loans were based on the projected market price of the commodity in question. Shortfall crops were fine for prices; bumper yields, not. In 1831 and 1832, prices of wheat and corn fell short, and the Bank lay overextended.

Biddle seems to have understood the issues that conspired to make his position difficult. He explained to a Congressional committee on 27 February 1832:

> The situation in the country at this period is very delicate. We have on the one hand an excessive importation, on the other hand a crop great in amount, diminished in value and coming in, at a time unusually late. This of itself produces great difficulty in meeting abroad the engagements of the country for its importations. But to this is added the intention of the Government to make heavy payments on the public debt, of which a large proportion is held

abroad, thus increasing the demand for foreign payments on diminished resources of the country. The preparation for these of course obliges the bank to be extremely reserved in its business.[258]

Biddle had either misjudged the quality of bills in which his inland branches did business, was unable to forecast crop yields, or he underestimated the drainage of specie from the country. In any case, he appeared reckless to his principal European creditor, Baring Brothers. Biddle exhausted and overdrew Thomas Baring's £250,000 open credit by £33,000 by September 1831, and uncovered debit balances reached £360,000 from commercial transactions – one third of them involving long bills for East Indian use. The start of 1832 showed Bank obligations to European financiers totaling $1,356,000.[259]

As Biddle reduced the Bank's commitments in October 1831, he asked Barings' agent, Thomas Ward, for an extra £200,000 credit that he pledged to repay by spring the following year. Barings' granted the request, but at a price of 5 per cent on the loan amount, 1 per cent commission on drafts passed against it, and a pledge from Biddle that the Bank would do business with no other London House for the duration of these exceptional measures. Biddle agreed, and promptly overdrew the Baring account in six months (March 1832) by a quarter of a million pounds.[260]

Many in the American press knew and publicized that the Bank was 'conspiring to make arrangements with European capitalists'.[261] What they did not know was the degree to which Biddle's rapid draw-down of Barings' credit, and subsequent requirements for liquidity, caught Barings off guard and irritated the partners. 'We are entirely at the mercy of an account which views us in the light of a reserve fund to be used to any extent', wrote Thomas Baring to Ward in Boston. 'This system is evidently useful to the Bank, as it answers all the purposes of an additional amount of specie in its coffers without the loss of interest ... but it is obvious that in many instances our pockets must pay a great share of the profits'.[262] Thomas Baring echoed the thoughts of New York Representative Churchill C. Cambrelang, who wrote of the Bank officers' credit overextension in 1831 as that of 'madmen' – who deserved 'to have conservators appointed over them'.[263]

Despite irritation with the overdrafts, Barings assisted Biddle still further. Difficulties in the winter and spring of 1832 had much to do with the government's order that the Bank retire all outstanding 3 per cent federal debt by July. Biddle bought time for the Bank until October with a postponement petition. In exchange, he agreed to pay interest on the postponed portion for the extra quarter. Meanwhile, he dispatched the Bank's cashier, Thomas Cadwalader, to London to arrange bridge financing for the large batch of bonds just months away from coming due.

Calwalader reached a refinancing agreement with Barings on 22 August 1832. The London partners asked British and Continental (mostly Dutch) holders of

United States 3 per cent debt certificates to defer $5 million worth of repayments until October 1833, a year past the bonds' maturity date. While the Bank maintained interest payments, Barings would take over the debt itself, buying at the best market levels available, at prices not to exceed 91 per cent. Barings would pay those foreign bondholders who insisted on repayment. The 3 per cent government debt certificates were to be returned through Biddle to the government. A side agreement stated that if Baring purchases did not exceed $5 million, they privileged the Bank to draw on them for the difference at 0.5 per cent commission.[264]

At first, Barings was loath to support the Bank. It seemed illogical given their soured opinion of its operations and its president. They wished also not to be associated with the often politically-motivated attacks in the American Congress on the Bank's profligate behaviour, justified or not. The refinancing deal by Cadwalader gave enemies of the Bank in Congress cause to assert that the Bank was not only irresponsible in domestic matters; that it was 'an agent of a foreign power', amoral and un-American. The issue fuelled a broader campaign by anti-Bank Democrats who desired to find proof that all bankers were of one common, sinister stripe, which President Jackson alleged them to be.[265]

Bates himself was puzzled by Ward's persevering support of the Bank, and Ward's suggestion that the partners finally had a splendid chance to profit in 1832 from their relationship with Biddle. Barings should take advantage of the lower rates the London money market afforded the partners compared with 1831, Ward said, and lend to Biddle at the enormous spread of 1–1.5 per cent higher interest.[266]

Ward's suggestion was a very practical one. He may not have viewed the condition or behaviour of the Bank of the United States as seriously as political discussions would have left the casual or more distant observer such as Bates to believe. Ward's close acquaintance Daniel Webster may or may not have been the source of his information, but his conclusions were clear: the Bank was neither so badly managed nor in such poor shape at the start of 1832 that it should not be rechartered. Before writing to Barings regarding debt refinancing, in fact, Ward evaluated the Bank's affairs as 'in the main well conducted and its several parts in a good working way & well adjusted to each other'.[267]

Barings may have formed its opinion from the fractious Congressional debates in the winter of 1832 when a long list of charges came forth against the Bank, such as those from Augustus Clayton, representative of Georgia. Overissue of notes, usury, misrepresentation, political favouritism, foreign influence and general managerial recklessness, Clayton said, militated against recharter. Fellow anti-Bank Democrats vociferously disputed the Bank's position as anything like the 'pillar of the American System' that senator Henry Clay of Kentucky said it was. Pro-Bank men answered the charges point for point, and the debate was sufficiently divisive that the House appointed a Select Committee of Ways and Means in February to look into the Bank's affairs.

The Committee vindicated Biddle and the Bank thoroughly. Later findings of Congressional investigations powerfully reinforced this opinion. Congress appointed an agent of the Treasury department, Mr Henry Toland, to investigate Bank conduct and condition. On 10 January 1833 Toland reported that the Bank was a safe depository for public funds. He described the Bank's debt as 'safe and wholesome', especially in the western states, and pronounced that the Bank was solvent, and maintained a greater supply of specie in proportion to its note issues than did the Bank of England. Further reports of the House Ways and Means Committee and Andrew Jackson's own secretary of the treasury, Louis Maclean, confirmed the earlier solid verdict.[268]

Barings Makes a Deal

Favourable verdicts notwithstanding, Barings had accommodated the Bank of the United States in 1832 at some cost. For the first time in its history, the new partnership had to borrow substantially in the London money market because of the scale of the American operation. The House used the so-called 'deferred threes' as collateral for a 4 per cent £150,000 loan from the City's foremost discounter, Overend, Gurney & Company, made payable when the Bank of the United States' loan came due in the autumn of 1833.[269]

It is possible that Overend, Gurney's loan to Barings may have been larger if it had not been for the deposits that Europeans fleeing the Continent entrusted to the House just before the operation with Bank of the United States. For Barings' 'backstopping' Biddle, it is interesting to note that by the start of 1833 (the middle of Barings' loan period), the Bank of the United States had recovered 60 per cent of the specie it had lost by the outflows of 1832. Interestingly, the Bank recorded the highest net profits in its history as well! So did Barings. Net dollar profits increased together as the table below shows.[270]

Table 3.4: Profits of the Bank of the United States and Barings, 1829–33 (in dollars).

Year	BUS	Barings
1829	2,706,455	123,144
1830	2,806,794	311,582
1831	2,935,022	257,337
1832	3,577,511	468,725
1833	3,196,067	570,076

In March 1832, while the Reform bill occupied the House of Commons and cholera raged in London, the long-term money market eased. American state and corporate issues became suddenly more favourably received.[271] A mutually beneficial deal materialized between Barings and the Bank which showed their relationship could be remunerative to the London House after all.

Through the mediation of its cashier at New Orleans, Samuel Jaudon, the Bank arranged for Barings to take a majority stake in a $7 million bond flotation of the newly-chartered Union Bank of Louisiana. When Ward signed the contract in New York on 24 August 1832, the Union Bank represented the largest single block of American bonds ever marketed by Barings on an overseas bourse. Created by Edmund Forstall to service agricultural interests in New Orleans, the New York bankers Prime, Ward & King took one third, and Barings two thirds of the total 5,500-share bond offering. More importantly, Barings captured the exchange account of the Union Bank – at the time, the largest chartered bank in New Orleans.[272] The British House thus strengthened its position in the Louisiana market, in which it had operated as agent to the Consolidated Association of Planters since 1828.[273] Together with the powerful New Orleans branch of the Bank of the United States, which processed more bills on personal security than any other in Biddle's branch system, in 1832 Barings lay at the heart of financing in the most important entrepôt of the American cotton trade.[274]

The year of difficulties with Biddle over the 3 per cents faded as the partners saw business double in the United States market. By Ward's count, American clients now numbered nearly one thousand, and over his first four years as agent, Ward estimated he had granted $50 million in credits. Ward's success at attracting clients was so pronounced that, by autumn 1832, the numerous clerks at 8 Bishopsgate were twenty days behind in entering bills receivable from the United States.[275] Many of these credit extensions were of the uncovered variety, and thus relied heavily upon Ward's screening, client accountability and honesty.

We have seen that Barings' decision to maintain a resident agent in the United States formed part of a broader plan to systematize and diversify its operations for increased safety and predictability of earnings. Bates, Mildmay and Thomas Baring divided operations among themselves into certain spheres, established the affiliate in Liverpool for international operations (including the newly-augmented exchange capacity at New Orleans), and standardized the firms rules in regard to credit and correspondents. With professional credit-rating services decades away, the firm relied on Ward for particularly American information and operational knowledge in the early 1830s.

If the Bank of the United States were allowed to encounter genuine troubles for any of a variety of reasons – management incompetence, misjudgement or the demands of a hostile political climate – Barings' ever-growing list of American clients would likely suffer. For self-interest as well, Barings preserved its clients' credit and liquidity as it had done in the past. When the firm encountered difficulties, for example in the late 1820s as Mexico's government agent, Barings appeared prepared to extend itself to whatever reasonable amount in order not to be associated publicly with a losing enterprise. In the Mexican affair, however, the firm's patience was not infinite. A Baring competitor in the Anglo-American market, Lizardi & Company, offered to take over the Mexican agency in the early 1830s, and the partners gave up their position willingly. For the time being in the United States, also, the partners supported Biddle and the Bank. Both benefited by the partnership, and American commerce and finance maintained solvency.

Despite difficulties, if one client relationship in the United States for Barings could be labelled as 'most important', it was likely the Bank of the United States. Indeed, during the Biddle presidency, the Bank was virtually synonymous with American finance. It was precisely this fact that rankled certain politicians but, certainly for anyone doing business in the American market, one paid attention to the fortunes of the Bank. Barings' relationship with Biddle gave it a quick way to monitor the American market. For now though, the restructuring of Bank obligations in 1831–2 was a way for the new partners to begin learning to observe the sometimes unpredictable scene of the emerging United States and the role that politics could play in a new country.

For now also, the timing of the firm had been good. It brought new personnel on board in a trough period in trade as we have seen above, and the partners aimed to profit as 'value players' when revival took hold. A prominent British financial journal commented on the helpfulness of Britain's most eminent bank in the autumn of 1832. 'The House of Baring brothers', it editorialized, 'has been one of the great channels for accomplishing all that could be effected by an extension of credit, and the application of British capital throughout the American Union'.[276]

In the coming years, Barings and Ward found themselves in what could be called a cacophony of events – all of which, in different ways, would affect business conditions in the United States. Maintaining the health of its American accounts had become more important to the overall health of the firm than four years before. Ever cautious, the partners had to decide continually whether to stay committed and helpful to the United States market, or pull away to more benign and profitable venues.

4 SILVER LININGS (1832–4)

> We have never lived in times of greater excitement than the present, and on so many subjects.
>
> Hezekiah Niles[277]

At the start of 1832, Bates believed that if only certain obstacles could be swept away, trade would go well and prosperity increase throughout the Anglo-American economy. Initially, the firm considered controversies in the early years of the Jackson administration as temporary and part of the normal frictions of American politics and doing business. The years 1832–4, however, showed themselves to be more serious than expected. They touched European diplomacy over Belgium, South Carolina's nullification, tariff reform and the Second Bank controversy. They gave the new partnership its first experience of American recession and recovery. The years of 1832–4 were more than simply a time to be endured before resuming regular business. They revealed valuable information to Barings about the United States, and when to curtail operations even as competitors expanded. These years seem to have enabled the firm to avoid, in the main, the woes of 1837.

Impediments to Business

The first decade of the new Barings partnership was not wanting for various opportunities or hazards. Disturbances of almost any kind could upset assumptions and plans in England, or in any market in which the House did business. Legislation on the national or local level could affect commodity prices, rates in money markets and trade conditions. A bank with international ambitions and commitments needed the traits of watchful steadiness and quickness of mind in its personnel to navigate the changeable nature of world events.

The period of reaction besetting Europe after the 1815 Vienna settlements made the Continent at times difficult for commerce. Revolutions and rebellions in France, Poland, Germany and the Papal States in the early 1830s, as well as British rivalries with a restless Russia in the Balkans and eastern Mediterranean, called for continuous monitoring for the banker who had long-distance trade contracts or who desired to establish new ones. Latin American trade was perennially handicapped by instability of governments and dubious credit quality. Compared with other world regions, the United States seemed politically stable and, for the Barings, familiar territory for investment and commercial ties.

The question of Belgian separation and sovereignty from the Netherlands had preoccupied European diplomacy since 1830 and, at various times throughout 1831, threatened to cause general war. No matter how furiously Ward accumulated accounts in the United States or however fruitful the trade, an unstable Europe caused market uneasiness, and affected Barings' decision-making.

On 15 November 1831, the five Concert powers[278] had signed the protocol defining Belgian territory as well as its neutrality – and the Belgian dispute ceased as a diplomatic problem. Until the end of the decade, however, Belgium stood in a state of unease because the Dutch king, William, did not accept its loss and filibustered the territory repeatedly even after the powers ratified the protocols in May of 1832. This irritated British statesmen, such as the foreign secretary, Lord Palmerston, but, without the support of the three eastern courts to join in coercive measures against a recalcitrant Holland, Britain would not resort to war.[279]

The eastern powers acceded to a division of the Low Countries in part because of British and French restraint over Russian and Austrian interests in Poland and northern Italy – and, for the time being, this diplomatic equilibrium held. Shortly after Barings had arranged the huge deal with Prime Ward & King for the Union Bank bonds and exchange account deal, however, an order in council placed on embargo on the cross-channel trade with Holland, and British and French troops seized Dutch ships. An Anglo-French force also blockaded the Scheldt River, bombarded the great citadel of Antwerp, and caused the Dutch to surrender that stronghold to the Belgian king. The London Stock Exchange stood unaffected, though insurance rates upon policies to Holland increased by a factor of ten. The Dutch embargo caused great distress in British ports such as Hull and, at a large November meeting, merchants and bankers in London solicited the British king to discourage any coercive actions against Holland disruptive to British trade.[280]

Bates mentioned the possibility of a Bank of England tightening in the event of war, but supposed he would know in advance of any Bank action since Mildmay was a director. Additionally, the firm had sufficient margin to withstand storms since it neither borrowed nor leveraged its books.[281] The threat of war was an irritating impertinence, but it was to the very possibility of it that Bates attributed the unexpectedly soft demand for the firm's Louisiana bond offering. Without Belgium, Bates predicted 'three or four years of successful trade'.[282] Britain was determined to compel Holland to evacuate the territories assigned to Belgium by treaty via an embargo against Dutch shipping and trade.[283] Still, as of the middle of June 1833, Bates reported from Europe that 'the Dutch King continues obstinate, the French king unpopular', and general business remained ill at ease.[284]

Bates viewed the military and diplomatic situation in Belgium also in a broad sociological way, and drew conclusions in his diary about where Barings should seek business.

> Came to the conclusion with Mildmay that the state of things in most parts of Europe is very unsafe for commerce; that the contest between the Governors and the Governed in England, France, Italy, etc, will end in the overthrow of all order and society for property and that all dealings in merchandise should be entered into with great caution; the following articles are likely to be favorably influenced by these changes: corn, wool – and American securities and American business will be safer than any other – and should be cultivated with greatest zeal.[285]

But the reform impulse was at least as present in Jacksonian America as it was in Europe, and from Barings' point of view, the business climate became less than ideal. Bates's idea to retreat to the safe harbour of the quickly-growing and stable United States would become more difficult than he imagined.

On 24 November 1832, the legislature of South Carolina voted to invalidate recently-passed federal tariff legislation which it believed was unconstitutional. South Carolina reacted to a particular bill signed by President Jackson in July, but the issue of import duties was a long-standing area of difference between the northern and southern states.

Throughout the 1830s, the north regarded a protective system as essential to the development of its industry, and was tied to such ideas as the right to regulate trade, security of property, national self-sufficiency and defence, and the economic independence of the Republic.[286] The south resented measures which raised prices for northern goods that it needed, and grew to see the tariff as a device by which the federal government subsidized the economy of a rival section.

Southern farmers were 'price takers'. That is to say, they were obliged to sell cotton at prices determined by strict supply and demand in an open market. On the other hand, they were forced to buy on a closed market where prices on manufactured goods were determined by tariff laws that reduced foreign competition. Moreover, they were forced to 'sell twice' – first their cotton for foreign credits, then their foreign credits in the northern money market. Ongoing transaction costs by this process embittered the south against the tariff.

The 1832 bill partially repealed the protective 1828 tariff to which southern states objected. More generally, its purpose was to reduce revenue to an already solvent federal treasury. The new bill lowered the overall tariff schedule by 25 per cent but retained the high rates on woollens, iron goods and cottons, and it was these features that caused South Carolinians to baulk.[287]

Sectionalism had yet to achieve the virulence of later years, and in the 1830s few states – not even those of the south – agreed with South Carolina's extreme action. Most were concerned with the perils of going into unchartered waters and setting precedents difficult to undo. Sympathy for South Carolina's constitutional stance was one thing; defiance of duly-passed federal law was another.

Precedents aside, the tariff question did not precisely coincide with north-south geography. Divisions existing within states were significant enough at this time to frustrate predictions about a state's leanings in the tariff debate, except in the most general way. Northern industry, for example, adamantly supported a protected market, but Yankee shipping interests fought vigorously to safeguard their ocean-borne import trade. Southern cotton most of the time preferred – even demanded – a free market, but southern men of a slightly different vision dreamed of a southern textile market someday, which would need protection. In 1816, John C. Calhoun of South Carolina was an outspoken advocate of tariff measures; Daniel Webster of Massachusetts had been an eloquent free trader. In the 1830s, both men had switched sides. The political economy of the 1830s was sufficiently fluid and the interests within states sufficiently diverse that South Carolina found herself, in the main, unsupported in her quest for nullification.[288]

Shortly after Congress approved the use of force in February 1833 to collect revenue in an individual state, the Senate leadership scrambled to built support for a some kind of middle measure to avoid military action. A 'compromise tariff' materialized under the steerage of senator Henry Clay of Kentucky, and passed Congress in March 1833. The free list was expanded, and duties on imports would be reduced gradually – at two-year intervals – for ten years until they stood at a uniform 20 per cent ad valorem rate. Apart from phased reductions, Clay's bill contained the striking feature of freezing of the tariff for ten years.[289]

Hezekiah Niles, the Baltimore editor of a widely-circulating weekly, was glad to have the tariff issue settled one way or the other. Niles was pro-tariff, and believed the 'compromise' legislation would hurt American enterprise. In the short run, he endorsed anything that banished uncertainty – the bane of commerce and business planning. 'We are well assured that very large sums of money or credits, or means, are now suspended by movements in congress on the tariff question', Niles wrote in 1832. 'We have heard of two or three cases by which half a million is suspended in its desired use in Pennsylvania; and have understood that much money is waiting for investment in manufacturing operations in Tennessee and Missouri.'[290] So it was everywhere, wrote Niles. 'All extensions have been stopped. Everyone is hauling in.'[291]

Barings made all sorts of calculations in relation to American trade. The 'pretty little bill', as Daniel Webster sarcastically called the tariff reduction legislation, pleased Joshua Bates very much. After all, it appeared to achieve for the United States the similar ends that Bates had desired for some time for England when he advocated reform of the English Corn Laws. In Bates's view, the tariff decision by the American Congress was a long-term plus for British manufacturing since it would cause structural change in the transatlantic relationship between the two countries. He believed the Americans were a people naturally disposed to agriculture; that they 'dabbled' in industry of various types only because misguided British policy discriminated for years against American farm products, and the United States needed something to do with a surplus population. If England reformed the Corn Laws, thought Bates, Americans could abandon their 'less natural' manufactures – however flourishing – and return to their origins as a farming people, supplying the free-trading British with foodstuffs of all sorts. Bates criticized the British restrictions on goods from the United States since they gave the Americans incentives for manufacturing in the first place. Though he admitted under parliamentary questioning that repeal of the Corn Laws would not totally eliminate American industry at this point, he testified that shrewd British tariff policy could cause American manufactures to 'drop off'.[292] Ideally, Great Britain and the United States were complementary economies: industrial and agricultural respectively.

The Americans appeared to have moved closer to complementarity by being first to lower tariffs, thereby in effect blunting the British Corn Laws for them.[293] The perception of what this move meant, good or bad, varied. The anti-tariff forces in the United States argued the compromise tariff spared the Union from potential fracture. They also considered a reduction of tariffs as quite reasonable because the federal government was on the verge of generating a surplus on the former high tariff schedule.[294] Tariff advocates, by contrast, viewed developments with 'deep concern' and predicted

> That a reduction of the duties to the proposed standard must inevitably produce excessive importation, the necessary consequence of which will be to create a large foreign debt, to subtract the specie, derange the currency, prostrate American labor, suspend improvements, and eventually involve the nation in bankruptcy and ruin, thus inflicting even a severer series of disasters upon the nation than those which befell the United States between 1816 and 1820.[295]

Hezekiah Niles wondered why legislatures tinkered with the prosperity the nation enjoyed. 'How', he asked, 'are the Americans to pay for British goods under the present *British* tariff? What have we *more* to export which Britain will receive'?[296]

To the author's knowledge Thomas Ward was mute on the tariff, though, as a New Englander, he probably favoured protection – as his acquaintance Daniel Webster certainly did. Unlike Webster, Ward was in a difficult position, since any tariff reduction on the American side appealed to his British employer. Bates expected that South Carolina 'would be properly managed', and had predicted the tariff would come down 'to appease popular clamour'.[297] It is likely his impressions at least in part came from Ward, who, in turn, was informed by Webster. The network also extended to the prominent merchant and Baring correspondent in New York, Jonathan Goodhue, who, as secretary of the New York Friends of Domestic Industry, probably supplied his close friend Ward with current and confidential information from the organization's frequent meetings. Goodhue was a likely reason at this time for Ward's frequent trips south to New York from Boston. Barings associate Russell Sturgis served as secretary to at least one anti-tariff meeting in Boston.[298]

In any case, Barings' view of American developments from London was clear, clipped and broad-stroked. 'The tariff question is now settled in the U. States', wrote Bates in his diary. 'It will produce an immense demand for British manufactures'.[299] And manufactures were only the beginning. Other facets of the tariff bill interested the partners. It removed, for example, the duty on teas from China or from any other place east of the Cape of Good Hope, provided imports came in American ships. Perhaps not coincidentally, Barings now took an interest in shipping, and assigned Goodhue & Company (no. 174) as its shipping manager in the United States.[300] They soon expanded their participation in the China trade. Importantly, the tariff fixed the exchange for payment of duties at a new $4.80 to £1, whereas the average of the par of sterling for several years had been about $4.88.[301]

The House was now confident that it possessed ample resources to exploit with flexibility any new opportunities crossing their path, including increased volumes of trade. 'We are now organized on a scale that will enable us to do any amount of business', Bates informed his United States agent. 'Our Counting House resembles a Custom House or public office, but it goes regular and easy, and for *regular times* we have capital enough for double the amount of regular business'.[302] This great traffic was showing up in Barings' smoothly-rising profits. In 1832, profits for the firm were £96 million; for the next year, £114 million; and for 1834 they reached £136 million.[303]

Bates knew that the firm's confidence and graceful increase in profits attracted attention and created competitors. 'One cannot be successful', he said to Ward, 'without exciting envy, and some people will have the bad taste to shew it ... As 617 & 619 & 999 do not increase, you may rest assured that they do all in their power to insinuate things against us – and in a manner that indicates a want of tact and taste that gives to their ill will an exactly opposite effect from that intended'.[304] Thomas Wiggin (no. 999) was a fool and a boaster, thought Bates. He talks about his commissions, 'which is all a flourish', then struts in public 'what he thinks he knows about our House', and the methods of Barings' speculations. And 'he made a very good move for us since his American agent is a rogue' and such an 'uncertificated Bankrupt [that] no one will trust him. Lloyds people [already] complain.'

George Wildes & Company (no. 619) 'are very desirous of getting banking business, which they will not speedily acquire. There is a want of high feeling there which will forever prevent much business.' As for 617 (Thomas Wilson &

Company), '[they] do not appear to be doing much; they are very sharp in looking out for business. For some cause or other, however, they are not very popular.'[305]

With these three American Houses, and with competition generally, Bates felt that so long as people held the impression that Barings was doing well, it seemed other Houses 'must put something forward to counteract it'. As to others 'insinuating things against us', Ward encouraged the House to hold the moral high ground:

> I never say a word against any House, and when anything is said of what others can do, will do, or are doing, I treat it with the greatest kindness and respect and generally without remark. #619 and #617 are doing all they can to obtain business through the activity of their agents and partners, but the new business they get they will have to buy. We have taken the right course and, whatever agents and others are disposed to say, the publick mind is fixed very strongly in its conviction as to the high character, safety, and honorable mode of proceeding of your House. The agents of #619 and #617 can produce no ill effect.[306]

Barings did not have to buy business. The 'publick' was in fact showing up at Ward's and Barings' door. In May 1832, Ward reported that Barings' business in the United States would yield, with little risk, £40,000 in the coming year.[307] Bates knew this prediction was plausible. The month before he had written to Ward from London that the services of the House were in much demand. 'We have Americans here without number looking for consignments, and they give me trouble enough without concerning myself with the maneuverings of the competition.'[308]

In anticipation of a settlement on war-torn Belgium, Barings was getting busy, as was all Europe it seemed. Niles reported 'very lively' activity in British trade and manufacturing because of modifications in the American tariff. The New York *Commercial Advertiser* said in the United States that 'the *reduction* of the duty upon iron and staple items of hardware has been followed by a *rise* in the market of 10 per cent, some articles have risen 20'. It reiterated Niles's impression of a price advance in Europe, which it attributed to the belief that foreign articles would see an increasing demand in the United States.[309] Barings reports indicate it was becoming more and more profitable for Americans to export – even to their own country! Americans no doubt added to the scramble for goods to export to the United States that showed up in price increases in Europe in the wake of American trade liberalization. Unlike the tariff increase of 1828, when foreign exporters scrambled to the American market before they were shut out by higher rates, the early 1830s excited traders for a different reason entirely. The United States now opened the door to exporters in March 1833, and promised to keep it open for a decade.

Continued American Expansion

American port cities did a great spring business in 1833 – better, it was said, than the year before.[310] New York, Philadelphia, Boston and Baltimore were all 'filled with strangers', newspapers reported. With the end of winter, southern and western merchants travelled to north-eastern cities and purchased imports on funds from the previous year's commodity exports. Prices of imported goods were higher this year, especially among those items on which duties had been most reduced.[311]

Prices for non-farm exports from Britain increased throughout 1833 because of excitement over American tariff liberalization, and the total value of British exports surged 39 per cent in 1833 from year-earlier levels. But price increases were confined only to 1833, as the export surge was part of a larger pattern of British recovery after seven years of depressed prices in the wake of the burst bubble of 1825–6. Industrial output rose steadily after 1833. Increased production kept prices steady until the middle of 1835, when a sharp inflationary rise developed.[312]

A large part of British investment after 1833 focused on domestic concerns such as joint-stock banks and railways. This contrasted with the expansion of 1824–5 based on foreign investment. The finance of such British internal investment was girded in the spring of 1833 with the renewal of the charter of the Bank of England for a period of ten years.[313] Import and export statistics indicate the start of a massive boom in the British general trade sector in 1833 that did not abate until 1837, and included in it substantial exports to the United States.[314] The pick-up in the British economy signalled opportunity for those who extended credits for the American export trade, such as Barings.

Trade required two markets of course, and the American one was increasingly exciting. President Jackson had sent missions abroad since 1829 to open doors for American business. Envoys negotiated formal treaties 'of Amity and Commerce' with Prussia (1829), Colombia and Russia (1831), Chile and Turkey (1832), Belgium (1833), Muscat and Thailand (1834). As part of the steady expansion of American trade with the Far East, Jackson began to explore ways to open Japan to the west, twenty years before Commodore Perry would do so by force.

Trade treaties could only add to a burgeoning American economy, where activity was everywhere noticeable, measurable in many ways, and commented upon often. Shipbuilding boomed. In Boston, 130 ships lay under construction, averaging 350 tons each.[315] Baltimore built even larger ships for accounts throughout the country – some steam, some upwards of 600 tons.[316] Some eastern shipyards built for western waters, especially after the completion of the important Ohio Canal in July 1832.[317] At Louisville, for example, there operated, by the summer of 1833, 'thirty-five huge steamboats, at one time receiving or discharging cargoes having to do with the enormous area south to Natchez and north to Cleveland,

Cincinnati, and Lake Erie'.[318] Revenue from canal traffic increased: the aggregate amount from tolls of New York canals was $147,945 for the month of August 1833 – a 40 per cent increase over August 1832 – even as the rate of tolls had been reduced.[319] Similar spikes took place in newer markets such as Ohio, where canal revenue for May 1833 increased by nearly two-thirds year over year.[320]

Not only was the United States developing its manufacturing capacity, but the means to finance it within a bullion-based economy. Gold streamed from mines in the southern states, most prodigiously from North Carolina. By the middle of 1833, the United States produced an amount equal to one-sixth of the entire quantity produced by Europe and the Americas.[321]

Demographically, the American market was expanding as well. In 1833, the United States population stood at just over 14 million, less than Great Britain's at the time, but it was expanding twice as quickly.[322] Not surprisingly, the growth differed by region of the country. In the previous decade, New England's population had grown by 19 per cent, the mid-Atlantic states slightly more quickly, but both more modestly than the country as a whole, which had increased by a third. The growth of the new states of the west and south-west was startling and increased the average: the population of Ohio increased 409 per cent in ten years; Indiana, 500; Michigan, 764; Arkansas, 1,344 per cent.[323]

Figure 4.1: View of Cincinnati by Henry R. Robinson (after J. C. Wild). Hand-coloured lithograph (1835). I. N. Phelps Stokes Collection, New York Public Library.

Increasing population accompanied increased production of many sorts. All-important cotton production had one of its best years in 1833 – increasing an exceptionally strong 14 per cent. This continued the string of winning years that began in 1830, as shown in Table 4.1.

Table 4.1: American Cotton Production, 1830–7 (in thousands of bales). Source: US Census, *The Statistical History*, p. 518.

Year	Bales
1830	732
1831	805
1832	816
1833	931
1834	962
1835	1,062
1836	1,129
1837	1,428

Annual reports issued from the Treasury attest to the variety of products besides cotton circulating in the American market of the early 1830s. Imports exceeded exports, though both increased steadily.[324] Individual states dedicated funds for larger customs Houses from New London and Newburyport, Massachusetts, to Key West.[325] Manufacturing output, by one estimate, climbed almost 60 per cent in the decade to 1839.[326] Though most Americans remained farmers, parts of the north-east were completing the vital early stages of industrialization. Typical were wool and cotton factories employing up to several hundred workers, and a few with over a thousand.[327] Though growth of New England cotton, for example, had slowed from its peak in yards produced, the young United States already ranked ahead of France in the cotton-spinning business by 1831. Mills in Lowell, Massachusetts, alone produced 7 million lbs of raw cotton annually by the middle of 1833, not to mention 5,000 tons of anthracite coal.[328]

Table 4.2: Annual Mean Growth Rates (%) of New England Cotton Industry, 1815–36. Source: Rostow, *The World Economy*, p. 138.[329]

Years	% Increase
1815–18	45.2
1818–25	38.3
1825–30	15.2
1830–6	12.2

As in textiles, the United States saw factory-produced articles such as boots, shoes, carpets, flint glass, lead, sugar, molasses and salt. Observers pointed to the increasing presence of the United States in a number of advanced sectors, especially textiles. But American determination to align with the most modern technologies showed itself also in their laying down the beginnings of a railway network after 1830 which, over time, improved inter-regional trade even more than canals had done ten years previously. In 1831, trackage in the United States stood at 72 miles, but it nearly doubled in 1832, and doubled still again by 1834.[330] The first lines began in the north-east. By the middle of 1833, rail systems were already subscribed as far south as Florida, and as far west as Schenectady, New York.[331] Many more were planned, especially for Ohio, to supplement a maturing system of wagon roads.[332]

Mastery gained from manufacturing engine technology for steamboats on the inland waterways translated readily to expertise in locomotive technology, and American-made engines soon outfitted many of the early railroads.[333] Factories at both Pittsburgh and Cincinnati were turning out over 100 steam engines per year by 1834 for this purpose.[334] The demand for iron products was so great that they remained both a locally-produced item throughout the antebellum years, and a lucrative imported item, often shipped from Liverpool, financed by merchants bankers such as Baring Brothers & Company, and Alexander Brown & Sons.[335]

So that Americans and the world could see the advancement of the United States in 'the useful and ornamental arts', regular exhibitions took place – for example at the American Institute in New York City that would certainly, according to a regular attendee, 'attract praise and eulogy even in the great cities of London and Paris'.[336] Here the spectrum of American ingenuity, inventiveness and trade – which had garnered 535 separate patents in the decade before 1830, and would yield many more – was systematically organized and displayed.[337]

As the largest measure of American progress, gross national product increased by an exuberant 8.2 per cent in 1833 to $1.37 billion.

Table 4.3: Rates of American Gross National Product Growth, 1830–6. Source: Berry, *Production and Population*, p. 19.

Year	Growth (%)
1830	2.8
1831	4.8
1832	6.6
1833	8.2
1834	–
1835	12.5
1836	9.2

To these gross national product growth rates, exports contributed less and less each year. From their peak in 1817, exports had dropped by over 6 percentage points (or over 50 per cent) from 13.1 per cent of gross national product to 6.4 per cent in 1833.[338] The United States was concentrating on its increasingly vibrant and ever-larger and deepening domestic market.

This was not lost on Joshua Bates, Ward or Hezekiah Niles. Nor was it lost on the American Institute, which began its displays and awards for domestic achievements in 1829, the year Barings made its new initiatives in the United States; the same year they hired Ward through Goodhue, and the year Barings locked in its correspondent agreement with Prime, Ward & King. With so much attention on the tariff and foreign trade, Niles reminded his readers that 'even at New York, "the great commercial emporium", the *home* market for farmers is three times more valuable than the foreign one … that even though trade had been opened to the West Indies, goods such as flour for example were taken up mainly at home'.[339] Niles continued:

> The consumption of wheat produced in the middle, southern and western states by the working people of the eastern states has increased ten fold since the establishment of manufacturies New England … The states north of the Potomac, now using about 300,000 bales of cotton, create a larger demand for that staple than is that of all the rest of the world, England excepted. New England now receives from other states, not less than two millions of barrels of flour a year. Her consumption before the war was hardly two hundred thousand.[340]

Though a north-south sectional issue, the tariff was becoming less and less important to American economic wellbeing because the value of internal trade was growing at three times the rate of foreign trade.[341] Americans should realize, said Niles, that commodities sold at Boston were as valuable as those sold at Liverpool, and moreover their growth or manufacture used American sweat, money, and talent. After twenty-five years, the United States was breaking away from an economy which could have been crippled by a change in the pattern of foreign trade in Jefferson's day. Its internal market was enlarging rapidly – both in production and consumption – and Americans would see that, as it grew, the United States market could increasingly set commodity prices, with a proportional lessening dependence on foreign exchanges.[342]

It is not clear if Joshua Bates read the columns of Hezekiah Niles, or if Ward sent him copies of the *Weekly Register*, but Bates held views similar to Niles which he expressed to Ward in the summer of 1833:

> A proof of the improved condition of mankind, only consider in 1825 the crop of Cotton in the U.S. was 550/m Bales, but now is double that quantity and the whole consumed in the year. Silk has increased there in about the same ratio; and sugar and coffee in like manner.

Bates concluded that American productivity was outstripping population growth – 'the whole condition of mankind was proof'.[343]

Ward needed little convincing. After all, economic growth was all around him in Boston. While visiting Goodhue, Ward no doubt surveyed the New York scene as well. He could read in the *New York Spectator* that merchants prospered almost regardless of the business they were in, since, during the first half of 1833, enterprise of almost every description was good. Trade volumes were up, earnings of ocean carriers were up, and the new railway securities became 'all the rage'. The stock of the Bank of the United States became a market favourite. According to the *Spectator*:

1250 shares [of the Bank] have been sold at 108–109! The rise, we believe, is without parallel, and has been occasioned by the Report of the Committee of Ways and Means. The Bears who have been contracting to deliver stock ahead will wish they had been Bulls.[344]

Bank of the United States shares moved up in sympathy with the general market, and with other bank stocks such as the Phoenix Bank, the Manhattan Company and City Bank. Generally rising share prices showed a logical enthusiasm for the nation's long-term prospects. But speculation in the Bank's shares was a bit different from other stocks because the Bank's very existence was in question between 1832 and 1834. Congress had agreed to recharter, but Andrew Jackson dug in his heels in opposition with a presidential veto in July 1832.

Markets and prices glide on differences of opinion among market participants. And market volatility and speculation results from uncertainty. The American economy held out excellent potential indeed, and the American tariff beckoned foreign trade. Even the Bank of England's recharter obligingly provided domestic stability from which British investors could venture abroad. But what stopped Barings from committing to the expanding United States more fully than it did was uncertainty about the fortunes of the Bank of the United States. As the most important single entity in American finance, the fate of the Bank hung over the economy, and frustrated planning for those in trade and business. As 1833 progressed, the situation became more and more unclear.

Jackson, the Bank and Money Disruption

The contest between the Bank of the United States and President Jackson destabilized the American financial system briefly and gave pause to Barings, who became ambivalent in their dealings with the United States. They had to deal with Biddle as a client to which they extended considerable credit privileges for dealings in the private credit markets. On the other hand, Barings was torn because it held the government treasury account as well, which provided a certain cachet for the firm's American business despite Bates downplaying its actual financial significance.

Shortly after Jackson vetoed the recharter bill in July 1832, relations between the Bank and Treasury became strained over the issue of a dishonoured draft on France. On 31 October 1832, the secretary of the Treasury (Louis McLane) asked Nicholas Biddle about the most convenient means to secure payment of the nearly 25 million francs due the United States under the spoliation claims treaty of 1 July 1831.[345] Biddle advised a draft on the French government, which the Treasury made on 7 February 1833. The bill was purchased by the Bank at the highest price of the day. The Bank sent the bill to Barings with instructions to sell it in London, because the Bank had ample balances with Hottinguer & Company in Paris at that time and preferred to build up its sterling resources. When the bill was presented, the French government refused to pay because no appropriation had been made. The Treasury was informed that the bill had been protested and taken up by Hottinguer & Company to save the honour of the Bank.

Friction between Treasury and the Bank ensued when Biddle presented to the United States government the customary 15 per cent claim for damages and interest on a disputed transaction, which amounted to approximately $170,000. On the advice of the attorney general, the Government denied any foundation to Biddle's claim in June 1833. The Bank defended itself, however, through Barings' legal counsel in the United States, Daniel Webster, who publicized the fact that the Bank was merely following the same commercial practices it would for any other client or customer.

However troubling to the administration, the French indemnity issue did not colour the start of Hezekiah Niles's twenty-third year as publisher of the *Weekly Register*. As he did every August when Congress was recessed, Niles gave readers an annual forecast of things to come. He had to admit that this year his report was rather bland. 'There is no peculiarly exciting subject before the public right now', he wrote, 'The several parties seem to be in a state of repose, that they may recover their strength for the ensuing session [which] will be a very interesting one'.[346] The markets rallied throughout the summer as if to nod assurance to the recessing congressmen that all would be well. By autumn, however, the situation had changed. The Biddle-Treasury tiff over the French draft went unresolved and much more serious problems arose between the Bank and the Jackson administration.

A member of President Jackson's inner circle, Amos Kendall, proposed a controversial plan for the transfer of federal funds from the Bank of the United States to state-chartered banks, dubbed 'pet banks' by critics. Jackson accepted the plan in early summer 1833. He dispatched Kendall, without the knowledge of secretary of the Treasury William Duane, on a highly-publicized tour of the eastern seaboard to determine those banks willing to act as federal depositories.[347] Kendall secured commitments from seven banks.

In September, with Congress still adjourned, Jackson gave approval to remove the deposits. Mr Duane's replacement at the Treasury, Roger B. Taney, issued instructions to the collectors of the public revenue to cease using the Bank of the United States as a depository, beginning on 1 October. After this date, deposits to the credit of the government should be made to the following private banks: the Girard Bank in Philadelphia, the Commonwealth Bank of Boston, the Merchant Bank of Boston, the Bank of the Manhattan Company in New York, the Mechanics Bank in New York, the Bank of America in New York and the Union Bank of Maryland in Baltimore. By December, the government had transferred all public funds from the federal Bank to banks partisan to the Democratic party.[348]

At first, bankers hesitated over the deposits transfer. After all, no precedent for this bold and possibly illegal stroke existed. What of a Congressional backlash? Kendall assured them of the president's stolid determination to distribute the deposits, and to distribute them widely among those banks which wanted a share. Furthermore, bank directors realized that, as depositories, they would be ongoing beneficiaries of the surplus revenues accumulating in the Treasury. In the second month of 1834, the new 'deposite' banks numbered twenty-two; by the expiration of the Bank of the United States' charter in 1836, there were ninety-one.[349]

The deposits transfer came roughly eighteen months after Jackson delivered the Bank veto in July 1832.[350] The message was popular among sections of the electorate whose knowledge of financial matters was rudimentary; among debtors, and those susceptible to rhetorical notions such as 'monied aristocracies' or 'foreign influences' endangering American freedoms. Those constituencies which had a specific interest in seeing Biddle fall from his perch atop the nation's exchange markets, such as state banks, also supported the veto. Some who had followed Jackson politically believed the president wanted merely to substitute a Democratic national bank for the Bank of the United States. Jackson had hinted several times after all in 1831 that he might leave the job to Congress, in which his party held a majority.[351] For many active in business, though, the veto only represented an unwelcome surprise and, as such, a destabilizing event.

Money was already expected to be 'tight' in the autumn of 1832 due to an outflow of specie to cover increased European imports from recent tariff liberalization. With the veto, money would tighten further. Throughout the summer, newspapers described the effect almost hysterically. East coast property values dropped. It was said that 'in Baltimore, sales of property were severely affected by the apprehension of a scarcity of money ... New enterprizes and investments of money, *making demands for labor,* have been retired and inflict injuries on those classes of the people least able to suffer any loss ... that several hundred persons, chiefly mechanics or manufacturers thrown out of employment because of the veto to renew the charter. Projected buildings and improvements will be *suspended* permanently if it is rendered certain the bank will be destroyed ... Prudent persons with money gather it in, and hold it fast.'[352]

In the western states, the veto reduced agricultural prices by as much as 20 per cent, and advanced borrowing rates. Of the veto, Pittsburgh and Cincinnati reported 'a paralyzing influence of this ill-advised and unexpected measure ... severely to be felt by the most enterprizing' – for example in the lumber industry. Editors in the southern city papers of Louisville and Natchez commented on merchants' caution to commit to large transactions, constrained by uncertainty and derangement of money and money markets.[353] Some commentators linked the abandonment of the American system, the tariff and the Bank – and saw gloomy prospects. 'With the general balance of trade against our country', they editorialized, 'the prostration of our DOMESTIC MANUFACTURES complete, the arrest of INTERNAL IMPROVEMENTS, and the extermination of a SOUND NATIONAL CURRENCY, the prospect a-head is that we shall have a distressing winter.'[354]

For four months after the veto of 10 July, the Bank understandably played a cautious game, which had an impact on the market directly and, no doubt, psychologically. Not only was its future suddenly uncertain but it was still in the midst of retiring large amounts of federal debt at the behest of the administration, over half of which was in the hands of foreign owners.[355] The Bank began to loosen in October and lend freely again, particularly in western branches such as Lexington, St Louis, Cincinnati and Louisville.

The election of November 1832 returned Andrew Jackson to the presidency for a second term. Congress failed to overturn the veto of the Bank, and Jackson determined to take advantage of election momentum to take further action against the 'monster' rather than let it fade away, charterless, in peace. In his annual message he recommended the sale of the government's stock in the Bank and floated the idea of removal of the federal deposits altogether. A report from Henry Toland, a Democrat and former director of the Bank appointed by the House to examine the debts and general condition of the Bank, advised that the deposits remain where they were, concluding the Bank was more solvent than the Bank of England.[356] Treasury secretary Louis McLane and the Senate Banking Committee presented similar findings.[357]

The Bank was indeed in good condition. So were the nation's finances – which had improved greatly in the last six years or so, and of which the Bank was nominal steward. Aggregate expenditures for the six years ending 31 December 1832 were $162,400,000. Aggregate revenue, chiefly from customs, totalled $157,690,000. The average annual expenditure for six years to 1832, then, was $27 million on revenues of $26 million. Remarkably, the same six years saw $80 million of public debt paid down ($13.3 million paid per year from revenues), so that debt remaining at the beginning of 1833 was slightly more than $7 million dollars. Thus, the average annual expenditure needed for all government purposes was approximately $13.5 million, and the current reduced tariff would produce estimated revenue for the upcoming year of $18 million. Moreover, the national debt was a sum less than the current market value of Bank of the United States stock owned by the government.[358]

Surpluses and fiscal health seemed likely for the United States in the near future. Starting in 1833 as well, British public finance showed surpluses which lasted for five consecutive years.[359] Domestic agricultural prices fell gradually over this period, led in 1833 by exceptional wheat harvests throughout Europe. By contrast, non-agricultural prices rose: iron and coal because of increased railway construction, cotton and woollen textiles with a new wave of capital development.[360] As to the circulation, the Bank of England held steady from 1831 to 1835, while joint-stock bank note issues increased 10 per cent.[361] Both sides of the Atlantic economy seemed poised for greater growth and created optimism among British investors and merchants, including Barings. London finance men could also look forward to a large British government loan of approximately £20 million coming to market in 1833 in compensation for the act abolishing slavery passed recently by Parliament.[362]

Large opportunities lay open for the partners at 8 Bishopsgate in a healthy United States. However, Thomas Wren Ward knew by his contacts in Congress and the large eastern American cities that problems were close at hand. An action against the Bank was coming. Despite Hezekiah Niles's bland forecast, rumours that the Jackson administration contemplated seizure of the deposits persisted through the summer of 1833 and clarified themselves somewhat with Kendall's tour. What a transfer portended for the American economy in the intermediate term was less certain. Ward reported in early September from New York only that he detected a slowdown in business, and money was becoming gradually more costly or 'scarce'.[363] This impression is consistent with the credit contraction that got underway in August. As Hezekiah Niles wrote his Congress 'recess' issue in August 1833, the directors of the Bank voted not to increase the number of discounted bills, and shortened maturities of new bills of exchange to ninety days. The Bank clamped down in anticipation since it could not predict what the Treasury would ultimately do – which, of course, was to withdraw all federal funds from the Bank over the next several months.

The deposits removal was a different magnitude of importance from past actions of the Jackson administration regarding the Bank or the American financial system as it stood in 1833. The bold stroke triggered a firestorm of partisan debate, a search for precedents, and led ultimately to a Senate censure of the president. It also threw into doubt, for some, the staying power of the economic prosperity reported by merchants that summer. On deposit removal stories in July 1833, the Bank of the United States' stock became what the New York *Commercial Advertiser* called 'a fruitful source of speculation', especially when a list became public showing how the assets, once controlled and managed by branches of the Bank of the United States, might be distributed on a state-by-state basis.[364] For a year after this posting – from August 1833 to roughly July of 1834 when the Bank of the United States ceased its defensive posture – the markets were in limbo, distorted by uncertainties, pressures and scarcities of various kinds.

The second half of 1833 saw two overlapping developments that made decision-making more difficult, and turned business in the autumn of 1833 from an atmosphere that should have been exuberant and fluent into one that was jittery and full of strain. The first development, already mentioned, was the physical transfer of the federal funds out of the Bank of the United States. The second was a large mysterious rise in the price of cotton. Both phenomena began in August 1833 and lasted for months. Both caused Barings great concern.

What had happened after the Bank veto happened again, except now in a more serious form with the deposits affair. The funds of the Bank were not to be withdrawn all at once, to be sure, but were meant to run off. That is, the government would draw out its remaining funds as it needed them for operations without replacing them, and current government receipts would go to the new depositories. The effect of this removal of public funds, as we have seen, obliged the Bank to reduce its assets in proportion to what it owed the government. To accomplish this, it would have had to refuse loans applied for and collect some already made. The Bank knew it would lose the government balances, of course, but how many withdrawals would come from individual depositors seeking safety it did not know. Thus, until there was more certainty, a contraction of credit seemed a sensible, almost inevitable, reaction to such drastic action as the administration took – and was likely attended by pain or inconvenience.[365] Biddle and the board's decision for a general curtailment of loans throughout the banking system in fact caused a financial panic, bringing a period of business buoyancy to an end.

Effects of the imminent deposits transfers were gradual, with much discussion over what *might* happen, what *might* develop; how an economy, otherwise quite healthy, *might* sputter. There was more specie entering the country than exiting, wages were reasonable and the currency stable. And yet, there began to float around 'reports of curious occurrences', and what one observer called 'a wonderful pressure for money at a time when it should be exceedingly plentiful'.[366]

The *National Gazette* soon wrote that, by the extraordinary action of removal, the Jackson administration had placed the entire revenue of the United States in a precarious position.[367] The president's annual message to Congress asserted otherwise – that 'through the increased accommodations of the state banks ... no public distress has followed the exertions of the bank'.[368] Journalists and members of Congress challenged the president's account: his characterizations of his state banks' solvency, the behaviour of the Bank of the United States and the solid condition of the economy itself.

Financial interests throughout the nation seemed also to take issue with Jackson. Money and credit worries now preoccupied business, and many cities reported trouble. Charleston reported pressure, as did Baltimore, Boston, Cincinnati and New York. Ward had reported in September to Barings that 'Money wd. bring readily one per cent pr. mo. for six months paper'.[369] By November, the situation had worsened. The anti-Bank *New York Standard* reported what it considered good news that 'first-class notes could be discounted *for less* than EIGHTEEN per cent. per annum'![370] Norfolk banks whose notes paid Virginia military personnel found their notes would not pass outside the state at *any* price.[371] Philadelphia reported all notes of local banks selling in the city below par.[372] The themes of business 'proceeding with extreme caution', or 'suddenly at a halt' – so familiar after the veto – were cited again everywhere.[373] Despite the Treasury surplus, credit was not available, as an extended discussion by Niles explained:

Money was scarce because of a general fear of using it. And the pursuits of labor are deranged, which must be because the [loss of employment] acts to produce a contraction of the economy ...

The plentifulness of money was materially and powerfully assisted by the existence of the best circulating medium, or currency, in the world. The bills, drafts and notes of the bank of the United States, and the exchanges of that bank, in the year 1832, amounted to the enormous sum of 255 millions of dollars at an average cost of one-eleventh of one per cent. to the public. But the bills and notes of this bank are, of necessity, becoming scarce. It may be said that they are going out of circulation, being gathered up by the bank itself, or held as severely in the vaults of the local banks as their own circumstances will permit ... So far as the state banks dare to do business, the charge for notes is much enhanced, while the shavings of bank notes are much thicker than they were a short time ago, all at the cost to the public, and for the benefit of brokers and others – who, producing no value themselves, feed upon the labor of other men ...

We speak not thus in general disparagement of the state banks: but their notes, when distant from the places from whence they issue, are not either money, or currency, in most cases ...[374]

The domestic exchanges of [the Bank] directly amounted to 241 millions in 1832, and the indirect exchanges, through its notes, passing to distant places, and there serving all the purposes of money, to, perhaps as much more, and the whole was substantially at par ...

The general derangement of business has already rendered more injury to the people than if the president were right about the Bank's being an unsafe depository, and Biddle had lost all the deposites himself! ... The wholesomeness of the currency has been violently transferred to stock-gamblers and money-shavers.[375]

Predictions that money strictures would affect hiring as well as cause outright labour layoffs came true by February 1834. Notices of discharged workers became common in cities such as New York, Pittsburgh, New Haven and Baltimore, with employers not being able to make sales or obtain money to pay wages.[376]

Naturally enough, traders, merchants, businessmen and anyone involved in money transactions felt the 'pressure' of Biddle's defensive contraction. The stock and exchange markets were still other gauges of damage done. They summarized the sentiment of the season, which must have been at low ebb in the middle of January, as the table from the *Commercial Advertiser* makes clear:[377]

	Sept. 28, 1833	Jan. 17, 1834
Exchange on England, prem.	7¼	1½%
New Orleans Canal	114	95
Delaware and Hudson canal & bank	120	73
Railroads		
Mohawk	113½	94
Saratoga	110½	103

Boston and Providence	108	89
Deposite banks		
City	111	96
Manhattan	122	124
Mechanics	123	116
Bank of America	116	109
New York	125	118

'A disordered currency is one of the greatest of evils', Daniel Webster had warned in 1832, and a disordered economy was beginning to bite.[378]

'Mr Biddle, Mr Jackson, and the removal of the public deposites is the present leading matter of interest in Washington this season', Thomas Ward wrote to Joshua Bates, 'and will give rise to able and ardent debates'.[379] Ward was correct. Professionals, tradesmen and labourers gathered in hundreds of meetings throughout the country to consider the deposits shift, and expressed their concerns in memorials to the twenty-third Congress and their local legislatures. Tens of thousands of private citizens signed petitions, and most viewed the deposits removal negatively. 'Without reference to politics or party' became the slogan for meetings held from Vermont to Louisiana, New Jersey to Ohio. 'People do not eat nor drink money', Niles wrote. 'That is, if someone in NY and someone in VA have money, their concern is that it is worth par at both places ... All they want of money is that it may have a sure value'.[380]

Not even Jackson's majority in Congress endorsed the abruptness of his actions and many members were swayed to censure the president after testimony by former Treasury secretary William Duane, who took issue with White House methods and was fired for doing so. Many banks in the largest cities – for example, Philadelphia and New York – thought the Bank of the United States too restrictive and indeed not worthy of recharter. Still, they believed the removal of deposits as the single most important cause of currency rupture and urged immediate restoration. State legislatures generally urged restoration as well, without recharter, and found the swagger and abrupt manner of the Jackson administration questionable.[381]

The methods of the Jackson administration did not inspire confidence among British investors, nor did the financial confusion that resulted from them. English newspapers advised their country's manufacturers and shipping Houses to refrain from sending out goods to the United States since there was no money to pay for them.[382] The *London Morning Chronicle* and the *Manchester Chronicle* spoke of serious injuries to trade due to the administration's hostility to the Bank, advised British mercantile Houses to hold off American commitments until things clarified, and reported that suspensions of large projects had caused considerable suffering among labourers. Phrases in London papers such as 'unparalleled embarrassments of the American commercial classes' and 'increasing misery of every

class' abounded. They warned also that the trumping of finance by American politics drove a wedge between transatlantic friends and customers, finding that

> A rancorous spirit of party pervades everything, has destroyed reasonable-
> ness in government, and makes [even] undoubted financial solvency and
> integrity no security against ruin for British investors.[383]

London noted that the Bank of the United States was once abused for the liberal-
ity of its accommodations; and now it was abused for curtailing them. Indeed,
The Times found the 'fiat government of the president [Jackson]' likely to per-
petuate the lamentable situation in the United States, and regretted greatly that a
'vast and profitable trade – so bright in its prospect only a few months ago – had
been so clouded'.[384]

A group of prominent New York bankers, including James Brown, Albert
Gallatin, Jonathan Goodhue, Philip Hone and James G. King, met on 18 March
1834 to discuss the economic affairs of the nation. They had opinions on the
nature of what was going on in the nation's banking system and issued a care-
fully-prepared statement.[385] The Bank of the United States may have contracted
generally, they said, but effects in New York – 'the centre of all the moneyed
transactions of the United States' – were mild. The contraction of loans did not
inordinately exceed the contraction of deposits. Furthermore, curtailment of
Bank loans was 'a necessary consequence' of the change in the depository, which
came as a result of the hostile attitude and gross financial ignorance about the
credit system of President Jackson and the new Treasury secretary Roger Taney.
As the group opined:

> It was without any necessity or investigation that the Executive thought
> proper to interfere ... The threat of the removal of the deposits, and especially
> their actual removal, created apprehensions of danger, immediately to the
> Bank itself and more remotely to all the monied institutions and concerns of
> the country ... Men saw that the relations between the government and the
> Bank were henceforth to be hostile; that between it and the selected banks
> they were to be those of mistrust; and that without a national Bank the stabil-
> ity and safety of the monetary system of the country would be endangered.

Not only had Jackson broken 'the great ramifying chain of mercantile credit', said
the *New York Spectator*, the bankers found three other causes of distress.[386]

Securities of the United States, many issued in the south-west in early 1833,
were now nearly impossible to pass on the major money markets of Europe,
including England, due to the war on the Bank and ensuing instability.[387] For
sure, many American banks could use these bonds as collateral for borrowing,
but the bonds themselves were difficult to sell, and created unproductive assets
on their books.

The committee also cited the change in the arrangement for paying import duties put into effect by the Tariff of 1832. The new law disposed of the lag time of up to eighteen months that importers once had to pay duties. Since March 1833, importers had to pay duties more promptly – on average within four-and-a-half months; sometimes in cash, sometimes immediately – as with woollens. This ended what had been, in effect, a credit to the importer which they had used as operating capital. Liquidity shrank dramatically among importers, who pressured trading-city banks for accommodation.[388]

Above all, though, the bankers found in the current distress a serious lack of business confidence. 'Private credit has been deeply affected', the report found, which caused a breakdown of the credit mechanisms which stemmed from certainty and trust. American commerce, currency and moneyed institutions had been cut loose from the moorings of a government founded in law. The country it seemed was subject to the whimsicality of one man – the president – and 'nothing could be more alarming to men of business'. Hesitancy born of low confidence was not for want of cash. 'Specie', the committee report emphasized, 'is more abundant than perhaps at any former period'. (Indeed the Bank was stockpiling it.) Paper money, perceived as unreliable, diminished confidence, 'locked up' the system, and would do so until common sense returned. In the absence of a functional, lending banking system, those importers and exporters who had to discount did so in the secondary exchange markets. In commercial cities, they sought out note 'shavers' who charged between 2 and 3 per cent per month to do business at the start of 1834. This effectively made the cost prohibitive of what had been, for ten years, a principal driver of American prosperity – stable paper currency – and people ceased to use it.

With astonishment and gall for President Jackson and his secretaries, Albert Gallatin compared the unnecessary financial violence of wrapping up the Second Bank's affairs with his own orderly wrapping up of the First Bank when its charter expired in 1810. In New York, he expressed concern about the nation's priorities, and credit abroad.[389] Daniel Webster was more concerned about the constricting effect of the so-called 'Bank War' on the country's economy. He told the Senate on the day of the Union Committee Report, 'It is like a strong man chained'.[390]

Jackson vowed never to restore the deposits, even when faced with entreaties from a cross section of political parties. 'Neither persuasion nor coercion, nor the opinions of the people, nor the voice of the legislatures could shake his fixed determination', memorialists from Philadelphia reported. '[He] would', they said, 'sooner seek asylum in the wilds of Arabia'.[391] A censure resolution showed the judgement of Congress that Andrew Jackson acted improperly in the deposits removal matter. Nevertheless the dissemination of federal funds after 1834 continued, and the Bank of the United States started a slow phase-out of its operations as government steward, including its branch system.

Figure 4.2: Andrew Jackson (1767–1845) by Ralph E. W. Earl (*c.* 1788–1838). Oil on canvas (1836). The Hermitage, Nashville, Tennessee.

The 'moral heroism' with which Jackson was credited over the deposits by his most ardent supporters, such as senator Thomas Hart Benton, did not appear to improve the health of the pet banks into which the federal funds poured. Despite Jackson's assurance that the state banks were adequate to replace the Bank of the United States, markets did not agree.[392] The depository successors to Biddle's Bank operated in the public sphere and, as the Union Committee asserted, public confidence was lacking. By 1833, most of the deposit banks with tradable shares outstanding were shaky, despite massive government support.

There was fear in major cities such as New York and Philadelphia that Biddle might make concentrated demands upon certain newly-selected depository state banks. Quick specie calls to banks indebted to the Bank could be awkward, even fatal to the state banks' ability to carry out lending and bank note functions. To counter this possibility, Treasury secretary Taney gave the deposit banks large drafts up to $500,000 on the Bank to hold and use in case of need.

There was some question as to why, if money was scarce, the state banks could not ease the pressure and even profit, at least short term, from high lending rates.[393] The problem was that not only did the deposits transfer disrupt general business, it placed certain key state banks in an adversarial position to the Bank of the United States that caused a defensive lock-up of capital. Taney's drafts to the deposit banks had not enabled them to 'increase facilities to commerce, and accommodations to individuals', as he had intended. Rather, the more the banks used the administration's drafts and deposits to lend, the more they became indebted to the Bank of the United States.[394]

As borrowers drew on their borrowed funds, the volume of notes and cheques outstanding against the lending banks increased, and more of them came into the federal Bank's possession. In turn, the increased discounts of the pet banks tended to make it necessary for Biddle's bank to take the action which would give the pets occasion to use the treasury drafts Taney had given them in self-defence.[395] The result of all this was an erosion of confidence in the deposit banks by the business community. Notes of deposit banks such as Girard in Philadelphia and the Commercial Bank in New Orleans sold at the beginning of 1834 at 7–8 per cent discounts. The Union Bank of Baltimore approached bankruptcy.[396] The Bank of the United States, on the other hand, retained its £250,000 open credit with Barings, to which Democratic partisans pointed as proof of 'foreign influence'. Ward asked Biddle to use it sparingly, and the Bank drew approximately £82,000 by April 1834 to relieve credit constrictions in the business community.[397]

The dislocations brought on by the deposits removal were joined by the issue of cotton among the concerns of market participants and commentators. In 1833, the price of cotton began to skyrocket at the same time Amos Kendall scoured eastern banks for candidates for the federal funds transfer.

Table 4.4: Prices of South Carolina\Georgia Cotton, 1832–4 (cents per lb.). Source: Cole, *Wholesale Commodity Prices*, vol. 2, pp. 242–51.

Year	Jan.	Feb.	Mar.	Apr.	May	June	July	Aug.	Sep.	Oct.	Nov.	Dec.
1832	9	9	10	10	10	11	11	11	11	12	12	12
1833	12	12	12	12	12	12	13	16	16	16	16	16
1834	12	12	12	12	14	14	14	15	14	14	15	18

London sources reported cotton 'extremely busy' at Liverpool in August.[398] New York cotton prices for 1833 jumped from 13 cents per lb. in July to 16 in August, and held this level for the next five months. Charleston started July at

11 cents, jumped to 17 in October, before falling back to 13 cents for November and December. Similar moves occurred in the cotton markets of Philadelphia, Cincinnati and New Orleans. In no other major commodity, except perhaps indigo, was anything like this volatility observed in 1833.[399]

Reasons for the rise in the wholesale price of cotton were obscure. Their effects were not. Mills in the east and south reported suspended operations because of cotton's high price on the one hand, and the low price of cotton goods on the other. British prices for cotton were also high and conditions in textile factories were, like those in America, reportedly 'embarrassing and dull'.[400] Some blamed American millworkers' misfortunes on foreign manufactures and the lowering of the tariff.[401] The source of the price rise however was obscure. The supply of, and demand for, cotton increased from 1832 to 1833 after all. The supply-demand balance did not seem to justify so extraordinary a price increase as occurred from August to December 1833.[402]

Some linked the cotton price rise to lingering concerns over South Carolina nullification. But the most common explanation involved speculators on both sides of the Atlantic taking advantage of the confusion in the American banking system to drive cotton prices to artificial and unsustainable levels. British and American newspapers reported what appeared to be 'gambling akin to what it was in 1825' in most commercial articles – 'most intensely in cotton'.[403]

Likely a combination of many factors, few doubted that a major driver behind prices was Nathan Rothschild. Rothschilds, after all, lay behind the cotton rise in 1825, or so contemporaries believed.[404] The *Circular to Bankers*, an influential organ of English country banks, devoted an entire issue to the possibility of a Rothschilds influence on prices, and found the idea plausible. There was no doubt that Thomas Ward linked Rothschilds to mischief 'of some kind' with one of Barings' competitors, but he had no concrete information about the cotton rise. Many observed the disruptions of 1833–4, and looked for answers. Most likely agreed with Barings' counsel, senator Daniel Webster, who considered 'the condition of the country indeed singular'.[405]

With hindsight, one can see that the price rise in Liverpool cotton probably did not come from Rothschilds in 1833–4, South Carolina nullification or the Bank deposits, but simply from increased British consumption in the face of reduced British cotton stocks. From the middle 1830s, the situation reversed itself, as consumption greatly lagged behind increased stocks. New sources of supply from India and Egypt, as we shall see, had a bearing on financial developments in the United States (Table 4.5).

Table 4.5: United Kingdom Cotton Consumption and Cotton Stocks, 1827–43 (in millions of lbs). Source: Rostow, *The World Economy*, pp. 132–3.

Year	UK Total Cotton Consumption	UK Cotton Stocks
1827	197	164.8
1828	218	147.1
1829	219	115.5
1830	248	118.8
1831	263	114.4
1832	277	103.7
1833	287	94.4
1834	303	82.3
1835	318	89.6
1836	347	116.3
1837	366	115.6
1838	417	160.9
1839	382	125.8
1840	459	206.9
1841	438	216.7
1842	435	242.3
1843	518	342.1

No matter the actual reasons for the 'singular' condition of the United States in 1834. The result was uncertainty – the bane of business and banking – which required caution and reassessment.

Barings' First Trimming

'If anyone had predicted such a state of things four months ago, he would have been considered stark mad'.[406] So reported Hezekiah Niles as he assessed the business landscape at the beginning of 1834. If Niles's assertions were true, Bates and Barings must have been mad – but only inadvertently so. They pulled back, a bit, roughly six months before the confusion with the Bank of the United States began and appear to have avoided difficulty. They trimmed their American operations not for reasons connected with Andrew Jackson alone. Political conditions coloured the firm's decisions. It appears that three other factors – of internal housekeeping, previous commitments and spiralling cotton prices – held at least equal sway.

Ward's rapid accumulation of clients in the United States between 1829 and 1832 caused the firm some concern that their American business might be growing too fast, and excesses could develop. Ward assured the House that 'all was safe for trade', yet included mention in his correspondence to 'several remittance delays'. In September 1833, Ward referred to the expected deposits removal by the Jackson administration as sensational, and told the partners not to worry. The Bank – their client – was solvent and safe.

The partners asked Ward to delay issuance of new credits to American merchants because they wished to avoid overcommitment, and, above all, maintain liquidity. Tardiness and slight bloating in the account book occurred at the same time the House took on the underwriting of the huge Union Bank of Louisiana loan in Europe. Of the original 5,500-share bond offering, Barings took an initial 4,200, and exercised its option to buy the rest in the middle of 1833. Barings had to be prepared to honour drafts on the Union Bank of $1 million based on these bonds, as the original contract of August 1832 stipulated.[407] The Louisiana loan coincided with Barings' 'backstopping' Biddle in his liquidity squeeze of 1832–3 for paying off American government 3 per cent debt in Europe for the Jackson administration.

The Louisiana loan commitment, the debt liquidation assistance to Biddle and the credit trimming accompanied Bates's belief in the middle of 1832 that prices would soon be rising in England and the United States. Bates told Ward that he believed that 'we are to have an advance in the prices of goods generally, and next year we must draw in.'[408] Bates was dead right about prices in the United States; mildly so about England (see Tables 4.6 and 4.7 below).

Table 4.6: Index of United States Wholesale Commodity Prices, 1825–45 (base: 1834–42). Source: Smith and Cole, *Fluctuations in American Business*, p. 158.

Year	Jan.	Feb.	Mar.	Apr.	May	June	July	Aug.	Sep.	Oct.	Nov.	Dec.
1825	100	100	104	114	115	117	113	110	107	109	105	106
1826	103	103	98	97	94	93	95	92	90	92	94	93
1827	94	95	95	95	92	91	89	90	91	91	92	94
1828	88	90	88	88	87	88	88	88	89	91	91	95
1829	95	94	93	92	89	89	85	85	85	85	86	85
1830	85	84	84	82	84	83	82	83	85	87	88	88
1831	86	88	89	90	89	90	87	87	89	91	92	91
1832	96	93	92	90	90	90	88	88	90	92	94	93
1833	94	91	92	91	93	93	93	96	98	99	98	98
1834	94	91	88	86	87	87	88	89	92	93	94	97
1835	99	98	100	103	107	110	115	115	113	111	112	116
1836	118	116	121	128	122	118	116	119	122	128	130	127
1837	128	131	129	119	102	102	103	103	98	101	106	108
1838	107	103	101	100	100	101	102	102	107	113	115	117
1839	118	125	124	123	120	118	114	112	112	108	104	101
1840	92	93	90	85	84	82	81	82	86	89	90	89
1841	88	90	88	87	88	84	84	86	91	90	87	85
1842	84	80	78	75	74	73	73	72	70	69	68	69
1843	69	67	67	68	70	71	72	73	74	73	74	73
1844	74	75	75	76	74	73	72	73	72	73	74	74
1845	72	72	74	78	78	76	76	77	79	78	83	86

Table 4.7: Index of United Kingdom Wholesale Commodity Prices,
Domestic and Foreign, 1825–45 (base: monthly average 1821–5 = 100).
Source: Gayer et al., *The Growth and Fluctuation*, vol. 1, p. 468.

Year	Jan.	Feb.	Mar.	Apr.	May	June	July	Aug.	Sep.	Oct.	Nov.	Dec.
1825	109	112	116	116	117	114	112	113	113	113	113	111
1826	108	103	101	101	100	97	96	99	101	97	100	99
1827	99	100	103	104	102	101	101	99	97	95	96	96
1828	94	95	95	95	93	93	93	96	95	102	103	104
1829	106	102	97	95	97	93	95	95	95	93	90	92
1830	91	93	90	92	95	95	98	99	95	94	95	97
1831	97	99	100	99	94	97	92	95	92	93	95	93
1832	94	92	94	93	93	94	92	91	89	89	88	89
1833	89	87	87	88	87	88	88	91	93	89	90	88
1834	87	87	89	87	86	89	87	87	86	84	85	85
1835	83	83	85	85	87	84	86	88	84	83	83	85
1836	84	89	93	98	97	98	97	96	95	96	98	101
1837	101	99	97	95	93	95	92	94	93	90	91	92
1838	92	95	95	96	97	97	98	101	98	98	101	106
1839	107	105	104	105	103	104	104	105	105	104	103	102
1840	102	102	103	104	102	104	105	105	105	101	99	98
1841	99	99	100	99	97	97	96	100	98	96	96	96
1842	95	94	91	91	90	90	91	88	86	85	83	83
1843	81	79	79	78	77	80	81	84	79	79	80	79
1844	80	79	83	83	84	84	83	80	79	79	79	81
1845	82	81	81	80	80	83	83	85	85	88	88	86

London ordered Ward to cut back Barings' commitments in the United States
in order that the House manage ongoing projects safely. As American newspapers had reported was characteristic, Barings was like other foreign firms which
returned bond remittances to American drawers for sale in the United States at
this time. Also, Ward reduced the number of uncovered mercantile accounts, and
opened new accounts on a covered basis only.[409] Fees increased for services in
order to increase margins for error. The commissions that Barings charged the
Bank of the United States for accepting and paying long bills used 'east of the
Cape' jumped from 0.5 to 0.75 per cent. All sorts of collateral was taken to secure
an account – sometimes financial, sometimes tangible.

Ward lamented that the partners had instructed him in the spring of 1833 to
have nothing to do with American securities until further advised. Like in England,
where a railroad and bank mania was underway, the United States was securitiz-
ing industrial enterprise, and offering shares to foreign financiers. Due to Barings'
long-standing position and reputation in the American market, there was still much
potential business, but Ward had to refuse to take part. 'There is no loan that has
been proposed for 6 mo. past that has not been offered to and pressed upon me ...
but in no case have I done anything', wrote Ward.[410] What he did do was bid for
loans in concert with other firms such as Prime, Ward & King and Thomas Biddle
& Company. Professor Ralph Hidy presents these groupings as early examples of
Barings acting as a loan syndicator. This may be true, but the present author finds
it more likely that these groups, assembled specifically by Ward at this time, may
have been brought together for other reasons: to give the illusion of Barings taking

part in the securities markets at a time he had orders to cut off completely, and to keep Barings' hand in American securities nominally while they waited for the next market up-tick and the opportunity to participate again fully.

Illusions were important at this time. For a banker, a reputation was the best currency. Barings had to maintain itself as a player in the American market, which, despite inevitable bumps along the way, would likely provide superior returns over time to those who took part. Ward was sensitive to maintaining Barings' position for its own sake, but also because he was the bank's most visible representative in the United States. If Barings would not provide American states and traders with the facilities they wanted, Americans would go elsewhere and, at this time, competition was, in Ward's words, 'increasing from all quarters'.[411]

Wildes & Company and Wilson & Company cut their commissions on acceptances to secure a share. Wiggin & Company acquired portions of bond offerings from several small New York Houses that would have, in past years, gone exclusively to Barings, but were now parcelled out because of Barings' reluctance to take the entire offering in light of earlier commitments. Wiggin & Company permitted American merchants to issue drafts of six months date – much longer than Barings would permit except on a case-by-case basis to the Far East or western South America. In 1832, the '3Ws' established presences in Boston to compete for consignments, credits and securities. A year later Ward complained that 'the check [to Barings' operations] was given at a time when others were desirous to let out with flowing sheets'.[412] Ward maintained that his House's standing was solid, that not even Rothschilds had the confidence of their merchants. In the middle of 1833, though, his correspondence to London clearly revealed agitation and worry about an increasingly tight business landscape.[413]

Ward worried because he felt restrictions imposed on him by London could cost the House business. Ward would, as instructed, insist on receipts for all uncovered credits, though he admitted they were embarrassing to impose on clients of proud reputation.[414] Barings had just entrusted the supervision of its cotton operations in the United States to Ward when London imposed cotton purchase price limits that Ward considered too low. However, his requests for latitude evidently went unheeded. The spike in cotton prices appeared suspicious to Bates. He clearly wanted a lower price point than the current very high 13–16 cents. Cotton inflation fitted his prediction the year before of increased commodity prices in general. Prices fell irregularly in Britain between 1833 and 1835. Since the markets were linked and prices tended to track in tandem, Bates questioned the sustainability of a rising American cotton price. The House would act cautiously until he understood it. In line with press reports, Ward wrote to London that he could not confirm rumours of a cotton corner, but he said Rothschilds was indeed initiating business contacts with Barings' competitors operating throughout the United States. It stood to reason that anyone engaged in the cotton trade would be cautious, especially if he had recently set up a major facility for its trade, as Barings had done at Liverpool in 1832.[415] Prices had a speculative feel to them in the summer and autumn of 1833, and this was not Barings' style or mode.

Barings was not alone in its caution, though it came earlier than it did to others. The partners' most formidable competitor in the United States, Brown Brothers & Company, curtailed as part of a restructuring of the firm following the death of Alexander Brown in April 1834. George Brown, who resigned from the Mechanics Bank in New York to head the firm after his father's death, agreed with Bates about the action in cotton prices and advised his southern agents not to over-advance on consignments to Liverpool. The firm was recording peak profits, and was hardly interested in jeopardizing them in what appeared to be a touch of speculation. Like Barings, Brown Brothers had learned the dangers of unusual commodity price swings by the bad fortunes of other firms. It had not participated in the 'madness of speculators' in 1825, had thereby avoided the 40 per cent decline in cotton prices in 1826, and had actually showed a profit for a year which crushed less prudent shippers and merchants.[416] Brown Brothers had been in the market in 1833 as Barings curtailed. Now, in 1834, Brown Brothers placed strict limits on advances to cotton exporters, wary that 'competition [was becoming] so great, people are willing to go to any length to get consignments'. The firm remained largely out of the market until they judged sobriety had returned.[417]

George Brown and the Joshua Bates steered their firms based to some extent on where they thought prices were heading, but it is unclear precisely how they drew such conclusions.[418] In the early nineteenth century, there were no techniques for judging aggregate worldwide demand, so most businessmen focused their attention on the supply side of the market equation. In this regard, the gross indicator here – crop sizes – indicated that bountiful harvests meant lower prices; small harvests meant prices would go higher. As Professor Perkins indicates, however, demand was notoriously volatile and many times did not correlate with supply.[419] To remedy this difficulty, neither Barings nor Brown Brothers practised market timing in the sense of withholding commodities from the market in order to wait for favourable prices. They viewed this common practice as speculative and dangerous – each generally selling a customer's cotton, for example, soon after it arrived at Liverpool. Instead, Barings and Brown Brothers – like other merchants and bankers – expected prices to move within an accustomed band and they counted on intuition, born of experience, to tell them when prices had moved outside of their traditional fluctuation. The assumption was that over time the market would revert to some sort of mean, in line with past patterns. It is not surprising, then, that Bates found a 23 per cent rise of the cotton price in one month outside any healthy norm. Sensibly he had turned cautious, especially given Barings' other commitments at the time.

Southern crops for the 1834–5 season appeared promising. Prices were imperfectly forecast in the antebellum period, but based on supply they would likely ease. Any unnatural influences that caused the spike in cotton prices in the summer and autumn of 1833 appeared to be abating, for cotton returned in January to its pre-spike price of between 10 and 12 cents. Good harvests in Europe too would contribute to muted food prices for the upcoming three years.[420]

What also returned to normalcy was the Bank of the United States. Shortly after the New York bankers' meeting of March 1834, Biddle suspended the Bank's curtailment policy. The Bank was in good condition to do so, for it held nearly $13 million in specie, and its balance with European bankers, such as its partner Barings, stood higher than ever – at $3,827,000.[421] In May, the Bank's notes not only circulated undepreciated; in some parts of the country, they passed at a premium.[422] In July, Biddle ended restriction. Immediately, money was noted to be 'more plentiful than it was'.[423]

The Bank's resumption took place as Congress adjourned its first session with an important piece of legislation involving the coinage of money. Part of Jackson's campaign against the Bank of the United States had to do with a distrust of paper money. Biddle believed that a modern financial system required a mix of coin and fiduciary instruments. Jackson preferred only gold and silver specie to circulate – a so-called 'hard-money policy'. He supported a proposal to overvalue gold in the United States to attract the metal from Europe and to induce the public to use gold instead of bank obligations for their business. The American currency was a bimetallic one, and had been so since 1792, when the price of 1 oz of gold was set at 15 oz of silver. Since then, the amount of gold in the country had gradually been depleted because of an unfavourable ratio to silver, especially in trade relations with Europe.

On 1 August 1834 the Gold Coinage Act passed into law, raising the silver price in terms of gold to 16 to 1. With the price of gold in the United States slightly higher than the price of silver, for example in England, it became more profitable to import gold than silver into the United States. By this measure, Congress hoped to address what it viewed as a specie shortage, and regularize a specie currency that had become somewhat chaotic over several decades with foreign silver coins entering into circulation, making the banking basis of notes whimsical.[424] For British investors, the depreciation of American gold coin had the effect of raising the value of the English sovereign from $4.44 to $4.87, or 8.5 per cent. Thus American securities or states' debt sent to England for sale became cheaper.[425]

Congress revalued gold as a concession to petitions from businessmen in New York and Boston to ease monetary conditions in the United States at a time of financial difficulty. In general economic terms the credit stringency of 1833–4 does not appear to have been as serious as partisan press reports of the time portrayed. Commodity exports continued to mount, imports increased and internal commerce expanded. Transactions connected specifically with the money econ-

omy were the ones most affected by the credit pressure slowly ending in 1834
– and some had been shaken.

Many conservative business and financial interests believed Biddle to have
behaved badly, having restrained credit too long. Restive state banks and states'
rights politicians found a large federal institution disagreeable. New York in particular wanted the Bank's control lessened or eliminated so that its own financial
community could assume such control, and erect an even larger Bank in place of
Biddle's. As for Ward, he found Biddle too prone to risk and to politics, though
Ward admitted a large bank had its usefulness. Above all, he detested instability.
'I am not a advocate of the present bank', he wrote to Bates, 'but *some* institution
must exist to preserve and keep up a sound currency'.[426]

Ward was part of the New England Whig establishment which had little use
for Democrats or Jackson, whom they viewed as fomenting trouble amidst the
country's plenty. Ward's fellow Bostonian, Webster, worried that, without the
Bank of the United States, the guardianship of public money would be under
'the absolute power' of the chief executive, or the Treasury secretary, who could
keep them 'where he pleases, as he pleases, and change the place of their custody
as often as he pleases'.[427] Ward believed the Jackson administration to be mor-
ally questionable, and said so to Barings. He wondered how long this brand of
American politics would last.[428]

Ward's fellow New Englander Joshua Bates wondered what was going on with
the Jackson administration regarding the Bank of the United States in 1833, and
he was likely inclined to agree that after the veto the United States was edging
towards, in Biddle's word, 'anarchy'. After all, the Bank of England had been up
for recharter in 1833 and the outcome of the rechartering debates in Parliament
had been legislation that allowed the Bank's operation to continue while permitting other banks to flourish as well. The English joint-stock banks gained the right
to establish themselves in London in 1833, provided they did not issue notes. The
privilege of issue remained with the Bank of England alone. Unlike the doctri-
naire Jackson administration, which determined to do away with the Bank of the
United States, the British maintained room enough, through compromise, for
a central bank and a second tier of country banking institutions. In reality, the
Banks of England and the United States were different in important ways, but
from Bates's vantage point in Britain, the scene must have been horrific.[429]

The very fact that Bates left his home country for England may testify to his
ambivalence to informal American ways. He and Ward were mortified for example by the increasing appearance of the firm's name in the press. Rather cryptically,
Bates confided to his diary: 'If this continues, we cannot' – referring possibly to
Ward's news that the press was linking the affairs of the Bank of the United States
with the affairs of Barings.[430] The policy of Barings had always emphasized discretion, neither confirming nor denying news regarding the House. Ward was
assiduous about this. Ever since the Bank veto in 1832 and Barings' assistance

to Biddle with payment of government debt, though, the House had appeared in newspapers as part of Congressional matters on finance. Though this did not often happen, it was more than in past years, and noticeable to the partners.[431]

Others knew of Ward's sentiments. Neither Goodhue nor Prime, Ward & King were supporters of the administration and were intimates of the Barings agent. Ward travelled to Washington often, and in February 1834 Edward Everett solicited him to organize an effort to raise money to counter the Jackson administration's general anti-business tone, 'for the sake of property and the restoration of a government of law'.[432] And, of course, Barings' longstanding relationship with Biddle, especially after the incident of the French indemnity, likely did not sit well with anti-Bank men.

Ward's anti-Jackson associations probably also had something to do with the startling disclosure that the United States Department of State had decided it would transfer its account from Barings to N. M. Rothschild & Sons in 1835.[433] As earlier remarked, Ward had for some time believed Rothschilds was considering an American commitment, but had few specifics.[434] Rothschilds may have made arrangements with the American government earlier if Ward confirmed the House's business dealings in the United States a year before the transfer announcement, since Rothschilds as a rule rarely conducted commercial business in a country without also lending to its government.[435] Barings retained the navy department account.

Politics, the association with Biddle, and the French indemnity payment problems caused Rothschilds' trump of Barings on the United States government account. Bates and Ward were nonchalant about the loss – even glad to be less accountable to a client that had become more troublesome than it was worth in profit. 'It [the loss to Rothschilds] is connected with party politics on the other side', wrote Bates in his diary. 'It shows the petty views of the administration and what the people will do when they get into power. We shall have [the account] back again in 2 or 3 years.'[436] Nevertheless, the loss represented part of the general onset of increased competition in the United States, and general slippage in Barings' share of the American market.

Ward did not care for Jackson's brash form of politics, but he remained optimistic through the past couple of problem years. He believed the nation was larger than one man, and his correspondence tended to be generally benign. The historian can reasonably assume that, if Barings suffered no major mishaps, Ward was likely solving problems independently – in the interest of sparing the House as much worry as he could, and of following Bates's general rule to keep writings brief.[437] So Ward, for various reasons, supported the bullish case of the United States. Specifically, he showed more confidence in American manufacturers to do well under the new duty, assuring Bates that, in his view, 'it is not in the power of tariffs, nor the absence of them to destroy manufacturers'. Nor did nullification

give merchants but slight pause, and was now in any case solved without significant effect.[438]

Class and propriety were large issues with the House, as they were also for
their American agent. Barings was practical, though, and associated with many
kinds of men, but preferred the caution, deliberateness and formality of former
Federalists. As we have seen, Ward associated with several anti-Jackson men. For
now, this network seemed tight, and growing, despite the problems that gave
Barings reason to trim their operations slightly over the Bank issue.

The Louisiana loan, for example, had the added benefit of bringing the Barings
network in the United States closer together. Bates and Jonathan Goodhue had
recommended Ward to Thomas Baring personally, but the important relationship of Ward with the New York bankers Prime, Ward & King had remained less
than cordial since his hiring in 1829. Ward felt that Prime treated him as an inter-
loper in the American market; as the representative of a banking organization in
the early stages of taking away 'the most profitable branch of [Prime's] business'.
For his part, Ward had little use for what he described to Bates as 'the disgusting,
cunning, managing sort of ways' of Nathaniel Prime. But, in 1832, Prime retired
from the banking firm he had founded, and during the Louisiana loan negotiations Ward felt there was now the basis for a better mutual understanding with
the remaining partners. The two Houses were stronger, he felt, by the crucial by-
products of cooperation: increased sharing of information and more forthright
exchanges.[439]

Walter Barrett, chronicler of New York business families, confirmed Ward's
feeling that the departure of the effective, but apparently overbearing, Nathan
Prime may have tempered the aggressiveness of a firm so dominated by his personality. Edward Prime took over from his father, and both Samuel Ward and
James G. King remained. The present author does not know Ward's opinion of
the new Prime, except that Edward was a business associate of the securities broker for the Bank of the United States, Thomas Biddle of Philadelphia, cousin of
Nicholas Biddle, with whom both Ward and Barings associated frequently. Of
the remaining partners, Ward and King, Ward considered them responsible, ami-
able men. The conservative Samuel Ward was the future founder of the Bank of
Commerce. James G. King was an intimate of Edward Everett – scholar, senator
and future ambassador to Great Britain – as well as a long-time and close friend
of Daniel Webster. Ward knew Everett and Webster well.[440] Barings' American
agent was well connected.

On an operational basis though, Ward had complaints at times about his
employer, Barings. There is evidence in the partners' succinct praise of their
American agent that Ward handled the unusual situation of the Bank-Jackson
contest of 1833–4 to his employer's great satisfaction. 'We cannot sufficiently
thank you', they wrote to Ward in 1834, 'for the ability and zeal you have displayed in protecting our interest during a period of difficulty and excitement'.

Such appreciation was no doubt deserved, but for Ward it may not have been enough. The business landscape was changing, and so was Barings' standing within it. The following assemblage by Professor Hidy illustrates the types of problems that peppered Ward's correspondence again and again with Barings in 1833, and caused him continuous angst in an age of slow communications. Ward:

> It is very important that your agent shd. understand your views and that all points shd. be fully discussed, which is impossible to be done by letter ... [But] Permit me to offer for your consideration one or two remarks. Your House and your agent have laboured hard to build up a business in this country. It has succeeded almost beyond hope. It is secured and needs only care and a right course to make it a source of permanent and immense wealth. We have given the impression of great resources – a desire to do all safe business – and on the most liberal plan. We have spread far and wide and embrace almost all the good business of the country – both commercial and in stocks. Are you not making too sudden and great a change? Does it not give the appearance of want of steadiness of purpose? Will not your stock business be retired to other Houses who are willing to hold and when occasion requires to borrow? A House like yours shd. at all times show the greatest steadiness and appearance of strength and perfect ease. Is it not desirable that your commercial correspondents shd. feel that in times of scarcity and indeed whenever your agent sees a sufficient reason, that they can have some advantage from the resources of so great a House in delay or accommodation? Is it not very important to keep up the impression that there is nothing like Barings? and is there no danger that the charm may be broken? Your agent has had a difficult task, and it would be a pity to lose any of the advantages already gained. Is it not important to keep other and stronger Houses that now exist in the field of American business from competition from you?
>
> I would be as rigid as necessary for safety, but even there some hasard [sic] must be taken. Credits must sometimes be given before others are remitted for. But is not the great object safety and that being in the main attained, is it not desirable to give way in minor points? I cannot judge to be sure for you, but it seems to me that times may occur in the course of such a business as yours, when safety wd. be the only thing to be looked after, and when you would be obliged to borrow or avail of other resources. I do not anticipate such a case, but such things have been and are possible.[441]

In a sense, Ward was speaking of the past. The firm *used* to have all the good business. Now they were obliged to share. Barings was only losing share because they *chose* to do so, and because the American market was maturing to include more players than ever. Barings thus had to accommodate to a relative share decline. Absolute numbers might increase as the United States attracted and grew in size. The retarding of the House's past dominance was what Ward appears to be trying to avoid, and he suggested ways of preserving this through, among other things, steadiness of reputation and improved communications within the firm and across the Atlantic.[442]

The capriciousness of American finance and politics obliged Barings to articulate what kind of House it was to be, as well as whether it would change its style of business in the increasingly competitive American marketplace that concerned Ward so very much. After 1834, it became clear that Barings would maintain its stance as a premier firm. If its competitors authorized drafts on remitted securities at 0.5 per cent commission as the situation eased in July 1834, Barings charged twice as much for the same function. Only Prime, Ward & King was given lower rates.[443] Barings would maintain a preferential style, taking on the business of relatively few, well-to-do and low-risk clients.[444] It was for safety's sake, for example, that the partners maintained their policy against 'double accounts'.[445] Exclusivity with Barings ensured superior transparency. After all, the extent of clients' commitments could be better known, and indiscretions avoided that arose when a client did business with an unknown third party. Ward knew his customers well, and could therefore extend advances and credits more often on an unsecured basis, especially in the east where unsecured credits were the rule. Established clients also took less monitoring. This explains how Barings could operate in the United States with relatively few personnel and from a distance.

By contrast, other Houses welcomed the smaller account, lessening risk by the diversification of large numbers. In the long term, this proved the correct approach for such firms as the American-based Brown & Company. In the United States, a rising middle class and immigration transfused the ever-changing economy generation after generation. Barings themselves wondered about this phenomenon in a letter to Ward in the 1840s. 'If we deal only with persons of wealth', they asked, 'and some one else takes all the rising generation, where shall we be 10 years hence when Browns have got all the now small accounts but then great merchants'?[446]

For sure, these worries would crop up in the 1840s, but the unusual, unstable 1830s seemed to require stricture and adherence to past principles. Barings' principles, after all, had brought them the sparkling success in the United States that other firms sought for themselves. The partners were not ready to tinker with what had worked for them in the past, especially during this time of acute financial 'experimentation' taking place in the United States under Jackson.[447] Whether this reluctance had something to do with a specific desire to insulate the House from the less-than-elite attitudes and practices of American democracy, the present author does not precisely know. What is clear is that safety, not market share, was paramount with the partners and that Jacksonian politics were thought to endanger safety. The highbrow Ward at this point believed safety could be maintained while keeping reasonable market share, and he was evidently bothered by the partners' disinclination to give him satisfactory leeway to apply rules in ways he saw fit. Ward, however, always deferred to his employers' 'prudence', and acknowledged it was this quality which ultimately ensured the House's success.[448] This perhaps provided the 'out' for London to take Ward's petitions less than seriously.

The London partners ran a merchant banking firm with worldwide interests in which Ward's United States was only one part, albeit important. Profits in 1832 were £98,000 and £119,000 the year after.[449] In 1832, Bates had boasted to Ward that 'BB & Co. are as much beyond what they ever were as a Commercial House as Prime is beyond Shipman or any other smaller concern ... Our Counting House resembles a Customs House ... business comes from all quarters and in all languages.'[450] The problem was how to keep control in a flood.

Barings chose a restrictive and narrow approach in the United States perhaps because their business was diversified already – indeed global. Other American Houses were called such because their gambit was less wide, and the United States was their principal concentration. Barings trimmed back in the United States simply because they could do so without great hardship; because they could shift capital elsewhere; and because the warning signs of danger coming from American finance were so clear. The House closed the books on a strong 1833. If the United States required trimming back a bit after a strong year, reduced commitments would give the partners a chance to do something they wanted to do anyway: reduce the flood of business to manageable proportions.

With the slight American trimmings, Barings' operations worldwide remained extensive. They totalled approximately $10 million, not including credits granted to merchants who purchased in England.[451] This total broke down as follows at the end of 1833: $1.9 million for the West Indies, South America and Europe; $7.3 million for the Far East; and almost $500,000 to commission Houses in Santiago, St Croix, New Orleans and Batavia. Hidy estimated that credits granted to correspondents for use in England tallied $2.5 million (£500,000). Profit across the firm decreased 23 per cent from the previous year on 41 per cent less acceptance and commission income.[452]

Barings' posture in the United States, despite restrictions, remained active; and at the end of 1834, Barings anticipated great things around the world. Freer trade was coming and the firm could go anywhere. Money, like sugar, fish, tobacco or rice, seeks its best market, and Bates was beginning to wonder if the United States – once so promising – was this best market after all. It was true that nullification in South Carolina, the tariff question and the Bank veto and deposits question were swept away, and no longer caused the problems that once presented businessmen huge reasons to worry. Even the diplomatic questions in Europe had gelled into reasonable permanence.[453] The turbulence and uncertainty of 1832–4 from a number of issues fell away in the United States, and now presented a more open field to investors and traders. Hezekiah Niles had noticed a turnaround in the economy at the end of July 1834, close to the time the Bank resumed, and Congress acted to reform the coinage.[454] The wealthy merchant Philip Hone also noticed the positive turnaround, and was thrilled because it contrasted so much with the previous year that had ended in such uncertainty – with 'stocks falling, panic and bankruptcies, the holidays gloomy'.[455]

The recovery year of 1834 ended with hope. 'Money is extremely plentiful', reported the *New York Journal of Commerce* just before Thanksgiving 1834. 'Large sums remain idle for want of borrowers.'[456] The 'large sums' would not remain idle for long, however, as the United States stood on the cusp of one the greatest speculative binges of the nineteenth century. As Barings was cutting back in the American market, all problems seemed banished.

5 CHANGING TOO SOON (1835–6)

Everybody is speculating, and everything has become an object of speculation from Maine to the Red River.

Michel Chevalier[457]

The Commercial Pendulum is in continual vibration. That the present state of things must change is certain – when cannot be foreseen – perhaps next year.

Thomas Wren Ward[458]

Except for the French indemnity question, the American economy at the end of 1834 had an open field to run if it wanted to do so. And it did. A former New York mayor spoke for many when he had said that the year 1833 had ended in an air of uncertainty and confusion. What Mr Hone did not know was that the United States was about to embark on a speculative expansion on a scale not seen in over a decade, and which at least one twentieth-century commentator has compared to the run-up to the depression of the 1930s.[459] The year 1834 ended with Treasury secretary Levi Woodbury proudly announcing the government's solvency, and the world saw the 'happy and unprecedented spectacle' of a developing country without a public debt.[460] Throughout the ensuing boom of 1834–6, Barings charted a course of watchfulness and caution. Bates and Ward were apprehensive about Jackson, and about what his successor might do. The competition for American business also intensified among British merchants bankers, about which Ward fretted. It seemed that the United States was where abundant opportunity lay.

In the long run this was so. But in the middle 1830s there developed a trap of sorts created by circumstances coming together that made American finance and commerce appear vibrant and appealing. With others making money quickly all around them, these years tested Barings' rule to stay disciplined, liquid and avoid leverage by borrowing. However, as Ward eventually cautioned, these circumstances were fragile and subject to collapse with little warning. They were harmful to all except the most attentive of participants, like Joshua Bates, who seemed to sense the unusual nature of the boom and decided to cut back operations before he absolutely had to do so. The House missed the last gains of the American run-up of 1835–6, but avoided the losses when panic struck in spring 1837. In comparatively good financial health, Barings was able to assist the Anglo-American financial economy return to proper functioning, as it had done on other occasions.

American Demand Unbound (1835)

The United States interested British merchant bankers, but Americans themselves were restless to grow and prosper. Throughout the veto and deposits fractiousness, the number of banks in the United States continued to increase. In 1829 there were 329 state banks with capital of $110 million, in 1834 there were 506 capitalized at $200 million, and by 1837 a total of 788 banks with $300 million in capital. State banks notes nearly tripled from 1830 to 1837.[461]

With the retreat of the Bank of the United States and its branches after 1833, state legislatures chartered more and more banks, and increased capitalizations of those already extant. News of new bank applications and formations came constantly. During the difficulties of 1833–4, Ohio formed ten new banking institutions with an aggregate capital of $4.4 million; the Bank of Kentucky of 1834 had capital of $5 million. Indiana, Tennessee, New Jersey and Maryland all chartered banks capitalized at $2 million. Maine added seven new banks in 1833–4 for a total of twenty-nine, and continued chartering at a furious pace to handle a suddenly hot market in timber lands. New Orleans had $25 million of bank applications in progress. Petitions for new banks to the New York legislature at the end of 1833 numbered eighty with an aggregate applied-for capital of $46 million. Thirteen already-existing New York institutions desired capital increases.

State governments encouraged the formation of banks since they helped foster commerce and were the facilitators for the raising of capital funds for public works and companies. The federal government also encouraged the expansion of banking by accepting their notes in payment for public lands – particularly in the south and west – thereby building up their state bank reserves through deposits of public money.[462]

The London *Times* noticed the American build-up. After all, the banking expansion in the United States mirrored Britain's own.[463] A boom in the formation of joint-stock banks followed the Bank Charter Act of 1833 both in the provinces and in London, and reached a peak in 1835–6.[464] In the United States, the British paper informed its readers: 'since the fate of [the Bank of the United States] was sealed, it has been thought necessary in the states to come to the assistance of public credit by authorizing state loans and banks'.[465]

So long as the deposits question was a live issue in 1833–4, however, American capital deployment by the ever-multiplying bankers had remained timid – 'locked-up'; the cost of borrowing very high, the country in limbo. Repeatedly the phrase 'wonderful scarcity of money' came forth from an amazed business press. There had been no actual shortage of money, simply a reluctance by institutions to deploy it under precarious conditions. Everything was said to have been 'in a false position – the government, bank of the United States, and state banks all out of place, deranged, and jostling against each other'.[466] With the fate of the Bank more certain by 1835, confidence returned and the pent-up demand for money could be satisfied. What had changed over this time, however, was the American financial landscape: an explosion in the number of institutions qualified and hungry to quench the money demand on the one hand, and the diminution of what some had seen as a mitigator of excesses, the Bank of the United States, on the other.

The release of demand appeared in American import figures. Importations averaged $59 million a year from 1822 to 1830, and $83 million from 1831 to 1833. From 1834 to 1837 they increased to a staggering $130 million on average, with the year 1836 alone contributing an explosive $177 million. Moreover, imports far exceeded exports (see Table 5.1).[467]

Table 5.1: United States Imports and Exports, 1832–8 (in millions of dollars). Source: US Census, *The Statistical History*, pp. 904, 907.

Year	Imports	Exports
1832	95	72
1833	101	82
1834	109	88
1835	137	102
1836	177	115
1837	130	111
1838	96	105

As discussed in Chapter 2, the United States ran a trade deficit for most of the nineteenth century which generally averaged 3 per cent of its total foreign trade. In the four years 1834–7, the gap grew unusually wide, to 10 per cent of total foreign trade, with 1836 reaching a staggering 17.6 per cent of total trade represented by more imports than exports. Here was pent-up demand with a vengeance; a demand requiring financing by American institutions and by eager European lenders who engaged in trade such as Barings.[468]

Customs duties provided ample revenues for the federal government, and allowed the sale of public lands to citizens at low prices. The country's public land sales rose moderately in the years 1828–33 but, as with imports and bank formations, the increase between 1834 and 1836 was on a different scale. In the autumn and winter of 1833, the Bank of the United States no longer received public deposits, which were switched to a group of designated state banks. Biddle relinquished responsibility for the currency, the Bank gradually lost the ability to police state banks by presenting their notes for redemption, and the Bank ceased its former role as a brake on the money market. Terms of borrowing eased. Land buyers paid the government in borrowed bank notes which were deposited in the 'pet banks'. Since banks considered government deposits the same as specie, they became reserves on which credit could be extended. A potentially dangerous loop developed. Land speculation and currency and credit expansion increased the government surplus, which in turn increased bank reserves, causing inflation and a fantastic increase in public land sales – which spasmed to a peak in 1836 (see Table 5.2). In 1828 just over $1 million worth of acreage was sold; in 1836 sales reached $25 million.[469]

Table 5.2: American Public Land Sales Receipts, 1828–42 (in thousands of dollars). Source: Smith and Cole, *Fluctuations in American Business*, p. 185.

Year	First Quarter	Second Quarter	Third Quarter	Fourth Quarter	Total
1828	207	191	248	574	1,219
1829	311	309	873	669	2,163
1830	479	351	520	1,059	2,409
1831	406	1,029	1,029	902	3,366
1832	597	524	630	1,052	2,803
1833	608	799	768	1,998	4,173
1834	1,054	982	955	3,073	6,064
1835	1,990	3,144	4,083	6,949	16,165
1836	5,847	8,423	5,859	4,805	24,934
1837	3,479	834	699	928	6,941
1838	548	524	700	2,239	4,011
1839	1,823	1,672	1,282	1,710	6,487
1840	950	794	468	536	2,747
1841	416	313	367	416	1,512
1842	253	591	263	345	1,453

The surge of land sales in the Ohio and Mississippi river valleys did not come from settlers of modest means who sought land only for farming homesteads long term. As with commodity traders of any age, professional speculators in the 1830s, with banking connections, could take advantage of the $1.25 per acre price, and did. Each bank counted the notes of other banks engaged in land transactions as reserves and expanded its loans accordingly. The ever-more numerous speculators were unrestrained by official oversight, and the multiplying banks had few legal requirements as to reserves before 1837, and together created in the arena of public lands what one banking historian has called an 'airy fabric of mutual debt'.[470] Skyrocketing land sales in the west also contributed to commodity inflation.[471]

Many found joy in the emergence of the United States from its 1833–4 confusion. *The Times* noticed a shift of psychology so marked after 1834 that it spoke of the 'restoration of confidence' within the United States almost as a phenomenon or a distinct period of time.[472] Harriet Martineau was thrilled by the rushing and bustle of things.[473] Michel Chevalier saw the speculation as an expected part of the kind of feverish economic activity and capital accumulation that took place from time to time in any growing nation; and he wrote in the summer of 1835:

In the midst of all this speculation, while some enrich and some ruin themselves, banks spring up and diffuse credit; railroads and canals extend over the country; steamboats are launched into the rivers, the lakes, and the sea; the career of speculators is ever enlarging, the field for railroads, canals, steamers and banks goes on expanding. Some individuals lose, but the country is a gainer; the country is peopled, cleared, cultivated; its resources are unfolded, its wealth increased. Go Ahead! Go Ahead![474]

Ward's Urgings

Bates and several other merchants on the British side had testified in 1833 to what they saw as general good health in the Atlantic economies.[475] The prosperity of the British economy appeared balanced, they said, at least until the end of 1834 – with manufacturing and mining active, good wages, and without the 'influence of speculation' that was developing in the United States.[476]

There were nevertheless rumblings of activity. American imports added heft to the British economy and the pick-up in trade worldwide enabled British exports in 1836 to exceed finally the historic peak of £51.6 million reached in 1815.[477] The success of the Liverpool and Manchester railroad in 1832 started a mania in railroad shares which in time spread to insurance and banks, since credit was needed to finance such a boom. Between 1825 and 1835 Parliament passed fifty-four railway acts, and enacted thirty-nine more during the next two years (Table 5.3).

Table 5.3: Number of Companies, Mileage and Capital Sanctioned by Railway Acts in Great Britain, 1833–43. Source: Matthews, *A Study in Trade-Cycle History*, p. 107.

Year	Companies	Mileage	Capital (£ millions)
1833	4	218	5.5
1834	5	131	2.3
1835	8	201	4.8
1836	29	955	22.9
1837	15	543	13.5
1838	2	49	2.1
1839	2	54	6.5
1840	0	0	2.5
1841	1	14	3.4
1842	5	55	5.3
1843	3	90	3.9

The number of joint-stock banks in Britain rose from thirty-two in 1833 to seventy-nine by the end of 1836. Joint-stock company formations and price increases in 1833–6 appeared so precipitous that some writers drew parallels to 1822–5, and warned of a similar reversal to that which had taken place after those years. British bullion left the country to chase foreign securities, particularly in the United States where currency devaluation made American assets cheap. Overarching this activity was the Bank of England's unwillingness to check or manage the expansion by raising its Bank rate. Starting in 1834, the Bank received 'extra deposits' arising out of a loan for the West Indian compensation and money borrowed by the Bank from the East India Company selling a large portion of its commercial assets. Until relatively late in 1836 the Bank allowed the new provincial joint-stock banks to do a liberal business with British merchant banks – rediscounting up to eight times their paid-up capital on top of a large portfolio of advances and bills.[478]

Ward predicted great demand for the upcoming spring season in the United States, and disagreed with Bates's conviction in March 1835 that prices on cotton *must* go lower.[479] At between 18 and 20 cents for all grades, Bates's assumption for lower prices seemed reasonable. After all, this was higher than in the days of the suspected Rothschilds corner. Bates proved wrong when cotton moved a bit higher in a summer rally before pulling back in the autumn.

Later in March, Ward made the first mention of which the present author is aware of speculation. He said that new highs in staples and the lack of resolution of the French question created a potentially unsavoury combination.[480] Ward's first mention of inflation in the real estate market came in the spring also – especially noticeable, he said, when he visited Goodhue in New York. Still, it did not concern him. He viewed the American scene in the first half of 1835 as an exuberant rebound from the tensions and uncertainties of recent years. Ward saw the country as Chevalier did: 'expanding in all directions, money plentiful & consumption increasing'.[481]

The problem was that Ward believed that Barings' 'very great machine' was less committed to taking advantage of America's potential than it had been when he was hired in 1828. He continued to believe the House was letting the treasure of the United States go to ever-more aggressive competitors because of rigid rules – for example, the one forbidding double accounts. Ward wrote:

> You suggest we sh^d not grant credits for 1 per cent to Houses dividing their business in London. This I do not think w^d be practicable. There must be good correspondents who could have two accounts. Those who are really good can get the Credits of others & those who are not good or w^d be obliged to pay extra we should not trust – we must I think go on and adhere to the principle of safety, but give way to other [principles] when a circumstance requires it.[482]

Ward expressed his exasperation at Barings' stubbornness, competitors and missed opportunities in a note in May 1835:

> In this country we had outstripped all calculation. We have the opportunity to do all the business. There may be a correspondent here & there drawn into Land or Stock speculations which may ultimately lead to evil, but so

far as I can judge we have none such. If you decline an acct. others are glad
to have it. We must be willing to do as others do. In cotton this year we cd
have easily done three times the business, which would have been a fortune
(& at less advances than others were willing to make.). – There must be good
correspondents who have two accounts. [Mr] Low calls on you or Hechscher
– or Oliphant – or B.T. Reed – or John Brown, & want you to do a certain
thing – you decline – they tell you another will do it – you reply that it is very
well, – you prefer not to do it – Wilson, Wildes or Wiggin do it, this leads to
other business for them![483]

Ward still viewed 1833 as a pivotal year in which Barings had pared back just as
it 'seemed to be monopolizing [American] business'. Problems of that year were
cleared away. Now Ward saw benign conditions ahead and urged action. 'General
peace, industry & trade will increase commodities and consumption & give good
employment to your ships and ours, and a demand for the productions & manufactures of both countries'. Ward acknowledged that large imports created an
unfavourable American trade balance, but he was unconcerned, since, in a specie-
based trade system, 'imbalances correct themselves'. The House had survived war
fears in Europe in 1830–2, nullification and the Bank war with the American
government, and faced huge possibilities with little risk. 'If the Bank US. pursues
the course we are led to suppose', Ward wrote (i.e., eases credit), 'there need be
no difficulty in the money market for a year, & perhaps two years – which is long
enough to look ahead ... and I do not perceive any thing in the general state of
trade to occasion any difficulty which the Bank of England cannot easily regulate'.[484] With things seemingly snug, Ward predicted a prosperous trade in the
autumn. The New York *Herald* agreed, writing: 'Commercial matters are for the
present very easy and comfortable'.[485]

In spring and summer 1835, Ward urged Barings to extend itself to meet growing competition. What must have made his urgings less than useful to London
were his hedgings, that tended to negate the seriousness of his advice. Earlier he
had petitioned for leniency in rules, but steeled the partners against his argument by admitting that the partners' 'prudence' had worked well for the House
for years. Similarly, in the prosperous late spring of 1835, he pushed the House
to become more aggressive in their United States' accounts in the face of other
Houses, but seemed to contradict himself by speaking of imminent danger. In July
– just two months after the May 1835 correspondence – Ward sent to London
a letter that probably made Bates pause in any fuller commitment to the United
States. He wrote:

> I am sometimes surprised to find that Goodhue, Griswold, Sturgis, and
> Appleton (all sound men) all speak of the prosperity of the country not only
> as unprecedented – but unwilling to admit the probability of any great future
> *reaction*. The general business of the country we all consider in a sound state
> – but it seems to me that we shall go on importing & spending in various

ways in proportion to the high prices of our crops, – & when the time comes
that we have too many goods – cotton falls in price, we shall then have trouble & scarcity of money, and the country storekeepers, Jobbers & Importers
full of goods, a great falling off of demand and ability to pay – when it is to
come I do not yet see but my reason tells me that it must come. –

In regard to *Land Speculations*, there is no doubt much based on proper
grounds. – that is to say, the value of the property has not been till now
appreciated – but it is also true that very much is artificial & when times
change & money is scarce there will be a great falling off in prices & those
obliged to sell will many of them be ruined. Still my belief is that the community will not be shaken with these revelations, as we can bear a great deal,
and the growth of the country is prodigious. – the Railroads seem to increase
themselves astonishingly.[486]

Ward turned out to be quite accurate for the future, but is this the kind of information he should have discussed if he was convinced the House should increase
its commitments? After all, Bates was no doubt already apprehensive about stock
speculations in London in 1835 and how they would play out. This letter from
Ward was unlikely to give him comfort or the tools to make confident decisions
about the United States. The pattern became typical in Ward's correspondence:
'prosperity is solid, but'; 'trade imbalances correct themselves, but'; 'generally
sound condition subject however to unforeseen events and changes'.[487]

Ward had no sooner sent off the above ambiguous letter to Bates than he sent
another to the entire House where he explained:

Things on this side at the moment are *in a better state* than they may appear
to you – but engagements are large, & imports of all kinds will continue to
increase – *and I look with some fear to the future*, though nothing is now out
of order in the commercial concerns of the States.[488]

Did Ward mean to imply here that the American economy was fine? Did he mean
to assure London that the concerns of the firm were in order, as he so often did
to convey readiness no matter what happened? It is hard to say. Engagements
were large he said, and he said also that this was a source of fear. Yet in the past
few months he had urged Barings on to greater commitments to take advantage
of American prosperity and thwart Wildes, Wiggin and Wilson. Reversals and
hedging are numerous and breathtaking to the casual reader, yet must have exasperated the London partners still more, who expected useful information from
their American agent on which to base decisions. Neither Bates nor Mildmay or
Thomas Baring asked for clarification from Ward on the points he raised in the
29 May or 24 July letters. They may have simply used the correspondence as a
tether to the United States in a most general sense. The conclusion the partners
may have drawn was that Ward was superb operationally – after all, America was

still profitable – but *they* would be the ones to shape overall trade and investment strategy.

The House Waits

The strategy for the United States did not call for pull back just yet. Despite a small paring, confusing messages from Ward, and competition, Barings maintained its American presence in 1835. It simply had to be careful, and to utilize the resources already in place in the area of its cotton, securities, merchandise, credit operations and knowledgeable personnel. Competition was increasing but so was the size of the market; good money could still be made. The years 1834–6 were very profitable for the firm overall with profit up 80 per cent to £164,312.[489] If Ward was rightly exasperated about the competition, it appeared the United States had room for many players.

Merchandise operations saw changes in volumes and emphasis.[490] The London House received standard commodities such as tallow, hemp and iron on joint account with Stieglitz & Company for re-export to the Continent or the United States. Ward continued to buy and send out wheat and flaxseed until at least September 1835.[491] At the end of May, he became reluctant to deal in high-priced coffee or sugar.[492] There is some indication that after 1834 Barings was more willing to trade on its own account, and seek profit for themselves directly, rather than increasing credits to American merchants.

Trading on its own account coincided with the House deepening its involvement with ships, originally connected with the establishment of the Liverpool office for cotton marketing operations. Before 1833, Barings co-managed four ships with Goodhue & Company. Now the firm took ownership of two vessels: one by purchase – the *Falcon*; the other by construction – the *Alexander Baring*. Both formed part of a long-term plan to take advantage of the changing trade structure in Asia after the indigo House failures in India opened the market to private Houses. Barings' new commitment to ships likely was the result of this new opportunity, as well as an indication that key relationships with large firms such as Russell & Company were bearing fruit.[493]

The boom year of 1835 was as brisk in the China trade as it was everywhere else, and Asia appeared in Ward's correspondence more than any other year since his hiring. Huge western demand for tea at post-monopoly low prices prompted merchants such as Griswold and Brown Brothers to dispatch extra ships to the east, albeit secretly so as not to disturb markets and alert speculators.[494]

With eastern trade executed as a rule on an uncovered basis, contacts were crucial, and Barings' were solid. Indeed Barings' powerful connections allowed their Far Eastern business to be self-propelled. 'Nothing need be said or done', Ward wrote confidently. 'Russell & Co will bend their influence & that of Houqua to promote your interest & procure Canton consignments. You may rest entirely safe in all you do with Houqua – and also with Russell.' Whether flattery or fact, Ward reported that Barings stood in China as it did everywhere – 'in higher credit than any other.'[495]

Though muddled in other issues at times, Ward was very clear about the partners' trade at Canton. The relationship of Russell, Houqua and Barings yielded quick and huge dividends, and, like other things Barings touched, endured the coming storm. Ward estimated the average per-voyage Boston-Canton-Boston profits on Barings' ships at £20,000.[496] A partner of Russell & Company listed the firm's yearly 'income' (net profit) from 1834:

Table 5.4: Russell & Company Profits, 1834–8 (in thousands of dollars). Source: Downs, *The Golden Ghetto*, p. 177.

Year	Profits
1834	88
1835	132
1836	180
1837	200
1838	200

Russells' competitors despaired of the awesome lock on profits this triangle possessed, which only deepened with the absorption of Russell, Sturgis & Company by Russell & Company in 1839.

As for import credits at this time, Barings' activity remained steady. Iron continued to come in from Liverpool based on demand for American railroad construction, especially around Baltimore and Boston. Import credits for English dry goods remained at 1833 levels. Latin American operations until the end of 1835 stayed large, with various Houses having authority to advance against consignments from the Caribbean to Argentina. At this time, Ward began to spend more and more time in New York, tending to business there with Samuel Ward and Jonathan Goodhue, but the House kept its principal agency in Boston.

At this time also, Ward began searching for reliable correspondents in Canada, and wrote to the partners in May that he would try to go north during the slow summer season. In one way, it made little sense to expand business to Canada unless the partners had plans to shrink their American operations. After all, Ward had written just three months before that he was having difficulty handling the large business the House already had on his watch. For this reason, the Canadian initiative probably did not come from Ward. If the initiative came from London, as Professor Hidy has claimed, were the partners planning a cutback in the United States, with expansion into Canada, India and China as part of a diversification strategy? After all, Ward was not furnished with the extra help which would sensibly be forthcoming had the House planned a comprehensive expansion in North America.[497]

International operations provided options for the House. A major way Barings could maintain profitability in the United States was to develop its new Liverpool office. It had intended this, after all, as a major receiving point in the Anglo-American cotton trade, but with the 1833–4 turbulence the House had not really used the Liverpool facility. Ward went to London to meet with the partners in late 1834. (The reader will recall that Ward had earlier encouraged the partners, without success, to visit the United States.) After a difficult start, the 1834–5 season saw a great success in cotton, with a huge year-over-year increase in exported cotton from £50 million to £70 million, threatening the dominance of the strongest House in the trade to that time, Brown Brothers.[498]

Barings' Second Trimming

In October 1835, worldwide operations worked well enough for Barings to declare that the capital of the firm had climbed to be 'nearly that of Boston'.[499] But there was no doubt that the boom times of 1835 were drawing competition intent to make it harder and harder for the partners to carry on their winning ways.

Often this competition came in the areas of securities, acceptances and exchange. The transfer of the main United States government account to N. M. Rothschild & Sons in 1834 was noted earlier. This House acquired the shares of several state banks in 1834–5 as well – for example, the Commercial Bank of Albany and the Merchants' Bank of Baltimore. By June 1835, Rothschilds had four branches of its own in the United States – at Boston, New York, Philadelphia and Baltimore. Later they bought Union Bank of Florida 8 per cent bonds.[500] Aware of Rothschilds, of course, Barings were not particularly concerned, since the two Houses operated in separate spheres – Rothschilds in exchange accounts and securities, while Barings was more interested in merchandise credits. Still, after a late start, Rothschilds lodged itself in the United States in a rather high-profile way by establishing as their American agents the premier stockbroking House on Wall Street, J. L. & S. I. Joseph & Company.[501]

Prominent and powerful as it was, Rothschilds was not considered an American House by the British and American financial communities, since most of its business concerned Continental Europe and its United States business was not central to its planning or interests. Those six British firms that competed with Barings in the United States converted from commission merchants to commission bankers after the 1825 crisis, and during the period of relative decline of the British textile trade. They included the Houses of Timothy Wiggin & Company, George Wildes & Company and Thomas Wilson & Company. These '3Ws' were aggressive in sending agents to the United States who had the power to grant letters of credit after 1834. The House of Lizardi & Company, well known in Paris, established a House at New Orleans in 1835, having made a reputation in South American securities. Morrison Cryder & Company emerged in late 1835 from a combination that included the wealth of James Morrison and the connections, through the Alsops and Wetmores, of John Cryder in South America, New York and the Orient.[502] Finally, Brown Brothers, with their Brown, Shipley branch in Liverpool, was Barings' closest and most able rival in the United States.

These six firms financed a large part of the Anglo-American transatlantic trade. Besides involvement with trade credits, they were also hungry for the flood of American state and municipal debt securities issued for a variety of purposes and needs after 1834, and contributed to a great increase of foreign capital in the United States in these boom years. As Niles pointed out in spring 1835:

> Ten times the amount of foreign capital has been introduced into the United States than was invested at the time of the veto. We do not complain of that. Capital is wanted in a new and rapidly growing country. Pennsylvania '*is sold to the British*', as Washington city is to the Dutch – but the money, if rightfully expended, is rightfully borrowed. In New York there are very large investments of English capital; one of the *deposite* banks belongs, 'body and breeches', to a 'most noble marquis'. Louisiana is said to have a banking capital of 50,000,000 dollars, a large part of which is foreign.[503]

In regard to securities, Barings inclined toward restraint. Ward's visit to England in the summer of 1834 had not only tried to organize the firm's cotton operations. It also included discussions with the partners about how Ward should handle the purchase of American securities and new loans under the firm's new policy of caution in the United States. Ward could go ahead with security purchases, yes, but now with the following conditions: (1) that sales take place in the United States; (2) Ward take a one-fourth stake; and (3) the total of his and Barings' share was no more than $200,000. Ward would have to believe in the commitments he made to a greater extent than formerly, a hurdle which the partners perhaps thought would make their rigourous American agent even more so.[504]

The reasons for Barings' restraint were numerous by the end of 1835. The London Stock exchange was becoming saturated with securities, which decreased their marketability for underwriters.[505] Spanish and Portuguese funds enticed the capital of British investors, as well as shares offered closer to home, such as railroad companies and banks. The West Indian Loan offered investors still more options as well as a bond offering for Upper Canada of £400,000.[506] This all spelled tighter money for the United States as far as Barings was concerned.

The barometer for the partners' sentiment along these lines was represented by the still-troublesome bonds of the Union Bank of Louisiana. Only by convoluted methods was the House able to unburden itself of the 1832 loan on European bourses. However, as the Louisiana loan had provided a reason for trimming before the Bank war in 1833, it seems to have played a similar role subsequently.

Ward is strangely silent on the Louisiana loan issue in the correspondence, perhaps because the difficult job of marketing it in Europe was not his. For Bates, though, there was less doubt. The machinations required to get these obligations to yield the slight profit which they eventually did were prodigious and, more importantly, indicated danger in the international money market. Bates's diary reveals his concern.

> Business is very brisk. Everything is rising and looks prosperous throughout the world. Too much so to last. Our ordeal with the UB is too hard and long to be right. I am not clear what this means.[507]

The Union Bank was an albatross and warning beacon, though Bates did not apparently consider it an impediment to participating in a broad transatlantic boom in trade and investment. To the contrary, the albatross might be a blessing. Perhaps it was Bates's nature to assume negative when seeing positive; diseased when seeing healthy; hollowness when seeing solid, but he was not sure about the United States' situation in 1835. And his nature was to be decisive.[508]

It was indeed difficult for Bates to be uncertain about what to do about the American scene, but he was now – and Barings hedged. It stopped taking on large projects like Louisiana alone. The partnership now entered into a series of relatively small, and syndicated, loans that became characteristic of Barings' securities activity in the boom period. If risk were taken, let it be shared. Of these, the most important was a 20 per cent stake of a thirty-five year 6 per cent $3 million Maryland bond with Prime, Ward & King, William Appleton and Ward. Maryland was remembered in London as the first American state to tap English capital for railroad construction. Apparently the loan was taken at a high price.[509] Barings exposed its capital on one other small offering in Kentucky in 1835, but Ward refused practically all other very numerous approaches from state and municipal borrowers.[510]

In these years, Barings' role was one of non-committal passive receiver from forwarding firms such as Prime, Ward & King. Certain bonds consistently sold well abroad – New York, Massachusetts, Ohio, Pennsylvania and the Bank of the United States. These issues were the ones that Prime most often sent to Barings, and which Barings was able to sell either in London or on continental bourses. Many, though, had to be sent back as sellable only to Americans, such as Florida 6 per cents, deemed high risk as the Creek Indian War raged in the state. In November, an astonished Ward confirmed that the House held practically nothing in securities, writing:

> You should congratulate yourselves with your views, and being in so snug & safe a position. The amts you hold is small and of good kinds – I have discouraged 299 from sending – but you have a joint stock ac‘understanding with them that I have left with you.[511]

He said he would look over the stocks jointly held and let the partners know if he thought any best be returned to the United States.

Lean as these commitments were, Ward was laying the groundwork for an expansion when, and if, the House deemed it safe. In these boom years, Barings prepared for a United States without Nicholas Biddle. It established relationships with several banks which had been once derisively termed 'pets' but now were simply a part of the American financial landscape.

Ward believed incorrectly that the state of Pennsylvania would not charter the Bank of the United States. He reported earlier to London that the Bank of America desired an account as well as the Manhattan Company, and Ward was inclined to view their applications as desirable to accept for the long term. They had the 'right sort of influence on public opinion, and were safe', Ward said, 'and of a character to give full weight to your advantages in New York'.[512] Ward mentioned that Rothschilds was establishing itself with these deposit banks as well – for example, Girard's of Philadelphia.

Competition for accounts at influential institutions was keen. For this reason, Ward was concerned amidst Barings' trimming operations in the United States to keep a network of institutions active so that Barings could maintain its exchange operations in the United States. For this reason also, he planned to bid on former branches of the Bank of the United States in Boston and New York to complement the relationships Barings had already with the deposit banks. He later found out in a meeting with Biddle in 1835 that the Bank would keep these properties as long as it was in business.[513] Professor Hidy has described the expansion of Barings' exchange operations after 1834, with anchors at New York, Boston, London and New Orleans, as a platform for the future expansion of Liverpool cotton operations when the partners wished.[514]

Barings had reduced exposure in merchandise credits and securities by the end of 1835 because it believed England and the United States were on the verge of lower prices because of a skittish money market, and because it did not want to be in a 'lock up' (illiquid) situation on its capital. Even at discounts, markets were hesitant:

> These American securities [Maryland and Kentucky bonds] we were accidentally enabled to effect to a friend who determined to place a fraction of these funds in such securities; in the open market we are not aware of any important transactions. Florida 6% are offered at 58 without finding buyers. Our money market is easy but notification of your riots and the chance of war with France will we think prevent any demand for American securities for some time unless very low prices are submitted to.[515]

Apart from money market questions, the firm grew nervous in 1835 as a land owner in the United States, and sold into strength. Barings and Hope & Company sold the Maine lands that had been in the portfolio since Alexander's tour in the

1790s. The frenzy of American public land sales troubled London, but a sale now would allow the firm to repurchase in the likely event of lower prices later.[516]

Barings also detected a shift of British investor psychology. They wrote to Prime, Ward & King concerned the United States was less the haven that European and British investors viewed it to be in the first years of the decade. British investors, Barings said to Prime, were beginning to demand higher risk premiums for American stocks. British investors were also somewhat nervous about whether there would be friction when the Bank of the United States charter actually expired at the start of March 1836.[517] In the future, investors would see lower prices and so, for now, avoid American securities. Thus went Barings' order and advice:

> We continue of [the] opinion that it will not be advisable to hold on to American Stocks for active accounts and that it will be best to look to future operations to cover any present losses. We act upon this principle for the exchange account and are disposed to do so where you are alone interested under the impression that you will be able to replace stocks cheaper within a year. Circumstances may occur to alter our views but the public are sellers though in small quantities and there are no buyers. Anything would produce a panic.[518]
>
> Cotton appears to us liable to fall for it is evident that production has got ahead of the Consumption. Bombay cotton to be ahead of last year's levels. The magnitude of the trade is such that no capital can stop the fall independent of the natural tendency downwards of an article of which production exceeds consumption. You cannot do wrong in selling what you hold of our account. Clear it off if you please.[519]

Barings believed in deflation for the short term; so did Ward. 'The general tendency for the coming year will be to a decline in prices', Ward wrote to the House. 'If your views as to Cotton are correct, business must be lessened considerably ... I want to get the old accounts closed up ... We are now on the top of a wave. It requires care in descending.' Ward was interested in safety. He was not interested in participating in the fool's game that he believed America was becoming as all sorts of speculations continued. 'The competition is very great & there is little calculation to be made on what others are willing to do', he said. Ward seemed uninterested in playing on the terms of others.[520]

There was power in being a pacesetter. Others, after all, had come to the United States because of the success Barings had achieved. Both Bates and Ward were wrong in timing their pullback, of course. The wave would crest much higher in 1836 than the London House imagined. But if 'wrong' in cutting back meant safety, it was a form of being right.[521]

All bets were off suddenly the next month when the greatest fire that New York had ever seen swept the city. It started at nine o'clock on the wintery evening of 16 December in the five-storey warehouse of Comstock & Adams in

Merchant Street. Flames jumped from building to building, 'like flashes of light-ning' recorded the retired auctioneer and diarist Philip Hone, and roared down to South and Water Streets. Firemen, exhausted by fighting two fires the previous night and decimated by a cholera epidemic that had recently ravaged the city, found the municipal wells, cisterns and hydrants frozen. The fire burned out of control for fifteen hours, and was stopped only by gunpowder levelling buildings to deprive the blaze of fuel. It was not completely extinguished for two weeks.

When all was over, citizens took stock of a mass of burning ruins in lower Manhattan over quarter of a mile square. Some compared the New York fire to the great Moscow conflagration of 1812, but were shocked because this had hap-pened in peacetime. The number of buildings gutted was nearly 700, with Front, Water and Pearl Streets worst hit, and almost every structure south of Wall and east of Broad to some degree a casualty. Estimates of losses in buildings and mer-chandise ranged between $18 million and £26 million, more than three times the cost of the Erie Canal. Twenty-three of the city's fire insurance companies went bankrupt. Four thousand clerks were temporarily thrown out of work, along with thousands of cartmen and porters. Joshua Bates wondered what would happen in the months and weeks ahead to this flourishing commercial city.[522]

Figure 5.1: 'View of the Ruins after the Great Fire in New-York Dec[r] 16th and 17th 1835, as seen from Exchange Place', by William James Bennett (after Nicolino Calyo). Hand-coloured aquatint (1836). Print Collection, New York Public Library.

America Moves 'Too Fast'

The year 1836 opened with a rally on Wall Street that made a mockery of those who feared any fire could dampen for long the animal spirits of the United States. It opened also with Texas declaring itself free from Mexico. Almost every state legislature talked of increasing their state bank capital – including New York, which reported a backlog of applications at Albany. By March, legislatures had incorporated new banks with a total capitalization of $100 million. From 1830 to 1836 the state banks increased their paper issues from $60 million to $140 million, their loans from $200 million to $457 million.[523] All new banks would see their shares likely floated, then snapped up by Wall Street, where banks were all the rage as the fuel of an increasingly speculative economy. Trade was expected to be huge for the spring. Not since its opening as a port of entry would New York harbour be so busy. To match their huge trade, New Yorkers now talked of a large new bank, capitalized near $50 million. After all, Philadelphia had just accepted Biddle's new charter. New York finances could not stay piecemeal and compete, it was said. 'The brokers are mad – the merchants mad – the landlords mad – the tenants mad – everything is bedlam! Up-up-up'! Thus 1836 began.[524]

For sure, there were dissenters from this exuberant mood. They talked of a market rally not solidly based, and public lands selling too quickly or for the wrong reasons. But mostly the spirit was optimistic. In February, more evidence appeared for the optimistic camp, as it seemed that, finally, the last serious impediment to prosperity was removed. War with France over the Napoleonic indemnity – still rumoured as imminent just a month ago – had been averted, the issue once and for all settled.

Philip Hone credited settlement of the French question with buoying the American economy. Ward did also. The usually understated Hezekiah Niles gushed that 'there is no reason to apprehend that, at present, a stoppage of this prosperity can be brought about'. He wrote further:

> Great Britain, the United States, and France are in a state of extraordinary prosperity. Money, and the means of acquiring it, are abundant in these nations. Vast improvements are taking place in them all. Facility is added to facility, to cheapen the labor of transportations and bring commodities to market. The accomplishment of one rail road or canal only points out the necessity of another. Interest continually is added to interest, in geometrical proportions; and in ten thousand ways. Population is increasing, civilization advancing, and the general state of society improving in each – while the rest of the world seems nearly at a standstill.[525]

From this time forward, the ever-higher upward spiral of the United States economy hypnotized Americans and a significant number of foreign participants.

The tariff worked efficiently. American imports were heavy and money from duties filled deposit banks to overflowing. Treasury secretary Levi Woodbury had announced trade and budget surpluses over a year previously. Month after month saw the deposit banks' further accumulation. The money was piling up to such an extent that it was becoming difficult to find banks in which to deposit the growing funds, since many of them could not meet qualifications as to capital.

The government surplus became an active issue about April 1836. Both political parties were concerned about the size of the surplus – the Jacksonians because they opposed federal expenditures for internal improvements, and the Whig opposition because they feared the control the surplus gave to the party in power. For the business community, the fear was market dislocation. The surplus should be made part of the circulation soon, it believed. Otherwise it became the stuff of speculators, who flourished in uncertainty and vacuum. The banks themselves were bound up as well, not knowing how much to lend since, as repositories for the surplus, they might be ordered to pay out on short notice. For them, the possibility of deposits seizure was not a chimera. It was a precedent which these banks had helped to establish with the deposits transfer order of the Jackson administration in 1833. Who was to say this could not happen again to serve a 'high political principle' from one party or the other?[526] The Boston *Daily Advertiser* thought it detected a slight falling off of business and trade due to the scarcity of money. But the vice president, Martin Van Buren, assured an audience in Cincinnati that the present financial system was more than sound; the country was prosperous since its release from what he called 'the thraldom' of Biddle.[527]

In June, both political parties agreed to a plan to distribute to the states in four equal parts any sum in the Treasury above a balance of $5 million, in proportion to the number of a states' representatives in Congress. Distributions would begin the first day of January 1837, and continue in April, July and October. It was called a loan in deference to Jackson's opposition to federal largesse. The surplus stood at about $50 million when the law passed. The states welcomed the distribution since most were in debt from internal improvements projects.[528]

Largesse continued in the form of aid to fire-stricken Manhattan, which rose phoenix-like from its December catastrophe, symbolizing the indomitable character of enterprise and the mercantile strength of the city. Representatives from the city went to Washington and Albany seeking assistance. Hone's delegation upstate was the more successful. The state authorized the city to float a loan of up to $6 million, a new precedent in disaster relief. Municipal authorities borrowed $1 million. The Canal Commission also contributed. 'All the best and most influential men in the city', wrote Hone, including Baring associates James G. King, George Griswold and Jonathan Goodhue, turned to the business of rebuilding. Nicholas Biddle travelled north from Philadelphia three days after the fire, and extended loans of $2 million for merchants and for the benefit of insurance companies. New York business went on virtually uninterrupted. Within a week of the fire, workmen were clearing away still warm rubble; the stock exchange resumed trading after four days. In a year, five hundred new buildings – 'now of stone, fine and commodious' – had replaced those destroyed, including a new Merchants' Exchange in Greek Revival style built of Massachusetts granite.[529]

Most importantly, city officials stoked an already healthy real estate market into a frenzy with the announcement of plans to transform the area of Manhattan ravaged by fire via massive building initiatives. In February, lots in what came to be called the 'burnt district' were selling, according to Hone, 'at most enormous prices, greater than they would have brought before the fire, when covered with valuable buildings'. One parcel of twenty lots purchased earlier in the decade for $93,000 now yielded $765,000 at auction.[530] The cost of living had risen steadily through 1834 and 1835, but shot up 66 per cent in the first two months of 1836. What happened in New York was an exaggerated form (from the fire recovery) of what was happening all across the country. Thomas Ward, and other careful observers, had noted pressure in real estate for some time. A year earlier, he had used the word 'bubble' in fact to describe the real estate picture to the London partners, and used Brooklyn's year-over-year rise of 'from 500 to 1000 perCent' as an example.[531] If the percentage increase here is certainly exaggerated, at least something was going on. Real estate had been bubbling, noticed by a comparative few, but in 1836 it took centre stage, and was commented upon in the press as a new venue for speculators.[532]

In 1835, aggressive capital had poured into banks and canals, but above all railroads, which saw more track laid that year than in any other before 1840 (see Table 5.5).[533] Smith and Cole's stock index tends to generally confirm this asset rotation. Prices weakened at the end of summer 1835 after a double top; they weakened still further in December 1835/January 1836; then gradually sank – never to recover their 1835 highs.[534] The real estate market appears to have inspired a furious rotation of investors out of securities into property, and this cash flow sent prices still higher.

Philip Hone was aware personally of urban inflation. In searching for a site on which to build a new home, he found a sellers' market in real estate. 'Everything in New York is at an exorbitant price', he wrote on 12 March 1836. 'Rents have risen fifty percent for the next year. I have sold my House, it is true, for a large sum [235 Broadway for $60,000. He bought it for $25,000 in March 1821]; but where to go I know not. Lots two miles from City Hall are worth $8,000 to $10,000. Even in the eleventh ward, toward the East river, where they sold two or three years ago for $2,000 to $3,000, they are now held at $4,000 to $5,000.' He goes on to say that other items, such as food, are rising also – 'Everything is in the same proportion. The market this morning is higher than I have ever known it.'[535]

Table 5.5: Railroad Miles Built in the United States, 1830–43. Source: H. V. Poor, *Manual of Railroads*, 1874–5, p. xxvii, in Sumner, *A History of American Currency*, p. 118.

Year	Miles Built
1830	0 (23 in operation)
1831	72
1832	134
1833	151
1834	253
1835	465
1836	175
1837	224
1838	416
1839	38
1840	516
1841	717
1842	491
1843	159

The stock market became a sideshow to the land boom. 'Land', the press reported, 'is where the bustle is, and the stockbrokers sit on their hands' with an active market also in commodities.[536] The speculation in land was astonishing and has been charted above by land sales in Table 5.2. Everyone borrowed money, often without an ability to pay. Some invested it in slaves, some in land alone – often with the object of increasing the culture of cotton or other quick-rising staples, or flipping acreage around to sell at tomorrow's higher price. Ward observed to London that merchants were ploughing profits less into their businesses than into real estate.[537]

Huge transactions and price hikes on land took place everywhere, and revealed an increasingly national market economy. New York, Philadelphia and Boston property markets hit record highs in the middle of 1836. Indiana, Ohio and Mississippi were also torrid. What of the just-admitted states of Arkansas and Michigan? The *Detroit Journal* explained that 'buying and selling [was] the order of the day ... that the city was authorized to obtain a loan of one hundred thousand dollars for extensive improvements ... and that it is filled with speculators toe to toe'. An Arkansas land office boasted that doubling one's money in land in a week was not unusual. Between 1831 and 1837 the valuation of land in city of Mobile increased from $1.3 million to $27.5 million. Even the land business in the frontier town of Chicago had turned into hysteria, having grown from a small military outpost in 1832 into a city of nearly four thousand people three years later. 'New York has extended her long-armed speculation along the lakes to Chicago', Niles reported. 'About 150 building lots, 40 feet front and of a suitable depth, have been sold for 300 or 400 dollars each ... The whole country is agog for land.'[538]

The whole country may have been agog, but not Barings. It thought America was going entirely 'too fast', and expressed this view to associates such as Prime, Ward & King.[539] Barings competitors, however, appeared to have thought differently. Barings' letterbooks provide little specific information about competitors. One has the impression the House set its own tone and pace, and was confident in doing so. If competitors wished to tag along or not, Barings seemed to care not a whit. Compared with London, Ward was a bit more explicit in his concern for competition on the turf of the House. It is reasonable that, as agent for the United States, it was his responsibility to keep the partners apprised of the United States scene and bring up American issues. His correspondence is sparse on specifics and it is very difficult to assemble a picture of competitors or the competitive landscape. Nevertheless, there are numerous items worthy of mention.

Barings began losing accounts, and bids for accounts, at the beginning of 1835. To the author's knowledge, Ward's first mention of a competitor's concrete effect on Barings came in January. There had been numerous account dismissals of clients for rules violations or recklessness during Ward's tenure. Ward usually reported only very good or very bad news, and took care of most business discreetly. That he mentioned competitors indicated that something had perhaps changed, or had become more pressing. Interestingly, a letter of 21 January concerned an account cast off by Ward, and picked up by Wilson (no. 617) or Wiggin (no. 999). The reason Ward dismissed the account listed as 'Mark Healy' is not supplied, but clearly the fracture was a give-away on Ward's part, not a loss to a competitor.[540] The pattern of Ward's culling the American lists and the competition picking up Barings cast-off scraps occurred throughout the boom years 1835 and 1836. Indeed, a somewhat amazed Ward left the impression that, to an extent, Barings' competitors could be counted upon to pick up almost anything. 'The agent of 999 steps freely into all openings I provide & is rather annoying in this way.'[541]

Voluntary withdrawals due to risk affected exchange accounts. Both the accounts of the Consolidated Association of the Planters of Louisiana and the Bank of Charleston (a 'pet' deposit bank) went to Wilson & Company because of what were called 'more favorable terms' of the Wilson bid. As Hidy pointed out, this meant Barings was reluctant to increase the size of credits for the institutions, lower commission costs and decrease interest rates. The Consolidated account would have complemented Barings' large stake in the troublesome but useful Union Bank of Louisiana, but the account moved out of Barings' range of prudence as Lizardi began to bid against Wilson.[542] Barings also refused to take some loans or loan *tranches* because of what they saw as adverse market conditions for reselling them.[543] Rothschild & Company, along with Wiggin, took for example a large Boston loan at a considerable premium.[544]

Risk on credit advances, for instance on cotton, also startled Ward during this time. In June 1836, he wrote to the partners of a deal recently made on cotton in which a firm advanced on the full cost of 13,000 bales at 17 cents. In the last year that Barings participated fully in the cotton market, 1834–5, Ward's limit was 15 cents for upland cotton. (This meant he and his agents, like Comly and Hagen, were closed out of the market by December when the price moved to 15 cents a pound – and Barings remained safe, without expensive goods on their hands.) Ward was startled because the cotton market had not seen 17-cent cotton consistently since the bubble of 1825, so to advance at a rate of 100 per cent at such a high level seemed irresponsible. On top of this, the firm who financed the cotton agreed to hold it for four months.[545] A fierce Barings competitor, George Brown of Brown Brothers & Company, likewise cited the aggressiveness of rival firms from the import side. He singled out the agent of George Wildes & Company for offering largely uncollateralized credits to importers over and over again.[546]

It is true that the American Houses, including Barings of course, supplied important funds for carrying on American state enterprises in the form of securities. And states indulged in a spending spree beginning in the 1820s which continued through the 1830s. Particularly during the Jackson years, the states were on their own to fund internal improvement construction. In 1830 aggregate state indebtedness was $14 million; in 1838, it reached over $170 million.[547] Dollar value of debt increased staggeringly, as did the number of states involved with debt finance, as Table 5.6 indicates.

Table 5.6: Outstanding State Debt Incurred in Five-Year Periods, 1820–38 (in millions of dollars). Source: Tenth Census of the US (1880), vol. 7, p. 523, in Myers, *A Financial History*, p. 143.

Years	Debt
1820–5	12.8 by 7 states
1825–30	13.7 by 6 states
1830–5	40.0 by 12 states
1835–8	108.4 by 16 states
Total	174.9 by 18 states

Some of this debt was held in the United States, but the greater part was in foreign portfolios, placed there by sales to clients by British merchant bankers such as Barings, Wilson, Brown Brothers or Rothschilds. The American government was of course a well-known borrower in Britain and Europe, but individual American states were less known. The merchant bankers vouched for the states as intermediaries to foreign investors. As was indicated in Chapter 2, Britain was generally eager to lend because her power to export was related to the amount of her loans, especially to developing nations. To a capital-hungry nation like the United States, eager for imports, borrowing was important. The American Houses supplied the critical funding to American traders, who in turn supplied the states with income by the tax revenues that spun off from commerce. The problem was that overconfidence and competition of the English Houses for American trade led to practices which over time became dangerous.

The reader will recall that before the War of 1812, and for some years after, it had been the custom for American merchants to send agents to England to purchase the goods they desired. The auction system was also a major tool for foreign goods to enter the United States. During the 1830s, auctions in the United States declined in importance and the agency system became more prevalent and slightly modified.

Gradually Anglo-American banking houses in London and Liverpool specializing in the United States facilitated trade based on the elaborate organization of credit. These British merchant bankers sent or hired agents to work for them in the United States, such as Thomas Ward of Boston for Baring Brothers or Richard Alsop in Philadelphia for Morrison Cryder, and they were given authority to grant letters of credit. An American merchant who wanted to buy goods in England through his agent there applied to the English banking agent of one of these Houses now resident in the United States. A letter of credit permitted the American agent in England to draw upon the London office of one of these Houses for the amount of credit by a bill of exchange at, say, ninety days. When the English manufacturer, who made the goods the American wanted, presented this bill at the London office, the bill was paid, with the understanding that the American merchant who ordered the merchandise in the United States would place funds in London to meet these bills at maturity.

When this method was first adopted it was customary for English houses which granted the credit to transmit these 'bills of lading' and invoices to their agents in the United States to hold as collateral security for the ultimate payment by the American importer. But in time, this conservative practice was done less and less as the scramble for American market share and clients intensified. Anyway, it seemed an affront to an established trader's integrity to require collateral, an insult to be avoided if another House was willing to extend credit without it. The bills of lading and invoices came gradually to be sent directly to the American merchants, and the English Houses were left with no tangible cover for the amounts they had accepted to pay. The consequence was that American Houses of little standing or capital could obtain credits with the British Houses without any security whatever.

Other risky practices soon appeared, with the establishment of the so-called 'open credit system'. This lessened the safety of the naturally self-liquidating one-to-one nature of the trade bill of exchange based on commodities. By the open credit system American importers obtained credits with a number of accommodative agents of British Houses, and played one off against the other, paying off their bills when due with the bill of another. Under this system it is no wonder that American trade expanded tremendously, as indicated by the figures above (Table 5.1). It is also little wonder that if excesses developed an event could occur that upset the information on which borrowers and creditors made plans, such as a natural disaster, unexpected financial failure or credit stoppage.[548]

But there was no doubt: Barings was focused and resolved to keep *its* patterns, *its* conservative ways of doing business, because they were successful – despite a giddy business climate, despite competitors, despite a loosening of safe practices. Joshua Bates wrote on this dogmatic position:

> In general we act on the most liberal principles, but with some people these principles will not answer. As to rank I am inclined to think the House cannot well get higher, and every day the difference between us and others will become more apparent.[549]

Thus wrote Bates in the summer of 1833, amidst the first trimming back. One feels that Bates is aware of the elite status of the firm here, but that with success came the requirement to protect what one had gained. Other firms had less lengthy or illustrious pedigrees. His words to Ward were ones of preservation, safety and leadership – qualities to which Ward was sympathetic by disposition. Make no mistake, he admonished Ward: the whole world watched what they did.[550]

London's Restraint and Jackson's Gold

Bates had reviewed the general direction of the firm recently with the man who hired him five years before, Sir Alexander Baring – now Ashburton – and received his blessing.[551] Bates was a confident and sure-footed man. Still, he was aware of his position as the first outsider in a family firm, and of the need to prove himself. He was likely quite gratified by Ashburton's imprimatur. In his correspondence to Ward he reflects some of what was at stake for him in the firm's success:

> All my partners are unanimous in this, that as we are young comparatively, and fortune and your good judgment seem to favor us we shall try and see what we can make of the business. As to fortunes, all consider that point as secure and they will labor now for glory. If we do not go beyond the previous Generation of Barings I shall be much disappointed.[552]

In this, Bates focused on posterity and legacy. This may explain the firm's obsession with safety, and in pulling back before it absolutely had to do so. The firm's methods were secure and in no need of change. Didn't Bates once say that 'business was tumbling into their hands' and Ward ask for an assistant to help with the heavy client load? The partners would not tinker for frivolous reasons. Bates would leave a risky situation rather than stretch for risky profits. They did not need to stretch. Others did.

Legacy may also explain Barings' cardinal principle of 'no borrowing' and the firm's vaunted liquidity. Time and again, Bates told Ward that the firm never borrowed, nor should it give the appearance of doing so. Here was a unusual characteristic of Barings, something that few other firms could pull off, and a practice that the firm was loath to squander for short-term gain. It was one of the explanations for their unchallenged position in British financial circles. Bates assured Ward there was nothing of greater importance. It was one reason for the envy Barings inspired among competitors, but it was also a profit centre. Superior prestige led to superior clients, for the firm could pick and choose. Safety was something clients paid for, and Barings certainly could charge higher account fees than other Houses – for example, for letters of credit. Prestige was also, of course, crucial in a business like merchant banking where foreign bills of exchange were a trader's currency at great distances such as the Far East. At great distances, Barings had no rivals. Bates also discouraged borrowing because borrowing required divulgence of information to lenders, and this did not sit well with the premium Barings placed on discretion.[553]

A high degree of liquidity was the prime benefit of the firm's 'no borrowing' policy. Barings could function without reliance on the short-term money market, but could lever up if required. In 1832, Bates reported the firm as hugely busy, but, based on the firm's financials, he said it could take on twice as much.[554] Like Rothschilds, Barings was loath to invest directly in industrial enterprises such as railroads. One reason for this was a feeling that this was simply an inappropriate venue for a merchant bank.[555] More importantly for the purposes of this book, by staying clear of such investments, Barings avoided the positions that 'locked-up' large amounts of other firms' resources, and which forced those other firms to borrow in order to finance letters of credit or exchange operations. Finally, and critically, Barings could support unsecured credits to its clients in the United States, as had become customary for the China trade.

Repeated urgings from Ward to liberalize policy went nowhere partly because of his contradictory letters; partly because of Bates's concern with legacy; partly because the firm was doing well as it was. At the end of 1835, Ward was agitated by how active such banks as Wiggin, Wilson and Rothschilds were becoming, and wrote: 'The other Houses are less particular in all respects in safe accounts than you are. The London Houses in the American trade are borrowers of money and have great advantages over you.'[556] The partners made no response.

The events of the second half of 1836 showed the wisdom of restraint and established practice. June of that year heard the chilling phrase 'money panic' associated with indecision over how the federal surplus should best be parcelled out, but was quieted by the action of the American Congress on the distribution by July.[557] That month, with Congress recessed, the president ordered Treasury secretary Woodbury to issue the so-called 'Specie Circular', directing land agents to accept only gold and silver in payment for public lands. The Circular was consistent with the preference of Jackson for hard money. Its immediate purpose was 'to prevent frauds, speculations, and monopolies in the purchase of the public lands and the aid which is said to be given to effect these objects by excessive bank issues and credits; to prevent the injury of actual settlers in the new States and of emigrants in search of new homes'.[558] Jackson hoped to cut back paper money issues, and establish gold coins as the principal standard of value and exchange for the United States. In practice, however, the Circular placed American banks in a rather awkward position where rapid contraction was necessary, and opened the door to panic, foreclosure and deflation. It would, over time, greatly concern financial authorities in England as well.

Gold now flowed from east to west, where it was used to buy land from the government. The Treasury deposited the gold it received for the sale of public lands into western banks, which feared to use it, since they knew that on 1 January 1837, federal withdrawals would begin as part of the distribution of the surplus passed earlier by Congress. Added to this, the circular order limited the amount which could be deposited in *any* bank, so western banks were constantly subject to Treasury demands to surrender any excess funds for redistribution to other institutions.

The combination of the two bills – the Distribution Act and the Specie Circular – created a locked-up, perverse financial situation in the country. 'It caused a drain of specie on the banks of New York at a time when it was important that that point should have been strengthened', raged Albert Gallatin. An eastern newspaper marvelled at the extraordinary situation:

> The state of the domestic exchanges apprehends evil. Specie is going around the country – from city to city – just like a bill of exchange. Not many days ago, about $5000 in English sovereigns were deposited in a Bank in Wall Street. This was a single deposit and easily recognized. In one week this sum, like a box of pills, went through the vaults of several banks here – got to Boston – was paid back to New York, and performed several other peregrinations too tedious to mention. This is a sample of the doings of the specie in the country. It is eternally on the move. There is no steadiness – no order – no regularity in the payment of bank balances – or the calls for specie between cities.

Another contemporary wrote: 'The monetary affairs of the country were convulsed – millions upon millions of coin were *in transitu* in every direction and consequently withdrawn from useful employment. Specie was going up and down the same river to and from the South and North and the East and West at the same time.'[559] Specie behaved only clumsily as a paper substitute, and made its way throughout the country but, because the Treasury was in effect hoarding gold, the wonder of the economic multiplier put in motion by paper and credit – quite understood at the time – was not allowed to work its magic.[560] Moreover, exchange now worked between American states as if they were different countries. Nearly at par under the Bank of the United States, currency now passed between Ohio and New York, for example, at 3 per cent against Ohio.[561]

A sense of flux settled over the American business scene in the summer and autumn of 1836. In August stocks sold off for no obvious cause but general edginess and unease. Banks in the west issued post notes to get around the Treasury's instructions and provided continued fuel for speculators. Paper money streamed into New York under the auspices of the Josephs from New Orleans based on Mexican gold, and newspapers reported widespread counterfeiting of gold coinage.[562] Imports and real estate remained strong for the time being. The *Herald* reported 'everything is rising – our staples, both north and south, money, and labor', but there was 'agitation and gloom'. Western land agents crawled all over the east, the *Herald* said, 'promoting humbug projects and towns ... and the accumulated disorders are beginning to be felt ... Every ten years there is a general explosion in banking, currency, and mercantile affairs. The time is probably now come again.'[563]

Business-oriented publications had strong opinions about the cause of the present unease. 'The famous compromise bill of 1833 is the mother of the whole mischief', recounted one paper. 'That law caused the surplus revenue – the surplus revenue caused the removal of the deposits and the quarrels about the U.S. Bank – these quarrels caused the Distribution Law and the Circular.' Another source, the *Daily Express*, agreed with this chain of reasoning and found that, overall, the present state of the money market and the unsettled currency was due to the interference of the government – 'the constant sums paid to the public revenue taken away from active business transactions and exorbitant rates paid for any money at all ... Our commerce suffers because we are governed by politicians, not men of science or knowledge, and because people encourage and foster such miserable conduct in their rulers.' For another New York paper, the cause of the trouble in the United States and abroad had to do with the competition for specie begun in 1834 with the passage of the American Gold Coinage Act. This 'cunning law', it said, 'caused British sovereigns to make wings and fly away' westward to the United States. This was President Jackson's objective. It became the Bank of England's concern.[564]

In his annual report, Treasury secretary Woodbury catalogued the immense build-up of specie in the country since 1833 and confirmed the effectiveness of the Gold Coinage Act in attracting gold from across the ocean. Specie had increased from $30 million in October 1833 to $73 million in October 1836. Gold coined for circulation since 1834, said Woodbury, exceeded the total amount coined since Jefferson.[565]

With the notable exceptions of items such as the 1834 legislation and the Specie Circular, gold is a somewhat illusive and subterranean theme in the nation's financial architecture at this time, as it is today. It acted quietly on the economy, and threaded its way through newspaper reports and the business correspondence as a theme of the period. Under an American presidential administration determined to place the country on a metallic basis, however, the issue of gold, and its sources, came to the fore.

One of the problems that appeared to hold back moneyed interests in the United States before 1836 was the French indemnity. The Jackson administration settled the indemnity question in 1836. The United States imported, through Rothschilds, approximately $4 million in gold in two instalments from France by February 1837. All of this reportedly was coined for circulation.[566] French payments made up for once robust gold production along the Appalachian Range of the upper south that had been tapering off since 1833 as land used for mining was used to grow high-priced cotton in the boom.[567] Still, reports of specie 'pouring' and 'streaming' into the United States, of 'huge specie surpluses', were not infrequent. Niles published monthly tallies of 'coins minted' in 1834, 1835 and 1836 to keep readers informed of what happened to imported treasure.[568] However, besides France as already mentioned, where was specie coming from?

Surging immigration season after season, 'exceeding all expectations', was one source. Arrivals came with gold or silver and often pledged it immediately towards the purchase of land.[569] In the spring of 1836, Samuel Jaudon, agent for the Bank of the United States of Pennsylvania, completed negotiations for loans of 12.5 million francs from Paris and £1 million from London, arranged through Barings and the discount House Overend, Gurney & Company. It was an enormous financing effort to settle the outstanding obligations of the Bank under the expired charter but, as far as specie was concerned, the *Herald* assured its readers it 'will be sent to the mint to be coined'.[570]

Contemporary evidence and current scholarship tend to point to two other, and apparently principal, sources of specie: Mexico and China. Professor Peter Temin writes that most specie that had supported United States expansion came from Latin America and Mexico at least from 1827. These inflows (usually silver) were offset by specie outflows from the United States to China until the early 1830s, when specie flows to China fell off.[571]

During the 1830s Britain found that China would import Indian opium from them, and the Chinese found this product so desirable that they abandoned their long-held desire to hoard silver. China now used the flourishing United States trade to secure American specie that it would send to England to buy opium. The Chinese accomplished their objective to obtain opium, but Americans substituted their credit in London for the physical trans-shipment of silver across the Pacific which they had obtained from Mexico. The Mexican silver, which American traders had sent to the Orient for so many years to cover its continual trade deficit with China, was thereby retained in the United States; it augmented reserves of the American banking system, and allowed prices to rise and demand for imports to increase.[572]

In the 1830s, Britain sold China over $10 million worth of opium per year, which the Chinese paid for partly with merchandise exports, but mainly with silver. A specie proxy system was set up based on the Anglo-American credit bridge in place since at least 1828. American China traders with an account at a British merchant bank found it much more efficient and safe to send a bill on London to the Orient than ship bulky silver around the world. Russell & Company, for example, would buy opium from an English merchant with the bill and Chinese goods such as tea and silks with the opium. The Bank of the United States supplied the long-dated (180-day) bills of exchange for such operations, called 'China' or 'India' bills, which were backed by Barings with a drawing account of £250,000.[573]

These changing arrangements in the Far East accompanied supply-side developments in Mexico which appear to have affected the United States keenly.[574] Mexican silver provided the raw material for credit and inflation in the boom years of the 1830s. Steep inflation in the United States would have ordinarily led to a balance of payments problem with America's trading partners, with a resultant outflow of specie. High prices in the United States would have discouraged purchases of American commodities and merchandise. In the case of Mexico, however, inflation was even higher than in its neighbour, and resulted in an outflow of silver over the border into the United States. Temin has suggested this stemmed from increased production in Mexican mines due to new discoveries of silver, gold and copper.[575] This was a normal part of the country's economy, which treated specie simply as a commodity export.

Professor Hugh Rockoff has suggested, however, that the particular reasons for Mexico's inflation and specie outflow had more to do with General Santa Ana financing a government deficit with copper coins worth more than what copper yielded on the bullion market than with new production or increased mining. The significant difference between the face value of the coinage and bullion caused rampant counterfeiting of the currency and a galloping inflation that made price increases in the United States look tame. Purchasing power in Mexico dropped, and her balance of trade went drastically negative. This situation was brought under control only when the Santa Ana government marked down the value of the coinage in March 1837.[576]

The uncertain economic and political situation within Mexico (exacerbated by Texas) caused Mexican assets to seek a haven in the United States at least until 1837, and reports of Mexican silver leaving Vera Cruz abound in the American press.[577] A typical report read:

> Large amounts of specie are flowing into the U. States from *Mexico*. Between the 17th and 24th ultimo, $524,036 in silver, were received at New Orleans – and other considerable sums arrived in different places; and the remainder of the first installment of the French treaty of indemnity has arrived at New York, being $200,000 dollars in 'gold Napoleons.'[578]

Interruptions of the Mexican trade were expected by merchants because of developing tensions in Texas, but feared because of the havoc this could cause to merchants themselves and the banks who supplied them credit. A large mercantile House wrote to *Niles' Weekly Register* on 15 December 1835:

It becomes our duty to draw your attention to the apprehension which is felt of an interruption in our trade with Mexico, and the probability of a cessation in our supplies of specie, in consequence of the part which had been taken by our citizens in the affairs of Texas ... that our government should have overlooked such an interference because of a few adventurers and land speculators must be a matter of regret to every reflecting mind. Thus a trade, which for the last 20 months amounted to 8,536,706 dollars of exports and to 9,363,696 dollars of specie has been jeoparded [*sic*]. We are already feeling the effects. The debt of Mexico to this place for the sales of the last six months amounts to 3,500,000 dollars ... a stock of upwards 3,000,000 dollars of goods remain here without even a single buyer. This derangement when it comes will be felt throughout the union.[579]

Mexican trade and specie flow were fragile. Without Mexican specie, the United States' balance of payments would likely have been negative. Specie imports and specie not sent to China kept United States' bank reserve ratios healthy. Bills on London were specie substitutes that enabled British capital to go to the United States. These bills on merchant banks also allowed Mexican silver to stay in the United States. When the specie anchor came loose, as it did in March 1837, the system convulsed.

Threadneedle Street Awakes

The remarkable international specie system described above evolved in the 1820s and 1830s. Of the four major players involved, British financial authorities, such as the Bank of England, did not focus on China and Mexico. Rather, they riveted attention in the second half of 1836 on the Americans, since the United States appeared determined to pull gold in from everywhere it could using devices such as the Specie Circular.

To defend its specie reserves, the Bank raised its rate of interest twice: first in July from 4 to 4.5 per cent, then in August to its legal maximum of 5 per cent. The Bank had left rates unchanged since July 1827. It had held steady even as market rates increased over one and a half percentage points since 1833.[580] Gold exports, which had been modest in the early part of the decade, expanded in the first quarter of 1836, and Bank reserves declined from £7.8 million in April to £5.5 million in September, and troughed at £4 million during the first week of February 1837. The Governor of the Bank believed specie went to the United States at least until September; thereafter drainage was internal due to anxiety that caused hoarding by British bankers and the public.[581] The drain until September, Sir John Clapham observed, was mainly external – to the United States. After September, drainage was internal due to anxiety among British bankers and public hoarding.

Besides the gold drain, the bank raised rates over concerns in July that it had too many acceptances (discounted mercantile paper) on its hands for large sums from the seven American Houses based in Britain. The Bank lent to the discounters ('money dealers'), who in turn took the American Houses' paper, and the Directors became aware through the sheer scale of acceptances stored by these discounters at the Bank that the United States' situation had reached speculative proportions. The challenge was, of course, to unwind the situation without disruption.

The Bank interviewed representatives of the Houses and explained to them that excessive facilities given to foreign bankers, 'either as open Credits or in anticipation of the sale of States' securities in this country', were objectionable to Britain.[582] Many of the new joint-stock banks in England had been attracted by the possibilities of an American boom after 1834. They had found an outlet for their resources by purchasing American trade bills in large amounts from the American Houses with the intention of rediscounting them on the discount market or at the Bank of England. Advances on American securities by joint-stock banks reportedly amounted in many cases to nearly half of their capital.[583] In the summer of 1836, governor James Pattison announced the Bank would no longer discount any bills bearing the endorsement of a joint-stock bank of issue. The investigation of American affairs and the decision to raise rates were popular measures, not only for their impact on gold exports, but because it was thought that these actions would blunt the torrid expansion of joint-stock banking underway in England since 1833. Many thought the Bank rate rise was long overdue; some thought it too abrupt, or even unnecessary since the speculation showed signs of breaking under its own weight.[584]

Tighter money in any case concerned Anglo-American merchants, particularly those who needed low-cost money to finance the cotton trade. The news about Bank of England rate moves and its action to curb excesses in trade between the United States and Britain reached New York in September. This was not good news. With Parliament passing railroad incorporations in great numbers, English capital had more and more reasons to stay home. Now, it was said, moneyed men, 'like Rothschilds and Barings' were beginning to lose confidence in American monetary institutions under the accumulated aggravations of the Jackson administration.[585] The Specie Circular was one more large aggravation, which had caused the Bank of England to take steps after nearly a decade of inaction. Some believed the spread between American and British interest rates would keep capital flowing westward, but American inflation led to a falling off of British purchases in the United States.

Another blow struck British markets in September. That month, the governor of the Bank of England wrote to the agent of the Bank's branch in Liverpool, instructing him to reject the paper of the American Houses, which were specified by name. It is not known if this clumsy action had the sanction of the full Court, but the Liverpool agent to whom the letter was addressed did not treat it confidentially. The effect was, as one British periodical wrote, 'like magic'.[586] The public credit of the American Houses, previously high, now stood annihilated, tagged with the ignoble label of 'discredited firms'. The discretion of the banker was stripped away; a previously private affair was now public.

Immediately, money-dealers and discounters rejected paper they had once enthusiastically embraced, and the Bank itself soon came under pressure to take on the role of large discounter to stabilize the market. The breakdown of the credit chain in England alarmed American merchants and banks already burdened by the effects of the Specie Circular. That what was happening in England might be more rumour than fact was dispelled by an unusually frank letter by Timothy Wiggin which appeared in New York newspapers in late September. He explained that too unbending a stance by the Bank of England would cause his firm 'to not feel bound to continue our usual facilities to dealers in British merchandise'.[587] Rumours an ocean away were suddenly made concrete.

As the autumn of 1836 came on, the state of things in Great Britain grew difficult, and the first financial casualties appeared. The Agricultural and Commercial Bank of Ireland failed in November, and a run on other Irish banks was prevented only by the Bank of England sending £2 million of gold to assist them.[588] That same month the Bank directors learned of the distressed Northern & Central Bank of England – an institution deeply involved in American investment, and one of the first Houses affected by the Bank of England's restrictive discount policy. Headquartered in Manchester, it was a large bank with thirty-nine branches, yet just three years old. It had achieved its size very quickly, apparently through credit extension. The Bank consented to come to the Northern & Central's aid with an advance of nearly £1.4 million, fearing the failure of so large an institution might cause a general panic.[589] The problems at Northern & Central soon spread, however, to other banks, such as the private firm of Sir James Esdaile & Company, and in late 1836 and early 1837 Britain found itself on the verge of a monetary panic. Financial hesitancy caused economic hardships as credit dried up to British manufacturing districts, and caused extensive employment lay-offs in a variety of industries.[590]

Most American bankers were aware of accumulating difficulties in 1836, and knew Great Britain would likely take steps to correct them, or defend its specie reserves. In an open letter on 11 November, Nicholas Biddle warned that the increased money rates in London would over time inevitably result in fewer and smaller investments in the United States and likely would halt projects in need of funds. Higher British rates attracted those investors who otherwise might have purchased American securities and, at the same time, Biddle warned, American inflation would lead to a falling off of Europe's actual purchases in the United States, contributing to a worsened trade picture. Both factors would make it increasingly hard for Americans to pay their debts and maintain consumption at levels of the last two years. Not only was the Bank of England raising rates in a bid to stem capital flow. In September, after years of no change, other financial centres in Europe moved to defend their currencies and reserves – including Amsterdam, Hamburg and the Bank of Scotland.[591]

Growing tension brought nervous warnings on both sides of the Atlantic. With huge American imports, decreasing capital flows to the United States and now action by the Bank of England, British and American newspapers acknowledged the situation was fragile. 'Any failure in the cotton crop', wrote *The Times*, 'anything like a political or commercial panic, any alarm in England as to the safety of American joint-stock companies ... any one of these events would produce a call upon the United States for specie, and would be followed by such a scene of distress as the present generation has never witnessed.'[592] The *New York Herald* felt that the accumulated disorders put the country on the verge of panic that waited only for a trigger; that American banks' record profits would be their last for a while since they came from high interest rates born of a bankruptcy of confidence – that is, from a defensive posture.[593]

It was in light of this fragile situation that the Bank of England solicited the opinion of Joshua Bates at the end of October 1836. In a letter, the Barings partner found the problem rooted in American profligacy and excess consumption. He recommended help to the Houses in the American trade. He considered the present episode of speculation and extended commercial commitments as temporary, if still potentially dangerous, and informed the Bank the predicament had to do with the wildly large and voracious appetite of the United States market where, for the present, demand continued to outstrip supply. He stated that the terms of trade continued in Great Britain's favour, and urged that the Bank engineer 'a transition from high prices to low without any great loss' to the commercial Houses so Britain could maintain its advantage. Bates then volunteered Barings' services for anything the Bank might require in mitigating the developing pressure, and to communicate any desires of the Court directors to its client, the Bank of the United States.[594]

While the transatlantic financial situation sputtered, Nicholas Biddle and his cashier, Samuel Jaudon, busied themselves trying to reconstruct under a Pennsylvania charter the network of banking and exchange offices it had once commanded throughout the United States and Europe under the older Bank. At the height of the American boom – summer 1836 – Biddle dispatched Jaudon to Amsterdam, London and Paris to establish correspondent relationships that turned out to be useful in the years ahead. With loans it secured from Europe, Biddle re-established relations with Barings, and established an open credit of £250,000, 'with the right on the part of the Bank to draw for an additional £250,000 provided that at the time of drawing, current American Stocks were transmitted to cover the drafts'.[595] Barings' cooperation was striking in view of the growing uncertainty in British finance at the time, and a great endorsement of the newly-chartered Pennsylvania bank. At least one American newspaper applauded Biddle's 'magnificent effort' to organize what appeared to be an increasingly disordered American banking scene.[596] For Barings, their connection to the broad-based Bank of the United States *of Pennsylvania* was an efficient proxy for exchange operations in the American market and represented an increased commitment in the exchange area to one large customer at the same time it was cutting back on exchange customers generally.

In November, Philip Hone returned from visiting his daughter in Europe. He surveyed a much changed and troubled scene from what he had left four months before. Industrial businesses appeared comparatively untouched, but the affairs of the financial economy were increasingly jumbled and confused.[597] Foreign trade sputtered as uncertainty for the outlook of the American Houses grabbed headlines. His beloved New York City had seen a wonderful rebuilding in the year since the fire, but the country as a whole seemed to stand on increasingly unstable financial ground.

Since he had left, the Specie Circular had caused a metallic currency to crowd out the fiduciary paper currency of the boom. The once-robust and confident New York banks with which Hone was so familiar were now covetous of gold; craven behind very high lending walls up to 4 per cent a month. In northern cities, southern commercial paper was reported practically unnegotiable. 'Merchants are going around New York streets with their hands and hats full', the *New York Herald* reported, 'but few will touch it, unless now and then a small quantity for three times its value, at an exorbitant rate'. Hone found the merchants paying all their profits to the bankers in the form of discounts and premium on exchange.[598]

As Andrew Jackson prepared to give his eighth and final report on the state of the Union in December 1836, Ward wrote to Bates.[599] It was a strangely detached, somewhat vacuous letter, replete with generalities and commonplaces which did not match the problems facing Great Britain and the United States at the time, and was likely of little implementable use to the firm. Barings was safe from mortal harm in the American market for sure. Perhaps this explains the lack of urgency or emotion, but in several respects the content of the letter itself was less than accurate. Ward, who appears to have been very good operationally, was less good at useful suggestions and judgements within the partnership, and is also an example of someone being wrong despite an abundance of information.

On the one hand, he thought Morrison Cryder, Wilson, Wildes, and even Wiggin were 'safe', yet later stated that failures were beginning in American cities and no one knew when they would end or how severe they would turn out to be. He also declared that loans to the several states of the Union were safe, which was true for a time, wrong selectively for the long run (some states defaulted), and was not in any case enough information for the firm to use. Similarly muddled, and even rambling, Ward wrote:

> We may expect less trouble than we have feared – still we have yet to see the effect of great Land speculations & of imaginary values & we must get

down from them and from the general & great extravagance in living & high money prices of Labour & all articles – But as we have great industry & production & articles which the world must have, we easily recover from any excess & what w^d be almost fatal on your side is soon cured by our own rapid growth & vigorous health. The favourable & I think the true views [are] that we are beginning to have a check which as above mentioned will operate to let us down without great evil, or at least without any material loss ... The Bank of England has only to take care to keep itself strong, and the trade of the country will take care of itself.

He stressed both countries' basic good health and wealth in the long run, about which he was of course right. But Barings needed to prevent trouble in the short and intermediate terms in order to survive to take advantage of any long run. Predictions about easy recovery for the United States were incorrect (see Chapter 6 below), and Ward addressed here nothing of the specifics of what the Bank of England was actually doing as economic affairs between the two countries became more and more, and more, serious.

Operationally the letter was more informative, telling the partners what to expect as far as credit instruments. 'You will continue to have Bills on Browns', Ward wrote, 'and indeed on all the Houses, but less on 619 [Wildes] I think. – in about two months [January] we shall have cotton Bills coming in, and I think ere long we shall have the Bank US drawing.' He bought some Bank of the United States shares on joint account with himself 'because most sensible persons here thought they would rise' – which they did. He cited the outlook for grain, coffee, teas and sugar prices as likely lower, and the cotton figures for the upcoming season of 1,450,000 bales which could be found in any New York paper.

But empty comments continued to riddle a correspondence which must, at times, have been almost insulting to professionals at the helm of the pre-eminent merchant bank of the day. 'People are beginning to feel anxious and the general feeling is that engagements must be lessened', Ward wrote. 'You will take care not to accumulate property with Bills of Lading on falling markets & close up voyages & goods', admonished Ward. How would this read after all that had happened in 1836; after Bates himself had been called to give advice and a disquisition on trade mechanics to Threadneedle Street? It is difficult to fathom that the firm would have survived with this sort of soft advice and posture. Nevertheless, Ward's judgement of, and screening for, good American clients on-the-spot was an element that one must conclude played a large part in keeping Barings safe from the problems that developed as 1836 gave way to 1837.

In early December 1836, Barings arranged aid for Timothy Wiggin & Company, in cooperation with its five other competitors without Bank of England participation. In equal measure, Wildes, Wilson, Lizardi, Brown Brothers and Morrison Cryder agreed to accept drafts of £30,000 at four months date if Wiggin's other resources failed. According to Professor Hidy, Wiggin & Company used this drawing account well and reduced its engagements by over half from December 1836 to March 1837. Even this would not be adequate, however, and Barings would be called upon again to arrange financing over the next six months.[600]

The business community hoped that Andrew Jackson's annual message would signal some sort of policy change to ease pressure in financial and trade markets. It hoped for a reduced tariff that matched the needs of government, public works for expenditure of the surplus, and establishment of a national bank for stabilization of the exchanges.[601] Only in the area of the distribution would movement come. Listening to the address, congressmen might not have recognized that it was the United States the president described. Instead of addressing the pressure under which markets laboured, Jackson observed the 'high state of prosperity' and 'the broad advances' of the country, and 'the destruction of evil' during his administration. 'With no causes at home or abroad', Jackson wrote, 'to lessen the confidence with which we look to the future for continuing proofs of the capacity of our free institutions to produce all the fruits of good government, the general condition of our affairs may well excite national pride'.[602]

Barings would steer its own path as it had always done, and apart from the American government. It had already voted on the short-term prosperity of the United States with a cut back of its commitments, and each passing month confirmed this as a correct decision. Ward had long voiced disgust with what he called 'the continual agitation of General Jackson'. And Bates must have held out little hope of good things to come from Jackson's successor, Martin Van Buren. The Barings partner had closely observed Van Buren many times from London, and assessed him as 'designing, low, and insincere'.[603]

The year closed with urban real estate in the United States less buoyant than a few months earlier – still high, but kept high more by financial churning and refinancings than by genuine enthusiasm. Ominously, the stuff of hard currency in this American emerging market – commodity staples – were said to be dull and lifeless due to falling domestic and foreign demand. Sugar, coffee, ashes, tobacco and cotton all showed signs of pullback.[604] All markets were nervous. The coming year would be a memorable one.

6 BARINGS ALONE (1837–9)

We stand on the edge of a volcano. The gayety, the beauty, the style, the fashion of 1836, is gone forever.

New York Herald[605]

It must be a very long time, years perhaps, before the entire effect of these failures is known, for they will extend more or less over the whole world.

The Times[606]

The Bank of England applied to my House yesterday to assist them in negotiating a loan from the Bank of France!

Joshua Bates[607]

The difficulties of the last months of 1836 continued and culminated in 1837. What began in Great Britain finally affected the United States, and illustrated unmistakenly that the economic ties of the two countries, so long in place across the Atlantic ocean, remained close.

American business failures began in March 1837, first in the south, then the north and west. Prices, including cotton, dropped sharply in late April. Undetected before the price declines, overadvances on commodities now became apparent. Proceeds from commodity sales to pay bills drawn months earlier in the United States were now insufficient. British and American financial institutions tried to stabilize the situation, but all plans proved unsuccessful. Intact through foresight, caution, its own prejudices and luck, Barings used its resources to continue the pattern of helpfulness to the transatlantic economy it began three decades earlier.

Tense Calm

'Within a few weeks we'll know where we stand', wrote Thomas Ward to London at the start of 1837. He was confident of Barings' prospects, despite pressures on both sides of the Atlantic. Few, however, knew how these boom years – this 'American experiment' as *The Times* of London called them – would end.[608]

The retired civic leader and financier Philip Hone – a man of means – certainly knew where he stood at the start of the new year. He could not convert anything he possessed into cash without great sacrifice. The price of money was 2 per cent a month, more in some places, and was as much a topic of discussion as the price of stocks in the recent bull market or cotton. 'I am compelled', said Hone, resignedly, 'to bow to the men who have the money in their hands'.[609]

This phrase would have rung true in the ears of Joshua Bates, who made liquidity a cardinal principle in running Baring Brothers & Company. Many individuals and firms found themselves in debt or overextended in their commercial liabilities at the end of 1836, but Barings did not. To use a favourite word of Ward's, the London merchant banking House was 'snug'. Barings would watch in 1837, participate a bit, lose a small sum; but mainly its work was done. As problems clarified themselves and unfolded in 1837, Barings did not catch their fury because they had exited many commercial relationships in the United States approximately twelve months before. They were 'value' players – not interested in paying too much for assets: whether financial, like bills and notes, or real, like cotton or hemp. By their prescience, the House was able to assist in cushioning the panic that came in late spring 1837.

Prices broke first in Great Britain; then the United States. Tooke and Newmarch indicate the decline began at the end of 1836. Professor Silberling accords with this, and records declining index numbers of 112, 113, 109 and 101 for the four quarters ending on 30 June 1837.[610] The declines would have been more acute had it not been for the movement of the wheat price, which rose, despite a good harvest, from the unusually low levels of the previous year. Sugar, silk and cotton fluctuated sharply. The oversupply of American cotton at Liverpool was an important reason for the drop in cotton prices, as well as increased cotton shipments from Egypt and India.[611] Prices of indigo and tea, once the preserve of the East India Company, remained soft as large quantities brought in by Calcutta and Canton privateers weighed on markets. Despite generally depressed prices in the first half of 1837, there remained an element of speculation in British markets due to uncertainties over Anglo-American commerce and finance. Thomas Tooke records that erratic price movements in cotton and silk caused manufacturers to be on their guard and 'so distrustful of the high prices that they bought only what was strictly necessary to keep their mills from an absolute stand'. British exports to the United States whiplashed downwards by almost two thirds in 1837. Only in the latter half of the year did prices recover.[612]

British prices broke in the first quarter; American in the second. According to Smith and Cole, general wholesale commodity prices in the United States peaked in February 1837. They declined gradually in March and April, then broke violently in May – with the largest one-month percentage drop, over 14 per cent, in the 1815–62 period. As Table 4.6 showed, the 1837 downdraught came after a recovery in the second half of 1836 from four consecutive monthly declines of April through July. This may have been the nonsensically high prices about which the business press commented, and not a recovery at all. After the May 1837 collapse, prices remained flat until a mild recovery in late autumn – one season behind recovery in England.[613]

The United States imported 26 per cent fewer goods by value in 1837; imports from Latin America dropped by 20 per cent. From Europe imports decreased by a third; from Britain by 41 per cent. Goods from Asia actually increased slightly. American exports stalled in 1837, with a 10 per cent overall decline. They dropped to Latin America slightly; to Europe by 10 per cent; to Britain by 12 per cent. Exports to Asia, already low, dropped by half. The American merchandise trade surplus with Great Britain in 1835–6 turned to a deficit.[614]

On both sides of the Atlantic, currency and banking issues dominated legislative agendas. In the United States, calls for revision or repeal of the Specie Circular became common from politicians and merchants' associations, as safe, but static, specie accumulated in government vaults. American commercial interests favoured specie or paper substitutes to go to England to reignite demand in that country for American goods, which had begun to slump in the second half of 1836.[615] In Great Britain, several journals hinted that the worst might not be over for rates in the English banking system, as the Bank of England's concern for its specie reserves could prompt more curtailing.

The tightening was having some effect, as the foreign exchange in February turned in Britain's favour – against New York – making British goods imported by Americans dearer for the first time in many months.[616] A tug of war continued between the Bank of England and the United States for specie in their respective banking systems and, as we have said, competition for specie in the Anglo-American trade also ratcheted up rates in several European banking centres. For the time being, however, specie flowing out of the United States as a result of rate hikes by America's trading partners was offset by specie flowing into New Orleans and New York from Mexico and South America.[617]

The close connection between the capital markets of New York and London had been understood for some time in the United States. The devaluation of the Gold Coinage Act acknowledged this explicitly as it attempted to pull specie from England to the United States. Insightful commentators realized that over time this deliberate step might affect the two countries significantly. 'The barometer of the American money market hangs up at the stock exchange in London', said an opponent of the Gold Act in 1834.[618] The Bank of England clampdown in the autumn of 1836 brought stability for a short time with minimal disruption. By the beginning of 1837, the banks, such as the Agriculture Bank, were coming back on line. The City column of *The Times* reported that the British money market was calm. The London & Westminster bank could forecast almost optimistic times ahead for the company's shareholders in March. From newspaper accounts,

Ward also concluded that 'things were getting right' on the British side of the Atlantic.[619]

But American financial affairs were another matter. They were combustible, fragile, uncertain, skittish – and made even more so by apprehensions of renewed trouble in Great Britain. The British convulsion had been mild so far, and had involved mainly institutions doing business within the country. Those with large American obligations and connections, such as the ones of which the Bank of England was wary and watchful, like the '3Ws', were not yet clear of danger because the United States, though in a confused financial state, had yet to experience its downturn. The British market had corrected mildly, and its very adjustment placed the focus on what now happened in American markets. British and American observers predicted that, with British credit pulling back, the American 'shoe' had to drop. How was the United States to pay for its trade imbalance so swollen with British goods, and American traders so indebted to British merchant bankers? And if American orders for British textiles should drop off from the year prior, mustn't all-important cotton prices also fall, devastating the value of United States exports?

The Bank of England waited to see what would happen in the United States before deciding what to do in regard to the American Houses. It did not have to wait long. The American situation grew ever more tense throughout February 1837. Terrible American wheat harvests made grain imports likely. The eastern American banks stood stubbornly clamped down and defensive against paying out specie to the western states or to England, or issuing notes which could be redeemed. They did not know the plans of British financial authorities, but had to assume the worst as far as a further curtailing of credit in England. No matter, the United States' financial market was tied to the British one; the British one was affected by Bank policy; the United States had to cope with whatever the Bank decided.[620]

The western United States itself was reportedly 'circulation starved', with transactions taking place on a metallic basis. Contemporaries saw a symptom of the unnatural state of affairs in the American economy in the immense amounts of grain pouring into American ports from all parts of the world, and yet noticing that prices remained high. Baltimore, Albany, New York and Boston reported food riots due to commodity prices, and over complaints that grain accumulated in warehouses stood unsold and undistributed.[621] An English writer later commented that the massive imports into the United States in 1836 had not accumulated on the docks of the Atlantic cities during these years, but had travelled west and south to every part of the country financed by questionable credit. At the time, the lack of visibility of these stocks of imports gave the mistaken impression of healthy finance and trade. With the rigid discipline of the Specie Circular, large commodity imports stood now as an outward and visible sign of a large problem.[622] Several newspapers found this to show the degree of disruption of internal industry, trade and distribution due to a serious disturbance in the currency. The commercial system was heavy and impeded, they said. The *New York Herald* wondered 'Where is this to end'?[623] It ended in New Orleans, just as the new American president, Martin Van Buren, took office, in the middle of March 1837.

In response to the Specie Circular, westerners had redeemed their paper currency for gold at issuing institutions. New Orleans had provided much of the paper for the Mississippi Valley, and that city was the first to feel the impact of the demand for gold. To complicate matters, the price of cotton was weakening rapidly and led to the failure of several important mercantile Houses. In early March, some New Orleans banks admitted their inability to honour gold drafts from the interior. Then Herman, Briggs & Company, a leading mercantile firm, suspended payment on 16 March with liabilities reported to be between $4 million and $8 million.[624] They were factors of cotton planters and interior dealers and had accepted large drafts in anticipation of the arrival of cotton. Depressed demand and prices made their position untenable. The ten largest New Orleans cotton Houses and many smaller ones would collapse by April.

Trouble in New Orleans rippled to eastern cities. Messrs Joseph & Company, the New York agents of Rothschilds, were under acceptance from southern cotton Houses for several million dollars, and suspended a week after Herman Briggs went down. It was believed Josephs would not be able to resume, and liquida-

Figure 6.1: View of New Orleans by William James Bennett (after Anthony Mondelli). Hand-coloured aquatint (1841). I. N. Phelps Stokes Collection, New York Public Library.

tion of their large real estate holdings, notably in Harlem, convulsed the New York real estate market. On 23 March, the agents of Rothschilds in Philadelphia, Messrs Phillips, failed with liabilities of $2 million – again, from too great extension in land operations or in the south-western trade.[625]

In the course of March, the cotton trade appeared more and more disastrous amid rapidly falling prices and a dearth of reliable creditors. Dry goods went unclaimed and unsold. Land sales by dollar value in the west and south-west were barely half their first quarter total, and would fall a further two thirds by the end of September.[626] Ominously, on 25 March, foreign exchange reached 112 – too high a price for specie to stay in the United States for long unless under unusual circumstances. The money market was strung tight, with capital locked down and 'commercial relations between the northeast and the southwest threatening to separate from each other'. Indeed, shortly after Herman Briggs' suspension, Ward informed London that New Orleans was 'breaking up' and that distrust was growing up among the merchants. He added: 'You'll soon have the field to yourselves'.[627]

Some expressed relief that a 'healthy reaction' had at last begun in the commercial world; that 'with failures in London – failures in Liverpool – failures in New York – failures in Philadelphia – failures in New Orleans, the state of things was at last finding its natural motion and proper speed'. Talk of a purge had circulated in 1836, since some had concluded the scope of credit overextension and price inflation on both sides of the Atlantic had gone too far for a painless escape. But there was a question as to what form this purging might take: a convulsion or a lingering and protracted series of failures? No one quite knew, but many talked vaguely of a repeat of the downturn of 1825–6.[628]

Assistance Amidst Collapse

Barings had reduced commitments before real trouble began, and continued to trim generally. Specific instances of good judgement that allowed the firm to prosper are interesting to note. Ward never transacted any business with Joseph & Company directly. In his words, he 'could not see through them' and he could not know if they were building a real fortune, or an imaginary one based on land speculations. Early on, he had advised Goodhue not to take their bills where Barings was concerned, despite their being the largest operator of stocks in New York City, trafficking in payments up to $1 million a day. As for Herman Briggs & Company, Ward miraculously had identified this firm to London as 'unsteady' in January 1837, and discontinued the account. This made sense in light of Ward's pronouncement of 'nothing happening' in the cotton market.[629]

Ward's forecast in late January for prices on cotton proved wrong compared to that of Bates, whose insight on cotton's prospects was breathtaking. Ward saw steady prices in the range of 16–18 cents. On 21 February, Liverpool 'good fair' upland cotton stood at 17 cents. Proudly, Ward wrote to Barings that he saw no reason to change his January estimate, but he acknowledged the present 17-cent price was 4 or 5 cents above Bates's limit on cotton purchases and advances. In April and May, cotton collapsed below 12 cents, and stayed under pressure for the balance of the next two years.[630]

These examples of specific good judgement and the general cut-back of the last twelve months gave Barings latitude possessed by few other Houses. The firm continued to tighten but, because of their caution in the past, the partners and Ward could view the distress of the present as a kind of opportunity – a time of caution of course, but a chance for some bargain hunting. The House had sat out the 1836–7 cotton season. As the New Orleans market collapsed in March and April, Ward began nibbling in the cotton market at prices under 11 cents. He also began accumulating coffee and white sugars.[631]

This was filigree in a general pattern of continued operational restraint by the firm, which curtailed Far Eastern credits and reduced activity in the whole category of dry goods. Securities purchases ceased. Revelations gradually came to light – first anonymously, then with names – that many prominent Houses had multiple accounts with multiple merchant bankers in England, and that the accommodation bills – drawing on one banker to pay another – were a common culprit in the pyramiding of credit. The single account House, however, did not appear to Ward as necessarily troubled or a cause for alarm. Though he had questioned its efficacy in the past, Ward now concluded with enthusiasm that the Barings' prohibition on double accounts was vindicated.

Profit was not the House motive for business at this pressurized time; control and preservation of resources were.[632] To this end, rules became ever-more important, even to the point of publication. On 27 March, Barings released to the American press a copy of a 2 March circular announcing restrictions as to bill remittances for present and prospective clients.[633] It was an unusual move for a firm for which publicity was anathema, and probably contributed to the panicked atmosphere in American financial centres – coming, as it did, amid the bad news from New Orleans. At the same time, it may have indicated the fierce independence the firm had always exhibited; the realization by Barings that theirs was one of the few solid Houses operating, and that the marketplace needed leadership. Ward indicated this esteem to the partners:

> The course taken by your House is beginning to be understood & appreciated, and your wisdom applauded – the conservative & beneficial influence exerted by you on the trade of the world is generally admitted – the good decisions to cut off accounts have saved losses to yourselves and to many others.[634]

The credibility and weight of Barings was important as developments continued for the four American Houses already tethered to the Bank of England for help.

On 22 March, the London *Courier* reported that important month-long negotiations between Houses engaged in the American trade and the Bank of England had ended satisfactorily, at least for the present. The Bank would permit four Houses to discount specific sums – Wilson & Company £400,000, Wildes & Company £250,000, Wiggin & Company £200,000, and Brown Brothers & Company £400,000 – against a deposit of collateral security and subscription lists of guarantors.[635] The Bank reportedly was loathe to abandon its official line of non-interference, but considered the magnitude of the problems in trade and manufacturing so extraordinary that inaction would have ruinous public consequences. By taking the paper of the Houses in question, the Bank hoped to provide for a gradual diminution of engagements, and to restore confidence to the British and the American markets, from the latter of which would come the much-needed remittances for imports purchased. Barings, which was acknowledged to be 'out of the market' by the director of the Bank of England, Horsley Palmer, was included in the list of guarantors and had examined the books of all four Houses, and supported the Bank's decision to intervene. It is known that the partners endorsed at least £20,000 in promissory notes for Wilson & Company, for example, maturing in five, six and seven months from 23 March.[636]

While the Bank of England engineered a 'soft landing' for the British credit system, American merchants and bankers of Atlantic seaboard cities visited Nicholas Biddle in Philadelphia to look for ways to provide liquidity to the United States market after the cotton House disasters in New Orleans. With his House intact and solvent, Ward joined the Philadelphia proceedings on 23 March, as Barings became a partner and advisor to America – as it had been in England to the Bank of England.[637]

A bold plan emerged on 29 March 1837. The Bank of the United States, the Manhattan Bank, the Bank of America, the Girard and the Morris Canal & Banking Company agreed to sell their own obligations, in the form of bonds, in the London, Paris, Amsterdam and domestic money markets to a total of $11.2 million, including $1 million in specie.[638] Of the total of so-called 'post notes' payable up to 14 months date, Biddle contributed $5 million. He explained the plan in a letter to the chairman of the Merchants Committee, John A. Stevens:

> Recent events in the south and in Europe, have, in concurrence with reasons of an earlier date, produced a paralysis of private credit which deranges the whole system of our foreign and domestic exchanges. For this the appropriate remedy seems to be *to substitute for the private credit of individuals the more known and established credit of the bank*, until public confidence in private stability, has time to revive.
>
> To the foreign exchanges, the engagements of the bank will be ready by the next packet, and they will enable the country to make without injury, an

early provision for the adjustment of foreign exchanges by the natural operation of remitting its produce and coin. I shall recommend to the board a
similar operation in the domestic exchanges, by an enlarged and immediate
purchase of bills of exchange on the distant sections of the Union.[639]

The New York banks played a significant, albeit junior, role alongside the manager, Biddle. *The Times* of London reported that the Manhattan Bank, in addition
to the amount agreed to under Biddle's short-term post-note plan, had applied
subsequently at the Bank of England to issue twenty- and twenty-five-year bonds,
bearing yearly interest of 5 per cent. The newspaper wrote that the British bank
was amenable to a correspondent relationship with the American bank, and had
agreed to pay the capital and interest due quarterly on the Manhattan Bank's
bonds.[640]

In a follow-up letter to Barings after his correspondence with John A. Stevens,
Biddle emphasized that he believed the trouble in the commercial community
was temporary, and that the Bank had interposed with emergency measures as 'a
common friend of the interests on both sides of the Atlantic' to break the rhythm
of panic. Cotton bills, he said, were discredited for the moment but would firm
'now that the crop had fallen to its proper commercial value'. Things would
straighten out after the almost complete withdrawal of open credits from the system, and now that the American scarcity of money obliged the country to buy
only what it could afford. The total of the Bank's foreign issuance in London
came to about £1 million, and was payable through Barings.[641] Referring to the
London House, Biddle said he found no reason to seek a new channel when the
old one was so familiar and satisfactory. 'We might as well', he said, 'make the
operation with you as with the Bank of England. The strength of your House has
been eminently conspicuous'.[642]

An excited Ward wrote from New York that he thought Biddle's actions would
increase American confidence over the next few weeks, and that Liverpool and
London would see a revival of United States remittances to British merchants.[643]
The American correspondent for *The Times* echoed Ward's optimism – that the
broad issuance of post notes would help bring money into circulation.[644] The
British newspaper related what the Bank of the United States did for its merchants by way of liquidity and confidence to what the Bank of England had done
for British commercial players. Biddle's cashier, Samuel Jaudon, certainly an
insider, wrote to Joshua Bates that he felt that, if the four American Houses made
it through March, he would feel easier about them longer term.[645]

In March, Bates was travelling in France though he was in contact with his
colleague Thomas Baring and with Bank of England directors. By 1 April, Bates
indicated he was anxious to return to London, convinced that problems were
wider than just the United States. Americans were pulling back from France in a
frantic effort to accumulate cash, he said; and like England and the United States,

the Continent was likely to see further commodity price erosion, so he was anxious to unwind the firm's remaining positions, particularly in indigo and tea.[646]

The English money market embraced the American banks' offering, particularly Biddle's high-profile issue backed by Barings. European investors had grown accustomed to a yield of 6–7 per cent for risky American securities, and these had safe payouts at a not-too-distant date. Moreover, the stock of the Bank of the United States was especially desired because the Bank was thought to be in line for healthy profits as coordinating manager of such a large international placement of American bank securities.[647] Certainly, Barings was set to profit by the huge demand which drove securities to a premium. 'You will observe that the public has taken a right view of your proceedings', wrote Bates to Samuel Jaudon. 'Your bonds go off as fast as they arrive here. The stock exchange has taken hold of them and money being plenty, they operate as a cash remittance & their arrival produced a complete change in the face of commercial matters here'.[648]

Ward confirmed to Barings that Biddle had strengthened the Philadelphia bank by his large flotations, yet Bates's mention of a 'complete change' in London's commercial picture turned out to be short-lived.[649] Biddle and the Bank of the United States would not, and could not, part with gold which the Bank of England desired and needed because states were now demanding to have their shares of the federal surplus scheduled for March distribution come to them in specie.

So throughout April, England entered a waiting game: waiting for payment, waiting for packet ships, waiting for reliable information from the United States. Before undersea cable and wireless, packet ships were the principal means for transmitting payments, people and news over long distances. The arrangements by Barings, Biddle and Threadneedle Street in March were only as good as how much they improved the commercial and financial affairs of both countries. If the largesse to American Houses in Britain was to work, American remittances had to come eastward from across the ocean to cover these Houses' commercial obligations. The March arrangements of the Bank of England and the Bank of the United States bought time for trade to straighten out. By the end of April, though, time grew short.[650]

Prices had fallen out of the Liverpool market. At the beginning of April 1837, Ward reported rather vaguely that he knew of at least a hundred failures, but this was certainly an underestimation since, in January, he had sent a detailed list to London of New York failures alone, which numbered over two hundred.[651] Imports would be half last year's volume, and might cease altogether. Exports of cotton would fall significantly as the general breaking up of the New Orleans Houses caused factors and planters to hold back cotton as bankers held back specie. Ward received new cotton buy-and-advance limits of 9 cents.[652] The *Herald* reported the United States had contracted roughly $150 million more trade obligations than it had resources to pay – 'certainly beyond the remedy of a few millions of bank currency or specie'. The *Herald* sarcastically described the bank suspensions as part of 'General Jackson's commercial revolution' which amounted by spring 1837 to almost $51 million – the same as the federal surplus – with New York and New Orleans accounting for 40 per cent of this total. Ward expected some payment delays, but not great losses to the House.[653]

Meanwhile, London and Liverpool waited for remittances aboard packet ships from the United States that did not come, and talked about utter credit ruination. The usual payment day on the fourth of the month came and went without arrivals. Everyone looked for bullion or goods, not bill remittances unsellable in the London discount market.[654] As of 5 April, five New York mails were overdue, and fanciful rumours of ship sightings off Ireland, South America and Canada abounded. Lacking options, desperate joint-stock banks throughout England applied to the Bank of England for help, but the provision for applications, as *The Times* explained, depended upon United States payments. Indeed the Bank of England was preoccupied with the fate of the American Houses already assisted, and their drawing down obligations as a percentage of capital. *The Times* wrote on 8 April 1837:

> The transactions between the Bank of England and the American Houses have been brought to a sort of crisis, by the inability of them to furnish securities to the amount of the further advances required, the cause assigned for which was the non-arrival of the New York mails, and the disappointment of remittances. So important was the situation of affairs considered, even in a public point of view, that communications took place between the Bank Directors and the Treasury ... The directors remark that the hope of safety lies in the greater degree of prudence which may be found to have been used by the New York Houses [than the British ones], but we believe that it will turn out that they at all events have secured themselves from all danger in this very extraordinary situation.

The American banks were indeed secured – if this meant stubborn to give up specie, or to make loans except at rates up to 50 per cent annualized. Biddle had garnered great praise for his initiatives but, by 16 April, the Bank of the United States had issued the last of its domestic post notes that it hoped might bring money out from the hoards of 'those who were afraid to trust the merchants'.[655]

Any increased confidence from Biddle's action or the New York banks was of little use to the largest cotton House in New Orleans, which collapsed in the third week of April for liabilities of $15 million on assets of just slightly more. Charleston and New Orleans reported cotton at 11 cents, and there were no purchasers at this price. The cascade of non-payments was most severe in Mobile, where the New York *Journal of Commerce* reported nine out of every ten merchants had suspended according to the southern papers of 14 April.[656] On 23 April, Biddle went to see President Van Buren about reform of the Specie Circular to restore liquidity to the American and transatlantic economies. The business press held out little hope for his success.

Ward tried to put the best face on things and took care of problems without worrying his employers. By the end of April, though, he put aside his relatively cheery correspondence to London for a rather more resigned tone. He was grateful Barings had comparatively little to fear, but he acknowledged a certain inevitable turbulence through which the country would have to pass in order to emerge clean again. 'There are double difficulties', Ward said.

> Where payables come round before receivables it is difficult to get money even for the best Houses. There is an actual deficiency of money to liqui-date immense engagements. Most importantly, a distrust & panic adds to the want of money and increases difficulties.[657]

The first week of May, a frustrated, reflective and somewhat despondent Ward wrote London a follow-up: 'Everything has worked badly. – The Bank of England from not curtailing a year ago. – The London Houses. – and the sudden check to every thing on your side. – & the disturbance of our currency by the gov.ᵗ – all has worked evil. – and it has come to panic and confusion. Things are in a bad state here.'[658] In this lament, Ward left out those to blame who stood at the centre of attention. For the four American Houses which the Bank of England decided to help by discounting their acceptances, Ward had less patience.

From the beginning of troubled year 1837, the partners communicated to Ward that Barings' associates and correspondents should avoid the bills of Wilson (no. 617), Wildes (no. 619) and Wiggin (no. 999). As for Brown Brothers, Morrison Cryder (no. 1376) and Lizardi, the partners and Ward considered them stronger than the '3Ws', and the House imposed no comparable restrictions – other than the ever-characteristic Baring caution. In April, Ward acknowledged that Brown Brothers needed some help, but said he could 'carry them along'. He acknowl-edged also Lizardi's possible vulnerability to a cotton downdraft since the House was heavily exposed at New Orleans.[659]

Common during this time are Ward's reports that the six Houses were contin-uing to take accounts which would have gone to Barings 'in more normal times'. As late as March, New York trading Houses told Ward tauntingly that they were accommodated twice as liberally by Wildes and Wilson than by Barings; 'with no limit' by Wiggin even after Bank of England assistance.[660] To this, Ward used such words as 'weak' and 'backward', or phrases such as 'loosely managed'. Unlike Bates who advised the Bank to manage the trade Houses through careful intervention, Ward found the gradualist ways of the Bank of England neither appealing nor equitable for American Houses which, in Ward's estimation, would likely lose twice their capital without assistance or without a miraculous revival of confi-dence. 'Those without means must fail, and the sooner the better.' Barings had played smart, pulled back before it had to, and avoided difficulty. Yet, less prudent

Houses, less restrained Houses, less forward-thinking Houses received accommodation. He considered this 'truly appalling'.[661]

'These times have developed a want of a proper sense of propriety in them', concluded Ward. Difficult times such as these would, he said, bring out character. And the high character of Barings' accounts was showing. Gratified by the House's success in relation to competitors, Ward observed to his employers: 'It is remarked of Barings that they never ask remittances – while 999 [for example] always does. Your remittances are always up, and his are all backward.'[662] Barings' preference for a few select accounts and Ward's judgement paid off. They had received much criticism for publishing in newspapers the House requirements for doing business, but Ward indicated that by maintaining high expectations, Barings was able to gather clients of high calibre. Long-term quality seemed to recognize other long-term quality when the highly-successful merchant George Peabody transferred his account from Wiggin to Barings in April, and went on to build the firm that became the House of Morgan.[663]

Van Buren Holds Firm

Whether the '3Ws' should be helped or left to fade away was an open question among financial men in the early spring of 1837. It mattered little to those less involved with money and banking. All that many Americans saw around them suddenly were peculiar difficulties in the financial and commercial communities that had seemed to be doing well just a few months before. Those extended in their trade obligations – as some American Houses appeared to be – seemed genuinely suffering under Bank of England restrictions, and by the effects this tightening had on an American economy already made rigid by legislated specie requirements.

Populist, largely agrarian, sentiment swelled in these years among what Biddle called 'the less intelligent part of our population', who blamed foreign influences, in part, for the difficulties in American finances. The Jackson administration had claimed the danger of foreign influence as one reason for acting against the Second Bank of the United States and the removal of its deposits in 1833. Though a chimera, Jackson had nonetheless emphasized the voting power of British and Dutch shareholders of the Bank of the United States, and presented the issue almost in national security terms.[664] *The Times* saw this as an election tactic, typical of 'passionate, but unsophisticated American democracy'.[665] In the confused autumn season of 1833, amidst xenophobic rhetoric, Niles had remarked on the irony that the administration transferred government deposits from the Second Bank to other banks, one of which, the 'pet' Manhattan, was after all almost *entirely* foreign owned, and Niles pointed out that 'in this bank the foreign stockholders vote'![666]

In this political climate of spring 1837, it was not surprising that arrangements between the Bank of England, Biddle and the New York banks would draw some xenophobic suspicions. Cries of 'consolidation', so common in the American domestic sphere over the nature of government, were now couched in international terms about transatlantic financial deals among large bankers. For Barings, this was a refrain on the distasteful theme it had heard in the pressurized 1833–4 period. The partners now found the name of the firm in print again, and under unfavourable conditions. Jacksonian partisans in Congress and the press labelled Nicholas Biddle an agent of a foreign government, and representative of a new 'British Party' in the United States trying to take advantage of the present troubled times to gain influence. The so-called 'Barings and Biddle Bank' intended to strip gold from the United States, they said, and ship it to England and other 'foreign countries'. Such sentiments had in fact crystallized in the recently-emerged and nativist 'Loco-Foco' party.

Support of 'foreign interests' (American Houses like the '3Ws') by 'foreign funds' (Bank of England and Baring Brothers), even to the extent of causing suffering among foreign nationals (British people by raising Bank rates), supposedly was proof of the designs and determination of what Loco-Focos called the 'British Party'. They had caused this 'artificial panic' throughout the United States, and weakened the country through the reintroduction of 'spurious paper currency'.[667]

The Times found these arguments curious. How could Americans interpret tight restrictions on the commercial facilities of British merchants engaged in the American trade as supporting 'foreign interests'? The 'war on American commerce', of which the Bank of England was accused, in fact badly crimped British firms such as the '3Ws', as much as American merchants who did business with them. Threadneedle Street's directors simply expected United States commercial interests to fulfill contractual agreements made with British firms. *The Times* found little fault with the Bank of England if American merchants were unable to do so.[668]

The disruptive handiwork of the Loco-Foco's 'foreign conspirators' reached a climax in the first two weeks of May 1837. Despite efforts by British and American banking institutions to provide liquidity, the transatlantic financial system seized up amidst what was reported to be 'a total lack of confidence in the capacity of individuals to meet their engagements, and in the value of every species of property, whether merchandise or landed estate'.[669] New York State advertised a $500,000 loan at 6 per cent without receiving a single bid.[670] A last-minute petition, representing over 300 firms, requested President Van Buren to reform the Specie Circular. It claimed a six-month depreciation in New York real estate of $40 million; over 250 business failures since March; a $20 million decline in railroad and canal stocks; a decrease of 30 per cent in the value of warehouse merchandise; and at least 20,000 daily labourers discharged. The petition continued:

> We believe that it is unjust to attribute these evils to any excessive develop-
> ment of mercantile enterprise and that they really flow from that unwise
> system which aimed at the substitution of a metallic for a paper currency
> – the system which gave the first shock to the fabric of our commercial pros-
> perity by removing the public deposites from the United States bank, which
> weakened every part of the edifice by the destruction of that useful and effi-
> cient institution, and now threatens to crumble it into a mass of ruins under
> the operations of the specie circular, which withdrew the gold and silver of
> the country from the channels in which it could be profitably employed. We
> assert that the experiment has had a fair trial, and that disappointment and
> mischief are visible in all its results – that the promise of a regulated currency
> and equalized exchanges has been broken, the currency totally disordered,
> and internal exchanges almost entirely discontinued. We, therefore, make an
> earnest appeal to the executive, and ask whether it is not time to abandon the
> policy which is beggaring the people.[671]

On 4 May, Van Buren received the merchants' petition, but rejected a change of policy.

Banks now felt squeezed from two directions. Depositors in the United States had increased their withdrawals throughout April 'in a most alarming manner', and Europe demanded payment in specie for commercial commitments.[672] Under these twin pressures, Albert Gallatin negotiated a last-minute loan from the com-missioners of the Erie Canal Fund in Albany to ease the pressure on American banks' hard currency reserves, and to show Europe a good faith attempt at pay-ment of obligations. Before arrangements could be finalized, however, the large New York Dry Dock Bank collapsed on 8 May with discounts of $1.2 million on capital of only $200,000.[673] The situation was succinctly described by the finan-cial historian Bray Hammond: 'The British had stopped buying, had stopped lending, and expected payment of what was due them. The Americans found themselves unable to sell, unable to buy, unable to borrow, unable to pay.'[674]

On 11 May, Prime, Ward & King sent the news to Barings. 'The banks here have been unable to sustain themselves', Prime reported, 'and by a common move-ment yesterday were obliged to suspend specie payments'. The letter went on:

> The immediate cause of this movement was so great a want of confidence
> among the depositors that very large sums were withdrawn in coin during
> the last two days. [Had the demands come from note-holders only], no mis-
> chief would have resulted; but against a combined movement on the part of
> those using banks for depositing their usually large balances in these times of
> difficulty, there was no recourse but the one adopted.[675]

Thomas Ward agreed with Prime that Biddle could not long resist suspension, with specie of $1.5 million, deposits of $2 million, and circulation of $7 million. 'Great confusion must be for some time to come', the firm asserted. [676] The banks in New York City and Brooklyn suspended payment on 10 May; Albany, Hartford, Philadelphia, Providence and Baltimore suspended on 11 May; Mobile and Boston on 12 May; banks in New Orleans on 13 May, and so on. [677]

Some now compared United States currency to the French assignats of 1793 or the American continentals of an earlier day. Foreign exchange ranged wildly from 115–20 on sterling. Gold and silver were the only standards for circulating currency now, or personal cheques of well-known citizens. 'Businessmen suddenly have no difficulty getting money such as it is ... Gold and silver itself is now actively traded. Property has rebelled and is going around the world in search of its proper owner. The narrow limits of Wall Street are now extended from Maine to Louisiana. The whole nation is a stock exchange. We are in the beginning of a new age.' [678]

The suspension of payments by banks in the nineteenth century differed from bank suspensions in the twentieth. In the 1930s, for example, banks closed completely for a week, and many of them were declared bankrupt in the course of that week. In the nineteenth century, the banks refused to fulfil only one of their obligations – specie payouts – and continued to fulfil others. In fact, because they were no longer obligated to maintain the price of their notes and deposits in terms of gold and silver, banks would issue them more easily than before, with great effect on prices. In the middle of the 1830s, also, most states were in the process of adopting codes and procedures for bank suspensions, including penalties. [679]

Gloomy or not, the bank suspensions indicated an abnormal situation, a systemic imbalance of some kind that in Ward's view had to rebalance itself, not by legislation or regulation, but by time. [680] Ultimately, Ward saw good things because, like Bates, he saw a bright American future – made only brighter now for having suffered redemptive pain, and learned lessons. The suspensions brought relief to came to Samuel Jaudon, who craved the certainty of knowing outcomes – whether good or bad – so that planning could resume. The bank actions, he said, would have the effect of securing many of the debts which could not be collected with apprehension the rule, decisions always pending, and money locked up.

Philip Hone felt that the suspension of the banks was the climax of eight years of foolish Jacksonian policies; that the situation in the United States would in fact lead to the ruin of the British Houses that had done business in America for years, and in turn to those Americans who did business with them. He agreed the suspensions would perhaps restore a degree of confidence, liquidity and commercial activity but, he wondered, at what cost? The Jacksonian 'experiment' had made the United States a 'nation of Yankee swindlers' to England. 'The fever [of

1835–6] is broken', Hone wrote, 'but the patient is in a sort of syncope, exhausted by the violence of the disease and the severity of the remedies'.[681]

There is no question that the suspensions had an effect in England, since it was the eastern anchor of the transatlantic system. The confidence of European investors in American securities was badly shaken by the sudden – many thought cavalier – stoppage of specie payments. British manufacturers who had shipped large quantities of merchandise to the United States now saw little prospect of being paid in acceptable currency. William Brown, the representative of Brown Brothers & Company in Liverpool, reported that it 'was loaded up with bills on exports to America that had not been paid for'. Though now assisted in England by the talents of a brilliant young partner, Joseph Shipley of Wilmington, Delaware, there was every indication that the firm was on the brink of collapse. In all likelihood the American branches would be pulled under too.

In mid-May, Wildes & Company solicited additional Bank of England aid. On Tuesday, 30 May, Wilson and Wiggin followed Wildes' suit, explaining they could not meet their liabilities because they could find no discountable remittances, owing to the 'almost universal suspension of credit throughout the principal commercial cities of the United States'.[682] 'The Houses ['3Ws'] are technically solvent, but their assets are in the wrong place – the United States'. wrote the New York *Herald*. As gold was said to be in the wrong place as it piled up in the western states in 1836, so now commitments and assets of commercial firms were misplaced, piled up in the wrong country.[683]

As of 2 May, the Bank of England had extended aid to Wildes, Wilson and Wiggin to the end of the month, hoping for remittance payments, knowing the adverse commercial impact that the ruin of the American Houses would likely have on the American and British economies.[684] With the American bank suspensions, the situation changed. Particularly, *The Times* reported that it was the news of the Van Buren administration's unwillingness to yield over the Specie Circular and the New York merchants' petition that most affected the Bank directors. James Morrison wrote to his agent in Philadelphia that all that needed happen was for Biddle and Van Buren to work together.[685] But it was not to be. On Thursday, 1 June, the Bank of England decided, by the margin of a single vote, to render no further aid to the discredited firms.

Throughout the summer, few of the leading Anglo-American firms were able to avoid the dishonour of outstanding acceptances and repudiation thereby of their guarantees of customers' debts. Lizardi and Morrison Cryder were hit, not mortally, but they required help. The latter secured a loan from the Royal Bank of Scotland.[686] Brown Brothers was saved with a Bank accommodation of £2 million on good security. In a letter to the Bank of England, Joseph Shipley reported the firm's liabilities as equal to the partners' capital of $6,750,000. Shipley stressed that over two thirds of the firm's acceptances arose from financing American purchases of British manufactured goods. With Bank of England help, recorded losses for the year were put at $300,000.[687]

The '3Ws' never traded again. Despite a decline of liabilities from the first advances of aid in the autumn and winter of 1836, the Bank assessed the firms as too shaky for further extensions, and unlikely to receive payments from the United States in the reasonably near future. As of 1 June, liabilities of Wilson & Company were £1,256,000; Wiggin & Company, £908,000; for Wildes & Company, £620,000. These figures represented a decrease of only 2.6 per cent, an increase of 1 per cent, and a decrease of 6 per cent respectively – indicating barely any movement for better or for worse in the trade-remittance picture from the previous week.[688] The ratio of acceptances to partner capital of the '3Ws' at the end of 1836 is a stark picture and quite different from that of Barings, as indicated by Table 6.1.

Table 6.1: Capital and Acceptances of Leading Anglo-American Houses to 1836 (in millions of pounds). Source: Bank of England Archives, 'American Account 1836–42', ADV/B521. The figure for acceptances refers to 8 December 1836. The capital of Morrison Cryder is a contemporary estimate from *Circular to Bankers*, 10 December 1834. Lizardi, as can be seen, was much the smallest Anglo-American House. Data compiled by Chapman, *The Rise of Merchant Banking*, p. 41.

House	Capital	US Acceptances
Baring Brothers & Co.	0.78	0.39
Brown, Shipley & Co.	1.35	0.62
Wiggin & Co.	0.38	0.42
Wilson & Co.	0.30	0.72
Wildes & Co.	0.27	0.53
Morrison Cryder & Co.	1.00	0.56
Lizardi & Co.	–	0.15

Though these firms' commitments concentrated in the United States, Wilson, the largest of the three, had operations throughout the world. It was connected with Canada – holding the agency of several banks – as well as interests in Brazil and Denmark. It also operated in China and the East Indies through Jardine Matheson. Wildes and Wiggin were purer American firms.

Prices in foreign stock markets as reported in *The Times* went sideways to downwards over the bad news of the British failures and uncertainty for the future. One of the most international trading firms, Jardine Matheson, lost over £110,000 because of defaults of the '3Ws', and two other firms (Gowan & Marx and Bell & Grant).[689] Banks in both Lower and Upper Canada suspended, and at least one large hong merchant in Canton failed. Due to difficulties in the United States, Morrison Cryder had to curtail its business sharply at Canton until the spring of 1838. British difficulties thinned the field of westerners active in the eastern trades. Bank of the United States bills, once favourably received in Canton, were no longer issued after 1836. As British institutions pulled back, private American paper stood orphaned, and non-negotiable in Canton without backing of someone with an international reputation.[690]

After the United States banks suspended in May 1837, Joshua Bates confided to his diary that the failure of the American Houses would have less economic impact now than if they had failed in October 1836 – when Bates first recommended assistance by his letter to the Bank of England. Commitments of the American Houses, though not by any means eliminated, had been significantly reduced by May 1837. As pressure had increased on both sides of the Atlantic, Bates could watch with equanimity, since the firm was, in his words, 'pretty clear of everything'.[691] Indeed, the firm's margin of safety was such that they were able to help American merchants, and letters of gratitude to Barings for the firm's accommodation are common in the partners' correspondence. By contrast, as Bates discovered on his trip to France, Jacob Rothschild was less inclined to extend himself in any public way to help American merchants or brokers, even to the Josephs of New York.[692]

The outcome of the pressure might have been quite different without Barings' forethought and stability that seemed to calm markets. Timothy Wiggin himself wrote to Wells & Company in Paris that, had Baring Brothers not been 'above want there would have been no possibility of arranging the affairs of the discredited Houses, and that he must say B.B. & Co. have made a generous use of the advantage of their position'.[693] Since at least October 1836, Barings had been almost a peer of the Bank of England. Mildmay remained a director. Bates was chairman of the committee to investigate and supervise the affairs of Wilson & Company that resulted in the December aid package cobbled together by the six rival Houses. He was the advisor to the Bank on procedure having to do with the '3Ws'.[694]

Ward had conveyed for several years that one of his goals was to stand above the fray in the administration of the Barings account in the United States. In this way, the public would keep the House in the highest esteem. On his European tour in March, Bates found that 'people always excepted B.B.& Co. in speaking of the American Houses'. This was emphasized by the Bank of England in correspondence, and by their competitor Brown Brothers.[695] Indeed, James Morrison underscored in a June letter to his American agent at Philadelphia that Barings was exceptional in the outcome of the current difficulties:

> The last ten days has been like a horrid dream! All the W's are gone and with them many others, indeed, as far as respects the American Houses, one looks about to see who is left standing, not who has fallen, the list is a brief one now! We are almost alone. All who had not resources like myself or Barings are gone.[696]

Morrison found it miraculous, almost supernatural, that out of eight hundred Barings correspondents, to his knowledge only eleven had failed.[697]

Morrison's information was no doubt incomplete, but the magnitude of success holds. In the United States, Professor Hidy found only five Houses in New York listed with Barings as 'Suspended Debts', one in Mobile, nine in Boston, and one in Philadelphia. On these, potential losses totalled £37,410. Over half of this was on a single account, the cotton factor Samuel Comly, which was, over time, reduced. These loss totals compare to £120,000 lost by Lizardi on cotton alone, and £300,000 by Brown Brothers.[698] In sum, Barings' losses were phenomenally small. The cashier of the Bank of the United States, like James Morrison, was amazed:

> You seem to have fully anticipated the present posture of things – the alarm about the specie shipments – the almost total absence of Bills in which parties here could have confidence enough to be willing to buy them for remittances – and the necessity which would fall upon the Bank of the United States to come forward with an offer of its credit. It seems to me as if you had the gift of prophecy.[699]

When Alexander Baring hired the outsider Joshua Bates for the House in 1829, Bates wrote in his diary that he hoped 'that long years of experience in the international trade of the United States would yield something of worth'. He hoped the new opportunity as a Barings partner would give him the means and respectability to make a contribution.[700] Eight years after he was hired, the firm stood higher in the world of merchant banking than it would ever stand again. The unusual challenges of the 1830s in the United States not only furnished Bates with the chance to employ what he knew. The House avoided the misfortunes that befell others, avoided resort to the Bank of England, and emerged with enhanced prestige that served the firm well in the years ahead. In the disarray of the American bank suspensions in May 1837, Thomas Ward wrote to his employer, Baring Brothers & Company at Bishopsgate:

> There is a very great reliance on your House. It will be the sheet anchor of the commercial world.[701]

Aftermath

The financial panic of 1837 was not the end of trouble, but a dramatic beginning. There ensued a series of economic and credit problems between the United States and Great Britain that lasted until 1843 and involved the United States in what some consider the longest depression of the country's history. Barings would participate at key points all along the way.[702]

In the summer of 1837, Nicholas Biddle implemented an audacious plan to right the American financial Houses. In issuing post notes the April before, the

Bank of the United States and its associate banks, such as the Girard and the Manhattan, came into possession of mercantile notes representing loans made on cotton. To protect banks from losses it was necessary to check the fall in cotton prices, which had dropped 40 per cent in six months.[703] If the price of cotton could be stabilized – or, better yet, raised – not only would banks be strengthened, and the country recover more rapidly from crisis, it could generate hard currency in which American merchants could liquidate foreign debts. Biddle decided to advance funds to cotton planters so they would be able to hold their crops for a rise in price; meanwhile, in the summer and autumn of 1837, Biddle set up an establishment in Liverpool, to which the cotton could be consigned, under the direction of Samuel Jaudon. With its own organization, the Bank of the United States would move into the vacuum created by the weakened and moribund Anglo-American Houses, and control the American trade. Local 'corners' of raw materials had been practised long before Biddle's time. This arrangement amounted to pooling an entire export commodity on an international scale never before attempted. Its purpose was to manipulate foreign exchange to American advantage, and – because it counted on the revival of trade – it would benefit British interests as well.[704]

Not only was the plan audacious, it succeeded. Unfortunately, there began a new wave of speculation by southern banks that made large advances on cotton. Resumption of specie payments among eastern banks in the spring of 1838 led the public to believe that conditions were once again sound. In the main, by 1839, wholesale commodity prices had recovered to 1836–7 levels, except for cotton, which retraced only approximately 50 per cent of the 1837 decline.[705] With banks lending again, though, American merchants paid off their private obligations. Similarly optimistic, the states began to issue bonds for internal improvements and banking purposes. All these elements contributed to apparent recovery in the United States, and fostered a willingness by the foreign investors, mainly British and Dutch, to buy new state bonds.

Agents for the separate American states aggressively promoted the new offerings directly in Europe, with great assurances of adequate security. The promotions, including principal and interest conveniently paid in Amsterdam or London in guilders or pounds sterling, worked and the bonds were snapped up. The London press was split in 1838 and 1839 over the wisdom of such investments or the overall reliability of the United States considering recent difficulties. *The Times* was sceptical of the state loans since the internal improvements on which the loans depended would likely not be profitable or even cover costs for several years – especially in the newer, sparsely-populated states whose tax potential was limited. Foreign sentiment turned cautious-to-negative on American state loans.[706] Ominously, Egypt and India continued large shipments of cotton to Liverpool, over time frustrating the crucial cotton price recovery upon which the Biddle plan relied, and delaying balance of the American trade account.[707]

Figure 6.2: Nicholas Biddle (1786–1844) by Henry Inman (1801–46).
Oil on canvas (n.d.). Print Collection, New York Public Library.

The year 1839 saw a relapse of financial pressure and crisis in both England and the United States. Bullion in the Bank of England dipped from over $9 million to £2.5 million between January and October. Large payments to the Continent were needed for food because of poor British harvests.[708] From the European side, the demand for British textiles was weak because merchants deferred large purchases. They thought prices were too high and, besides, European spinners were now making their own products. In connection with high-priced cotton, Britain criticized the United States for keeping the price of cotton artificially elevated 'with waste-paper dollars'. As in late 1836, the Bank of England once again defended its reserves by raising its rates from 5 to 6 per cent. It also reinstated their direct action against credit to Americans in London, refusing to discount bills it considered to have arisen from cotton speculations.

The Bank of England's rate increases began to bite on commercial Houses in the United States, and failures were reported in Canton, Calcutta, Le Havre and Brussels. In Britain itself, conditions were bad. The year 1838 had been a time when investors bought American securities. They had also purchased securities in their own internal improvement companies of railways, which led to overbuilding. Depressed economic conditions in Britain generally led to a huge drop in demand from British cotton textile factories, which stopped buying American cotton.[709]

The Bank of the United States failed in the autumn of 1839, due to difficulties associated with state loans in Mississippi, Texas, Michigan, Illinois and Indiana as well as a drop in the cotton price, which by 1840 had fallen back to the low it had reached in 1837 before Biddle's operations began. Together with the clampdown of the Bank of England, the suspension of the Bank of the United States precipitated a financial panic which, unlike after May–June 1837, developed into an economic depression. The western and southern states were especially hard hit and their banks once again suspended, but even the wealthy states of Maryland and Pennsylvania had difficulty meeting payments. In the climate of depression, talk of repudiation of foreign debts by the states in the columns of the American press met with some approval, especially in Democratic party circles. It was offputting however to foreign investors, who now went from cautious to generally negative on American credit, and reduced the flow of capital to the American states to a trickle.

Financial historians claim that, however bold Biddle's plan was, it had neither domestic nor international support; that it only postponed to 1839 the kind of business readjustment which should have occurred in 1837, and perhaps made it worse. Barings too was skeptical, and cut its ties to Biddle over what appeared to be overly-risky operations.[710] The facilities supplied by the Bank had provided for the sale of American bonds, which generated large amounts of foreign exchange. Heavy importations of merchandise resumed as in 1835–6, and wages increased because of employment of men and resources on internal improvements. The United States became more heavily indebted to foreign investors than ever before in its history.[711] The only way the Biddle plan could have worked was if there occurred a recovery of trade in 1838–9. When there was not, the Bank could not hold back the world's market forces by countless extensions. The president of the Bank of Indiana commented on the country's condition:

> The depression which prevailed from 1837 to 1843 cannot be understood by any one who did not witness it. It was widespread and all-pervading. It affected all classes, but the greatest sufferers, next to the day laborers, were the farmers. Everything which the farmer had to sell – oats, hogs, chickens, wheat – had to be disposed of in barter or for currency at ruinous prices ... Day laborers were the greatest sufferers, for wages declined more than the

prices of the articles which they needed for their own support and the support of their families. Many were out of employment.[712]

Hugh McCulloch's words are supported by price behaviour in the United States after the 'Biddle recovery' of 1838, in Chart 6.1 below.

Chart 6.1: Unweighted Indices of Agricultural and Industrial Wholesale Commodity Prices (monthly), 1825–45. From Smith and Cole, *Fluctuations in American Business*, p. 65 (base: 1834–42 arithmetic scale). By permission of Harvard University Press.

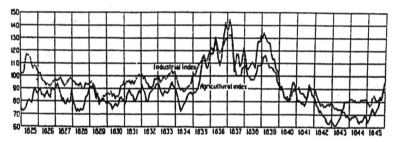

The Bank no doubt was a contributor to the problems McCulloch described. Just to what extent is not for this book to weigh. But the Bank's programme in the years to 1843 can be added to the European developments mentioned above, together with the disruptions of the Opium War and, in Anglo-American relations, the Caroline Incident and ongoing boundary disputes that erupted in 1838 over Maine and Canada.

It is pertinent to this study, however, to mention that Baring Brothers kept its hand in throughout – in an important advisory, official, almost detached, capacity. Its credit was high from its prescience on the events of 1837 and, though it did not recommit itself to the United States trade as it had in the years 1828–35, officials in the United States and Great Britain still valued Barings' advice and participation on American issues. Herein are five examples.

On the issue of American state bonds, Thomas Ward after 1840 personally coordinated what turned out to be a fairly involved marketing campaign, trying to convince individual states and American citizens, especially in the south, of the virtues of good credit and the short-sightedness of repudiation. Through Daniel Webster, Barings led the effort for the federal government to assume state debts contracted during the boom year of 1838 in order to increase their marketability in Europe. The proposal was published and, despite more castigation as part of a foreign plot, Barings repeatedly encouraged other bankers such as Hottinguer and Hope to support American enterprise, because of its long-term prospects, and overlook 'the indiscretions of democracy'.[713]

Barings also assisted in specie resumption in the United States in 1838. A year after the Bank of England's specie reserves had stabilized and increased, the Committee of Treasury evidently thought that the sooner American currency and banking were put in order, the better would be the chances of unlocking the assets of the discredited American Houses. In a secret operation, the Bank used Barings' agent in New York, Prime, Ward & King, to ferry to the United States 680,000 sovereigns in six ships, under Barings guarantee for arrival in late spring 1838. Prime would dispose of the gold and remit purchaser's bills to the Bank. Recognizing that British and American interests were interlocked, Thomas Tooke pronounced the Bank of England-Baring Brothers operation 'wise'.[714]

When difficulties from multiple directions began in 1839, Baring Brothers & Company once again offered assistance. Barings had stopped relations with the Bank of the United States in 1837 because it considered Biddle's cotton 'corner' too risky. However, in 1839 the Bank of the United States changed management, and Barings syndicated loans from Amsterdam, Paris and English financiers of more than £800,000 from June to December. Samuel Jaudon negotiated for the new president of the Bank, William Dunlap, who took over from Nicholas Biddle who had retired in March. Barings' effort put off the breakdown of the Anglo-American credit bridge for over a year before the state repudiations in 1841.

At home, Thomas Baring managed in July an important loan from the Bank of France to the Bank of England to ease the severe British specie drain that had started in January 1839.[715] Joshua Bates was proud of these two large operations in which the House played master intermediary. One has the impression that he felt the House was at the top of its game. 'The Bank applied to my House yesterday to assist them in negotiating a loan from the Bank of France', confided Bates to his diary. 'It cannot be denied that but for the exertions of my House the Bank of England would have stopped payment as also Jaudon, and bills on Peabody for a large amount would have gone back to America and the confusion would have been very great. I have now the satisfaction that by a bold action all these evils have been averted, and the Bank of England is now in a strong position'. Triumphantly, Bates concluded: 'It will be the Bank's own fault if it go wrong again'.[716]

Finally, and again triumphantly, Barings was able to assist in settling myriad political differences between England and the United States, and averted possible war. In 1842, Lord Ashburton and secretary of state Daniel Webster – the associate of Nicholas Biddle, Thomas Wren Ward and Joshua Bates, and general council to Barings in the United States – negotiated the Webster-Ashburton Treaty. It established the permanent border between Canada and the United States – in question since Ghent – from Maine and New Brunswick west to the Rocky Mountains. Without knowing it, Ashburton helped the future economy of the American middle west by drawing the boundary line between Lake Superior and the Lake of the Woods, giving the United States the magnificent iron-ore deposits of Minnesota, so vital to the America's industrial strength in later years.

All these things Barings could not have done if it had not survived the Panic of 1837, and emerged with enhanced prestige. No other House was equipped to render such solid assistance. A British House, Baring Brothers & Company worked consistently to strengthen the transatlantic economy and the long-term fortunes of the United States and Great Britain, and trade around the world.

CONCLUSION

Our states are very rich and very safe – debts are nothing to their resources.
Thomas Wren Ward[717]

More Reform

The results of events of the panic year 1837, and those of the depression years beyond, were numerous. A common conviction gripped both sides of the Atlantic that a better understanding of money and markets could help avoid panics and depressions in the future. Certainly the 1830s was already a period of financial reform in the United States and Great Britain, and the events after 1837 made the search for answers more pressing.

For Great Britain, the years 1836–41 saw several parliamentary banking inquiries, centred first in 1836–8 on the new joint-stock banks; and in 1840–1 on currency circulation and the Bank of England.[718] The investigations culminated in the important Bank Charter Act of 1844, which separated the Bank of England's note issue from its banking business. Note issue would remain tied to gold reserves except for a £14 million fiduciary issue. The Act required that the Bank publish weekly summaries of accounts. It also marked the decisive stage in the gradual elimination from circulation in England and Wales of all notes other than the Bank's own, since the Act limited the issue of notes by joint-stock banks. The Act proved too inelastic, however, as the 1847 and 1857 panics would show, and was suspended and reinstated several times.

In the United States, Congress repealed the Specie Circular in May 1838 over President Van Buren's protest. Many state banks designated as government depositories had failed, and were thereby discredited. In 1840–1, experiments in the disposition of government funds took the form of the Independent Treasury Bill and legislation for a third Bank of the United States. Neither initiative passed into functional law, and Congress readopted the former system of using state banks as government depositories. From the expiration of the charter of the Second Bank in 1836 to the National Banking Act in 1863, regulation of banking in the United

States was left to the private sector and the states. Congress finally established the Independent Treasury System in 1846, whereby government funds were held in several sub-treasuries around the country, which conducted business only in gold and silver. The Independent Treasury separated government finance from the rest of the American banking system.

The widespread failures of 1837–43, including the supposedly safe Safety Fund System in New York and the Suffolk System in New England, caused a general public revulsion against bankers and banking in the United States on the one hand. On the other hand, after the Bank of the United States there lingered a reticence to allow an explicit connection between the government and a large institution in the manner of a central bank. Thus, separate spheres of banking emerged in the aftermath of panic and depression: the Independent Treasury, and the so-called 'free banking system', requiring no legislative charter for establishment of a banking institution – only capital enough to purchase government bonds against which to issue notes as currency.

Who to Blame; Well-Informed People Make Poor Decisions; Good Timing

Who or what was to blame for the 1837 panic? The answers are many. *The Times*, the *Edinburgh Review* and Thomas Wren Ward, among others, blamed the Bank of England for acting late, clumsily and too severely. Others assigned responsibility to the discounters ('the money lenders') for overextending. On the American side, many blamed Andrew Jackson for the disruptions to the economy and financial system in his wrangle with Nicholas Biddle. The Bank of England blamed too-liberal credit extensions of the American Houses and the intransigence of Van Buren over repeal of the Specie Circular. *Hunt's Merchants' Magazine* in 1844 suggested dual responsibility for the 'chain of indebtedness', which it said was fed by Britain, encouraged by America, and 'was as foolish as it was fragile'.[719]

Most economic historians writing years later agree that the root of the panic was a dramatic shift of specie flows, having to do with changes in international trade and finance roughly in the decade after 1825.[720] As we have seen, specie was a common topic of discussion, but contemporaries, including Barings, did not consider this international factor as an immediate cause of difficulties nor did they cite it as a reason for decisions made or initiatives undertaken.

In March 1837 the Mexican government under Santa Ana indeed reformed its currency to avoid counterfeiting, and reduced the amount of Mexican silver flowing into the traditional specie entrepôt of New Orleans. This same month, the American panic began with the first major cotton House failures ('displacements') in New Orleans. Besides the dynamics of specie flows, cotton played a large role in triggering the end of the American upswing. Since 1833, large overstocks in Liverpool from exuberant American exports, and cotton from the new non-American sources of India and Egypt, were terribly vulnerable to collapse when confidence ran out in late April and May (see Table 4.5). The fear of reduced bank liquidity was based on a cessation of Mexican silver, liquidity problems already present from the Specie Circular, Bank of England restrictions on British credit and the realization of large overstocks in the chief commodity upon which the Anglo-American credit bridge mainly rested – cotton. These were the essentials of the Panic of 1837.

Difficulty in finding parties to blame for what happened in the 1830s, or even sorting through different explanations for the same event, leads us to the idea that people quite knowledgeable and close to the best information can be wrong in their judgements and decisions. Ward himself was increasingly muddled, even contradictory, in his correspondence to London. Apart from this, he often was simply wrong in his assessments. His prognosis for the safety of the '3Ws' in 1836 was incorrect. He believed that high rates for money in late 1836 would continue to bind investors to American projects and securities, but the London headquarters was sceptical. His prediction of recovery in the cotton market in January 1837 proved premature, and would have been disastrous had the House not forbidden purchases except at much lower prices. In the longer run, Ward's confidence in 1835 that the individual American states would have little trouble paying their debts was shown to be much too optimistic. The state defaults in fact were legion. They led to severe international obloquy for the United States and, as we have seen, entailed a marketing campaign that Ward himself would coordinate (see Chapter 6, 'Aftermath').

Other well-informed persons proved equally fallible as Ward. In March, before the suspension, the president of the large Phoenix Bank in New York City told Bates in Paris he believed Americans would 'be able to pay their debts promptly and there was nothing to fear'.[721] Even the pre-eminent bankers of Europe were capable of errors. When the relationship between Barings and the Jackson administration broke down over the Bank of the United States, Rothschilds hurried to offer its services as a way to enter the American market. It seemed to James, brother of the famous Nathan, that a Franco-American financial marriage was an ideal one. Those associated with the government and the Bank of the United States were, he said, 'the wealthiest people in America' and 'no less solid' than the Bank of France. According to a recent historian of House of Rothschilds, James began to imagine 'flooding the American market' with his Spanish mercury 'so that in six months we will be masters of the market'. At first, the French-American partnership went well. Rothschilds found itself receiving large quantities of American bonds from all over the United States and securities for new banking and canal companies. By late 1839, however, James and his nephews were beginning to discern why long-experienced Barings had cut back in the United States when they had. In addition to losing on sums advanced to such bankers as J. L. and S. I. Joseph in the panic of 1836–7, Rothschild & Company became enmeshed with the defaults of several American states during the depression in the early 1840s.[722]

As far as Barings' general decision-making accuracy, it appears the firm did not have to be overly precise, since the partners seem to have followed what we have called the idea of 'changing before you have to'. According to the evidence, the House's timing was not quite right. It curtailed commitments in the United States too soon. It was, strictly speaking, too cautious. After all, Barings' pullback in the last quarter of 1835 (prior to the New York fire) meant the firm missed the profits of 1836. They also avoided the downdraught of 1837.

It is interesting to relate Barings' actions to the business patterns developed by economic historians for the United States and Great Britain over the time span of this book. As stated in the Introduction, the purpose of this study was to present what the firm *believed was happening*; and how these beliefs effected what the firm did and when. The study has not sought to fit Barings' behaviour to a preconceived pattern. It has started from the periodical sources and company archives of the period. The author, nevertheless, considers that it may be of some use to present a very rough recapitulation of this book in the form of charts, with Barings' actions flagged (see Charts 7.1 and 7.2).

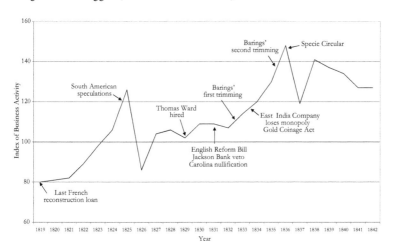

Chart 7.1: British Business Cycle Pattern, 1819–42. Source: index data in Gayer et al., *The Growth and Fluctuation*, vol. 1, pp. 354–6.[723]

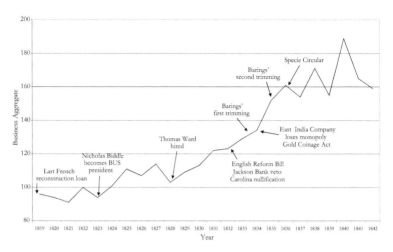

Chart 7.2: American Business Cycle Pattern, 1819–42. Source: an unweighted index of the author's construction made up of: (1) wholesale commodity prices from Smith and Cole, *Fluctuations in American Business*, p. 158; (2) cotton production, Rostow, *World Economy*, pp. 132–3; (3) gross national product, Berry, *Production and Population*, pp. 25–6; (4) bank, insurance, railroad share index, Smith and Cole, *Fluctuations in American Business*, pp. 174, 183; (5) volume export index, North, *Economic Growth*, p. 241. This index is expressed in terms of relatives of the period 1821–5.

Accompanying the charts is a table compiled from Willard Thorp's *Business Annals* (see Table 7.1). It provides Thorp's short-hand characterizations of economic conditions in United States and Great Britain for each year of our study, and accords usually with trends depicted in Charts 7.1 and 7.2. Economic patterns presented in academic sources, very much after the fact, confirm Barings' uncanny good judgement – indeed prescience – throughout the period under review.

Table 7.1: General Business Conditions in Great Britain and the United States, 1819–43. Source: Thorp, *Business Annals*, pp. 118–23, 156–61.

Year	Great Britain	United States
1819	Recession; depression	Severe depression; financial panic
1820	Depression; slight revival	Depression
1821	Slow revival	Depression; revival
1822	Revival; prosperity	Revival; mild recession
1823	Prosperity	Revival
1824	Prosperity	Prosperity
1825	Prosperity; recession; panic	Prosperity; panic; recession
1826	Depression	Depression; revival
1827	Revival	Moderate revival
1828	Prosperity	Prosperity; recession
1829	Recession; depression	Depression; revival
1830	Depression; revival	Moderate prosperity
1831	Recession; depression	Prosperity
1832	Depression	Moderate prosperity

Year	Great Britain	United States
1833	Revival	Prosperity
1834	Prosperity	Mild depression; revival
1835	Prosperity	Revival; properity
1836	Prosperity; financial panic	Prosperity
1837	Recession; panic; depression	Prosperity; panic; recession; depression
1838	Depression	Depression; revival
1839	Depression	Revival; panic; recession
1840	Depression	Depression
1841	Depression	Depression
1842	Depression	Depression
1843	Depression; revival	Depression; revival

Competitors' Risky Behaviour; Panic's Effect on Barings

Post-facto explanations for the American Houses' risky behaviour in the United States are numerous in the sources, but none very precise. Nevertheless, it is useful to look at three. The first explanation comes from Thomas Ward as he saw Houses extending beyond what he thought advisable. This had to do with the government distribution of the surplus to the states. The general thinking was that these payments would act as a prop to an overextended economy, acting as a rate cut, in present Federal Reserve parlance, to provide important liquidity in the face of the economic 'head wind' of the Specie Circular. Markets anticipated this boost, and may have been a reason merchant bankers advanced to firms based on a projected 17-cent cotton price such as the one Ward cited to London in the middle of 1836 (see Chapter 5).[724]

The second explanation for risky behaviour comes from Jonathan Goodhue, and may be called 'artificial confidence'. On the last day of May 1836, Goodhue wrote a letter to Joshua Bates in which he expressed the conviction that all prices, including real estate, 'must give way'. He found, though, that the relatively shallow panic of 1833–4 may have given the country confidence that it could survive economic surges and instability, and had instilled a certain tone of fearlessness in American enterprise.[725] Even before Goodhue's observation, Ward had noticed what he considered the lack of reality around him. He described a sort of somnambulism in members of the business community – hypnotized by what appeared to be a healthy economy and the wealth, bubble or not, accumulating around them. Perhaps this was why Ward commented that the '3Ws' were paying so little attention to the French indemnity question that he considered so important to long-term planning. Maybe it is the reason for Goodhue himself being so shocked by the very suddenness of the May 1837 collapse. Maybe it is an explanation why the panic blindsided even the best-informed and most experienced businessmen.[726]

A third explanation of behaviour is that competitors had to overextend aggressively in order to grab share from Barings. This was especially the case in the

United States where Barings had such a lead because of its long-term presence. As we have seen, Bates alluded to the envy excited among other firms, and considered it an inevitable by-product of success. British merchant enthusiasm for the American market came partly from the United States' growth rate as an emerging market, and partly from Barings' success, which others desired in vain to emulate. 'We aim', said Brown Brothers & Company, 'and with perfect right – at a rank & position equal to Barings, but it is impossible that we can maintain it if we are to be in the discount market week by week ... whereas they never discount & are known to have always large sums lying at call'.[727] The struggle by competitors takes us to a further set of issues related to business style, the 'lender of last resort' and 'moral hazard'.

The American Houses in this book did not wish to borrow, but in order to increase share they had to take risks, and so reduced their liquidity by leveraging their acceptances. This approach worked to gain clients generally in the United States, as well as at the specific expense of Barings. Quite early in 1837, Thomas Ward and others wished for overextended and irresponsible firms to be liquidated, eliminated, purged. The Court of the Bank of England and Joshua Bates were sympathetic to this draconian approach, but were less quick to act, fearing broad economic damage.

By rendering aid in late winter 1837, the Bank delayed what turned out to be the inevitable for some merchant banks. Here we reiterate that Barings was the only large Anglo-American merchant bank to go through the turbulence of 1836 and 1837 without Bank of England assistance. It is more important to emphasize, however, that Brown Brothers & Company lived to fight another day, despite taking risks that required bailing out. Brown Brothers captured customers long term in the United States, whereas Barings left the field in the name of risk avoidance, required no aid, and was, in terms of customers, penalized for prudence and good judgement – as Ward pointed out (see Chapter 6).

But this point raises a still more important issue related to business style, and long-term banking success in the American market. Barings and their agents granted credits only to merchants who gave them all their business – men of large means and established credit to whom they could, in most cases, safely entrust the consignment of goods shipped under credits to the merchants themselves. Knowing a relatively few clients had two crucial effects. Barings could issue more uncovered credits comfortably and thereby not offend a clientele accustomed to highly-personalized service. Familiarity usually carried with it safety, but its risk lay in the fact that one failure could have large results. Here is perhaps the explanation for Barings' obsession with liquidity: it was a kind of hedge that allowed Barings to grant uncovered credits for prestigious customers.

By contrast, Brown Brothers' policy involved opening numerous small credits 'with men judged of ability and integrity'. This method was labour-intensive and entailed considerable risk without proper due diligence, because not all

these numerous accounts could be known as well as Barings knew theirs. Brown
Brothers likened issuing credits more to the insurance business, where the purpose was to limit the exposure of any single account.[728]

Of the two approaches, Brown Brothers' proved the more fruitful and appro-
priate method in the United States over the longer run. Compared to Brown
Brothers, the Barings style missed the middle-class businessmen who aspired to
grow prosperous. Barings were less willing to entertain the smaller risky accounts
that contained great danger, but a chance for great gain as well. The very growth
of the United States was based on risk and uncertainty – as many developing
markets are – as well as a fierce entrepreneurism almost defined by stretching
convention and precedent. These were characteristics of Jacksonian America, and
were less than attractive to Bates or Ward.

Barings found strength in the proven, the better-known, the durable and
the less-risky. These preferences worked superbly well for getting the firm safely
through the problems of the Jacksonian 1830s. Such stalwart caution, however,
turned out to be a weakness in the long term in the American market, which
Barings gave up to firms like Brown Brothers and, later, George Peabody and the
Morgans. If it was the case, as it appears, that a major reason for Barings' withdrawal in the 1830s was 'vulgar American democracy', then it was a pull out with
serious long-term consequences since American democracy did not go away.[729]

Joshua Bates made little attempt to retake the American acceptance business
after the Panic of 1837, and after Barings' first trimming in 1834. To the contrary,
by the early 1840s, he refused business having to do with the United States, even
though he could apparently command good terms. In Bates's view, 'competition
for business was never less' – with all British firms 'in London and at Liverpool
sadly crippled'.[730] Bates toured the American Union in the summer of 1841 for
the first time in thirteen years, and was jolted by what he saw – mortified by
American states defaulting on debts in violation of what he considered sacred
contracts, and the 'unending slanderous remarks' about foreign capital. 'The general state of things in the United States appears to be as near chaos as possible',
he reported to Ward from London on the first day of August 1842. 'Everything
American is in disgrace here. I have not broached this to my partners, but I have
a great desire to avoid exposure for long periods in the United States.' Bates went
on to assure Ward that the House was 'admirably mounted' to prosper throughout the world in lieu of the American market.[731] This the House did after 1837
– the same year Victoria ascended the throne as Queen, and Britain embarked on
building an empire that spanned the globe.

Barings never returned to the United States with the energy or intent that it
had up to the Panic. The partners did come back enthusiastically to the booming
America of the 1850s, but the market was by then more fragmented. Barings was
matched increasingly by American-born players who exhibited less aversion to
'American democracy' and, as Americans, were more easily 'on the spot' in the

United States than a British bank could ever be. This trend likely was inevitable as American financial institutions matured, and more American players entered the market, but was affected somewhat in 1837 by the Bank of England's not allowing Brown Brothers to fail. Thomas Ward believed Threadneedle Street acted improperly.[732] By its support of Brown Brothers, the Bank essentially rewarded Barings' most serious competitor in the United States for what it considered a lack of prudence. Instead of disappearing like the '3Ws', Brown Brothers became the dominant merchant bank in the United States from the 1840s to the 1880s. Brown Brothers probably would have made Barings' task of cracking the American market much more difficult if it had attempted a full-fledged return, and this partially explains Barings' link-up with Kidder Peabody of Boston in the late 1880s.[733]

It appears, then, that Barings' well-timed judgement to withdraw and survive before 1837, ironically, spelled its ultimate demise in the American market. Due in part to what we would likely refer to today as a variant of 'moral hazard', Brown Brothers inherited Barings' mantle of dominance in the United States. This book has made the point that loss of dominance would probably have occurred as the American financial system matured, and as the United States became increasingly self-sufficient in its capital needs. To assert, in Professor Hidy's phrase, that Barings simply 'renounced predominance' in 1834 is precisely to miss the point of this maturing United States economy and financial infrastructure, or assumes that any single firm, however determined, could lay claim to what became a truly immense American financial landscape.

It is in relation to issues of dominance and influence that the present author has used the phrase Baring's 'American moment'. It appears that one reason that Barings held the sway that it did in the United States was because it established its presence and good name before others did. We discussed in Chapter 1 how the firm was active with American merchants and institutions practically before the United States was a country. The French reconstruction loans boosted Barings' contacts, prestige and capital further. In these respects, Barings' head start in the American marketplace resembles what is referred to today as an 'early adopter'. It accrued to itself the advantages and privileges of being the only firm of size – American or British – on the United States scene for over twenty-five years if we count from 1800. Only in the late 1820s did other firms seriously attemp to challenge and mimic Barings' success. Only with great resolve could the firm have maintained its position, and even then it is doubtful. John D. Rockefeller's early lead in American petroleum refining appeared unassailable in the 1890s until the Texas discoveries. In the time of Rockefeller, as in that of Barings, the United States grew faster and in more directions than any firm's capability to manage or control. Indeed, Barings voluntarily, and for its own reasons, pulled back from the United States. Its diminution over time, as Barings gave way to Brown Brothers, and Brown Brothers to J. P. Morgan, was perhaps inevitable. Barings' moment in the American sun, however impressive, was temporary.

Before connecting the triumphant 1830s to two less triumphant episodes of Barings' history as a firm, the author offers one final and speculative thought on the idea of the 'American moment'.

Barings' connection to the United States in the 1830s made sense. Francis Baring had established trade contacts as early as the 1770s. Ashburton married into Philadelphia society during his first American tour, had purchased extensive real estate for the House, and made numerous contacts at the highest levels of American business and politics. Joshua Bates was an American and hired Americans: Thomas Ward in Boston for the United States, Samuel Gair to supervise the crucial post of Liverpool. Barings was indeed an 'early adopter' as we have said, but the firm's commitment to the United States may have served another purpose.

The American commitment may have been a retreat of sorts in the face of competition on the Continent from Rothschilds, whose name laces these pages. The decision to become an American House as it fully did in 1828 may have been an example of leading from weakness more than from strength. It made sense for the British government to give the lead manager position for reconstruction loans to a British House after the war. The House of Rothschilds was associated with France and, in 1815, the world stood fatigued of things French. Rothschilds had no choice but to lie low, and defer to the victor's choice: Barings. But, despite the huge French loans pumping up Barings' finances and prestige, Rothschilds still outgunned and outclassed Barings financially (Chapter 1) as early as the 1820s, and it appears that Barings needed the French loans more than Rothschilds did.

In 1825, the Bank of England tapped Rothschilds, not Barings, for assistance. In 1836–9, the Bank of England indeed used Barings for counsel and Bank of France bridge loans, but by this time the principle English Rothschilds author of the 1825 loan, Nathan ('Natty'), was dead. As we have seen, Rothschilds did not establish a beachhead in the United States until comparatively late, perhaps because they wanted to see how others fared. Barings' experience in the United States appears to have been propelled by the slightly artificial momentum built up from the French wars.

In sum, and with little but circumstantial evidence, Barings may have committed as it did to the United States for what can be termed 'negative reasons'. Its biggest rival, Rothschilds, was not there yet. Negative or not, as these events have shown, from the moment the House operated in the United States to 1836, it acquitted itself brilliantly.

EPILOGUE: ARGENTINA AND SINGAPORE (1890, 1995)

> The affair shows how mistaken management was to give too much respon-
> sibility to a clerk.
>
> Peter Baring, 1995, on Barings' bankruptcy[734]

The performance of Barings was creditable in the Panic of 1837, yet there were two terrible lapses by the bank in later years worth reviewing briefly that may add clarity to the main story of this essay. The gulf between 1837 and later years seems prima facie so wide, the times so changed, and the problems so different, as to defeat comparison. However, the characteristics of Barings' proud conservatism revealed in the 1830s resonated in later years to monumental effect. Argentina was the first area of difficulty. Singapore was the second. The story of each is first sketched, results presented, and comparisons drawn where possible to the 1830s.

Argentina: 1890

In the 1880s, Great Britain's hot money was going to Latin America, specifically Argentina. First for the wool trade on the Pampas, then for various infrastructure projects such as railroads and electricity, British investment was worth about £25 million by 1880. In 1885 it stood at £45 million; by 1890 £150 million.[735] After some years away, Barings returned to the region in the late 1850s, and by the 1880s was keenly interested in Argentina. It maintained a correspondent relationship with a well-established Buenos Aires trading House, S. B. Hale & Company.

The director of Hale & Company was an American named C. H. Sanford who, in 1888, solicited Barings' senior partner, Lord Revelstoke (Edward Baring) to share a concession granted to Hale from the President of Argentina for harbours, docks, railways and other public works in the municipality of Buenos Aires. Hale & Company paid $21 million for the concession, for which it received 10 mil-

191

lion shares and debentures in the newly-formed Buenos Aires Water Supply &
Drainage Company for sale to the public.

Two years before Sanford's solicitation, Baring Brothers & Company had
completed a highly-successful flotation of shares in the century-old distilled
spirits concern of Guinness & Company. Revelstoke expressed no special confidence in Sanford, but his enthusiasm for the Guinness shares apparently buoyed
Revelstoke beyond reason. With the guarantee from the Argentine government,
the profits from Guinness seemed reproducible in South America – and anyway,
if recent history were an indication, public confidence in Barings was such that
the firm's name on a share issue was enough to guarantee its sale.

But, as Barings had run into a sluggish reception for the bonds of the Union
Bank of Louisiana in 1832, so in November 1888 the first *tranche* offering of the
Buenos Aires Water Supply & Drainage Company was unfavourably received.
Much of Barings' capital was locked up elsewhere in South America, and the £2
million share issue in the Water Supply Company threatened to overextend the
firm badly. Moreover, Revelstoke had not syndicated the offering. That is to say,
Barings did not share the risks by underwriting them with other Houses – something Barings had done since the French reconstruction loans, and a practice
common for financing sedentary and slow-to-profit utilities.[736]

In 1889 Revelstoke dispatched his son, John Baring, to Argentina to investigate. John confirmed a project of vast proportions on the scale of the Canadian
Grand Trunk Railway which also had been government-connected, and in which
Barings had mired itself for many unprofitable years. He also described a deteriorating political situation, though he assured his father valiantly that there was
no chance of default on the utility bonds. Soon this information proved of little
comfort or accuracy. The political condition of the country went to pieces in late
1889, compounding an already dubious economic situation, and no British investor would touch Argentine assets.

At the start of 1890, Barings' acceptances were £15 million on capital of £2.25
million, with £1 million in real estate. Apart from unsold securities, this acceptances level of 6.5 times partners' capital was considered unsafe at the time, and
other firms such as Schroeders and Kleinworts were criticized for similar ratios.
Committed to paying bills on contracts in other parts of the world amounting
to millions of pounds, Barings' dead money on Argentine shares that would not
move on the London exchange spelled bankruptcy.[737] The partners realized what
they had done, and stood aghast, in the early autumn of 1890. In Philip Ziegler's
words, the firm gave the impression 'of a doomed passivity, the resignation of
men who see an avalanche about to descend upon them but can do nothing to
save themselves'.[738]

For London the stakes were quite high: its pre-eminent bank – the 'keystone of
English commercial credit' – imperilled.[739] Barings' bills, like parts of the British
Empire, were scattered throughout the world. Because of high stakes, Barings

was rescued in November 1890 by a consortium organized by the governor of the Bank of England, William Lidderdale, and a somewhat reluctant chancellor of the Exchequer, George Goschen, in the government of Lord Salisbury. With the government committed, Rothschilds joined in, the rest of the City followed (private and joint stock), and a fund amounting to £17.3 million – more than £1 billion today – met Barings' commitments. Ironically for our story, the firm of Brown, Shipley contributed to the rescue pool and its parent, Brown Brothers in Baltimore, wrote: 'It is frightful to think what might have been the consequences if Barings had not been carried through'.[740]

The cause of what became known in London newspapers as the 'Baring smash' was an unfortunate set of events in Argentina, but also something hauntingly similar to what would befall Barings again a century later. William Lidderdale in 1891 found trouble with Barings brewing for a long time, with Argentina a last straw of sorts. Barings would have run into trouble anyway, he said, 'because the business was entirely managed by Revelstoke and he did not seem the least to know how he stood. It was haphazard management, certain to bring any firm to grief'.[741] With £15 million worth of Barings foreign bills, to say nothing of its outstanding loan calls in the domestic British economy, the variety of banks that contributed to save Barings did so, in large part, to save the general health of their own businesses.

Liquidation of the old firm took three years, and by the turn of the twentieth century there were no visible signs of injury. But, as reputation takes much time to build up, so memories lingered. Barings suffered a severe diminution in stature, and the air of invincibility which had been theirs since Napoleon was forever broken. In 1890 Barings sold equity in itself to fellow bankers to raise liquidity, but bought these stakes back to become once again its own master in 1895. As for the Bank of England, the crisis once and for all established the institution as the country's lender of last resort.[742]

In 1897, the first Lord Revelstoke died. His son, John Baring, seems to have absorbed the shock that humbled his father's House. He assumed leadership and established the firm as a profitable but plodding organization until 1929. Upon his death, *The Times* recalled that, for many years after his assuming control, he refused to take part in certain enterprises. He was never sure if the firm had recovered enough in the eyes of the City and the world. Until he was, the second Lord Revelstoke declared that he would 'take no risks'.[743]

Singapore: 1995

One hundred years after Argentina, the firm maintained its risk-averse posture under the conservative leadership of Peter Baring, nephew of John. In the bullish 1980s and 1990s the City changed from its gentle buttoned-up style to the more swashbuckling approach of the Americans who, in the form of large firms such as Goldman Sachs, Morgan Stanley and Bankers Trust, were leading the City's growth. No longer was the British banker indiscreet to talk about making money. It was assumed this was the very reason for the banker's job.

Barings was now a boutique – however distinguished – among larger public institutions. It had opted not to compete with the large banks which offered clients a full range of financial services. It also did not participate in the clamour of overpriced takeovers and mergers that took place after the 'Big Bang' in 1985 which deregulated much of British finance and promised to put London on par with New York and Tokyo for prominence in the world of money. Barings continued a niche business counselling brokers and banks, treasury trading operations and asset management.[744]

Amidst general abstention, Barings in 1984 bought a modest but highly-profitable team of researchers and dealers specializing in Asian securities from the stockbrokers Henderson Crosthwaite. Led by Christopher Heath, this team became the core of Baring Securities, which by 1989 had offices throughout the world and was contributing half of Barings group profits of nearly £70 million.[745]

The fall of the Japanese stock market in January 1990, however, made things difficult for Baring Securities. Profits became less regular and large, and some years experienced losses. Friction between the headstrong Heath and Barings chairman Andrew Tuckey (Peter Baring was chairman of the holding company, Barings, Plc.) over funding for Baring Securities and whether trading at the brokerage was a conventional agency commission or a proprietary one led to the firing of Heath in March 1993. The banker Tuckey then folded Baring Securities into Baring Brothers & Company to form a new business called Barings Investment Bank. Cleared by the Bank of England, Tuckey hoped the combination of the volatile bonus-driven brokerage and the more regular fee-based bank would provide smoother, yet higher, overall earnings for the holding company than if each remained separate. The problem was that the combined company of May 1993 now had a common capitalization, whereas the former architecture of the firm kept the securities subsidiary separate from its parent, and funded by the parent up to strict limits. With consolidation, risks and profits mingled, and 230-year old Barings entered uncharted waters in terms of personnel culture clashes between bank and brokerage, investment instruments and battles with competitors with deeper pockets and more experience.

These developments established the background for the series of troubling events that followed. A year before Heath's departure, July 1992, Baring Securities sent a young English trader named Nicholas Leeson to their newly-opened Singapore subsidiary, Baring Futures (Singapore), Ltd. Hired the same year as Peter Baring became group chairman, Leeson had cut his teeth at Coutts & Company, moved to Morgan Stanley and then landed work as a clerk at

Barings' derivatives-settlements desk in London in 1989. Leeson had an unusual assignment in Singapore: he was asked to head the office's settlement operations and be, in addition, the Baring Futures' floor manager on SIMEX (Singapore International Monetary Exchange). This arrangement was extraordinary since the two tasks were, as a rule, separate. The function of traders was to make money; the function of settlements employees to see that traders stayed honest and within the bounds of accepted firm and Exchange practice. Irregularities began immediately upon Leeson's Singapore arrival; with each one, a chance to arrest the slide towards disaster was missed.

Leeson manipulated Barings' funds to finance his own trading through bypassing the company's reporting system by way of a dummy account. His trades were in complex proprietary financial instruments known as derivatives – specifically options and futures. Originally developed to reduce risk in commodity markets in the nineteenth century, in the late twentieth century derivatives represented investment vehicles in their own right. Heath had been a pioneer in options in Japan, and Barings had benefited smartly. Here was where the bankers split from the brokers by culture. Bank personnel admitted generally – and took a certain haughty pride at doing so – that they did not understand these modern financial tools. Perhaps this applied most to Peter Baring, who had achieved the chairmanship over his more progressive brother, Nicholas, precisely because he was more risk averse. The supervisor for securities at the Bank of England admitted that he also did not understand Barings' securities business. Even Leeson's boss in Singapore sent out from London, Simon Jones, could not explain the complexities of derivatives trading.[746]

Dazzling, almost unbelievable, profits rolled in from the Far East after Leeson's arrival and numbed all concerns. Aided by the Singapore operations, group profits at the beginning of 1995 totalled £100 million, a record for the firm. But on 23 February 1995, Baring Brothers – the oldest merchant bank in the City of London – collapsed under £869 million of accumulated losses from option trades on the Nikkei 225 index. How could this happen? The two general causes were the recklessness of Leeson's fraud and the impotence of Barings' management. According to accounts by Stephen Fay and the *Financial Times* team of John Gapper and Nicholas Denton, explanations ran deeper, and are surveyed below. They have to do with three elements that drive most financial markets: panic, ignorance and greed.

When the London investigating team began to uncover the extent of damage Leeson had done over three years in Singapore, panic was the initial reaction at Barings' headquarters at 8 Bishopsgate. The final totals came after a week of digging, but the early liability estimates of £400 million made clear that obligations on derivative contracts exceeded Baring capital. An earlier case of panic in 1993 set the stage for this later fatal one, however.

Heath's Baring Securities unit sustained several losing years as it adjusted to changing conditions in Asia at the end of the Japanese bull market. Losses are often the prelude to management shake-ups and lay-offs in any organization. For Barings, however, losses were the pretext for a take-over by the bankers who, according to writer Stephen Fay, 'dreamed of a securities business that was risk-averse'.[747] Andrew Tuckey and Peter Baring found Heath's broker-salesman style anathema and grating (as Thomas Wren Ward had found Nathaniel Prime's), but did not grasp that the style itself had much to do with making money. Instead, the brokerage arm was gutted of Heath and his top men. Brokerage lost its autonomy under the consolidated structure, and became administered from London by new people in the areas of settlement and treasury all headed up by a specialist, not of the brokerage culture, but in banking and corporate finance, Peter Norris.

The reorganization of 1993 shook Barings. The firm took a volatile culture of derivatives trading into its core that it neither understood nor respected but, by the superior earnings that this alien business produced, Barings hoped it could become a contender against its larger American competitors. Barings' banking-oriented management acted precipitously in 1993 to tame what it viewed as Heath's 'reckless' brokerage after it had a few sub-par years. It did not change management of the brokerage arm or attempt to restructure operations. Instead, London combined brokerage and banking to reduce overall volatility to the parent company and, in so doing, brought into its fold that which would undo the whole enterprise.

Information is the kernel of modern securities markets and competent decision-making at any time. Besides precipitate action towards the brokerage arm, managerial ignorance found Barings ill-equipped to compete, prosper, or even survive. Despite the firm's historical commitment to steadiness and low-risk banking, the consolidated organization did not take risk-management seriously even though numerous members of the firm in executive positions professed to less-than-intimate knowledge of the securities business. They thought their eastern operations risk-free in fact – a grinding arbitrage of off-setting positions set up between Osaka and Singapore. In reality, by January 1994, their floor manager and settlements director, Nick Leeson, had booked no fewer than 50,000 futures and options in the Nikkei 225 through a dummy account. This occurred before Leeson was given the title of proprietary trader. Moreover, he never received clearance to trade options anyway.[748]

Barings relied on branch offices for information about what was going on in its trading operations. Practices were not standardized, and offices had different conventions depending on the preferences of branch managements. Several incidents occurred before the catastrophe that indicated a need for closer monitoring of settlements: one in Mexico City and one having to do with the firm's risky but potentially profitable clearings of transactions involving Latin American brokers and Wall Street securities firms. There occurred a settlements mess so serious with the latter transactions that the Securities and Exchange Commission in New York threatened Barings' United States license if it was not promptly resolved. Not until three years after Leeson's arrival in Singapore did London purchase computer systems by which it could reconcile executed trades with clients' orders from anywhere in the world. (Leeson himself admitted that his former employer, Morgan Stanley, would have detected him in a matter of weeks.)

Without adequate technology, personnel assumed the burden, but were singularly lax in the task of running a competitive operation in the long run. The arrangement that allowed Leeson to start to cover his losses in a dummy account in August 1992 never varied, but was never really scrutinized. Two audits of the Singapore operations, one by Barings' internal auditor, the other by Coopers & Lybrand, failed to discover problems or reconcile accounts. Leeson requested funds from London to finance margin calls on client accounts (he was the actually the client), and London never reconciled the actual accounts with the funds sent to finance them. Brenda Granger, who ran the section which specialized in futures and options, talked to Leeson regularly, but admitted she did not fully understand what he was doing. Though a bit sceptical, nevertheless she funnelled hundreds of millions of pounds to Singapore to fund Leeson, and the routine was never questioned.[749]

The settlements department watched whenever a transfer was made from a client's account. Then a check call confirmed a requested transfer. But when transfers were being made from one area to another within Barings – from Baring Securities in London to Baring Securities (Singapore) for example – there existed no checks. The chief operating officer, Geoffery Barnett, reportedly informed the Bank of England that he was unfamiliar with the way funds moved throughout the group on a day-to-day basis. In retrospect the Bank of England was also remiss in its responsibilities as a regulator. Despite misgivings, it had, after all, granted Barings the so-called Treasury concession to consolidate its banking and securities operations – the first granted in the City. The Bank also looked the other way for Barings on enforcing its own rule that prohibited banks from committing more than 25 per cent of its capital to a single customer.

Panic and ignorance contributed to the Leeson catastrophe. Still, a third element – greed – gave management a powerful incentive to believe that what Leeson was doing in Singapore *had* to be legitimate, real and known to his immediate supervisors. Besides, middle managers at least thought the large amounts in which Leeson dealt *must* have approval from someone higher than them, and they were loath to interfere or probe too deeply.

No one probed too deeply. Bonuses were at stake. In 1994 fifty-eight Baring employees were due bonuses on top of their annual salaries of between £250 and £500 million; five of between £500 and £750 million; and four, including Peter Baring and Andrew Tuckey, of over £750 million – all due to Leeson's fake profits.[750]

The largest bonuses went to the bankers in London, not to brokers in outlying offices. They went to the people who were supervisory, who held watchdog positions. Senior managers denied that bonuses had anything to do with the collapse, but such astronomical numbers stretch plausibility. What was clear was that the Big Bang culture of the 1980s greatly benefited the bankers at Barings, however much they disdained the brokerage culture. The point is that they had incentives for passivity because Leeson was a goose laying golden eggs at a comfortable distance from London, unable to bother Bishopsgate with the rough and tumble stockbroker culture of Heath.

Panicky responses to risk, lack of information and greed combined to affect Baring management's decision-making in London. But there were other key exogenous elements – outside London – that enabled the Leeson story. The Singapore Exchange and the Singapore staff at Baring Securities itself may have abetted the catastrophe when coupled with London's passivity. There are indications that SIMEX permitted questionable activities in its derivatives trading because the increased share volumes that Leeson generated brought prestige to a relatively young exchange struggling to snatch business from Japanese markets. The Exchange fêted Leeson with the title 'Trader of the Year' in 1994, and gave similar accolades to Barings – all while the inquiries it *did* make to Baring Securities about unusual account activities were stonewalled, evaded or disregarded.

There are indications also that Leeson's Singaporean staff, including the financial controller of Baring Securities, Rachel Yong, was naïve and unquestioning in changing account balances for Leeson, transferring funds or altering software programmes to mask dealings.[751] In regard to the executives at Singapore, James Bax and Simon Jones were veterans of the Heath days. They tended to resent intrusions from London people, who they viewed as less-than-informed about trading operations, and, for this reason, tended to protect Leeson as one of their own. In 1994, a London audit recommending that Singapore separate its back office operations from floor trading stood unimplemented, ignored.

Ignorance, greed and docile obedience played into the hands of Leeson. One is reminded of Nicholas Biddle's audacious attempt from 1837–9 to control the transatlantic cotton market and improve United States' revenues. Though of a different stripe, this twentieth-century Nicholas was equally bold. From 1994, Leeson wagered the depressed Japanese market would experience little volatility and, if there was to be activity, it would be to the upside. Accordingly, he positioned himself with derivatives to take advantage of his hunch, and bought calls on the Nikkei 225 index. According to Denton and Gapper, by September 1994, Leeson's trades accounted for a massive 7.2 per cent of SIMEX's volume in this index in Japan. 'The scale of the operation Leeson was running was, frankly, awesome', writes Stephen Fay. 'By the end of January 1995, what he was actually doing was fighting off both SIMEX and Coopers & Lybrand, as well as directing the biggest single futures-and-options operation in the Singapore, Tokyo, and

Osaka markets ... The Bank of England report [after the collapse] makes a remark about Leeson which is almost flattering. Referring to his options trading, it comments: "To manage an exposure of the size Lesson constructed is technically and mentally demanding".[752]

It also took fraud, forgery of documents, fabrications, evasiveness, brazen lying and a charismatic personality. Leeson had probably learned about the sluggishness of management and the 'holes' in operations when he worked first at Morgan Stanley, but most especially as a Barings settlements clerk in London from 1989 to 1992. He knew the backwardness of Barings' technical operation. He likely also perceived the nature of an organization such as an international investment bank, where managers are seldom in the same place at the same time, and where decisions can be delegated, put off and avoided for weeks, months or even years. For the same reasons, problems can go undetected. Consequently, someone who is determined will tend to have 'lead time' before the organization catches up.

As indicated, Barings executives on bonus schedules perhaps did not wish to 'catch up', and this added to the natural inertia of management that allowed Leeson leeway to act. Leeson was an organized agent in a firm disorganized by its consolidation of banking and brokerage in 1993. From accounts after the collapse, it appears that his determination was inclined in a direction opposite to Barings' historical one that was so healthy, based on reputation and integrity. It is possible that those in Barings, so keen to preserve this proud legacy, simply could not conceive that what Leeson was doing was possible within such an upright setting.

In the middle of January 1995, however, an earthquake at Kobe, Japan, sent the Nikkei into a spiral that Leeson could no longer control, and only his fleeing to Thailand alerted management once and for all that the firm should address its Singapore trading operations decisively.[753]

Pride Maintained

Connections between Argentina, Singapore and the story of the 1830s are varied and instructive. Perhaps the first common element is the quickness of climax to each crisis. Jonathan Goodhue commented to this effect that there was so little time to react before everything locked up in the United States or the Bank of England took action. Likewise, the time from the bankruptcy of Barings on 25 February 1995 to the frantic meeting of City bankers at Threadneedle Street, to the sale of Barings to the Internationale Nederlanden Groep (ING) was a mere week. Argentina was a bit different since time almost stood still after Revelstoke realized the irreversibility of his rash action with the Buenos Aires Water Company. There were no quick decisions here per se, but a month-long time period from Barings' solicitation of assistance to the Bank of England's decision to grant it. With Argentina, quickness came rather in the form of a reputation lost after over a century of scrupulous building.

These three instances of stress point also to the importance of subordinates. At their cores in fact, the crises in Argentina and Singapore had charismatic men: C. H. Sanford and Nicholas Leeson. They were indispensable to each episode, but enabled only by managers in a particular context. Revelstoke received Sanford's news about the investment opportunity in Argentina enthusiastically just after Barings' spectacular success with Guinness. With Singapore, others hired Leeson. Leeson's personality allowed him to advance through channels and manoeuvre with his trades. However, as Guinness had carried away Revelstoke, so also top management in London found Leeson appealing as a way to regain the profits the firm had reaped in the past from Christopher Heath. There is little evidence that such exuberance was possible in the 1830s with Ward and Bates. To them in fact, charismatic men were by their nature suspect. Bates's inclination was to see dark when presented with light, bad where there appeared good, danger in the presence of apparent safety.

Importantly as well, Sanford and Leeson represented Barings executives chasing the competition: with Revelstoke it was Rothschilds; in Singapore the large American firms. This was unthinkable to the partnership of the 1830s. Bates and Ward followed no one. Others followed Barings – in the United States at least. To behave any other way was not to operate on one's own terms or at one's station. By the late nineteenth century, and certainly by the late twentieth, however, the banking world had changed. In the 1890s and 1990s, Barings did ironically what the '3Ws' had done in the 1830s, for similar reasons and with similar disastrous results. Barings abandoned good judgement to gain share against larger, more established rivals. The later Barings put business before control; Bates never did. As we saw, Ward chafed under what he considered too-tight hands-on management that cost the firm market share.

After Argentina, Singapore and Peter Baring's too-loose style, Bates seems prudent. The 1830s and 1990s were, after all, times of restructuring. Bates and Ward carefully built relationships based on close monitoring and trust. With the 1990s restructuring, the attitude is one of aloofness and detached supervision. Thomas Baring painstakingly established anchors in the United States on his 1828 tour. In Argentina, this was performed only as *post-facto* reconnaissance by John Baring. In Singapore, what would now be called 'due diligence' was of the scantiest kind.

In the area of management continuity, Alexander Baring (Ashburton) clearly intended the character of the firm not change from what he and his father had established, and hired a man with whom he was very familiar, Joshua Bates. Bates, Ward and the partners determined to increase business, but in a fashion that was an organic extension of what came before them. To the contrary, with Peter Baring and Andrew Tuckey there is a sharp and deliberate discontinuity in the consolidation of banking and brokerage for the sake of improved earnings.

In closing, we return to the issue of risk and corporate culture. We have shown that Barings' good timing and conservatism enabled it to survive the Panic of 1837 with enough strength to counsel the Bank of England in regard to weaker British merchant banks, and to benefit the transatlantic economy generally. We have also shown that Barings reduced its extensions of credit to merchants in the Anglo-American trade because it had other options internationally from which to derive earnings. We have found the House terribly concerned with reputation that fostered conservative behaviour. Finally, we have found that an important reason for Barings reducing exposure in the United States was an uneasiness over an American politics that destabilized the financial system, fostered an anti-foreign bias and lacked accountability in debt repayment.

Based on excellent character analysis of American clients by Thomas Ward and extreme wariness over high prices by Joshua Bates, the House indeed remained intact. Barings was rigid with rules and maintained a slightly contemptuous attitude to democracy. These were strengths during the 1830s, since they played a part in keeping the firm safe. In the longer run, however, they were heavy liabilities since they tended to stifle innovation and flexibility. If Barings was inclined to loosen its ways at the end of the nineteenth century by turning to cutting-edge industrial finance, this inclination was thwarted and conservatism reinforced by the missteps in Argentina. By the late twentieth century, Barings' attempt to compete with the large swaggering 'vulgar' American firms by entering the brokerage business was bound to be difficult for lack of experience, and for its commitment in the 1890s to run a low-risk firm. The firm's elite and long banking history worked against any easy integration of a fast-moving securities business.

The securities business is a most democratic of enterprises. No one is entitled to anything except what he provides to the firm. A securities firm's profits indeed depended on people who had once performed the function even of clerks, and these 'clerks' were now entitled to bonuses.

At the beginning of the nineteenth century, Barings and their merchant banking peers entered business for a variety of motives: money, public service and social position. In the period of this book to 1840, these attitudes were noticeably changing to a more rough and tumble egalitarian attitude for anyone doing business in the United States.

By the late twentieth century, these particularly American attitudes had become the way to compete on a global scale. The Panic of 1837 provides a first glimmer of this change towards the rough and tumble in global finance. Baring Brothers' reaction to this panic was superb, as if it could predict the future. In the future, however, the House anchored itself to a past ideal that, in the end, led to its destruction. The birth of modern finance – so American and democratic in its aspect – had left Baring Brothers behind.[754]

NOTES

The following abbreviations are used in the notes:

Baring Archives   Baring Archives, House Correspondence, ING Barings, Ltd., 60 London Wall, London.

Bates Diary   Joshua Bates, Diary, ING Barings, Ltd., London.

Niles   *Niles' Weekly Register.*

NAC   Baring Papers, 'Letters received from agents in Boston', National Archives of Canada, Ottawa.

MHS   Thomas Wren Ward, Papers and Diary, Massachusets Historical Society.

1.   Editorial reprinted in the *Washington Globe*, 22 August 1835.

2.   T. Creevey, *The Creevey Papers: A Selection from the Correspondence and Diaries of the Late Thomas Creevey, MP*, ed. Sir H. Maxwell, 2 vols (London: Murray, 1903), vol. 1, p. 287.

3.   G. Blainey, *The Tyranny of Distance: How Distance Shaped Australia's History* (Melbourne: Sun Books, 1966).

4.   For an engaging survey of the slave trade on the cusp of abolition, see P. Johnson, *The Birth of the Modern: World Society 1815–1830* (New York: HarperCollins, 1991), pp. 303–36. For the development of free trade as an idea, see D. A. Irwin, *Against the Tide: An Intellectual History of Free Trade* (Princeton, NJ: Princeton University Press, 1996).

5.   S. Fay, *The Collapse of Barings* (London: W. W. Norton, 1996); J. Gapper and N. Denton, *All That Glitters: The Fall of Barings* (London: Hamish Hamilton, 1996).

6.   The idea of displacement is discussed in H. P. Minsky, 'The Financial Instability Hypothesis: Capitalist Processes and the Behavior of the Economy', in C. P. Kindleberger and J. P. Laffargue (eds), *Financial Crises: Theory, History, and Policy* (Cambridge: Cambridge University Press, 1982), pp. 13–47. See also D. Glasner, *Business Cycles and Depressions: An Encyclopedia* (New York: Garland Publishing, 1997); D. H. Fischer, *The Great Wave: Price Revolutions and Rhythms of History* (New York and Oxford: Oxford University Press, 1996); J. A. Schumpeter, *Business Cycles, I* (New York: McGraw-Hill, 1939).

7.   C. P. Kindleberger, *A Financial History of Western Europe*, 2nd edn (New York: Oxford University Press, 1993), pp. 264–5; A. Smith, *An Enquiry into the Nature and Causes*

of the Wealth of Nations (1776), ed. E. Cannan (London: Methuen & Co., 1904), p. 465.

8. A. M. Schlesinger, Jr, *The Age of Jackson* (Boston, MA: Little Brown, 1945); R. Hofstadter, *The American Political Tradition and the Men who Made it* (New York: Knopf, 1948); F. Redlich, *The Molding of American Banking: Men and Ideas* (New York: Hafner Publishing Co., 1951); B. Hammond, *Banks and Politics in America, from the Revolution to the Civil War* (Princeton, NJ: Princeton University Press, 1957); R. V. Remini, *Andrew Jackson*, 3 vols (New York, Harper & Row, 1977–84); Brands, H. W., *Andrew Jackson: His Life and Times* (New York: Doubleday 2005).

9. W. B. Smith, *Economic Aspects of the Second Bank of the United States* (Cambridge, MA: Harvard University Press, 1953); P. Temin, *The Jacksonian Economy* (New York: W. W. Norton, 1969); H. Rockoff, 'Money, Prices, and Banks in the Jacksonian Era', in R. W. Fogel and S. L. Engerman (eds), *The Reinterpretation of American Economic History* (New York: Harper & Row, 1971), pp. 448–58. One should note also the work of William Graham Sumner who, in 1896, was one of the first to stress international forces in explaining the events of the 1830s. See W. G. Sumner, *A History of Banking in the United States* (New York: n.p., 1896).

10. Viscount E. V. D'Abernon, *Portraits and Appreciations* (London: Hodder & Stoughton, 1931), pp. 14–15.

11. Johann was not exceptional in his settling in England. For a brief account of foreign-born merchants permanently resident in England by the middle of the eighteenth century, see T. S. Ashton, *An Economic History of England: The Eighteenth Century* (London: Methuen, 1955), p. 140.

12. V. Nolte, *Fifty Years in Both Hemispheres, or Reminiscences of the Life of a Former Merchant* (New York: Redfield, 1854), p. 157.

13. A. Shortt, 'The Barings' (unpublished manuscript, Baring Papers, National Archives of Canada, Ottawa), pp. 29–30. Information found by Shortt in the Baring Archives in a notebook kept by Sir Francis. Cited in R. W. Hidy, *The House of Baring in American Trade and Finance: English Merchant Bankers at Work, 1763–1861* (Cambridge, MA: Harvard University Press, 1949), p. 488, n. 33.

14. The Barings were obliged to become exchange dealers and dealers in bills since bill brokers did not become a distinct part of the London money market until the turn of the nineteenth century. See W. T. C. King, *History of the London Discount Market* (London: Frank Cass, 1936), ch. 1; L. Pressnell, *Country Banking in the Industrial Revolution* (London: Clarendon Press, 1956), pp. 84–105.

15. Figures prepared by Barings unnamed internal company personnel. Information supplied by ING Barings archivist, Dr John Orbell (now retired).

16. P. Ziegler, *The Sixth Great Power* (New York: Knopf, 1988), p. 373.

17. B. R. Mitchell and P. Deane, *Abstract of British Historical Statistics* (Cambridge: Cambridge University Press, 1962), p. 402.

18. Hidy, *The House of Baring*, pp. 52–3.

19. J. Orbell, *Baring Brothers & Co., Limited: A History to 1839* (London: Baring Brothers & Co., Ltd, 1985), p. 17.

20. The First Treaty of Paris had imposed no reparations on France, but Waterloo made the Allies less forgiving. See H. Nicolson, *The Congress of Vienna: A Study in Allied Unity* (London: Constable & Co. Ltd, 1946), pp. 98–9, 238–41.

21. N. Ferguson, *The House of Rothschild, 1798–1848* (New York: Viking, 1998), p. 114; Kindleberger, *A Financial History of Western Europe*, p. 215.

22. Hidy, *The House of Baring*, p. 62.

23. Cited in A. D. Gayer, W. W. Rostow and A. Jacobson Schwartz, *The Growth and Fluctuation of the British Economy 1790–1850*, 2 vols (Oxford: Clarendon Press, 1953), vol. 1, pp. 110–13.

24. Kindleberger, *A Financial History of Western Europe*, p. 215.

25. L. H. Jenks, *The Migration of British Capital to 1875* (London: Nelson, 1927), p. 36; 16 July 1819. Autobiographical memoirs of Swinton Holland in Ziegler, *The Sixth Great Power*, p. 392, n. 32.

26. Wellington and Rothschild were hardly alone in their opinions. Amidst the French loan negotiations in 1818, the Duke of Richelieu reportedly made his famous statement about Barings' financial preeminence: 'There are Six Powers in Europe. Great Britain, France, Russia, Austria, Prussia, and Baring Brothers'.

27. See Baring Brothers & Company, table of 'Capital, Profits and Losses; Commission Income, 1792–1890', by John Orbell and ING Barings' in-house staff, Baring Archives. The real fall of income was considerably greater taking into account wartime inflation.

28. Francis Baring left an estate of approximately £625,000, of which £400,000 was in land; £27,000 in art, furniture and jewels; and £68,507 in House capital, Orbell, *Baring Brothers & Co.*, p. 20. The *Gentleman's Magazine* of 1810 (p. 293) eulogized Francis, stating: 'At his death, he was unquestionably the first merchant in Europe; first in knowledge and talents, and first in character and opulence', cited in Ziegler, *The Sixth Great Power*, p. 51.

29. Nolte, *Fifty Years in Both Hemispheres*, p. 262. The Baring acquisition of the Dutch firm of Hope & Company in 1814 is interesting, indeed ironic, in light of the Dutch financial services combine, Internationale Nederlanden Groep (ING), buying Barings in 1995 for £1 plus assumption of debt after Baring Securities' disastrous derivatives-trading problems in Singapore. Hope & Company, after being under Barings' British supervision since the early nineteenth century, became fully Dutch again. See Conclusion and Epilogue below.

30. B. Mallet, *Thomas George, Earl of Northbrook: A Memoir* (London: Longmans, Green and Co., 1908), pp. 3–4.

31. D. C. M. Platt, 'History of Barings', 2 vols (unpublished manuscript in the Baring Archives), vol. 1, p. 57.

32. Alexander had apprenticed at a banking House in Germany, at the House of Hope & Company and at his father's firm in London.

33. Barings' familial connection was a legacy, of course, of America's colonial history with Great Britain. Particularly after 1815, the Anglo-American link matured into an elevated and peaceful competition between peers often called 'the special relationship', which continues to the present. The Barings are one famous example of this transatlantic link. The marriage of Winston Churchill's father, Randolph, to Jenny Jerome of Brooklyn, NY, in 1874 was another.

34. S. Bruchey, *Robert Oliver: Merchant of Baltimore, 1783–1819* (Baltimore, MD: Johns Hopkins University Press, 1956), pp. 149–51.

35. H. Adams, *The Life of Albert Gallatin* (1879; New York: J. P. Lippincott, 1943), pp. 548–52.
36. Alexander Baring to Henry Hope, 9 January 1797, in Ziegler, *The Sixth Great Power*, pp. 65–6.
37. Ibid., p. 54. Upon returning from his American tour, Alexander Baring began a political career. He served in Parliament from 1806 to 1835, sitting for Taunton. He spent the early part of this career as a Whig, the latter part as a Tory. For much of his career he advocated the elimination of commercial monopolies and restrictions to free trade. In 1820 Baring delivered a House of Commons speech for free trade in light of Thomas Tooke's recent petition to Parliament on behalf of London manufacturers. Consistent with his House's business interests in the United States, Baring opposed wartime restrictions upon American trade and traders in the years leading up to the War of 1812. In this regard, some of his arguments may be found in his *An Inquiry into the Causes and Consequences of the Orders in Council and an Examination of the Conduct of Great Britain towards the Neutral Commerce of America* (London: J. M. Richardson and J. Ridgway, 1808).
38. Ziegler, *The Sixth Great Power*, p. 67.
39. Hammond, *Banks and Politics in America*, pp. 207–8.
40. D. Kynaston, *The City of London: A World of its Own* (London: Chatto & Windus, 1994), pp. 1–36.
41. Baring to Pierre Labouchere, 15 February 1804, Northbrook Papers A4/1, in Ziegler, *The Sixth Great Power*, p. 71.
42. Of the $15 million agreed upon, $3.75 million represented the United States government's assumption of myriad of its merchants' claims against the French government. Thus, France garnered $11.25 million on the Louisiana transaction, Adams, *The Life of Albert Gallatin*, p. 318. In order to purchase Louisiana, the United States Treasury issued debt greater than the total foreign debt when Alexander Hamilton took office in 1790. By 1803, however, the good credit of the United States was so firmly established abroad that it was able to take this debt in its stride. The Republican administration of Thomas Jefferson spoke of a debt of $15 million as 'a trifling sum', even though the Louisiana Purchase increased the national debt to its highest level before the Civil War. In January 1835 the entire national debt was paid off, and the government's debt to Europe was entirely liquidated. See A. Hamilton, *Works*, ed. H. C. Lodge, vol. 9, pp. 26–7, quoted in J. C. Miller, *Alexander Hamilton and the Growth of the New Nation* (New York: Harper & Row, 1959), p. 562.
43. For a history of the firm of Prime, Ward & Sands, see W. Werner and S. T. Smith, *Wall Street* (New York: Columbia University Press, 1991), *passim*, esp. 50–4; D. Adams, *Finance and Enterprise in Early America: A Study of Stephen Girard's Bank, 1812–1831* (Philadelphia, PA: University of Pennsylvania Press, 1978); J. K. Medbery, *Men and Mysteries of Wall Street* (New York: Fields, Osgood & Co., 1870).
44. M. G. Myers, *A Financial History of the United States* (New York: Columbia University Press, 1970), pp. 76–8.
45. Alexander Baring to A. J. Dallas (president of the Bank of the United States), 9 April 1816, cited in Platt, 'History of Barings', vol. 1, p. 72.
46. 'Second Report from the Secret Committee on the Expediency of the Bank Resuming Cash Payments', *Parliamentary Papers*, 3 (1819), p. 119.

47. The Manhattan Company invested heavily in New York State loans in the 1820s as it transformed itself from a municipal water company to a major banking institution. Today the Manhattan Company is part of JPMorganChase, the third largest bank in the United States.

48. See Jenks, *The Migration of British Capital*, p. 360, n. 25; Nolte, *Fifty Years in Both Hemispheres*, pp. 297–9.

49. For line items in the Bank of the United States balance sheets that read 'Due Baring Bros' and 'Due Hope and Co', see *Niles*, 18 (21 October 1820), p. 117; 19 (3 June 1820), p. 249; 26 (6 March 1824), p. 7

50. F. Sheppard, *London: A History* (Oxford: Oxford University Press, 1998), p. 236. Niles estimated total loans contracted in England for South American states were £21 million from 1822 to 1825. Of this $95,975,861, 70 per cent went to Brazil, Columbia and Mexico, *Niles*, 29 (4 February 1826), p. 364.

51. Gayer et al., *The Growth and Fluctuation*, vol. 1, p. 185; *Niles*, 29 (8 October 1825), p. 88.

52. Jenks, *The Migration of British Capital*, pp. 24, 44–56.

53. *Niles*, 29 (10 September 1825), p. 23.

54. J. H. Clapham, *The Bank of England: A History*, 2 vols (Cambridge: Cambridge University Press, 1944), vol. 1, p. 94.

55. Quoted in F. G. Dawson, *The First Latin American Debt Crisis: The City of London and the 1822–1825 Loan Bubble* (New Haven, CT: Yale University Press, 1990), p. 106; For a list of British joint-stock companies 'formed in 1824 and the beginning of 1825', see *Niles*, 29 (19 November 1825), p. 183.

56. *Hansard* (16 March 1825), col. 1063.

57. W. Smart, *Economic Annals of the Nineteenth Century, 1801–1830*, 2 vols (London: Macmillan & Co., 1917), vol. 2, pp. 295–9; *Niles*, 29 (17 September 1825), p. 34; (24 September 1825), p. 52; (15 October 1825), p. 113; Clapham, *The Bank of England*, vol. 1, pp. 98–9.

58. T. Tooke and W. Newmarch, *A History of Prices and the State of the Currency*, 6 vols in 4 (1838–57; London: P. S. King & Son, 1928), vol. 2, p. 162.

59. H. Arbuthnot, *The Journal of Mrs. Arbuthnot 1820–1832*, ed. F. Bamford and the Duke of Wellington, 2 vols (London: Macmillan, 1950), vol. 1, pp. 426–8; vol. 2, pp. 10–11.

60. Both newspaper excerpts cited in Tooke and Newmarch, *A History of Prices*, vol. 2, pp. 171–3, n.

61. *Niles*, 29 (3 December 1825), pp. 210–11.

62. The arrangement with the Bank of France involved shipping gold to London in exchange for silver. The higher price of gold in England than in France (15.2 to 1, instead of 14.625 to 1) favoured the exchange. See Clapham, *The Bank of England*, vol. 1, p. 101; Tooke and Newmarch, *A History of Prices*, vol. 2, p. 162; Ferguson, *The House of Rothschild*, p. 137.

63. The concept of the 'lender of last resort' is generally credited to Sir Francis Baring, who coined the French phrase cited in the text in his 1797 *Observations on the Establishment of the Bank of England*, in which he advocated the idea of a central institution from which sound banks could borrow in a crisis. The idea was developed further in later works of the nineteenth century. See H. Thornton, *An Inquiry Into the*

Nature and Effects of the Paper Credit of Great Britain (London: J. Hatchard, 1802); W. Bagehot, *Lombard Street: A Description of the Money Market* (1873; Homewood, IL: R. D. Irwin, 1962).

64. Smart, *Economic Annals*, vol. 2, p. 344.
65. *Niles*, 29 (10 September 1825), p. 23.
66. Sheppard, *London: A History*, p. 236.
67. King, *History of the London Discount Market*, p. 38.
68. Ziegler, *The Sixth Great Power*, p. 374.
69. H. S. Ferns, *Britain and Argentina in the Nineteenth Century* (Oxford: Clarendon Press, 1960), p. 141.
70. Orbell, *Baring Brothers & Co.*, p. 26.
71. Most of Barings' Mexican investments were impossible to sell at a profit and remained on the books of the House until the middle 1840s, when £170,000 was written off. Mexico's position as a potentially strong economy among the Latin American states stood on its historical reputation as a producer and exporter of silver. In the late 1830s Barings willingly relinquished its agency of Mexican financial affairs to the House of Lizardi & Company. Mexican delinquency in its bond obligations to European states culminated in the three-way invasion of the country by Great Britain, Spain and France in 1861/2 – with the latter installing its representative on the Mexican throne in 1863, Orbell, *Baring Brothers & Co.*, pp. 26–7, 41.
72. Gayer et al., *The Growth and Fluctuation*, vol. 1, p. 214. See also Chapter 2 below.
73. Nolte, *Fifty Years in Both Hemispheres*, p. 17.
74. Mallet, *Thomas George, Earl of Northbrook*, p. 10.
75. Bates Diary, 1 January 1838.
76. Orbell, *Baring Brothers & Co.*, p. 27.
77. The form of these merchant banking firms was typically the partnership or, very commonly, a family-centred enterprise. The choice of form was in large part due to slow and uncertain communications between trading centres and the need for absolute familiarity and trust between firm members. It was also not unusual for firms to employ only members of a particular religious sect, ethnic or cultural group. The Quakers – for example Rathbones, Overend Gurney and Cropper Benson & Company – were made cohesive as trading and banking organizations by their religious beliefs, but were held together also by family ties. Scots (James Finley & Company; Wallace Bros & Company), Greeks (Cassavetti Bros; Ralli Bros), Dutch-Huguenots (Andres; Bosanquet Family) and Jews (Kuhn, Loeb & Company; Rothschilds; Sassoons) all represent groups which formed notable, numerous and homogenous banking and merchant Houses based on their cultural make-ups. London was the preferred destination of restless merchants and financiers from other nations, and Great Britain was transfused throughout the nineteenth century with new commercial talent. Among notable merchant banking Houses, ones whose members were part of the German diaspora are of disproportionate importance in the nineteenth and twentieth centuries in both Great Britain and the United States compared with talent from other nations. Some notable Anglo-German Houses include N. M. Rothschild of Frankfurt, the Seligmans, Speyers, Kleinforts and Schroders. It is no exaggeration to say that by the middle of the nineteenth century, the Barings as gentiles and members of the Church of England were a distinct minority among first-rank merchant

banking Houses. Professor W. D. Rubinstein finds that, of the thirty-one million-aire merchant bankers who died between 1809 and 1939, twenty-four were Jewish and four were Anglicans. See W. D. Rubinstein, *Men of Property: The Very Wealthy in Britain since the Industiral Revolution* (London: Croom Helm, 1981). See also Y. Cassis, *English City Bankers, 1890–1914* (Cambridge: Cambridge University Press, 1994), *passim*; S. Chapman, *Merchant Enterprise in Britain: From the Industrial Revolution to World War I* (Cambridge: Cambridge University Press, 1992), pp. 81–166. For context and comparative development of banking as an institution, apart from families, see K. E. Born, International Banking in the 19th and 20th Centuries (New York: St Martin's Press, 1977); D. S. Landes, 'The Old Bank and the New: The Financial Revolution of the Nineteenth Century', in F. Crouzet, W. H. Chaloner and W. M. Stern (eds.), *Essays in European Economic History 1789–1914* (New York: St Martin's Press, 1969), pp. 112–28; R. Cameron, with O. Crisp, H. T. Patrick and R. Tilly, *Banking in the Early Stages of Industrialization* (New York: Oxford University Press 1967).

78. Jenks, *The Migration of British Capital*, p. 67; Ziegler, *The Sixth Great Power*, p. 77.
79. *Circular to Bankers* (23 June 1837).
80. Ferguson, *The House of Rothschild*, p. 162; Ziegler, *The Sixth Great Power*, p. 374.
81. S. Chapman, *The Rise of Merchant Banking* (London: Allen & Unwin, 1984), p. 40; E. J. Perkins, *Financing Anglo-American Trade: The House of Brown 1800–1880* (Cambridge, MA: Harvard University Press, 1975), p. 19.
82. Bates Diary, 7 September 1829.
83. Ward to Bates, 7 June 1833, MHS.
84. Baring Brothers & Company, table of 'Capital, Profits and Losses; Commission Income, 1792–1890'.
85. Hidy, *The House of Baring*, p. 507, n. 17.
86. By 1829, foreign investors held more than half of New York's outstanding Erie Canal debt, M. Wilkins, *The History of Foreign Investment in the United States to 1914* (Cambridge, MA: Harvard University Press, 1989), p. 57.
87. Jenks, *The Migration of British Capital*, p. 361. See also Wilkins, *The History of Foreign Investment*, p. 54; R. C. McGrane, *Foreign Bondholders and American State Debts* (New York: Macmillan, 1935), esp. pp. 1–264; and for a contemporary state-by-state debt survey, see A. Trotter, *Observations on the Financial Position and Credit of Such of the States of the North American Union as have Contracted Public Debts* (1839; New York: A. M. Kelley, 1968), ch. 7.
88. Wilkins, *The History of Foreign Investment*, p. 53; United States Bureau of the Census, *The Statistical History of the United States from Colonial Times the Present* (New York: Basic Books, 1976), p. 1118.
89. Trotter, *Observations on the Financial Position*, pp. 1–18. The United States had a history of scrupulously paying its obligations. It had established its creditworthiness early in the money markets of Europe at the insistent steerage of Alexander Hamilton.
90. B. U. Ratchford, *American State Debts* (Durham, NC: Duke University Press, 1941), p. 88; *Niles*, 54 (21 July 1838), p. 322, in Wilkins, *The History of Foreign Investment*, p. 54; Adams, *The Life of Albert Gallatin*, p. 656.

91. The sale of securities not only provided the funds for covering the large deficit in the American balance of payments on the merchandise account, but was the means whereby America gathered gold unto itself – to large extent from its major trading partner, Great Britain. This disturbed the Bank of England by 1836, and is discussed in Chapters 5 and 6 below.

92. J. R. McCulloch, *Dictionary of Commerce and Commercial Navigation*, 5th edn (London: Longman, Brown, Green, and Longmans, 1850), p. 28; Trotter, *Observations on the Financial Position*, p. 376; Myers, *A Financial History*, p. 69; R. C. McGrane, *The Panic of 1837: Some Financial Problems of the Jacksonian Era* (Chicago: University of Chicago Press, 1924), p. 13; L. Schweikart (ed.), *Banking and Finance to 1913* (New York: Facts on File, 1990), p. xxxi, table.

93. As Fritz Redlich has pointed out in his classic account, *The Molding of American Banking*, American banks increased the number and type of financial instruments dramatically in the 1820s and 1830s, including post notes, certificates of deposit, notes payable at places other than the place of issue, and scrip used as an exchange medium. The period saw also the proliferation of so-called 'country banks' that based credit issuance on private credit and land, rather than relatively concrete commercial transactions. These inland institutions coexisted with the older and less numerous 'money banks' of the Atlantic seaboard cities. By the 1840s the welter of negotiable instruments had diminished to regular bank notes and the bank cheque. However, for Redlich, the experimentation in finance during the late 1820s and 1830s in the area of negotiable instruments prompted him to assign to the period the overriding 'leitmotif' of 'safety', and significant efforts of reform at the federal and state levels were made to that end. See Redlich, *The Molding of American Banking*, pp. 44–5 and *passim*. After its implementation in New York in 1829, the idea of a safety fund spread to other states, including Vermont in 1831, Indiana in 1834 and Michigan in 1836.

94. L. Schweikart, *Banking in the American South from the Age of Jackson to Reconstruction* (Baton Rouge, LA: Louisiana State University Press, 1987), p. 48.

95. Jenks, *The Migration of British Capital*, pp. 75–6; Schweikart, *Banking in the American South*, p. 49.

96. The southern model funded many corporations throughout the United States. States fronted for private banks, canal and railroad companies. They substituted the strong credit of a known sovereign entity for that of an unknown farming enterprise in order to borrow in distant money markets, such as Great Britain. States sold bonds and the proceeds passed to the banking, canal or railroad companies; the state government would then take the firms' stocks or bonds as security. American banks and merchants bought the state securities, which they could resell in Europe or use as collateral for borrowings in the United States and Europe. See Wilkins, *The History of Foreign Investment*, pp. 54–5.

97. For the importance of foreign trade during the colonial and confederation periods, see J. J. McCusker and R. R. Menard, *The Economy of British North America, 1607–1789* (Chapel Hill, NC: University of North Carolina Press, 1991), pp. 71–88.

98. D. T. Gilchrist (ed.), *The Growth of the Seaport Cities, 1790–1825* (Charlottesville, VA: University Press of Virginia, 1967), pp. 54–79.

99. Mitchell and Deane, *Abstract of British Historical Statistics*, pp. 313–14; A. H. Imlah, *Economic Elements of the Pax Britannica: Studies in British Foreign Trade in the Nineteenth Century* (Cambridge, MA: Harvard University Press, 1958), pp. 37–8.
100. US Census, *The Statistical History*, p. 907.
101. G. R. Taylor, *The Transportation Revolution, 1815–1860* (New York: Rinehart, 1951), p. 450.
102. Jenks, *The Migration of British Capital*, p. 67.
103. Taylor, *The Transportation Revolution*, p. 450.
104. D. C. North, *The Economic Growth of the United States, 1790–1860* (Englewood Cliffs, NJ: Prentice-Hall, 1961), pp. 282–8.
105. To 1881, United States exports are recorded as 'unmanufactured textiles' and agricultural commodities such as wheat, tobacco and cotton. Only from the middle 1880s did American exports become statistically significant in the areas of processed products and manufactures. See US Census, *The Statistical History*, pp. 898–9.
106. From 1825–30, exports declined 21 per cent, imports 30 per cent From 1830–6, exports advanced 73 per cent, imports 182 per cent. Continuing the pattern, in the depression of 1837–43, exports declined 33 per cent; imports a devastating 76 per cent to the lowest import level in the nineteenth century, 28 per cent, as a percentage of United States total foreign trade. See Taylor, *The Transportation Revolution*, pp. 444–5; US Census, *The Statistical History*, pp. 884–6.
107. From Mitchell and Deane, *Abstract of British Historical Statistics*, pp. 313–14; North, *The Economic Growth*, p. 233; US Census, *The Statistical History*, pp. 884–6.
108. It is interesting to note the resilience of British trade in the period 1815–60, during which Britain only once suffered a multi-year volume decline in its total foreign commerce. This came in the three-year period 1854–7, associated with financial panic of 1857. Otherwise the British trade record of these four and a half decades is one of almost uninterrupted advance. This consistency cannot be said of the United States trade pattern before 1843. After this devastating trough year – particularly on the import side – American trade adopted the British pattern, however, and experienced no multi-year declines in total trade for the balance of the antebellum period. Between 1843 and 1860, the total value of United States trade more than quintupled from $125,259,153 to $687,192,176; total exports increasing from $82,825,689 to $333,576,057; total imports from $42,433,464 to $353,616,119. See Taylor, *The Transportation Revolution*, p. 446; Imlah, *Economic Elements in the Pax Britannica*, pp. 37–8. See also Gayer et al., *The Growth and Fluctuation*, vol. 1, chapters 3–4.
109. Based on five-year averages from 1796 to 1853 in Imlah, *Economic Aspects in the Pax Britannica*, pp. 37–8.
110. US Census, *The Statistical History*, pp. 904–7; Mitchell and Deane, *Abstract of British Historical Statistics*, p. 313. American export figures in *The Statistical History* are based on the selling price (or the cost if the good is not sold) of the commodity shipped.
111. N. S. Buck, *The Development of the Organisation of Anglo-American Trade, 1800–1850* (New Haven, CT: Yale University Press, 1925), pp. 136–7. Due to political instability associated with independence movements in Latin America to the early 1820s, North America was the primary recipient of British goods accumulated during the war.

112. 'Report from the Select Committee on Manufactures, Commerce, and Shipping', *Parliamentary Papers*, 6 (1833), q. 511 (G. Shaw).
113. *Niles*, 27 (9 January 1825), p. 289.
114. Conveying the intensity of competition for example in the spinning and weaving sectors, Parliament committee members repeatedly heard phrases such as 'good business, but no money', or 'all trade is depressed in profit to a serious extent despite full demand for labour'. See 'Report from the Select Committee on Manufactures', qq. 621–2 (K. Finlay); qq. 2003–4 (T. Wiggins); qq. 5188–5237 (H. Houldsworth).
115. A secondary market for commercial paper (a discount market) is generally accepted to have been functioning in Great Britain by the middle 1820s. The Bank of England, however, assumed full discounting responsibilities only after the Bank Charter Act of 1844, when it became a competitor for loans with the already-functioning discounters in the British money market. The loan percentage charged for discounting at the Bank of England was known simply as 'Bank rate'. It typically stood higher than the market rate to discourage borrowing except as a last resort. See King, *History of the London Discount Market*, pp. 78–9, 161–9.
116. M. G. Myers, *The New York Money Market, I: Origins and Development* (New York: Columbia University Press, 1931), pp. 58–72. For a further discussion of the American exchange market, see A. H. Cole, 'Evolution of the Foreign-Exchange Market of the United States', *Journal of Economic and Business History*, 1 (1928–9), pp. 384–421.
117. Cited in Buck, *The Development of the Organisation*, pp. 147–8, from *Niles*, 13 (27 December 1817), p. 284, quoted from a speech in Parliament. See *Hansard's Parliamentary Debates*, 1st series, 33 (9 April 1816), p. 1099.
118. 'Report from the Select Committee on Manufactures', qq. 847–8 (J. Bates).
119. Imlah, *Economic Elements in the Pax Britannica*, pp. 94–5. Imlah's price index for exports dropped by 60 per cent between 1801 and 1831. See also A. H. Imlah, 'Real Values in British Foreign Trade, 1798–1853', *Journal of Economic History*, 8 (November 1948), pp. 133–52. For increased competition among British manufacturers, see also testimony by Joshua Bates in 'Report from the Select Committee on Manufactures', qq. 744–1057.
120. Jenks, *The Migration of British Capital*, pp. 67–8; and the later assessment by Chapman, *The Rise of Merchant Banking*, pp. 14–15, 39.
121. US Census, *The Statistical History*, pp. 904, 907.
122. [J. R. McCulloch], 'Enquiry into the Circumstances that have Occasioned the Present Embarrassments in the Trade between Great Britain and the United States of America', *Edinburgh Review* (American edn), 65:132 (July 1837), pp. 263–73, on p. 268.
123. Bates to Ward, 21 June 1832 and 2 June 1833, MHS. The stream of Americans to London became a torrent when a steamboat service from New York to Liverpool became available in 1838. To fill out this dynamic picture further, see S. Chapman, 'British Marketing Enterprise: The Changing Roles of Merchants, Manufacturers, and Financiers, 1700–1860', *Business History Review*, 53 (Summer 1979), pp. 205–34.
124. The bill of exchange was the engine of commercial finance in this period and for many years, and was connected with the idea of exchange. For an overview of these issues,

see *The Bill on London*, 4th rev. edn (London: Gillett Bros, Discount Ltd, 1976); P. Einzig, *The History of Foreign Exchange* (London: Macmillan, 1964); L. E. Davis and J. R. T. Hughes, 'A Dollar-Sterling Exchange, 1803–1895', *Economic History Review*, 2nd series, 13 (1960–1), pp. 52–79; A. H. Cole, 'Seasonal Variation in Sterling Exchange', *Journal of Economic and Business History*, 2 (1929–30), pp. 203–18.

125. Bates Diary, 4 September 1829.

126. The Far East stayed in the purview of Joshua Bates's family for some time. Bates's great granddaughter married the (British) Rajah of Sarawak on the north-western coast of Borneo in 1911. The revenue figure for Bates and Baring is cited from Ziegler, *The Sixth Great Power*, p. 143. Though the author is unable to confirm the revenue figure, a list and description of clients accumulated by Bates and Baring in the Baring Archives attests to the extensive scope and international character of the contacts retained by Baring Brothers in 1828.

127. Bates to Ward, 21 September 1846, MHS.

128. *Edinburgh Review*, no date, in Chapman, *The Rise of Merchant Banking*, p. 70.

129. Bates Diary, 8 June 1837.

130. Mildmay's membership of the Court of Directors from 1828 to 1849 re-established Barings' connection with the Bank of England that Alexander Baring (Baron Ashburton 1835) had forged as a director from 1805 to 1817. After Mildmay, Barings' presence on the Court was almost continuous for over a century: Thomas Baring, grandson of Sir Francis (1848–67); Edward C. Baring (1879–91); John Baring, 2nd Lord Revelstoke (1898–1929); Sir Edward Peacock (1929–46); George R. S. Baring, 3rd Earl of Cromer (Governor 1961–6). A complete catalogue of Bank officers may be found in R. Roberts and D. Kynaston (eds.), *The Bank of England: Money, Power and Influence 1694–1994* (Oxford: Clarendon Press, 1995), appendix 2.

131. The impression of 'middle-man' status for Mildmay was supplied by the recently-retired archivist of ING Barings, Dr John Orbell, whom the author wishes to thank.

132. A formal agency agreement appointing Ward is not extant, though a letter from Thomas Baring to Ward, dated 3 October 1829, confirms Ward's appointment and assigns him power of attorney for the firm in the United States. The introduction to the House Correspondence to North America (Boston) states Ward's appointment with power of attorney in the United States was 29 October 1829. See Baring Archives, HC5.1.2.

133. Baring Archives, HC5.1.20.4 (North America, Boston agents).

134. Ward's salary of £2,000 was the equivalent of $8,889 which, adjusted for inflation, is roughly the equivalent in 2007 of $200,000. Salary negotiations continued throughout 1830 and 1831 between Ward and London. Bates to Ward, 5 April 1832, MHS. For conversions of historical figures of dollars and sterling, see J. J. McCusker, *How Much is That in Real Money?: A Historical Price Index for Use as a Deflator of Money Values in the Economy of the United States*, 2nd edn (Worcester, MA: American Antiquarian Society, 2001).

135. Baring Brothers Letterbooks, fragment, Barings to M. Sussman, before letter of Barings to the New York banking house of Prime, Ward & King, 30 May 1832, cited in Hidy, *The House of Baring*, p. 507, n. 23.

136. C. P. Huse, *The Financial History of Boston from 1822 to 1909* (Cambridge, MA: Harvard University Press, 1916), p. 14.

137. Besides musings on the conditions in their home countries, also scattered in the pages of both men's diaries are extended descriptions and analyses of countries in Asia, Latin America and Europe (including Russia). Ward, for example, surveyed, one by one, individual countries' monetary regimes.
138. Ward Diary, 30 April 1838, MHS.
139. Ward to Bates, 17 May 1832, MHS.
140. Ziegler, The Sixth Great Power, p. 144.
141. Ward to Barings, 20 October 1835, NAC.
142. Goodhue to Bates, 15 December 1828, Baring Archives, HC5.2.12.
143. Ward also involved himself in Boston's broader civic life. From 1828 to 1836, Ward served as treasurer to the Boston Athenaeum, and for twelve years from 1830 held a similar position at Harvard College.
144. Ward to Bates, 25 July 1833 and 5 February 1832, MHS.
145. Bates to Ward, 2 June 1833, MHS.
146. Bates to Ward, 4 January 1832, MHS.
147. Bates Diary, 31 December 1832, cited in Kynaston, The City of London, p. 93.
148. Bates to Ward, 5 April 1832, MHS. The series of out-letter books begins in 1831. The letters were copied on tissue paper and, with the ink not always dry, pasted into the more substantial letter books. The copies often smeared and are generally difficult to read. From the 1890s typescript copies become common.
149. Baring Brothers & Company, table of 'Capital, Profits and Losses; Commission Income, 1792–1890', pp. 2–3.
150. Bates to Ward, 8 November 1831, MHS, cited in Hidy, The House of Baring, p. 130.
151. By 1821, the United States had recovered from the severe depression of 1819 but, except for an uptick in 1825, the decade of the 1820s saw continually declining prices – albeit gradual. Periodic recessions were minor in the 1820s and tended to be regional. The Ohio Valley, for example, saw three downturns in 1824, 1827 and 1830. From 1822 to 1830 the South saw the price of its principle staple, cotton, cut by over two fifths. See T. S. Berry, Western Prices Before 1861: A Study of the Cincinnati Market (Cambridge, MA: Harvard University Press, 1943), pp. 406–31; A. H. Cole, Wholesale Commodity Prices in the United States, 1700–1861 (Cambridge, MA: Harvard University Press, 1938), pp. 201–34.
152. See J. Killick, 'Bolton Ogden & Co: A Case Study of Anglo-American Trade, 1790–1850', Business History Review, 48:4 (Winter 1974), pp. 501–19, on p. 507.
153. Bates to Ward, 5 April 1832, MHS.
154. Ward to Barings, 17 September 1832, 3 September 1835 and 2 January 1837, NAC.
155. Ward to Barings, 24 December 1834 and 18 February 1835, NAC.
156. American seamen wasted no time after independence from Great Britain in launching ships for China. While under British administration, colonists were prohibited from sending ships east of the Cape of Good Hope. On 22 February 1784 an American ship, the Empress of China, left for China loaded with ginseng and furs, and entered Canton harbour five months later. Two Americans financed the voyage: Robert Morris (a friend of Alexander Baring) of Philadelphia and Daniel Parker of New York.
157. Bates to Ward, 21 June 1832, MHS.
158. Smith, Economic Aspects of the Second Bank, p. 34.

159. Ward to H. Lavergne, 7 September 1835, NAC.
160. Hidy, *The House of Baring*, p. 138.
161. Ward to Barings, 20 February 1835, NAC.
162. Ward to Barings, 7 December 1834, NAC.
163. Ward to Barings, 6 February 1835, NAC.
164. Ward to Barings, 21 January 1835, NAC.
165. Ward to Bates, 17 May 1832, MHS.
166. Hidy, *The House of Baring*, p. 140.
167. This section is based on ibid., pp. 140–4.
168. The legal validity of the credit receipt was not tested until 1843 when, in a case involving the House of Fletcher Alexander, the receipt was upheld as a binding legal obligation by the borrower.
169. Perkins, *Financing Anglo-American Trade*, pp. 254–6.
170. Ward to Barings, 31 January 1835, NAC. Occasionally, Ward made exceptions to the double account rule with large customers, such as the New York firm of C. A. & E. Heckscher, Hidy, *The House of Baring*, p. 167.
171. Bates to Ward, 11 October 1831, MHS. The author is not aware if Bates practised a policy of customer exclusivity before 1828 as part of Bates & Baring. For an account of the different customer approach by the major Anglo-American house of Alexander Brown & Company, see Perkins, *Financing Anglo-American Trade*, p. 119–20. The issue of revocation was important since any credit agreement in the form of a negotiable instrument likely affected many parties.
172. Bates to Ward, 4 March 1833, MHS; Ward to Barings, 7 December 1836, NAC.
173. Ward to Bates, 17 May 1832 and 7 June 1833, MHS.
174. For a classic exposition of the transformation of American internal trade from advancements in canals, rivercraft technology and railroads in the antebellum years, see Taylor, *The Transportation Revolution*.
175. The trade relationship between the United States and Mexico was a mirror opposite to that of the United States and China. Mexico was a specie contributor to the United States, since it was a taker of American goods. Until significant opium shipments into China through India in the early 1830s, China remained a taker of American specie since demand for Chinese goods was high in the United States. American (and British) traders had little success exporting significant goods to China. For a good overview of the China trade with explanations of business methods, see M. Greenberg, *British Trade and the Opening of China, 1800–42* (Cambridge: Cambridge University Press, 1951).
176. Schweikart, *Banking in the American South*, pp. 211–12. For a survey of finance in the southern United States, see R. Kilbourne Jr, *Slave Agriculture and Financial Markets in Antebellum America: The Bank of the United States in Mississippi, 1831–1852* (London: Pickering & Chatto, 2006); G. D. Green, *Finance and Economic Development in the Old South: Louisiana Banking 1804–1861* (Stanford, CA: Stanford University Press, 1972).
177. I. D. Neu, 'Edmond Jean Forstall and Louisiana Banking', *Explorations in Economic History*, 7:4 (Summer 1970), pp. 383–98.
178. As the firm added and lost partners – that is to say, changed ownership – its name changed. Various titles of the partnership include Prime & Ward (1808–16); Prime,

Ward & Sands (1817–25); Prime, Ward, Sands, King & Company (1826–33); Prime, Ward & King (1834–46); Prime, Ward & Company (1847). In 1847, Rufus King's son restructured and led the firm as James G. King until 1853. This sequential change of ownership is clear in the Baring Papers, National Archives of Canada, Ottawa, and is established also, with minor variations, in Redlich, *The Molding of American Banking*. It is also epitomized in F. Hunt, 'J. G. King', in *Lives of American Merchants* (1856; New York: A. M. Kelley, 1969), pp. 184–214.

179. Note should read: For operations of firms in nineteenth-century New York, see also W. Barrett, *The Old Merchants of New York City*, 5 vols (1870; New York: Greenwood Press, 1968), vol. 1, p. 16; C. Browder, *The Money Game in Old New York* (Lexington: University of Kentucky Press, 1986).

180. The author is not aware of the specific details of the 1830 arrangement with Prime, Ward & King worked out through Thomas Baring in his American travels. Regarding double accounts, these additional City (London) bankers included Barings' peer, Rothschild, with whom Prime, Ward & King split a Maryland state bond offering in 1835 (see Chapter 5 below), Hidy, *The House of Baring*, p. 509, n. 43; Prime, Ward & King to Barings, 16 January 1837, NAC.

181. Jonathan S. Goodhue (1783–1848) was born at Salem, Massachusetts, and received early training in commercial affairs as an apprentice to the Salem merchant and ship owner John Norris. He formed his first partnership in 1809 in New York with Peletiah Perit of Norwich, whose Connecticut links provided the firm with a great amount of New England business. From his apprentice days, Goodhue had travelled extensively to Aden, Calcutta and Canton. As Goodhue & Company, the firm acted as agent for the China House of Russell & Company, as well as agent for the Liverpool packet line across the Atlantic on the first and sixteenth of each month from New York and Liverpool after 1834. The firm dissolved in December 1861. It is interesting to note that when Goodhue first arrived in New York from Boston, he received his initial financial assistance from William Grey – the same man to whom Joshua Bates had been apprenticed until age twenty-four. According to Barrett, Goodhue was among the few New England merchants who survived the War of 1812, Barrett, *The Old Merchants*, vol. 1, p. 327 and *passim*; Hunt, 'Jonathan Goodhue', in *Lives of American Merchants*, pp. 345–66; Hidy, *The House of Baring*, p. 82.

182. Baring Brothers Letterbooks, Barings to Ward, 28 February 1832, NAC.

183. Barings to Ward, 4 April 1833, NAC.

184. The House had retained the Mexican government's agency since 1826, but tired of having to make payments on securities ahead of Mexico's remittances, Barings transferred the agency to Lizardi & Company in 1836. It is interesting to note that Barings' general avoidance of Latin American finance since the problems of the mid-1820s did not disqualify the firm from handling the transfer of $15 million paid by the United States to Mexico under the Treaty of Guadalupe Hidalgo for the territories of Texas, New Mexico and California in 1848. It may be noted also that the decade of this study, roughly 1828–38, represents part of a dormant period in an otherwise fertile relationship between Barings and Latin America. With the late 1840s, Barings re-established ties with the region, heavily concentrating in Uruguay and Argentina which, in the 1890s, had historic consequences for Barings and for all British finance.

185. Ward to Bates, 2 June 1833, MHS.
186. The population of the United States in 1816 was 8,659,000; in 1826, 11,558,000; in 1836, 15,423,000. See US Census, *The Statistical History*, p. 8.
187. Berry, *Western Prices*, p. 531 and *passim*. The land boom that characterized much of the 1830s was one of three periods of feverish land sales and speculation before 1860 in the United States. The other periods include 1816–18 and 1852–6. Each land sale increase was associated with population movement and new settlement into western territories. Each correlated positively with increasing prices for the major western staples of corn and wheat, but with a lag time of approximately one year. A fourth, shorter lived, land sale spurt and commodity price increase occurred during the Irish famine years, 1845–7. See W. B. Smith and A. H. Cole, *Fluctuations in American Business, 1790–1860* (Cambridge, MA: Harvard University Press, 1935), p. 55 (chart).
188. Based on weighted monthly price indices. For New York, see ibid., pp. 143–68. For New Orleans and Cincinnati, see Cole, *Wholesale Commodity Prices*, pp. 178–9, 185; Berry, *Western Prices*, pp. 97–102.
189. Cole, *Wholesale Commodity Prices*, p. 94. Cole finds that the regional price indices for the cities of Boston, New York, Philadelphia, Charleston and, of slightly later date, New Orleans and Cincinnati/Ohio Valley show 'complete unanimity in secular trend' towards convergence from at least 1745, and that the trend becomes more apparent in the years after 1822. Berry's study of Cincinnati prices is a potent indicator of when integration of the western states into the American national economy took place. Berry finds that, before 1825, prices in the young Cincinnati were the most independent of itself, New York and New Orleans. After 1850, the more mature Cincinnati's prices were the least independent. This indicated the west was working fairly intimately with other regions because it was now lashed to those regions by better roads, canals and rail lines, Berry, *Western Prices*, pp. 120–35.
190. US Census, *The Statistical History*, p. 899.
191. *Niles*, 56 (27 July 1839), p. 349; North, *The Economic Growth*, pp. 133, 237; T. S. Berry, *Production and Population Since 1789: Revised GNP Series in Constant Dollars* (Richmond, VA: Bostwick Press, 1988), p. 19. This gross national product figure derives from North's table A-VII, p. 232, which sets cotton prices among five exporting cities at $0.1764 per lb. See Cole, *Wholesale Commodity Prices*, p. 259. In this calculation, I have used Berry's bale weight for cotton of 500 lbs, stated in his *Western Prices*, p. 154.
192. Tooke and Newmarch, *A History of Prices*, vol. 2, p. 120.
193. Ibid., vol. 2, pp. 209–14, as cited in Gayer et al., *The Growth and Fluctuation*, vol. 1, p. 212, n.
194. Smart, *Economic Annals*, vol. 2, p. 474.
195. Tooke and Newmarch, *A History of Prices*, vol. 2, pp. 13–14.
196. Smart, *Economic Annals*, vol. 2, p. 472.
197. In 1833, Parliamentary witnesses unanimously described a difficult pricing environment for various British manufacturers over the preceding six years. By contrast, the range of agricultural prices over this time remained generally high. The relative strength of agricultural prices and the satisfactory position of the farmer allowed the revision of the Corn Laws in 1828 into a sliding scale of duties related to home prices.

See Gayer et al., *The Growth and Fluctuation*, vol. 1, pp. 234, 528; Smart, *Economic Annals*, vol. 2, p. 526.

198. North, *The Economic Growth*, pp. 93, 244; D. C. North, 'The United States Balance of Payments, 1790–1860', in *Trends in the American Economy in the Nineteenth Century*, Studies in Income and Wealth of the National Bureau of Economic Research, vol. 24 (Princeton, NJ: Princeton University Press, 1960), pp. 573–627, on p. 621.

199. US Census, *The Statistical History*, p. 1118; Berry, *Production and Population*, pp. 25–6.

200. R. H. Timberlake, *The Origins of Central Banking in the United States* (Cambridge, MA: Harvard University Press, 1978), p. 29; Smith, *Economic Aspects of the Second Bank*, p. 137.

201. Commenting on the 1825–6 pressure, Biddle wrote in 1828 about an interventionist bank policy: 'I have always thought the Bank of England misses the delicate and hazardous moment when, assuming confidence in itself, it might have inspired confidence in others', quoted in ibid., p. 140.

202. W. B. Smith reports that by the middle of 1832 roughly half of Pennsylvania's debt was domiciled overseas, ibid., pp. 101, 282, n. 8.

203. S. E. Morison, *The Maritime History of Massachusetts 1783–1860* (Cambridge, MA: Houghton Mifflin Company, 1921), pp. 276–7; Hidy, *The House of Baring*, p. 74.

204. Ibid., p. 68.

205. The Country Bankers Act restricted the Bank of England's monopoly of joint-stock banking to within a 65-mile radius of London. It also allowed these banks to set up outside that limit and issue notes. The Act authorized the Bank of England to establish country branches for the first time in England and Wales, which could issue their own notes. Competent descriptions of British bank development are found in M. Collins, *Money and Banking in the UK: A History* (London: Routledge, 1988); R. S. Sayers, *Modern Banking*, 7th edn (Oxford: Clarendon Press, 1967).

206. As they had no London presence, the House of Brown did not participate in securities' underwriting as did London-based banks. Brown remained an unalloyed trading firm – and a very tough competitor that dominated the American market from the 1840s onwards. For the rise of Liverpool, see Chapman, *Merchant Enterprise in Britain*, esp. pp. 73–93.

207. Bates to Ward, 7 November 1830, MHS.

208. Bates Diary, 14 March 1831; Bates to Ward, 21 June 1832, MHS.

209. Bates Diary, 30 August 1845, in Ziegler, *The Sixth Great Power*, p. 126.

210. Bates to Ward, 5 April 1832, MHS; Hidy, *The House of Baring*, p. 107.

211. Bates to Ward, 21 June 1832, MHS.

212. Ziegler, *The Sixth Great Power*, pp. 134–6.

213. Bates to Ward, 20 April 1833, MHS. Barings' profit figures for each twelve-month period may be followed in Joshua Bates's diary. It is from this source that the above figures derive. They differ slightly from Ziegler's unsourced figures on p. 136 of his *Sixth Great Power*, but are within 4 per cent of Bates's estimates. See Bates Diary, 16 February 1833, for profit of 1832; 18 January 1834, for 1833.

214. Bates to Ward, 21 June 1832, MHS.

215. Bates to Ward, 5 April 1832, MHS.

216. Ward to Bates, 5 February 1832, MHS.

217. Bates to Ward, 20 April 1833, MHS.
218. After 1833, prices for hyson (green) teas imported into the United States dropped from an unweighted mean of $0.98 per lb. in 1829–32, to an average $0.64 in the years 1833–6, Cole, *Wholesale Commodity Prices*, pp. 229–63.
219. Greenberg, *British Trade and the Opening of China*, p. 185.
220. J. M. Downs, *The Golden Ghetto: The American Commercial Community at Canton and the Shaping of American China Policy, 1784–1844* (Bethlehem, PA: Lehigh University Press, 1997), pp. 82, 127, 162, 170.
221. M. Keswick (ed.), *The Thistle and the Jade: A Celebration of 150 Years of Jardine, Matheson & Co.* (London: Octopus, 1982), p. 22; Greenberg, *British Trade and the Opening of China*, p. 98; Y. Hao, 'Chinese Teas to America – a Synopsis', in E. R. May and J. K. Fairbank (eds), *America's China Trade in Historical Perspective* (Cambridge, MA: Harvard University Press, 1986), pp. 3–25, on p. 25.
222. Hidy, *The House of Baring*, pp. 166–7.
223. Keswick, *The Thistle and the Jade*, pp. 65, 109–10.
224. J. Sturgis (ed.), *From the Books and Papers of Russell Sturgis* (Oxford: privately printed, n.d.), p. 209. Copy in Baring Archives. Russell Sturgis became partner of the House of Baring in 1851.
225. For a detailed discussion of the recharter of the East India Company, see 'China Trade and Government of India', transcribed from the *Liverpool Times*, in *Niles*, 44 (18 May 1833), pp. 183–4; also *Niles*, 44 (17 August 1833), pp. 406–7; 45 (12 October 1833), p. 103; Bates to Ward, 2 June 1833, MHS.
226. *Niles*, 44 (11 May 1833), p. 163; (22 June 1833), p. 272; (17 August 1833), p. 407; 45 (23 November 1833), p. 199; J. H. Rose, A. P. Newton and E. A. Benians (gen. eds), *Cambridge History of the British Empire*, 8 vols in 9 (Cambridge: Cambridge University Press, 1929–59), vol. 2, pp. 756–8. The six failed Houses listed in *Niles*, 45, are Alexander & Company, Mackintosh & Company, Failie & Company, Colvin & Company, Shotten & Company and, the largest, John Palmer & Company. A prominent member of the same Palmer family was Horsley Palmer of the Bank of England from 1830 to 1833, whose opinions contributed to the Bank Charter Act of 1833. See Greenberg, *British Trade and the Opening of China*, pp. 165–6. For indigo price data, see Cole, *Wholesale Commodity Prices*, p. 202 ff.
227. Bates to Ward, 21 June 1832, MHS.
228. Bates to Ward, 2 June and 10 July 1833; Ward to Bates, 25 July 1833, MHS.
229. Bates to Ward, 20 April 1833, MHS.
230. Bates to Ward, 21 June 1832 and 10 July 1833, MHS; Bates Diary, 8 September 1833, in Ziegler, *The Sixth Great Power*, p. 132.
231. Bates to Ward, 2 June 1833, MHS. Regarding the Corn Laws, by 1833 Parliament had revised the laws restricting foreign grains into Great Britain in 1828 with a sliding scale of import duties linked to grain prices in the home market. See table in Smart, *Economic Annals*, vol. 2, p. 438; Gayer et al., *The Growth and Fluctuation*, vol. 1, pp. 233–4.
232. Bates to Ward, 2 June 1833, MHS.
233. Bates said publicly that the Corn Laws encouraged American manufacturing, which would eventually compete successfully with British wares. If free-trade legislation could pass, so that Britain allowed American commodities into the country with

fewer regulations, Bates believed the United States would return to its more natural inclination of an agricultural nation, and the growth of American manufacturing would slow. See 'Report from the Select Committee on Manufactures', qq. 882–5 (J. Bates).

234. Ward to Bates, 25 May 1833, MHS.

235. Bates to Ward, 4 January and 21 June 1832, MHS.

236. Ward to Barings, 4 September 1832, Baring Archives, HC5.1.2.

237. Andrew Jackson, 'Annual Address to Congress, December 8, 1829', in J. D. Richardson (ed.), *A Compilation of the Messages and Papers of the Presidents*, 10 vols (Washington, DC: Government Printing Office, 1896–9), vol. 2, p. 1025.

238. Redlich, *The Molding of American Banking*, p. 135.

239. One of the first sources of the theory that note issues could be regulated by the course of exchange was Thornton's *An Inquiry into the Nature and Effects of the Paper Credit of Great Britain*. David Ricardo endorsed Thornton's argument in his *The High Price of Bullion: A Proof of the Depreciation of Bank Notes* (London: John Murray, 1810). Publishers in the United States took up these works in the first decades of the nineteenth century, when Biddle must have read and absorbed them. See Redlich, *The Molding of American Banking*, pp. 124–5.

240. 'The Curency', in *National Gazette*, 10 April 1828; United States 22nd Congress, 2nd session, Senate Document 17, p. 100, both cited in Redlich, *The Molding of American Banking*, p. 135. For the evolution of Biddle's thinking during the Jackson years, see R. C. McGrane, *The Correspondence of Nicholas Biddle Dealing with National Affairs, 1807–1844* (Boston, MA: Houghton Mifflin Company 1919).

241. R. C. H. Catterall, *The Second Bank of the United States* (Chicago, IL: University of Chicago Press 1902), p. 502.

242. Smith, *Economic Aspects of the Second Bank*, p. 151.

243. Additionally, cholera hit Great Britain in late 1831, and continued until April 1832, claiming nearly 3,000 victims. It should be noted that cholera was a regular feature of the nineteenth century – in Great Britain, the American south and Europe. It is difficult to say how the disease affected business conditions, decision-making or business outcomes. See *Circular to Bankers* (22 April 1831); *Niles*, 42 (31 March 1832), p. 81.

244. Gayer et al., *The Growth and Fluctuation*, vol. 1, p. 212.

245. Smith and Cole, *Fluctuations in American Business*, p. 159.

246. Ziegler's tables indicate a huge increase of income between 1831 and 1832, *The Sixth Great Power*, p. 375.

247. Smith, *Economic Aspects of the Second Bank*, pp. 134–46; Catterall, *The Second Bank*, p. 503.

248. Ibid., p. 502.

249. Smith and Cole, *Fluctuations in American Business*, p. 192.

250. Clapham, *The Bank of England*, vol. 2, p. 118; *Niles*, 42 (17 March 1832), p. 33.

251. Catterall, *The Second Bank*, p. 145. For British bill rates, see Mitchell and Deane, *Abstract of British Historical Statistics*, p. 460.

252. *Niles*, 42 (10 March 1832), p. 20 (emphasis in original).

253. *Niles*, 42 (10 March 1832), p. 20.

254. Berry, *Western Prices*, p. 415.

255. Philadelphia ranked first and New York third, according to the monthly statement of the Bank detailing branch business, as printed in *Niles*, 42 (21 April 1832), p. 150.

256. Berry, *Western Prices*, pp. 415–16.

257. Redlich, *The Molding of American Banking*, p. 140.

258. Smith, *Economic Aspects of the Second Bank*, p. 292, n. 30.

259. Hidy, *The House of Baring*, p 113; Catterall, *The Second Bank*, p. 502.

260. Hidy, *The House of Baring*, p. 116.

261. For example, see *New York Courier*, in *Niles*, 43 (9 September 1832), p. 73.

262. Barings to Ward, 14 November 1831, in Hidy, *The House of Baring*, p. 114.

263. Letter of 16 February 1832, cited in Catterall, *The Second Bank*, p. 145.

264. Bates Diary, 22 August 1832; Smith, *Economic Aspects of the Second Bank*, p. 158.

265. *Niles*, 43 (22 December 1832), p. 265; 44 (9 March 1833), p. 27; 'Mr Polk's Speech', *Niles*, 45 (11 January 1834), pp. 335–44.

266. Ward to Bates, 8 March 1832; Barings to Ward, 17 April 1832, NAC. Hidy wrote: 'Barings could not understand how Ward could treat with "so little remark" the critical disclosures of the House of Representatives investigating the affairs of the bank', Hidy, *The House of Baring*, p. 155.

267. T. W. Ward to Nathaniel Appleton, 3 February 1832, Appleton Papers, Massachusetts Historical Society, cited in Smith, *Economic Aspects of the Second Bank*, p. 155.

268. *Niles*, 43 (26 January 1833), p. 359; 44 (9 March 1833), pp. 27–8.

269. Hidy, *The House of Baring*, p. 120. It must be noted that the House under Bates did not discount its bill remittances, but always held them to maturity. This policy was apparently unique to the House and was enunciated to Ward in the difficult times of February 1837. 'The advantage of not discounting is that of having your credit unlimited', said Bates, revealing a disciplined, restrained and controlled approach. This approach was not followed by Barings' rivals. According to Professor Hidy, whose study goes beyond the years of this essay, the House did not show the slightest sign of wavering from this plodding policy at least to 1861. On rare occasions, the firm tapped the London money market if it needed funds, and used bonds as collateral. It did not borrow against its commercial transactions by discounting, Hidy, *The House of Baring*, pp. 149–50.

270. Barings' profit figures converted at $4.80/£1, Catterall, *The Second Bank*, p. 504; Ziegler, *The Sixth Great Power*, p. 375.

271. *Niles*, 42 (17 March 1832), p. 33; *Circular to Bankers* (9 and 23 March 1832).

272. Hidy, *The House of Baring*, pp. 110–11.

273 In April 1833, the Citizens Bank of Louisiana surpassed the Union Bank as New Orleans' largest chartered bank, with a capitalization of $12 million. See Schweikart, *Banking in the American South*, p. 136, table 7.

274. *Niles*, 42 (21 April 1832), p. 150; see also Bates to Ward, 21 June 1832, MHS, for evidence of the arrangement of the Louisiana loan through the offices of Biddle.

275. Hidy, *The House of Baring*, p. 122.

276. *Circular to Bankers* (5 October 1832).

277. *Niles*, 45 (18 January 1834), p. 345.

278. Great Britain, France, Prussia, Russia and Austria.

279. C. W. Crawley (ed.), *The New Cambridge Modern History, Vol. 9: War amd Peace in an Age of Upheaval, 1793–1830* (Cambridge: Cambridge University Press, 1971),

pp. 246–52; Herbert C. F. Bell, *Lord Palmerston*, 2 vols (London: Longmans, 1936), vol. 1, pp. 116–38.

280. *Niles*, 43 (24 November 1832), p. 200; (5 January 1833), pp. 302–3.

281. Bates to Ward, 5 April 1832, MHS.

282. Bates to Ward, 10 July 1833 and 21 June 1833, MHS.

283. 'From London papers' (William IV's speech to open Parliament), *Niles*, 44 (5 February 1833), p. 66.

284. Bates to Ward, 21 June 1833, MHS.

285. Bates Diary, 30 August 1831.

286. For a contemporary account of the favourable northern view of the tariff, see 'Memorial of the New York Convention' of 25 October 1831, a meeting of 'friends of domestic industry', presented to the committees on manufactures in both Houses of Congress, in *Niles*, addendum to 42 (1832), pp. 19–39.

287. The tariff of May 1828 was the fourth (after 1816, 1818 and 1824) in a series of ever-more protectionist measures passed by Congress to shield American business and industry from British imports after the War of 1812. With it, protection reached its highest point before the Civil War. The tariff of 1828 imposed a value-added tax of 50 per cent as well as a specific duty of $0.04 per lb. on raw wool, 45 per cent on most woollens, and sharply-increased general duties on hemp and pig and bar iron. The legislation of 1832 began a period of successively lower duties and included measures in 1833, 1842 and 1857. The trend towards lower tariffs lasted until 1860 and included an ever-lengthening free list. For a formal description of the tariff of 1832, see 'Report of the Secretary of the Treasury: on the Adjustment of the Tariff', in *Niles*, 42 (5 May 1832), pp. 188–9.

288. R. V. Remini, *Daniel Webster: The Man and his Time* (New York: W. W. Norton, 1997), pp. 219–21, 270, 299.

289. *Niles*, 44 (2 March 1833), pp. 4–7; (9 March 1833), p. 18.

290. *Niles*, 42 (21 April 1832), p. 121.

291. Ibid., p. 122.

292. 'Evidence before Committee on Manufactures, Commerce, and Shipping' (2 March 1819), in *British Parliamentary Papers. Industrial Revolution*, 3 vols (Shannon, Ireland: Irish University Press, 1968–70), vol. 2, pp. 54–5, qq. 882–5. Great Britain did not repeal the Corn Laws until 1846 under the ministry of Robert Peel.

293. For a partial list of British and American goods with their duties compared, see *Niles*, 43 (12 January 1833), p. 316.

294. [H. Clay], 'Debate in the Senate', *Niles*, 43 (16 February 1833), pp. 409–10.

295. 'Resolution from the New York Convention of the Friends of Domestic Industry', *Niles*, 43 (26 January 1833), p. 352; also 44 (9 March 1833), pp. 22–3.

296. *Niles*, 44 (22 June 1833), p. 266 (italics in original).

297. Bates to Ward, 4 January 1832, MHS.

298. *Niles*, 42 (9 June 1832), p. 275.

299. Bates Diary, 12 May 1833.

300. Hidy, *The House of Baring*, pp. 186–7; Ward to Barings, 10 September 1833, NAC. The author does not know if the ships jointly managed by Barings and Goodhue were registered in the United States for duty-free importing. Bates favoured American shipbuilding technology, which he considered twenty years ahead of British. It is

likely, however, that the attractiveness of the American market in the early 1830s, made even more so by tariff incentives, contributed to the United States carrying 90 per cent of its international trade under its own flag. *Evidence before Committee on Manufacturing, Commerce, and Shipping* (1833), q. 972; J. Strouse, *Morgan: American Financier* (New York: Random House, 1999), p. 458. For a contemporary discussion of American ship-building science, see *Niles*, 44 (13 July 1833), pp. 334–5.

301. *Niles*, 44 (23 March 1833), p. 49.

302. Bates to Ward, 21 June 1832, MHS (emphasis in original).

303. Bates Diary, 16 February 1833, 18 January 1834 and 2 February 1835.

304. Bates to Ward, 21 June 1832, MHS.

305. This two-paragraph section draws from Bates to Ward, 21 June 1832 and 5 April 1832, MHS.

306. Ward to Bates, 5 February 1832, MHS.

307. Ward to Bates, 17 May 1832, MHS.

308. Bates to Ward, 5 April 1832 and 2 June 1833, MHS.

309. *Niles*, 44 (23 March 1833), p. 52; (29 March 1833), p. 65 (italics in original).

310. *Niles*, 42 (31 March 1832), p. 79.

311. *Niles*, 44 (6 April 1833), pp. 81–2.

312. Gayer et al., *The Growth and Fluctuation*, vol. 1, p. 245; Mitchell and Deane, *Abstract of British Historical Statistics*, p. 314. The year 1832 was the beginning of what Gayer et al. called a 'major business cycle', which extended to 1837. All business cycles in the period 1790–1850, whether 'minor' or 'major', include increases in the volume of exports. See Gayer et al., *The Growth and Fluctuation*, vol. 2, pp. 534–5.

313. From *The Times*, London, as of 31 May 1833, reported in *Niles*, 44 (13 July 1833), p. 328.

314. Gayer et al., *The Growth and Fluctuation*, vol. 1, pp. 250–1.

315. *Niles*, 44 (2 March 1833), p. 2.

316. *Niles*, 44 (27 July 1833), p. 354.

317. News from the *Cleveland Herald*, in *Niles*, 42 (23 June 1832), p. 300. With the Ohio Canal completed, the *Herald* commented: 'There will be a chain of communication, which, for magnificence of design and greatness of enterprise, has scarcely a parallel in the works of art – a communication which will connect the waters of the Atlantic with those of the Mississippi'. For an overview of canals in the antebellum Midwest, see H. N. Scheiber, *Ohio Canal Era* (Athens, OH: Ohio University Press, 1969).

318. *Niles*, 44 (20 July 1833), pp. 338, 355.

319. Reported by the *Albany Argus* of 9 September 1833, in *Niles*, 45 (21 September 1833). For perspective on the 1832–3 figures, Erie and Champlain canal tolls in 1825 totalled slightly over half a million dollars, Taylor, *The Transportation Revolution*, p. 34. For infrastructure build-out in the United States, see C. Goodrich, *Government Promotion of American Canals and Railroads* (New York: Columbia University Press, 1960).

320. Tolls received on the Ohio canal were $16,933.80 in May 1833, and $10.147.43 in the previous year, *Niles*, 44 (27 July 1833), p. 355.

321. *Niles*, 43 (23 February 1833), p. 425; 44 (11 May 1833), p. 162.

322. US Census, *The Statistical History*, p. 8; F. Crouzet, *The Victorian Economy* (London: Methuen, 1982), p. 20; P. Deane and W. A. Cole, *British Economic Growth, 1688–1959*, 2nd edn (Cambridge: Cambridge University Press, 1967), p. 172. Britain's annual growth rate reached a maximum of 1.5 per cent between 1801 and 1831, then fell to 1.3 per cent between 1821 and 1851, and 1.2 per cent thereafter. By contrast, the United States grew at nearly 3 percent per year throughout the antebellum period. Immigration, partly from Great Britain itself, was a major contributor, especially in the period under study. The years 1830–40 saw a quantum increase of immigration to the United States as a percentage of total population growth, which continued for the balance of the century. See W. W. Rostow, *The World Economy: History and Prospect* (Austin, TX: University of Texas Press, 1978), pp. 20–1.
323. *Niles*, 44 (17 August 1833), p. 402.
324. *Niles*, 46 (26 July 1834), pp. 371–3. So far as an apparent trade deficit existed, 'invisible' profits having to do with shipping earnings likely mitigated a yawning gap. See Hezekiah Niles's comment, p. 372.
325. *Niles*, 44 (9 March 1833), pp. 18–19.
326. S. Bruchey, *Enterprise: The Dynamic Economy of a Free People* (Cambridge, MA: Harvard University Press, 1990), pp. 151–2.
327. The four large mills at Lowell at this time had 290, 480, 826 and – in the Merrimac Mill – 1,443 workers. Such New Hampshire firms as New Market, Cocheco and Great Falls were on average even larger with 672, 1,075 and 1,443 workers. See *Trends in the American Economy*, pp. 450–1.
328. *Niles*, 44 (6 July 1833), p. 315.
329. *Bell's [London] Weekly Messenger* reported that British factories spun 288 million lbs of cotton in 1832 (of which 10 per cent was Scottish), compared with the United States' 85 million lbs. The United States supplied three-quarters of the cotton consumed by British mills, *Niles*, 44 (16 March 1833), p. 37; comparative country data from the *Glasgow Chronicle*, as reprinted in *Niles*, 44 (1 June 1833), p. 224.
330. Rostow, *The World Economy*, p. 152.
331. R. L. Frey (ed.), *Railroads in the Nineteenth Century* (New York: Facts on File, 1988), p. 282; *Niles*, 44 (17 August 1833), p. 403.
332. *Niles*, 45 (31 August 1833), p. 5; Berry, *Western Prices*, pp. 71–94.
333. The Americans had watched closely the development of British railroad lines, especially after the Stockton and Darlington line opened on 27 September 1825, and the Liverpool to Manchester line five years later. Many American engineers visited England to see these in operation, and to study the machinery, including locomotives.
334. V. S. Clark, *History of Manufactures in the United States*, 3 vols (1929; New York: Carnegie Institution of Washington, 1949), vol. 1, p. 507.
335. *Niles*, 44 (22 June 1833), pp. 267, 269.
336. *Niles*, 44 (20 July 1833), p. 351.
337. Clark, *History of Manufactures*, vol. 1, p. 313.
338. Ibid., pp. 18–19; North, *The Economic Growth*, p. 233.
339. *Niles*, 44 (16 March 1833), p. 41 (emphasis in original).
340. *Niles*, 44 (27 April 1833), p. 130.
341. *Niles*, 45 (9 November 1833), pp. 165–6.

342. *Niles*, 44 (27 April 1833), p. 130; (18 May 1833), p. 182.

343. Bates to Ward, 2 June 1833, MHS.

344. *New York Spectator*, 24 June and 6 March 1833, in Smith, *Economic Aspects of the Second Bank*, p. 170.

345. These claims dealt with seizures of American ships and cargo by the French during the Napoleonic wars. France agreed to pay in six annual instalments. For a documentary overview of this question, see 'Relations with France', in *Niles*, 49 (23 January 1836), pp. 346–56.

346. *Niles*, 45 (31 August 1833), p. 1.

347. *Niles*, 44 (3 August 1833), p. 375; (10 August 1833), p. 402.

348. *Washington Globe*, 27 September, in *Niles*, 45 (5 October 1833), p. 81. The *Washington Globe* was considered the newspaper of the Jackson administration. For a list of banks selected as depositories of public money at the start of 1834, see *Niles*, 45 (8 February 1834), p. 396.

349. *Washington Globe*, undated, in *Niles*, 45 (8 February 1834), p. 396.

350. Richardson, *Messages and Papers of the Presidents*, vol. 2, pp. 576–91.

351. *Niles*, 43 (8 September 1831), p. 17. Jackson outlined his views for a Democratic national bank in his 'Plan for a National Bank' in 1829, which Amos Kendall edited. See also Redlich, *The Molding of American Banking*, p. 169.

352. *Niles*, 43 (22 September 1832), p. 49.

353. *Pittsburgh Gazette* and *Cincinnati Gazette*, in *Niles*, 43 (15 September 1832), p. 40; *Louisville Price Current* and *Natchez Observer*, in *Niles*, 43 (29 September 1832), p. 73 (italics and capitalization in originals).

354. *Niles*, 43 (22 September 1832), pp. 49–50 (emphasis in original).

355. Smith, *Economic Aspects of the Second Bank*, p. 156.

356. *Niles*, 43 (26 January 1833), p. 359. The reader is reminded of the distinction between solvency and liquidity. Solvency refers to a ratio of assets to liabilities. Liquidity has to do with the ability to convert assets readily to cash or cash equivalents. It is possible for an individual or institution to be quite solvent, but require a loan because of the form of assets held. In this case, one is said to be 'illiquid'.

357. *Niles*, 43 (22 December 1832), p. 265; (5 January 1833), p. 305.

358. Report of the House Ways and Means Committee, 28 December 1832, in *Niles*, 43 (5 January 1833), pp. 305–7.

359. Mitchell and Deane, *Abstract of British Historical Statistics*, pp. 393, 396. Note this is seen as the start of the major British business cycle of 1832–7, asserted by Gayer et al., *The Growth and Fluctuation*, vol. 2, p. 535.

360. *Glasgow Times*, in *Niles*, 43 (20 October 1832), pp. 113–14; Gayer et al., *The Growth and Fluctuation*, vol. 1, p. 243.

361. Mitchell and Deane, *Abstract of British Historical Statistics*, p. 450; Tooke and Newmarch, *A History of Prices*, vol. 2, p. 240. Legislation in 1833 permitted joint-stock banks in London and within the 65-mile radius around London previously denied to them by the Country Bankers Act of 1826. The 1826 Act allowed joint-stock banks to issue notes outside the radius. In exchange for this concession, the Bank of England set up branches for the first time.

362. For the impact of this loan on British public finance, see Mitchell and Deane, *Abstract of British Historical Statistics*, pp. 396, 399, n. (*e*).

363. Ward to Barings, 14 and 18 September 1833, NAC.
364. *New York Commercial Advertiser* of 18 July, in *Niles*, 44 (27 July 1833), p. 353; states list in *Niles*, 44 (3 August 1833), p. 381.
365. Hammond, *Banks and Politics in America*, pp. 418–19.
366. *Niles*, 45 (5 October 1833), p. 81.
367. Quoted in *Niles*, 45 (5 October 1833), pp. 81–2.
368. Richardson, *Messages and Papers of the Presidents*, vol. 3, p. 31.
369. Ward to Barings, 20 September 1833, NAC.
370. Reported in *Niles*, 45 (2 November 1833), p. 146 (emphasis in original).
371. 'North Carolina papers', and 'Eye Witness Communication', *Niles*, 45 (28 December 1833), pp. 295, 297.
372. *The Philadelphia American Daily Advertiser*, in *Niles*, 45 (4 January 1834), p. 309.
373. *Niles*, 45 (12 October 1833), p. 97.
374. The Bank of the United States branch system, of course, had eliminated these inefficiencies after roughly 1827.
375. *Niles*, 45 (23 November 1833), pp. 194–5; (28 December 1833), p. 288.
376. *Niles*, 45 (28 December 1833), p. 288, n.; (8 February 1834), p. 396.
377. Reproduced from *Niles*, 45 (1 February 1834), p. 389; see also P. Hone, *The Diary of Philip Hone, 1828–1851*, ed. B. Tuckerman, 2 vols (New York: Dodd, Mead, and Company, 1889), vol. 1, p. 85.
378. *Register of Debates*, 22nd Congress, 1st session, pp. 954–64, in Remini, *Daniel Webster*, p. 362.
379. Ward to Bates, 21 November 1833, Baring Archives, HC5.1.2.
380. *Niles*, 46 (22 March 1834), p. 49.
381. *Niles*, 45 (28 December 1833), p. 298; (4 January 1834), pp. 309–12; (11 January 1834), pp. 333–4; (8 February 1834), p. 397.
382. 'From London papers to 18th January', *Niles*, 46 (1 March 1834), p. 5.
383. Quoted from *Niles*, 46 (5 April 1834), p. 87; (10 May 1834), p. 172.
384. Quoted from the 'London Times of May 8', *Niles*, 46 (28 June 1834), p. 299.
385. The committee was appointed by the signers of a memorial drawn up at the Merchants' Exchange and sent to Congress in February. James Brown was a member of the merchant banking House Brown Brothers & Company; Philip Hone was former mayor of New York City, financier, philanthropist, civic leader and ardent Whig; James G. King was a partner of Prime, Ward & King. The section dealing with the New York bankers' report is taken from 'Report of the "Union Committee" of N. York', *Niles*, 46 (29 March 1834), pp. 73–80. In addition to the 'Report' itself, the present writer will include references to Niles where relevant.
386. As quoted in Smith, *Economic Aspects of the Second Bank*, p. 166.
387. *Niles*, 45 (28 December 1833), p. 289.
388. Apart from the Union Committee report itself, see also the helpful discussions of duties in *Niles*, 45 (7 September 1833), p. 18; (2 November 1833), p. 146; (9 November 1833), p. 163.
389. Albert Gallatin served as secretary of the Treasury from 1801 to 1814 under presidents Jefferson and Madison, *Niles*, 45 (15 February 1834), p. 421.
390. *Richmond Enquirer*, in *Niles*, 45 (25 January 1834), p. 363, n.

391. 'Report of the Philadelphia Committee', 22 February 1834, in *Niles*, 46 (1 March 1834), p. 9.

392. Hammond, *Banks and Politics in America*, p. 420.

393. 'United States Bank Items', *Niles*, 45 (15 February 1834), p. 410.

394. Hammond, *Banks and Politics in America*, pp. 420–1.

395. For an excellent discussion of these issues, albeit pro-Bank, see ibid., pp. 420–2; *Niles*, 45 (23 November 1833), p. 195.

396. The Girard Bank was not the original institution owned by Stephen Girard, who had died in 1832, but an institution under state charter, *Niles*, 45 (25 January 1834), p. 195; *Niles*, 46 (29 March 1834), p. 65.

397. R. W. Hidy, 'The House of Baring and the Second Bank of the United States, 1826–1836', *Pennsylvania Magazine of History and Biography* (July 1944), pp. 269–85, on p. 284.

398. 'Foreign News', *Niles*, 44 (3 August 1833), pp. 376, 424.

399. Cole, *Wholesale Commodity Prices*, pp. 245–49.

400. *Niles*, 45 (31 August 1833), p. 3; (7 September 1833), p. 17.

401. *Charleston Mercury*, in *Niles*, 45 (28 September 1833), p. 66.

402. A circular from Barings shows that Europe took 648,166 bales to the end of May 1833, against 589,581 bales at the same time in 1832, *Niles*, 45 (31 August 1833), p. 3.

403. *Manchester Guardian* and *Leeds Mercury*, in *Niles*, 45 (31 August 1833), p. 3; *Pennsylvanian*, in *Niles*, 45 (7 September 1833), p. 17.

404. *Niles*, 45 (14 September 1833), p. 33.

405. Ward to Barings, 14 September 1833, NAC; *Register of Debates*, 23rd Congress, 1st session, X, part 1, p. 984, in Smith, *Economic Aspects of the Second Bank*, pp. 167–8. The recently-published history of Rothschilds makes no mention of cotton activities of the House at this time. It does corroborate Ward's impression of activity in preparation for a commitment to the American market. This will be described in later sections of this volume. See Ferguson, *The House of Rothschild*.

406. *Niles*, 45 (4 January 1834), p. 309.

407. Hidy, *The House of Baring*, p. 166.

408. Bates to Ward, 3 June 1832, Baring Archives, HC5.1.2. Professor Hidy finds the partners were worried about price declines in the United States in the second quarter of 1833. There is little evidence for such price behaviour in the weighted or unweighted wholesale price data assembled by Smith and Cole in *Fluctuations in American Business*. See Hidy, *The House of Baring*, p. 165.

409. The reader will recall that 'coverage' of a credit has to do with the attachment of a bill of lading. See Chapter 2 above for these concepts.

410. Hidy, *The House of Baring*, p. 168.

411. Ward to Barings, 14 September 1833, NAC.

412. Ward to Barings, 18 November 1833, in Hidy, *The House of Baring*, p. 170.

413. Ward to Barings, 14 September 1833, NAC.

414. Ward to Bates, 20 November 1833, MHS.

415. Ward to Barings, 18 September 1833, NAC.

416. Perkins, *Financing Anglo-American Trade*, pp. 36, 98–9.

417. Ibid., p. 37.

418. This section borrows from ibid., p. 106, which relies on Peter Temin's article, 'The Causes of Cotton-Price Fluctuations in the 1830s', *Review of Economics and Statistics*, 49 (November 1967), pp. 463–70.

419. Perkins, *Financing Anglo-American Trade*, p. 96.

420. W. W. Rostow, 'Business Cycles, Harvests, and Politics: 1790–1850', *Journal of Economic History*, 1 (1941), pp. 206–21, on p. 210.

421. Catterall, *The Second Bank*, pp. 502–3; *Niles*, 45 (7 September 1833), p. 19.

422. *Niles*, 46 (10 May 1834), p. 169; (17 May 1834), p. 188.

423. *Niles*, 46 (19 July 1834), p. 346.

424. In preparation for the gold recoinage of August, Congress passed the Silver Coin Law in June 1834, which laid down new weight specifications for foreign coins 'to pass current as money' in the United States and 'be legal for the payment of debts and demands', *Niles*, 46 (7 June 1834), p. 253; (5 July 1834), p. 321. For a contemporary Jacksonian political view of the Gold Coinage Act legislation, see T. H. Benton, *Thirty Years' View, or, A History of the Working of the American Government for Thirty Years from 1820 to 1850*, 2 vols (New York: Appleton, 1854–7), vol. 1, pp. 440–70.

425. J. H. Palmer, *Causes and Consequence of the Pressure on the Money Market from 1ˢᵗ October, 1833, to 27ᵗʰ December, 1836*, cited in Tooke and Newmarch, *A History of Prices*, vol. 2, pp. 285–6.

426. Ward to Bates, 24 February 1835, NAC.

427. Niles, 48 (21 February 1835), p. 425.

428. Ward to Barings, [no day] April 1835, NAC.

429. Hammond, *Banks and Politics in America*, pp. 446–7. Edwin Perkins observes that the Browns also sometimes envied the British financial system in comparison to the American. See Perkins, *Financing Anglo-American Trade*, p, 128.

430. Bates Diary, 16 February 1833; Ward to Barings, 23 December 1832, Baring Archives, HC5.1.2.

431. *Niles*, 42 (21 July 1832), p. 378; (28 July 1832), p. 398; 43 (15 December 1832), p. 258; (22 December 1832), p. 265; (9 February 1833), p. 396; 44 (9 March 1833), p. 27.

432. Everett to Ward, 18 February 1834, MHS.

433. *Niles*, 47 (13 December 1834), p. 236.

434. Ward to Barings, 14 September 1833, NAC.

435. Ferguson, *The House of Rothschild*, p. 369. See also Ziegler, *The Sixth Great Power*, p. 150.

436. Bates Diary, 26 September 1834.

437. Bates to Ward, 5 April 1832, MHS.

438. In commenting on Nullification to Bates, the well-informed Ward concluded that the issue of slavery would cause 'restlessness from time to time that may grow troublesome, but [in the end] it [would] strengthen the Union'. He cited the fractiousness among the southern states themselves and their inability to unite with South Carolina. 'The doctrines of '98', Ward wrote in 1833, 'are out of fashion, the true principles of our Government are better understood, and the opinion is gaining ground among the Slave states that their only safety lies in holding on to the Union and in the support of the Free States', Ward to Bates, 25 May 1833, MHS. His intelligence note to Bates proved correct and useful in the short run. In the longer run, of course, he saw the

inaccuracy of his prediction. Ward died in 1856. Joshua Bates, who died in 1864, lived to see its complete undoing.
439. Ward to Bates, 28 May 1833, MHS. It is likely that Ward's distaste for Nathan Prime represented the culture difference that to this day divides brokers from bankers. Under Prime, the firm was highly profitable, and Prime himself was reputed to be the third wealthiest man in New York in 1830. Likely, Ward found Prime's methods to accumulate wealth anathema. As a pioneer in the securities market, Prime established his reputation as an aggressive 'stock and exchange broker' and amassed a fortune as a market maker in such shares as the Manhattan Company. He began as an independent operator, but in order to accommodate a growing roster of customers and services, such as investment banking, foreign exchange and loan contracting, he built progressively larger partnerships. It is not difficult to imagine that the great speculations of Prime in the stock, bond and real estate markets would be vulgar to the instinctively more conservative and discreet Ward. It is also interesting to note that the young Prime was a coachman to William Gray, a prominent Boston merchant and early director of the First Bank of the United States. Gray reportedly loaned Prime money to launch his career. This was the same William Gray who was the early employer of another man who made something of himself in the world of finance: Joshua Bates. See Werner and Smith, *Wall Street*, esp. pp. 50–4; D. Cooper and B. Grinder, 'Richard Grasso, Nathan Prime, and Stock Exchange Transformation', *Financial History*, 80 (Winter 2004), pp. 10–11.
440. Barrett, *The Old Merchants*, vol. 1, pp. 12–13. Samuel Ward of Prime, Ward & King should not be confused with Thomas Ward's eldest son, Samuel, who took over as Barings' American agent when his father retired from the firm in 1853.
441. Ward to Barings, 7 June 1833 and 9 and 13 April 1833, Baring Archives, HC5.1.2.
442. The historian of Barings in the United States, R. W. Hidy, considered that the House 'renounced preponderance ... by its own voluntary action in 1833'. This is misleading in the view of the present author since, in an ever-larger market, it was becoming difficult for Barings or any single House to dominate, at will, the marketing and shipping of American produce and securities. Barings' trimmed its operations because of many present obligations, increased remittance delinquencies and, perhaps, the hostile political environment. Barings could 'voluntarily' cut back its operations. It could also maintain its business as it was and, from the increased number of firms doing American business, see its 'preponderance' fall away into an increasingly fragmented market. Hidy suggestion of the renunciation of something that had already essentially happened makes the event less weighty than his dramatic statement implies, Hidy, *The House of Baring*, p. 171.
443. Hidy, *The House of Baring*, p. 176.
444. 'Wealthy, honourable, safe, and capable', or a similar permutation, was a typical grouping of words that Ward used to describe the Baring correspondent. Ward uses this phrase to describe John Hagen, a principal cotton correspondent with interests in Mobile and New York who drew on Barings. A similar description is made of Samuel Comly, another southern cotton correspondent. See Ward to Barings, 29 May and 20 March 1835, NAC.
445. The reader should not confuse the idea of 'double accounts' with the idea of a 'joint account'. See Perkins, *Financing Anglo-American Trade*, p. 12.

446. Hidy, *The House of Baring*, pp. 351, 562–3, n. 13.
447. The word 'experimentation' was a term of derision used by those who disagreed with the policies of the Andrew Jackson administration in matters of finance. London and Ward likely would have shown sympathy for such a term.
448. Ward to Barings, 29 May 1835, NAC.
449. Bates Diary, 16 February 1833 and 18 January 1834.
450. Bates to Ward, 21 June 1832, MHS.
451. This paragraph tallies information from Ward's list forwarded to Barings dated 25, 30 December 1833, and excerpted from Hidy, *The House of Baring*, pp. 171, 173, 521, n. 14. The present author has converted British pounds to dollars, rounding up from the market par of $4.88 to 5.00/£1.
452. Ziegler, *The Sixth Great Power*, p. 375.
453. Interestingly, just as business was unwinding from the difficulties of 1832–4, Europe had settled into a rigid, divided equilibrium. Belgium ended as a diplomatic problem by the end of 1831. The expansionist activities of Egyptian pasha Mehemet Ali in the Levant and Asia Minor culminated in the Russo-Turkish treaty of cooperation and defence at Unkiar Skelessi in July 1833. A year later, four western Mediterranean powers – Great Britain, France, Spain and Portugal – countered by forming a Quadruple Alliance. Both held for the chronology of this volume.
454. *Niles*, 46 (19 July 1834), p. 346.
455. Hone, *The Diary of Philip Hone*, vol. 1, p. 84.
456. 19 November 1834, quoted from Smith, *Economic Aspects of the Second Bank*, p. 172.
457. M. Chevalier, *Society, Manners and Politics in the United States: Being a Series of Letters on North America*, trans. from 3rd edn (Boston: Weeks, Jordan, 1839), p. 305.
458. Ward to Bates, 24 July 1836, NAC.
459. M. Friedman and A. J. Schwartz, *A Monetary History of the United States: 1867–1960* (Princeton, NJ: Princeton University Press, 1963), p. 300.
460. 'Report of the Secretary of the Treasury', 2 December 1834, in *Niles*, 47 (13 December 1834), p. 247. See also J. S. Gordon, *Hamilton's Blessing* (New York: Walker and Company, 1997), p. 201.
461. The charter rate of banks had increased hugely in the 1830s. In the nine years to 1829, legislatures chartered only twenty-nine more banks than existed in 1820. In the next eight years, this rate increased by a factor of nineteen. The annual rate of charter in 1820–9 was 3.2; in 1830–7 it was 57.4. In the 1840s the states one by one enacted general banking laws which followed the pattern of general, and non-political, incorporation laws. Before then, most state banks continued to be chartered by special act of their legislatures. See P. B. Trescott, *Financing American Enterprise: The Story of Commercial Banking* (New York: Harper & Row, 1963), p. 16; P. Studenski and H. E. Kross, *Financial History of the United States*, 2nd edn (New York: McGraw-Hill, 1963), p. 107; US Census, *The Statistical History*, pp. 1018, 1020; Myers, *A Financial History*, p. 94; J. J. Knox, *A History of Banking in the United States* (1903; New York: Augustus M. Kelley, 1969), p. 82.
462. *Niles*, 45 (28 December 1833), pp. 295, 297; (1 February 1834), p. 389; 46 (5 April 1834), p. 86; (28 June 1834), p. 86; 50 (21 May 1836), p. 201; Ward to Barings, 22 April 1833, NAC.

NOTES TO PAGES 120-6

463. *The Times*, 16 July 1836.
464. B. L. Anderson and P. L. Cottrell, *Money and Banking in England 1694–1914* (London: David & Charles, 1974), pp. 243, 280.
465. 'The "London Times" of 8ᵗʰ May', *Niles*, 46 (28 June 1834), p. 299.
466. *Niles*, 45 (25 January 1834), pp. 367–8.
467. A. Gallatin, *The Writings of Albert Gallatin*, ed. H. Adams, 3 vols (1879; New York: Antiquarian Press, 1960), vol. 3, p. 386. For additional perspective, see Niles's comment that American imports in the third quarter of 1835 equalled those for *all* of 1829, *Niles*, 49 (20 February 1836), p. 425. Of these 1835 imports, 80 per cent passed through the port of New York.
468. These figures are calculated from the tables of G. R. Taylor, which closely approximate Gallatin. See Taylor, *The Transportation Revolution*, pp. 444–5. Taylor uses the *Historical Tables of Commerce, Finance, Tonnage, and Immigration of the United States*, Treasury Department, Bureau of Statistics (Washington, 1894).
469. US Census, *The Statistical History*, p. 430.
470. Hammond, *Banks and Politics in America*, p. 453.
471. *Niles*, 50 (26 March 1836), p. 53.
472. *The Times*, 16 July 1836.
473. H. Martineau, *Society in America*, 3 vols (London: Saunders and Otley, 1837), vol. 1, pp. 259–61.
474. Chevalier, *Society, Manners, and Politics*, p. 309.
475. 'Parliamentary Committee on Manufactures' (1833), in *British Parliamentary Papers. Industrial Revolution*, vol. 2, qq. 390–1579 pp, 22-97.
476. Tooke and Newmarch, *A History of Prices*, vol. 2, pp. 253–7; *Niles*, 50 (19 March 1836), p. 33; (18 June 1836), p. 267.
477. Gayer et al., *The Growth and Fluctuation*, vol. 1, p. 214.
478. Ibid., vol. 1, pp. 243–73; W. M. Scammel, *The London Discount Market* (New York: St Martin's Press, 1968), p. 156; J. H. Clapham, *An Economic History of Modern Britain: The Early Railway Age 1820–50*, 2nd edn, 3 vols (Cambridge: Cambridge University Press, 1930), vol. 1, pp. 387, 511; Tooke and Newmarch, *A History of Prices*, vol. 2, pp. 274–8; King, *History of the London Discount Market*, p. 87.
479. Ward to Bates, 20 and 21 March 1835, NAC.
480. Ward to Barings, 21 February 1835, NAC. In this letter, Ward informed the London partners that France had recalled its minister to the United States.
481. Ward to Barings, 18 May 1835, NAC.
482. Ward to Barings, 29 May 1835, NAC (bracketed interpolation by author for illegible word).
483. Ward to Barings, 26 May 1835, NAC. Note these ideas are a continuation of the extended quotation cited in Chapter 4 above, but here Ward includes names of specific firms.
484. Ward to Barings, 29 May 1835, NAC.
485. Ward to Barings, 30 July 1835, NAC; *New York Herald*, 7 September 1835.
486. Ward to Bates, 24 July 1835, Part 5, Baring Archives, HC5.1.2 (emphasis in original).
487. Ward to Barings, 29 May 1835, NAC.
488. Ward to Barings, 24 July 1835, NAC (emphasis added).

489. Ziegler, *The Sixth Great Power*, p. 375. As usual, this net total is from a variety of sources: commissions on American and European banking, insurances, the servicing of loans and sometimes arrangements for their refunding, the running of sales of goods, stocks, dividends and acceptances.
490. This section is based generally, but not exclusively, on Hidy, *The House of Baring*, pp. 187–94.
491. Ward to Barings, 28 September 1835, NAC.
492. Ward to Barings, 21 and 29 May 1835, NAC.
493. Bates to Ward, 20 April and 2 June 1833, MHS.
494. Ward to Barings, 21 March 1835, NAC.
495. Ward to Barings, 30 May 1835, NAC.
496. Ward to Barings, 18 May 1835, NAC. For correspondence of an American contemporary of Sturgis in the China Trade, see P. F. Kerr (ed), *Letters From China: The Canton-Boston Correspondence of Robert Bennet Forbes, 1838–1840* (Mystic, CT: Mystic Seaport Museum, Inc., 1996).
497. Ward to Barings, 18/19 May and 18 February 1835, NAC; Hidy, *The House of Baring*, p. 192. Was the House also privy to plans of Lord Durham in regard to federation for Canada, and did the partners wish to stake a claim to new prospects in the reorganized dominion? The firm's huge stake in Canada for the rest of the nineteenth century – including the Grand Trunk Railroad – makes this question at least plausible.
498. Ward to Barings, 29 May 1835, NAC.
499. Ward to Barings, 20 October 1835, NAC. At the close of 1835 the capital of the House stood at £674,018, the equivalent of $2,995,636 in American currency. Adjusted for inflation, this is roughly the equivalent in 2007 of $70 million. British deflator from private communication with J. J. McCusker, 10 August 2007.
500. *Niles*, 48 (13 June 1835), p. 250; Ward to Barings, 30 July 1835, NAC; Wilkins, *The History of Foreign Investment*, p. 62.
501. For a succinct discussion of the differences between the House of Baring and the House of Rothschild, see Chapman, *The Rise of Merchant Banking*, pp. 16–34.
502. Ward to Barings, 7 December 1835, NAC. In 1833, Ward gave these figures: 'Alsop is no doubt rich, 200/m; Wetmore 100/m; Cryder, 80/m', Ward to Bates, 25 July 1833, MHS.
503. *Niles*, 48 (2 May 1835), p. 145 (emphasis in original).
504. Hidy, *The House of Baring*, p. 197. Hidy writes that this tight policy held for the next two years.
505. Ward to Barings, 5 July 1835, NAC.
506. Ward to Barings, 12 August 1835, NAC; *Niles*, 48 (29 August 1835), p. 452.
507. Bates Diary, 8 September 1835.
508. Hidy, *The House of Baring*, pp. 198–9.
509. Ibid., p. 199; Ward to Barings, 22 April and 5 July 1835, NAC.
510. Ward to Barings, 21 August 1835, NAC.
511. Ward to Barings, 5 November 1835, NAC.
512. Ward to Barings, [no day] April 1835, NAC.
513. Ward to Barings, 10 October 1835.
514. Hidy, *The House of Baring*, p. 200.
515. Barings to Prime, Ward & King, 17 November 1835, NAC.

516. F. S. Allis (ed.), *William Bingham's Maine Lands* (Boston, 1954), vol. 2, p. 1254, cited in Wilkins, *The History of Foreign Investment*, p. 65.

517. Barings to Prime, Ward & King, 22 October 1835, NAC; to Prime, 11 November 1835, NAC.

518. Barings to Prime, 5 December 1835, NAC. For evidence that Prime was a sympathetic ear to selling (or not buying) and waiting for lower prices, see Prime to Barings, 8 April 1837, NAC.

519. Barings to Mssrs Stieglitz & Company, 18 November 1835, NAC.

520. Ward to Bates, 10 October 1835, NAC.

521. Ward to Barings, 10 October and 6 November 1835, NAC.

522. For the account of the fire see E. G. Burrows and M. Wallace, *Gotham: A History of New York City to 1898* (New York: Oxford University Press, 1999), pp. 596–8; E. R. Ellis, *The Epic of New York City* (New York: Coward-McCann, 1966), pp. 240–2; Hone, *The Diary of Philip Hone*, vol. 1, pp. 180–2; *Niles*, 49 (26 December 1835), p. 180; Bates Diary, 9 January 1836. The ruin of the New York fire insurance industry led promptly to state legislatures permitting insurance companies to operate across state lines. The *Philadelphia Gazette* and the *New York Daily Advertiser* claimed the prohibition against business relations between American states was the same folly perpetuated by those who prohibited foreign investors from lending to the states in the form of subscriptions to bank stocks, for example, and to an aversion to foreign capital in general. See *Niles*, 49 (2 January 1836), p. 300.

523. Catterall, *The Second Bank*, p. 364.

524. *New York Herald*, 23 and 26–8 January and 6, 10 and 12 February 1836; *Niles*, 49 (2 January 1836), p. 297; (30 January 1836), p. 361; 50 (2 March 1836), p. 50; (26 March 1836), p. 99.

525. *Niles*, 50 (5 March 1836), p. 1; 49 (9 January 1836), p. 313; (13 February 1836), p. 424; (20 February 1836), p. 425; Ward to Barings, 16 March 1835, NAC; Hone, *The Diary of Philip Hone*, vol. 1, p. 200.

526. *New York Herald*, 4 April 1836; *Niles*, 50 (9 April 1836), p. 90; (23 April 1836), pp. 129, 135.

527. 'Mr. Van Buren and the Bank, &c', *Niles*, 50 (23 April 1836), p. 135.

528. Treasury secretary Woodbury opposed distribution of the surplus. He proposed instead to husband the surplus for a short time 'as a provident fund to be ready to meet any contingencies attending the great reduction contemplated in our revenue hereafter'. It is interesting to note the argument of the recent Federal Reserve chairman, Alan Greenspan, who proposed a similar 'letting the surpluses run' solution with current budget surpluses – preferring accumulation to tax cuts, and government spending the surplus as last option. See 'Report of the Secretary of the Treasury', *Niles*, 49 (19 December 1835), pp. 257–64.

529. Hone, *The Diary of Philip Hone*, vol. 1, pp. 185–6; Goodhue to Bates, 9 January 1836, Baring Archives, HC5.12.13A; *Niles*, 49 (26 December 1835), p. 285; 50 (16 April 1836), p. 113. Barings acted as foreign distributing agent in England for the £60,000 of sterling bonds that it issued in mortgage bonds for the Merchants' Exchange.

530. Hone, *The Diary of Philip Hone*, vol. 1, p. 200.

531. Ward to Barings, end of April 1835, NAC.

532. *New York Herald*, 13 June 1836.

533. Margaret Myers finds 113 railroad charters issued since 1830, of which 44 were chartered in 'that magnificent year, 1836'. These charters may have come from the exuberance of 1835, but evidently the companies themselves put off building in later years, Myers, *A Financial History*, pp. 114–15.

534. Smith and Cole, *Fluctuations in American Business*, pp. 44–51, 179.

535. Hone, *The Diary of Philip Hone*, vol. 1, pp. 203–4.

536. *New York Herald*, 15 June 1836.

537. Ward to Barings, 9 December 1835, NAC.

538. *Niles*, 50 (5 March 1836), p. 1; (30 July 1836), pp. 331, 363; 48 (16 May 1835), p. 188; (20 June 1835), p. 273; *New York Herald*, 16 June 1836; Chevalier, *Society, Manners and Politics*, p. 307; McGrane, *The Panic of 1837*, pp. 43–69; Studenski and Kross, *Financial History*, p. 99; D. L. Miller, *City of the Century: The Epic of Chicago and the Making of America* (New York: Simon & Schuster, 1996), pp. 48–88. Niles reported that speculation in American lands had reached England, including properties in Virginia, Georgia and Texas. A thousand acres of Georgia land sold for £50, *Niles*, 51 (5 November 1836), p. 160.

539. Bates Diary, 5 May 1836.

540. Ward to Barings, 21 January 1835, NAC.

541. Ward to Barings, 13 May 1835, NAC.

542. Ward to Barings, 14 and 30 July, 7 September and 10 October 1835, NAC.

543. Ward to Barings, end of April 1835, NAC.

544. Huse, *The Financial History of Boston*, pp. 52–3. Between 1832 and 1839, Boston debt increased from $641,000 to $1,502,000.

545. Ward to Barings, [no day] June 1836, NAC. The transaction turned out well, since cotton prices levitated for a further six months. See Cole, *Wholesale Commodity Prices*, pp. 255–9.

546. Perkins, *Financing Anglo-American Trade*, p. 118.

547. C. Lewis, *America's Stake in International Investments* (Washington, DC: Brookings Institution, 1938), pp. 18–20. Initially an advocate of eliminating the federal debt, Albert Gallatin later commented that debt paid off in one quarter (the central government) invited it into another (the states). Debt temperance in the federal government caused debt drunkenness in the states, and saw 'the rapid decline in public economy and morality; a wild mania for speculation; the outburst of every one of the least creditable passions of American character', Adams, *The Life of Albert Gallatin*, p. 656.

548. [McCulloch], 'Embarrassments in the Trade between Great Britain and the United States'.

549. Bates to Ward, 10 July 1833, MHS.

550. Bates to Ward, 20 April 1833, MHS.

551. Bates to Ward, 2 June 1833, MHS.

552. Bates to Ward, 10 July 1833, MHS.

553. Bates to Ward, 5 April 1832 and 10 July 1833, MHS.

554. Bates to Ward, 21 June 1832, MHS.

555. This was an example of the great split between the merchant banks and the new type of industrial banks that grew up in the 1850s, of which Credit Mobilier of France was the groundbreaking example.

556. Ward to Barings, beginning of November 1835, NAC.
557. *New York Herald*, 23 June 1836.
558. Knox, *A History of Banking*, pp. 81–2; 'Important Treasury Circular' in *Niles*, 50 (16 July 1836), p. 337; 'The Late Treasury Circular', *Washington Globe*, in *Niles*, 50 (23 July 1836), pp. 351–2.
559. Adams, *The Life of Albert Gallatin*, pp. 391–2; *New York Herald*, 10 November and 1 December 1836; E. G. Bourne, *A History of the Surplus Revenue of 1837* (1885; New York: C. P. Putnam's Sons, 1968), pp. 27–8.
560. Hezekiah Niles devoted much space to the issues of the multiplier and velocity. See, for example, *Niles*, 42 (21 April 1832), pp. 121–2.
561. 'Report of American correspondent', *The Times*, 9 September 1836.
562. *New York Herald*, 12 and 19 September 1836.
563. *New York Herald*, 19 August, 9 and 19 September and 12 October 1836. One is reminded of the height of the speculations in England roughly ten years before (1825) with this news of promoters of real estate and projects in the American west. In England, shares of imaginary companies in imaginary countries attracted cash. The best known of these frauds was securities relating to the imaginary South American kingdom of 'Poyais', mentioned in Chapter 1 above.
564. *New York Herald*, 12 and 25 October and 2 November 1836; *Daily Express*, 14 October, in *The Times*, 29 November 1836; 'New York Papers', *The Times*, 10 November 1836.
565. 'American Treasury Report to Congress', 6 December 1836, in *The Times*, 12 January 1837.
566. *Niles*, 50 (23 April 1836), p. 133; (14 May 1836), pp. 185, 187; (27 August 1836), p. 425. The total of the indemnity was approximately $5 million, but the third instalment, made on 2 February 1838, has little bearing for the immediate purposes of this book. The exact negotiated amount was 18,486,666 francs.
567. *Niles*, 49 (28 November 1835), pp. 218–19. A British newspaper commented in late 1836 on the phenomenon of people in the United States shifting their activities because of the mania. 'Farmers', it observed, 'instead of ploughing their fields and sowing them with seeds were engaged in surveying them off in town lots. Labourers, instead of assisting in cultivating the earth, were employed to dig down hills and fill up vallies, to open streets and construct wharfs and piers, on the site of various magnificent cities which speculation, now excited to madness, had projected. In this way hosts of men, equal in number to a large standing army, were changed from producers to consumers', *The Times*, 23 November 1836. Similar sentiments may be found in the American press. See, for example, *New York Herald*, 7 January 1837.
568. See, for example, *Niles*, 47 (21 February 1835), p. 427.
569. North, *The Economic Growth*, pp. 97, 245; *New York Herald*, 25 July 1836; *Niles*, 44 (27 October 1832), 142–3; 48 (9 May 1835), p. 161; 50 (4 June 1836), p. 234.
570. Samuel Jaudon replaced Thomas Calwalader as cashier of the Bank of the United States, *New York Herald*, 25 July 1836; A. M. Andreades, *History of the Bank of England 1640–1903* (London: P. S. King & Son, 1909), pp. 263–8; Smith, *Economic Aspects of the Second Bank*, pp. 188–9.
571. Temin, *The Jacksonian Economy*, p. 80.
572. Ibid., pp. 80–1, 173.

573. Ibid., p. 82; *Niles*, 46 (5 April 1834), p. 86.
574. This section draws on Rockoff, 'Money, Prices, and Banks in the Jacksonian Era', pp. 448–54.
575. Temin, *The Jacksonian Economy*, p. 80.
576. A large item in the New York *Journal of Commerce* supported the counterfeiting scenario. The paper claimed that Mexico possessed $480 million in bullion and coin. According to Niles, this was an absurdity on a per capita basis and in relation to Mexico's small banking system. If the country had so much bullion, it could borrow from anywhere, and certainly would not be running a government deficit. Such ballooning makes more sense if one considers the possibility of counterfeiting and the resultant artificial nature of the currency. If the financial system were known to be hollowed out by inflation and counterfeiting, it would make sense that creditors and investors would show little interest in the country. Hence, Barings giving up the Mexico agency account to Lizardi & Company. See *Niles*, 46 (14 June 1834), p. 258.
577. *Niles*, 46 (26 July 1834), p. 364; 47 (18 October 1834), p. 102; (21 February 1835), p. 428.
578. *Niles*, 47 (20 December 1834), p. 258 (emphasis in original).
579. *Niles*, 49 (16 January 1836), p. 339.
580. Clapham, *The Bank of England*, vol. 2, p. 429; Mitchell and Deane, *Abstract of British Historical Statistics*, p. 456; King, *History of the London Discount Market*, p. 80; *The Times*, 22 July and 2 September 1836.
581. Palmer, *Causes and Consequences*, p. 29, cited in R. C. O. Matthews, *A Study in Trade-Cycle History: Economic Fluctuations in Great Britain 1833–42* (Cambridge: Cambridge University Press, 1954), p. 93. Professor Peter Temin states that the United States did not import large quantities of gold from Britain in 1836. That this was believed to be happening, however, prompted action by the Bank. Temin writes that it is unknown where British gold went in 1836. Professor Hidy suggests bullion went to English and Irish joint-stock banks anxious to build up their reserves throughout the autumn of 1836 in anticipation of even greater tightening by the Bank. See Temin, *The Jacksonian Economy*, p. 137; Hidy, *The House of Baring*, p. 208.
582. Clapham, *The Bank of England*, vol. 2, pp. 153–4; *The Times*, 25 August 1836; *Niles*, 51 (15 October 1836), p. 98.
583. *The Times*, 24 October 1836.
584. For a discussion of the timing and rationale for the Bank of England's rising Bank rate, see Gayer et al., *The Growth and Fluctuation*, vol. 1, pp. 267–73. *The Times* of 29 August pointed out, disapprovingly, that total paper money in England and Wales in the summer of 1836 exceeded by 15 per cent the amount of the bubble year of 1825 (£46.2 million vs £40.5 million). While it endorsed the Bank of England's surprise rate-raise, it found the Bank itself to be the 'chief instigator' of the paper money expansion in the first place. In its discussion of the increase of money, the paper of this date made no mention of the proportional growth of the British economy since 1825.
585. *New York Herald*, 12 September 1836.
586. [McCulloch], 'Embarrassments in the Trade between Great Britain and the United States', pp. 269–70.

587. *The Times*, 28 October 1836.

588. *The Times*, 17 November 1836.

589. 'Proceedings in Reference to the Northern and Central Bank', Bank of England Archives (London), Committee of Treasury, G8/129; *The Times*, 1 December 1836; J. Giuseppi, *The Bank of England: A History from its Foundation in 1694* (London: Evans Bros, 1966), p. 96.

590. *The Times*, 15 November and 22 December 1836; Clapham, *The Bank of England*, vol. 2, p. 156.

591. *The Times*, 1 October and 22 November 1836.

592. *The Times*, 13 October 1836.

593. *New York Herald*, 12 October & 7/21 November 1836.

594. Letter of Joshua Bates to Governor James Pattison, 26 October 1836, Bank of England Archives, G8/29.

595. Biddle to Barings, 31 August 1836, NAC.

596. *New York Herald*, 11 June 1836 and 27 January 1837.

597. Hone, *The Diary of Philip Hone*, vol. 1, p. 234; *New York Herald*, 3 November 1836.

598. *New York Herald*, 1 December 1836.

599. Ward to Bates, 14 November 1836, Baring Archives, HC5.1.2.

600. T. Wiggin & Company to Baring Brothers Company et al., 23 December 1836, NAC.

601. *New York Herald*, 1 December 1836.

602. *Niles*, 51 (10 December 1836), p. 232–7; Richardson, *Messages and Papers of the Presidents*, vol. 3, p. 237.

603. Ward to Barings, 16 March 1835, NAC; Bates to Ward, 21 December 1831, MHS.

604. *New York Herald*, 9 and 29 December 1836.

605. *New York Herald*, 22 April 1837.

606. *The Times*, 3 June 1837.

607. Bates Diary, 20 July 1839.

608. Ward to Barings, 3 January 1837, NAC; *The Times*, 1 May 1837.

609. Hone, *The Diary of Philip Hone*, vol. 1, p. 240.

610. Tooke and Newmarch, *A History of Prices*, vol. 2, pp. 270–1; N. J. Silberling, 'British Prices and Business Cycles 1779–1850', *The Review of Economic Statistics*, 5, Supplement 2 (October 1923), pp. 223–47, on p. 233; *Annual Register* (1837), p. 181.

611. *New York Herald*, 25 November 1836.

612. Bates Diary, 20 August 1837; Tooke and Newmarch, *A History of Prices*, vol. 2, p. 272; Gayer et al., *The Growth and Fluctuation*, vol. 2, pp. 250–1. Silberling's index shows flat prices from June to June, with recovery in the second half of 1838. See Silberling, 'British Prices and Business Cycles'.

613. Smith and Cole, *Fluctuations in American Business*, p. 158.

614. US Census, *The Statistical History*, pp. 904, 907.

615. 'Memorial to Congress', *Niles*, 51 (28 January 1837), p. 343.

616. *The Times*, 23 February 1837.

617. *Niles*, 51 (3 December 1836), p. 224; *New York Herald*, 22 January 1837; *The Times*, 4 March 1837. News printed from the United States in *The Times* was delayed by approximately three weeks.

618. *Niles*, 52 (6 May 1837), p. 146.
619. *The Times*, 13 and 26 December 1836 and 2 March 1837; Ward to Barings, 21 January 1837, NAC.
620. *Niles*, 51 (11 February 1836), p. 369; *The Times*, 8 and 9 March 1837; Ward to Bates, 29 January 1837, NAC.
621. *Niles*, 52 (11 February 1837), p. 369; (18 February 1837), p. 400; (25 February 1837), pp. 403, 416; *The Times*, 4 and 17 March 1837.
622. [McCulloch], 'Embarrassments in the Trade between Great Britain and the United States', p. 266.
623. *Niles*, 52 (10 September 1836), p. 17; *New York Herald*, 2 and 13 February 1837.
624. This is Niles's liability estimate. The *Herald* simply reports $6 million, *Niles*, 52 (18 March, 1837), p. 33; (25 March, 1837), p. 49; *New York Herald*, 17 March 1837.
625. *Niles*, 52 (25 March 1837), p. 49; *New York Herald*, 22–3 and 25 March 1837; 'American Affairs', 23 March, in *The Times*, 22 April 1837; Ward to Barings, 22 March 1837, NAC.
626. Smith and Cole, *Fluctuations in American Business*, p. 185; Ward to Barings, 29 March 1837, NAC.
627. *New York Herald*, 25 March 1837; Ward to Barings, 22 and 30 March and 23 April 1837, NAC.
628. *New York Herald*, 22 March 1837; *The Times*, 12 December 1836.
629. Ward to Barings, 30 July 1835, 3 January and 13 March 1837, NAC.
630. Ward to Barings, 21 January and [no day] February 1837, NAC; Cole, *Wholesale Commodity Prices*, pp. 263, 267.
631. Ward to Barings, 2 and 9 April 1837, NAC.
632. Hidy, *The House of Baring*, p. 210; Ward to Barings, 9 and 10 April 1837, NAC.
633. *New York Journal of Commerce*, in *Niles*, 52 (1 April 1837), p. 66.
634. Ward to Barings, 10 April 1837, NAC.
635. *The Times*, 23 March and 6 June 1837; Hidy, *The House of Baring*, p. 217.
636. Ibid., p. 217; H. Palmer to W. Brown, 15 March 1837, Morrison Cryder Papers, Guildhall Library, London, MS 11720, folder 1.
637. Ward to Barings, 22 March 1837, NAC.
638. *Niles*, 52 (8 April 1837), p. 81.
639. Ibid., p. 81 (author's emphasis).
640. *The Times*, 24 April 1837.
641. The offering was coordinated with the correspondents of the Bank of the United States, Hottinguer & Company in Paris, and Hope & Company in Amsterdam, and came payable in francs and guilders. Bonds of the Morris Canal & Banking Company were payable in London at Messrs Morrison Cryder & Company; those of the Bank of America at Rothschilds in Paris. See Biddle to Barings, 1 April 1837, NAC; *The Times*, 24 April 1837; *Niles*, 52 (8 April 1837), p. 81.
642. Biddle to Barings, 1 and 29 April 1837, NAC.
643. Ward to Barings, 29 and 30 March 1837, NAC.
644. 'American Affairs', 23 and 24 March, in *The Times*, 22 April 1837.
645. *The Times*, 24 April 1837; Jaudon to Bates, 8 March 1837, NAC.
646. Bates to Thomas Baring, 1 April 1837, NAC.
647. *The Times*, 27 April 1837; Jenks, *The Migration of British Capital*, pp. 90, 95.

648. Bates to Jaudon, 2 May 1837, in Smith, *Economic Aspects of the Second Bank*, p. 192.

649. Ward to Barings, 9 April 1837, NAC.

650. Biddle to Barings, 29 April 1837, NAC. Throughout correspondence to Barings in the spring, Biddle stressed that, in large part, he, Jaudon, the Bank of the United States and the New York banks were trying to counter perverse monetary actions of the federal government. The country needed time, wrote Biddle, 'for trade to regain its rights, and [to] bring back the useless bullion now buried, hoarded & hid in the woods', Biddle to Barings, 1 and 29 April 1837, NAC.

651. Ward to Barings, 18 January and 9 April 1837, NAC.

652. Ward to Barings, 4 May 1837, NAC.

653. Ward to Barings, 9 April 1837, NAC; *New York Herald*, 3 and 4 April 1837.

654. *The Times*, 5 and 6 April 1837.

655. Smith, *Economic Aspects of the Second Bank*, p. 192.

656. *Niles*, 52 (22 April 1837), pp. 113–14.

657. Ward to Barings, 25 April 1837, NAC; Smith, *Wealth of Nations*, pp. 465 ff.

658. Ward to Barings, 4 May 1837, NAC.

659. Ward to Barings, 3 and 21 January, 9 April and 13 March 1837, NAC.

660. Ward to Barings, 6 March 1837, NAC.

661. Ward to Barings, 11 April, 26 January and 24 April 1837, NAC.

662. Ward to Barings, 13 February and 25 April 1837, NAC.

663. Ward to Barings, 29 March 1837, NAC; M. E. Hidy, *George Peabody: Merchant and Financier 1829–1854* (1939; New York: Ayer Co. Publishing, 1978), *passim*; Strouse, *Morgan*, pp. 44–74.

664. Foreign investors held shares for profit and stability of income only. They held no voting power as expressed in the charter of the Second Bank of the United States. See section 16, no. 12 of the charter in Catterall, *The Second Bank*, p. 486.

665. *The Times*, 1 October 1836.

666. *Niles*, 45 (16 November 1833), p. 178.

667. *Niles*, 52 (22 April 1837), pp. 119, 197; Ellis, *The Epic of New York City*, pp. 247–51.

668. *The Times*, 26 April 1837.

669. *The Times*, 1 May 1837.

670. H. W. Lanier, *A Century of Banking in New York, 1822–1922* (New York: Gillis Press, 1922), p. 205.

671. 'New York Committee' in *Niles*, 52 (13 May 1837), p. 166.

672. Hone, *The Diary of Philip Hone*, vol. 1, p. 252.

673. J. T. W. Hubbard, *For Each, the Strength of All: A History of Banking in the State of New York* (New York: New York University Press, 1995), pp. 91–2; Hone, *The Diary of Philip Hone*, vol. 1, p. 254.

674. Hammond, *Banks and Politics in America*, p. 459.

675. Prime, Ward & King to Barings, 11 May 1837, NAC.

676. Ward to Barings, 10 May 1837, NAC.

677. For this sequence, see *Niles*, 52 (3 May 1837), p. 161; Temin, *The Jacksonian Economy*, p. 113.

678. *New York Herald*, 9, 10, 15 and 24 May 1837; *The Times*, 8 July 1837.

679. Temin, *The Jacksonian Economy*, p. 114; Friedman and Schwartz, *A Monetary History*, pp. 328–9; Hammond, *Banks and Politics in America*, p. 478.

680. Ward to Bates, 7 May 1841, MHS.
681. Hone, *The Diary of Philip Hone*, vol. 1, p. 258; *The Times*, 22 June 1837.
682. Clapham, *The Bank of England*, vol. 2, p. 158; *Niles*, 52 (20 May 1837), p. 183; Perkins, *Financing Anglo-American Trade*, p. 40.
683. *New York Herald*, 15 May 1837.
684. James Morrison to Richard Alsop, 5 May 1837, Morrison Cryder Papers, MS 11,720, folder 1.
685. *The Times*, 3 June 1837; Morrison to Alsop, 19 May 1837, Morrison Cryder Papers, MS 11,720.
686. James Matheson to his Manila agent, 18 August 1837, in Greenberg, *British Trade and the Opening of China*, p. 169.
687. Clapham, *The Bank of England*, vol. 2, p. 158; William Brown to James Brown, 24 June 1837, Brown Brothers Records, Guildhall Library, MS 11,720, folder 1; Bates Diary, 18 June 1837; Perkins, *Financing Anglo-American Trade*, pp. 40, 119, 284, n.
688. *The Times*, 6 June 1837. Figures for percentage calculations based on liabilities of 22 May presented in Hidy, *The House of Baring*, p. 222.
689. James Matheson to his Manila agent, 9 September 1837, in Greenberg, *British Trade and the Opening of China*, p. 169.
690. *The Times*, 5, 6, 7 and 15 June 1837; Hidy, *The House of Baring*, p. 221; Downs, *The Golden Ghetto*, pp. 111–12, 213–14.
691. Bates Diary, 11 May and 15 April 1837.
692. Bates (in Paris) to Thomas Baring, 1 April 1837, NAC.
693. Bates (in Paris) to Thomas Baring, 27 March 1837, NAC.
694. R. W. Hidy, 'Cushioning a Crisis in the London Money Market', *Bulletin of the Business Historical Society*, 20: 5 (November 1946), pp.131–45.
695. Bates (in Paris) to Thomas Baring, 30 March 1837, NAC; Horsley Palmer to William Brown, 15 March 1837; Brown to Palmer, 17 March 1837, Morrison Cryder Papers, MS 11,720.
696. Morrison to Alsop, 9 June 1837, Morrison Cryder Papers, MS 11,720, folder 1.
697. Morrison to Alsop, 21 May 1837, Morrison Cryder Papers, MS 11,720, folder 1.
698. Hidy, *The House of Baring*, p. 234; Perkins, *Financing Anglo-American Trade*, p. 119.
699. Jaudon to Bates, 4 April 1837, NAC.
700. Bates Diary, 4 September 1829.
701. Ward to Barings, 21 May 1837, NAC.
702. For recent literature on the Jacksonian panic and its aftermath, see A. Grinath, J. J. Wallis and R. Sylla, 'Debt, Default, and Revenue Structure: The American State Debt Crisis in the Early 1840s', *NBER Historical Working Papers*, H0097 (March 1997); P. L. Rousseau, 'Jacksonian Monetary Policy, Specie Flows, and Panic of 1837', *Journal of Economic History*, 62:2 (2002), pp. 457–88; P. L. Rousseau and R. Sylla, 'Emerging Financial Markets and Early U.S. Growth', *Explorations in Economic History*, 42:1 (2005), pp. 1–26; J. J. Wallis, 'What Caused the 1839 Depression?', *NBER Working Papers*, HO133 (April 2001); J. J. Wallis, 'The Depression of 1839–1843: States, Debts, and Banks', Working Paper, University of Maryland and NBER (n.d.); R. E. Wright, *The Wealth of Nations Rediscovered: Integration and Expansion in American Financial Markets, 1780–1850* (Cambridge: Cambridge University Press, 2002).
703. Cole, *Wholesale Commodity Prices*, p. 263.

704. Redlich, *The Molding of American Banking*, p. 133; Biddle's cotton transactions are described in detail in Jenks, *The Migration of British Capital*, pp. 88–93.
705. Cole, *Wholesale Commodity Prices*, p. 135 (New York), p. 144 (Philadelphia), pp. 157, 162 (Charleston), p. 172 (New Orleans), p. 181 (Cincinnati); Ward to Barings, 7 and 11–12 January (hemp), 24 and 26 February (sugar), 6 February (iron), 23 February (coffee) 1839, NAC.
706. *The Times*, 15 December 1838 and 5 March 1839.
707. Ward to Bates, 6 January 1838, NAC.
708. Thomas Tooke pointed out that it was precisely a *good* harvest that helped ease pressure on the Bank of England in 1836–7. No help from came from nature when the pressure recurred in 1838–9, Tooke and Newmarch, *A History of Prices*, vol. 2, p. 308.
709. Memorandum from John Reid (Manchester) to the Governor, 11 May 1839, Bank of England Archives, C136/58.
710. Ward to Barings, 3 December 1838, NAC.
711. Smith, *Economic Aspects of the Second Bank*, p. 220; Hammond, *Banks and Politics in America*, p. 504.
712. H. McCulloch, *Men and Measures of Half a Century* (New York, 1888), p. 57, cited in Myers, *A Financial History*, p. 99.
713. The Baring Circular can be found in *Circular to Bankers* (10 January 1840). This latter thought regarding democracy is in Bates to Hope & Company, 27 May 1842, in McGrane, *Foreign Bondholders*, p. 33. It is interesting since the 'indiscretions of democracy' were one reason for Barings' pullout before 1837. It should be noted that, despite Barings' assistance in connection to the United States, Bates, like other businessmen in England, was disgusted by the repudiation of debts by American states. Many diary entries in 1842 touch this issue. See, for example, entries for 24 April and 4 and 25 July.
714. Clapham, *The Bank of England*, vol. 2, pp. 164–5.
715. Sir John Rae Reid (deputy governor of the Bank of England), to Thomas Baring, 22 July 1839; Thomas Baring to Sir John Rae Reid, 22 July 1839, Baring Archives, HC3.52.1B.
716. Bates Diary, 20 July 1839 and 7 January 1840.
717. Ward to Bates, 10 October 1835, NAC.
718. The reader is reminded of earlier reform legislation in the United Kingdom having to do with banking and finance. Important acts include the Country Bankers Act of 1826 (which restricted the Bank of England's monopoly of joint-stock banking to a radius of 65 miles of London, allowed joint-stock banks outside this limit and issuance of notes, and authorized Bank to open country branches, the first of which was Gloucester) and the Bank Charter Act of 1833 (which renewed the Bank of England charter to 1855 and permitted establishment of joint-stock banks in London, while prohibiting their issuing notes).
719. *Hunt's Merchants' Magazine*, 10 (1844), pp. 76–7, in Smith, *Economic Aspects of the Second Bank*, p. 93–4.
720. See, for example, Sumner, *A History of Banking in the United States*; Temin, *The Jacksonian Economy*. See Chapter 5 above.

721. Bates to Thomas Baring, 27 March 1837, NAC. The general suspension in the eastern states in May 1837 surprised bankers in the American west. For example, J. F. D. Lanier, president of the Madison branch of the Bank of Indiana, says in his memoirs that he had not 'in the least anticipated the suspension', and incidentally that the capital for the bank was almost wholly borrowed from abroad. See *Sketch of the Life of J. F. D. Lanier* (1871), in J. C. Brown and J. F. D. Lanier, *Two Private Banking Partnerships* (New York: Arno Press, 1975), pp. 12–14.

722. Ferguson, *The House of Rothschild*, pp. 370–4.

723. Gayer et al. divide the period 1819–42 into major and minor cycles as follows: 1819–26, major; 1826–9, minor; 1829–32, minor; 1832–7, major; 1837–42, minor. These cyclical markings reiterate Barings' good judgment as indicated. It is interesting to note that Thomas Ward joined the firm at the beginning of a minor cycle – consistent with the 'trough'/'good timing' of Chapter 3, and the firm's inclination to participate in the market as value players.

724. Ward to Barings, 24 July 1836, NAC.

725. Goodhue to Bates, 31 May 1836, NAC.

726. Ward to Barings, 10 October 1835, NAC.

727. Perkins, *Financing Anglo-American Trade*, p. 171.

728. J. C. Brown, *A Hundred Years of Merchant Banking* (New York: privately printed, 1909), p. 284.

729. This raises another crucial issue. The rise of joint-stock banking after 1833 eventually had an enormous impact on the financial services industry and capital markets, including private banking concerns such as Baring Brothers & Company Joint-stock banks had access to enormous capital which partnerships could not match. Baring Brothers, like similar British merchant banks, did not abandon its partnership structure completely. The last major American investment banking partnership, Goldman Sachs & Company, sold a 15 per cent minority stake to the public in May 1999 in an effort to tap capital markets to access resources available to already-public competitors such as Morgan Stanley, Credit Suisse First Boston and Merrill Lynch.

730. Bates to Ward, 1 August 1842, MHS.

731. Interestingly, Ward all but dismissed the American scene at least temporarily in the spring of 1837. Two weeks prior to the May suspensions, he wrote that, in his view 'it would be for the present a good time for you to operate abroad', Ward to Barings, [no day] April 1837, NAS; Bates to Ward, 3 November and 3 December 1841 and 1 August 1842, MHS.

732. J. H. Clapham's views were similar to Ward's in regard to Bank of England assistance, though he spoke not of the survival or demise of a specific competitor as did Ward. Clapham wrote that the Bank's assistance in 1837 was 'without precedent and damaging insofar as it encouraged American bankers to issue more securities in the British market in 1838 and 1839' – with the results touched upon briefly in the 'Aftermath' section of Chapter 6 above. For the problem of 'lender of last resort' historically, see C. P. Kindleberger, *Manias, Panics, and Crashes: A History of Financial Crises*, rev. edn (New York: Basic Books, 1989), esp. pp. 178–231; Clapham, *The Bank of England*, vol. 2, pp. 164–5.

733. Perkins, *Financing Anglo-American Trade*, pp. 45 ff.

734. Fay, *The Collapse of Barings*, p. 292.

735. Rostow, *The World Economy*, pp. 467–74; Ferns, *Britain and Argentina*, p. 397.

736. D. C. M. Platt (ed.), *Business Imperialism 1840–1930: An Inquiry Based on British Experience in Latin America* (Oxford: Clarendon Press, 1977), pp. 77–118.

737. Chapman, *The Rise of Merchant Banking*, pp. 79–80.

738. Ziegler, *The Sixth Great Power*, p. 242.

739. Baron Alphonse Rothschild to London cousins, 15 November 1890, in Chapman, *The Rise of Merchant Banking*, p. 79.

740. Roberts and Kynaston (eds), *The Bank of England*, pp. 45–6; Brown Brothers to Brown, Shipley, 21 November 1890, in Ziegler, *The Sixth Great Power*, p. 248.

741. Ibid., p. 245.

742. Scammell, *The London Discount Market*, pp. 188–9.

743. *The Times*, 20 April 1929.

744. Sheppard, *London: A History*, p. 345. For a Empire-wide survey of British banking up to the Big Bang, see G. Jones, *British Multinational Banking 1830–1990* (Oxford: Clarendon Press 1993).

745. Fay, *The Collapse of Barings*, p. 33. For perspective on growth over sixty years, the gross profits of Baring Brothers & Company in 1929 were £646,724, Ziegler, *The Sixth Great Power*, p. 378.

746. Gapper and Denton, *All That Glitters*, pp. 126–8; Fay, *The Collapse of Barings*, pp. 110, 116, 128. For a useful primer on derivatives markets, see J. Bernstein, *How the Futures Markets Work* (New York: New York Institute of Finance, 1989).

747. Fay, *The Collapse of Barings*, p. 267.

748. Ibid., pp. 122, 172–3.

749. Gapper and Denton, *All That Glitters*, pp. 280, 305–6; Fay, *The Collapse of Barings*, p. 180.

750. Ibid., p. 269.

751. Ibid., pp. 93–4, 165.

752. Gapper and Denton, *All That Glitters*, 140; Fay, *The Collapse of Barings*, p. 158.

753. All senior managers in London were implicated in the failure of Baring Brothers & Company. ING asked most to resign. Peter Baring was due to retire from Barings in 1995 and did so. Andrew Tuckey submitted his resignation to ING, but returned as a consultant to the corporate finance department. Nicholas Leeson served forty-three months of a six-and-a-half year jail sentence in Singapore for his part in Barings' collapse. Leeson, aged thirty-two, earned early release for good behaviour on 5 July 1999, and has since returned to his native Britain. See *Wall Street Journal*, 7 July 1999.

754. On 31 March 2005, the MassMutual Financial Group acquired Baring Asset Management Limited from ING Group for an undisclosed amount. The consummate British firm with the strongest of ties to the United States – Barings, once the Queen's bank – had crossed the Atlantic and was now truly American.

GLOSSARY

Unless indicated, definitions are those contemporary to this essay.

acceptance: a bill of exchange or time draft, which the person on whom the bill is drawn has agreed to pay at maturity. Upon acceptance, a bill of exchange becomes negotiable.

acceptance credit: a principle instrument issued by banks to merchants to finance foreign and domestic trade transactions. A letter of credit often provided evidence of an acceptance credit, and was issued in advance by the bank or the bank's agent to a merchant. Acceptance credit agreements were usually limited as to the percentage of a transaction the bank agreed to finance.

accommodation bills, accommodation paper (finance bills): bills drawn by an individual without an underlying trade transaction. The payer accepts, allowing the payee to discount the bill, as an accommodation. In the antebellum period, these 'finance bills' were considered to be somewhat risky since they looked like ordinary bills of exchange, yet had no basis in mercantile transactions.

An accommodation bill of lading can be issued by an agent prior to the receipt of the merchandise, usually to enable the seller to present his documentation to a bank before the specified time limit. This is a potentially dangerous practice since the bill of lading may be used as a basis for credit, and can lead to difficulties if the delivery of goods does not occur. See **bill of lading**; **real-bills doctrine**.

bank of issue: a bank empowered with the note issuing privilege. Central banks are the sole banks of issue today, but in the nineteenth century state and national bank notes made up most circulating notes. These banks retain the legal right of issuance today in the United States, but disincentives in the tax code make this uneconomical.

bank notes: a bank's own promise to pay (contrasted to an order to pay) to bearer upon demand, and intended for use as money. A note is concrete evidence of a debt or obligation.

Bank rate: rate of interest (discount) charged for rediscounting eligible paper by the Bank of England. It tended to exceed general money market rates for short term loans (discounts) because the Bank believed that the banking business, apart from note issue, was best carried out by private banks. The Bank rate formed the maximum discount rate in the money market. Bank rate is a term especially associated with English banking, but can be a general term for fixed central bank rates. The equivalent to Bank rate in the United States is the discount rate of each of the twelve Federal Reserve banks.

bill of exchange (or credit transfers): the primary instrument by which obligations were settled between debtors and creditors residing at a distance from each other without the transmission of money from the fifteenth to the nineteenth centuries. The bill of exchange was legally-binding evidence of indebtedness arising from a commercial transaction. As such, bills were highly negotiable, and could be bought and sold in what became known in the nineteenth century as the bill or discount market. Suppliers of goods regularly sold the bills they possessed on their customers in order to collect payment in advance of the bill's maturity date. Merchant banks provided this service to customers to whom they granted an exchange account. There existed two types of bills, foreign and domestic, the latter also called inland. Bills are classed also by their usance: 'time' or 'sight' – indicating either delayed or immediate payment upon presentation to a debtor. The vast majority of bills of exchange were time bills and, in the nineteenth century, were payable in pounds sterling. The terms bill of exchange and 'draft' are used interchangeably today, but the former usually connotes an order to pay arising from a foreign transaction; the latter is reserved for domestic business. Functionally, the bill retains its place in present commerce as the 'bank acceptance'.

bill of lading: a receipt issued by a carrier certifying that he has received the goods described therein from the within-described consignor, for transportation to a specified destination to a specified consignee, or to the order of any person. The bill of lading serves as a contract of transportation. It serves also as a general inventory of goods, source of information of the parties of origin and destination, routes goods will take, and time allotted for shipment.

cashier: in bank management, the second most important position behind the bank president.

consols: an abbreviation for consolidated British debt borrowed in perpetuity (annuities), and paying dividends semi-annually.

correspondent: a bank having a direct connection or close service relationship with another. Most country banks in the period of this book, both American and British, maintained correspondent relationships with banks in cities, either as a reserve or as a fund against which drafts could be sold and out-of-town cheques collected.

country banks: a general name for English banks which appeared in the second half of the eighteenth century to meet the needs of early industrialization. Originally country bankers operated a banking operation as an adjunct to their main occupation of a local trade or industrial enterprise. The country banks supplied a local circulating medium during the French Wars and before the Bank of England branch system after 1826. They were the principal link between London and the quickly-industrializing central and northern districts of England. Country banks complement the other three major parts of the English financial system, which include the Bank of England, private city banks and discounters.

discount: to sell a claim on a third party to a bank or discount house, which deducts the interest in advance.

discount market: the open market for acceptances and commercial paper, as contrasted with a bank's discounts for its own customers. Considered part of the money market.

discounters, discount houses (bill brokers): financial intermediaries in England who introduced those in need of funds to those with funds to spare, with the typical outcome of the transaction a bill of exchange. Prior to 1825, discounters acted as simple agents for country banks, gathering up bills put out for discount by the banks in capital-hungry industrial areas and sending them off to banks with surplus funds seeking investment. In the 1830s discounteres created a discount market with an institutional integrity recognized by the Bank of England, evidenced by its granting to the discounting firms Bank rediscounting privileges.

Exchequer Bills: name given to interest-bearing promissory notes issued since 1696 for various sums by authority of the British government. Bank of England advances are made upon exchequer bills. The safest and most liquid of assets, bankers could redeem them at the same prices they paid generally, since their face value did not fluctuate. By the end of the First World War, the treasury bill had replaced exchequer bills almost completely as the leading means of short-term borrowing by the British government, as the dominant form of short paper in the money market overall, and the greatest part of banks' liquid assets.

Funds (the 'Funds'): the name given to the public debt due from the British government.

futures, futures contract: a contract whereby a seller agrees to deliver a specified quantity of a particular grade of a certain commodity on a certain date at an agreed-upon price. When first developed, futures agreements sought to limit risk in participants in commodity markets by providing a degree of certainty to planters, buyers and ranchers. After 1975 futures markets developed in financial assets, which became risk management (hedging) tools, for example, in the management of currency and interest-rate volatility. In the United States, the trading of futures for the management of agricultural risk became standardized with the establishment of the Chicago Board of Trade in 1848.

hong merchant: one of a guild of Chinese traders holding an exclusive franchise from the Imperial Government and known collectively as the Cohong. The hong merchant secured every foreign ship that came to China, and was the foreign trader's main contact in the China trade. The hong merchant was responsible for the customs and orderly behaviour of the entire ship's company. He paid the port fees, generally bought much of a trader's cargo, and provided goods for the return voyage. The hong merchant acted as intermediary between the Chinese government and the outside commercial world.

jobber: term for a promoter of a particular set of goods or an asset class; slightly pejorative, viewed as hustlers.

joint-stock banks: incorporated commercial banks in England distinct from the Bank of England and the private banks. Today known as 'clearing banks', they increased in number throughout the nineteenth century after the Bank Charter Act of 1833. Joint-stock banks were public corporations with limited liability. Their capital was contributed by shareholders, who elected directors to decide policy and supervise operations. These banks generally paid interest on deposits (a new practice in the early nineteenth century) and relied on rediscounting to maintain liquidity.

merchant bank: private banks that developed from mercantile operations, also called 'issuing houses' or 'acceptance houses'. They often retained a dual character of trade and finance, and were the most international players in the financial world of the nineteenth century. Merchant banks were usually structured as private partnerships, were family centred and served a small, specialized clientele. Private, they resisted the trend towards joint-stock banking that increased in financial and economic importance from the middle 1830s onward.

option, options contract: the right, but not the obligation, to buy or sell specified securities or commodities in specified amounts, at specified prices and for a specified duration of time. Option contracts are considered 'derivatives' since their value depends (derives) from the value of the underlying asset they represent, whether a share index, bonds or real estate. There are two general types of options, 'call' options and 'put' options. In general, the buyer of a call option hopes the price of the underlying asset will rise. The buyer of a put option anticipates the price of the underlying asset will fall. Options are legally-binding contracts, may be bought and sold as financial instruments, and exist for almost any good or service.

par of exchange: in regard to national currencies, par of exchange is the equivalency of a certain amount of one country's currency in terms of the other's, fixed by the countries' respective mints. Sometimes called 'mint par of exchange'.

post notes: promissory notes due generally in six months' time, yielding interest and usually sold at a discount. They were a bank liability equivalent to time deposits, but they could be sold as investments. In the antebellum period, they offered high yields and were common obligations. They reached small investors since they came in denominations as low as ten dollars.

real-bills doctrine: a view that it is safe to allow the money supply to grow with the underlying volume of trade. As long as credit based itself on real bills of exchange representing actual concrete commercial transactions and movement of goods – not accommodation or finance bills – the economic effect would be salutary. Thomas Tooke and Nicholas Biddle were devotees of the real-bills doctrine. This doctrine is sometimes referred to as the banking school, and stands in contrast to monetarism.

rentes: the income stream from the bonded perpetual debt of the governments of France, sometimes used to describe the debt of other Continental countries.

sovereign: in the currency system of England, a gold coin with the value of one pound, no longer in circulation.

specie: gold and silver money. Often used as a synonym for money itself.

specie export point: the price at which it is less expensive to ship gold/silver (coin) than to purchase a banker's or merchant's bill.

tranche: French for 'slice'. A segment of a loan issued in a particular currency, and at a particular time and price.

usance, tenor, or currency: refers to the period between a negotiable financial instrument's creation (issuance) and its maturity.

BIBLIOGRAPHY

Manuscripts and Documents

Bank of England Archives (London), Committee of Treasury.

Baring Archives, House Correspondence, ING Barings, Ltd., 60 London Wall, London.

Baring Papers, National Archives of Canada, Ottawa.

Brown Brothers Records, Guildhall Library, London.

Joshua Bates, Diary, ING Barings, Ltd., London.

Morrison Cryder Papers, Guildhall Library, London.

Thomas Wren Ward Papers and Diary, Massachusets Historical Society.

Newspapers and Journals

Circular to Bankers (1831–2, 1837, 1840).

Edinburgh Review, 65 (1837).

Edinburgh Review (American edn), 65 (1837).

Hansard (1825).

Hansard's Parliamentary Debates (9 April 1816).

The Herald (New York), 1835–7.

Niles Weekly Register, vols 13 (1817); 18–19 (1820); 26 (1823); 27 (1825); 29–30 (1825–6); 42–52 (1832–7); 54 (1838); 56 (1839).

Parliamentary Papers, 3 (1819); 6 (1833).

The Times (London), 1835–7.

Secondary Sources

D'Abernon, Viscount E. V., *Portraits and Appreciations* (London: Hodder & Stoughton, 1931).

Adams, D., *Finance and Enterprise in Early America: A Study of Stephen Girard's Bank, 1812–1831* (Philadelphia, PA: University of Pennsylvania Press, 1978).

Adams, H. *The Life of Albert Gallatin* (1879; New York: J. P. Lippincott, 1943).

Anderson, B. L., and P. L. Cottrell, *Money and Banking in England 1694–1914* (London: David & Charles, 1974).

Andreades, A. M., *History of the Bank of England* (London: P. S. King & Son, 1909).

Arbuthnot, H., *The Journal of Mrs. Arbuthnot, 1820–1832*, ed. F. Bamford and the Duke of Wellington, 2 vols (London: Macmillan, 1950).

Ashton, T. S., *An Economic History of England: The Eighteenth Century* (London: Methuen, 1955).

Bagehot, W., *Lombard Street: A Description of the Money Market* (1873; Homewood, IL: R. D. Irwin, 1962).

Baines, T., *History of the Commerce and Town of Liverpool* (London: Longman, Brown, Green, and Longmans, 1852).

Baring, A., *An Inquiry into the Causes and Consequences of the Orders in Council and an Examination of the Conduct of Great Britain towards the Neutral Commerce of America* (London: J. M. Richardson and J. Ridgway, 1808).

Barrett, W., *The Old Merchants of New York City*, 5 vols (1870; New York: Greenwood Press, 1968).

Bell, H. C. F., *Lord Palmerston*, 2 vols (London: Longmans, 1936).

Benton, T. H., *Thirty Years' View, or, A History of the Working of the American Government for Thirty Years from 1820 to 1850*, 2 vols (New York: Appleton, 1854–7).

Bernstein, J. *How the Futures Markets Work* (New York: New York Institute of Finance, 1989).

Berry, T. S., *Western Prices Before 1861: A Study of the Cincinnati Market* (Cambridge, MA: Harvard University Press, 1943).

—, *Production and Population Since 1789: Revised GNP Series in Constant Dollars* (Richmond, VA: Bostwick Press, 1988).

The Bill on London, 4th rev. edn (London: Gillett Bros, Discount Ltd, 1976).

Blainey, G., *The Tyranny of Distance: How Distance Shaped Australia's History* (Melbourne: Sun Books, 1966).

Born, K. E., *International Banking in the 19th and 20th Centuries* (New York: St Martin's Press, 1977).

Bourne, E. G., *A History of the Surplus Revenue Act of 1837* (1885; New York: C. P. Putnam's Sons, 1968).

Brands, H. W., *Andrew Jackson: His Life and Times* (New York: Doubleday 2005).

Browder, C., *The Money Game in Old New York* (Lexington: University of Kentucky Press, 1986).

Brown, J. C., *A Hundred Years of Merchant Banking* (New York: privately printed, 1909).

Bruchey, S., *Robert Oliver: Merchant of Baltimore, 1783–1819* (Baltimore, MD: Johns Hopkins University Press, 1956).

—, *Enterprise: The Dynamic Economy of a Free People* (Cambridge, MA: Harvard University Press, 1990).

Buck, N. S., *The Development of the Organisation of Anglo-American Trade, 1800–1850* (New Haven, CT: Yale University Press, 1925).

Burrows, E. G., and M. Wallace, *Gotham: A History of New York City to 1898* (New York: Oxford University Press, 1999).

Cameron, R., with O. Crisp, H. T. Patrick and R. Tilly, *Banking in the Early Stages of Industrialization* (New York: Oxford University Press 1967).

Cassis, Y., *English City Bankers, 1890–1914* (Cambridge: Cambridge University Press, 1994).

Catterall, R. C. H., *The Second Bank of the United States* (Chicago, IL: University of Chicago Press 1902).

Chapman, S., 'British Marketing Enterprise: The Changing Roles of Merchants, Manufacturers, and Financiers, 1700–1860', *Business History Review*, 53 (Summer 1979), pp. 205–34.

—, *The Rise of Merchant Banking* (London: Allen & Unwin, 1984).

—, *Merchant Enterprise in Britain: From the Industrial Revolution to World War I* (Cambridge: Cambridge University Press, 1992).

Chevalier, M., *Society, Manners and Politics in the United States*, trans. from 3rd edn (Boston: Weeks, Jordan, 1839).

Clapham, J. H., *An Economic History of Modern Britain: The Early Railway Age 1820–50*, 2nd edn, 3 vols (Cambridge: Cambridge University Press, 1930).

—, *The Bank of England*, 2 vols (Cambridge: Cambridge University Press, 1944).

Clark, V. S., *History of Manufactures in the United States*, 3 vols (1929; New York: Carnegie Institution of Washington, 1949).

Cole, A. H., 'Evolution of the Foreign-Exchange Market of the United States', *Journal of Economic and Business History*, 1 (1928–9), pp. 384–421.

—, 'Seasonal Variation in Sterling Exchange', *Journal of Economic and Business History*, 2 (1929–30), pp. 203–18.

—, *Wholesale Commodity Prices in the United States, 1700–1861* (Cambridge, MA: Harvard University Press, 1938).

Collins, M., *Money and Banking in the UK: A History* (London: Routledge, 1988).

Cooper, D., and B. Grinder, 'Richard Grasso, Nathan Prime, and Stock Exchange Transformation', *Financial History*, 80 (Winter 2004), pp. 10–11.

Crawley, C. W. (ed), *The New Cambridge Modern History, Vol. 9: War amd Peace in an Age of Upheaval, 1793–1830* (Cambridge: Cambridge University Press, 1965).

Creevey, T., *The Creevey Papers: A Selection from the Correspondence and Diaries of the Late Thomas Creevey, MP*, ed. Sir H. Maxwell, 2 vols (London: Murray, 1903).

Crouzet, F., *The Victorian Economy* (London: Methuen, 1982).

Davis, L. E., and J. R. T. Hughes, 'A Dollar-Sterling Exchange, 1803–1895', *Economic History Review*, 2nd series, 13 (1960–1), pp. 52–79.

Dawson, F. G., *The First Latin American Debt Crisis: The City of London and the 1822–1825 Loan Bubble* (New Haven, CT: Yale University Press, 1990).

Deane, P., and W.A. Cole, *British Economic Growth, 1688–1959*, 2nd edn (Cambridge: Cambridge University Press, 1967).

Downs, J. M., *The Golden Ghetto: The American Commercial Community at Canton and the Shaping of American China Policy, 1787–1844* (Bethlehem, PA: Lehigh University Press, 1997).

Einzig, P. *The History of Foreign Exchange* (London: Macmillan, 1964).

Ellis, E. R., *The Epic of New York City* (New York: Coward-McCann, 1966).

Fay, S., *The Collapse of Barings* (London: W.W. Norton, 1996).

Ferguson, N., *The House of Rothschild, 1798–1848* (New York: Viking, 1998).

Ferns, H. S., *Britain and Argentina in the Nineteenth Century* (Oxford: Clarendon Press, 1960).

Fischer, D. H., *The Great Wave: Price Revolutions and Rhythms of History* (New York and Oxford: Oxford University Press, 1996).

Fogel, R. W., and S. L. Engerman (eds), *The Reinterpretation of American Economic History* (New York: Harper & Row, 1971).

Frey, R. L. (ed), *Railroads in the Nineteenth Century* (New York: Facts on File, 1988).

Friedman, M., and A. J. Schwartz, *A Monetary History of the United States: 1867–1960* (Princeton, NJ: Princeton University Press, 1963).

Gallatin, A., *The Writings of Albert Gallatin*, ed. H. Adams, 3 vols (1879; New York: Antiquarian Press, 1960).

Gapper, J., and N. Denton, *All That Glitters: The Fall of Barings* (London: Hamish Hamilton, 1996).

Gayer, A. D., W. W. Rostow and A. J. Schwartz, *The Growth and Fluctuation of the British Economy, 1790–1850*, 2 vols (Oxford: Clarendon Press, 1953).

Gilchrist, D. T. (ed.), *The Growth of the Seaport Cities, 1790–1825* (Charlottesville, VA: University Press of Virginia, 1967).

Giuseppi, J., *The Bank of England: A History from its Foundation in 1694* (London: Evans Bros, 1966).

Glasner, D., *Business Cycles and Depressions: An Encyclopedia* (New York: Garland Publishing, 1997).

Goodrich, C., *Government Promotion of American Canals and Railroads* (New York: Columbia University Press, 1960).

Gordon, J. S., *Hamilton's Blessing* (New York: Walker and Company, 1997).

Green, G. D., *Finance and Economic Development in the Old South: Louisiana Banking 1804–1861* (Stanford, CA: Stanford University Press, 1972).

Greenberg, M., *British Trade and the Opening of China, 1800–42* (Cambridge: Cambridge University Press, 1951).

Grinath, A., J. J. Wallis and R. Sylla, 'Debt, Default, and Revenue Structure: The American State Debt Crisis in the Early 1840s', *NBER Historical Working Papers*, H0097 (March 1997).

Hammond, B., *Banks and Politics in America, from the Revolution to the Civil War* (Princeton, NJ: Princeton University Press, 1957).

Hao, Y., 'Chinese Teas to America – a Synopsis', in E. R. May and J. K. Fairbank (eds), *America's China Trade in Historical Perspective* (Cambridge, MA: Harvard University Press, 1986), pp. 3–25.

Hidy, M. E., *George Peabody: Merchant and Financier 1829–1854* (1939; New York: Ayer Co. Publishing, 1978).

Hidy, R. W., 'The House of Baring and the Second Bank of the United States, 1826–1836', *Pennsylvania Magazine of History and Biography* (July 1944), pp. 269–85.

—, 'Cushioning a Crisis in the London Money Market', *Bulletin of the Business Historical Society*, 20: 5 (November 1946), pp.131–45.

—, *The House of Baring in American Trade and Finance: English Merchant Bankers at Work, 1763–1861* (Cambridge, MA: Harvard University Press, 1949).

Hofstadter, R., *The American Political Tradition and the Men who Made it* (New York: Knopf, 1948).

Hone, P., *The Diary of Philip Hone, 1828–1851*, ed. B. Tuckerman, 2 vols (New York: Dodd, Mead, and Company, 1889).

Hubbard, J. T. W., *For Each, the Strength of All: A History of Banking in the State of New York* (New York: New York University Press, 1995).

Hunt, F., *Lives of American Merchants* (1856; New York: A. M. Kelley, 1969).

Huse, C. P., *The Financial History of Boston from 1822 to 1909* (Cambridge, MA: Harvard University Press, 1916).

Imlah, A. H., 'Real Values in British Foreign Trade, 1798–1853', *Journal of Economic History*, 8 (November 1948), pp. 133–52.

—, *Economic Elements in the Pax Britannica: Studies in British Foreign Trade in the Nineteenth Century* (Cambridge, MA: Harvard University Press, 1958).

Irwin, D. A., *Against the Tide: An Intellectual History of Free Trade* (Princeton, NJ: Princeton University Press, 1996).

Jenks, L. H., *The Migration of British Capital to 1875* (London: Nelson, 1927).

Johnson, P., *The Birth of the Modern: World Society 1815–1830* (New York: HarperCollins, 1991).

Jones, G., *British Multinational Banking 1830–1990* (Oxford: Clarendon Press 1993).

Kerr, P. F. (ed), *Letters From China: The Canton-Boston Correspondence of Robert Bennet Forbes, 1838–1840* (Mystic, CT: Mystic Seaport Museum, Inc., 1996).

Keswick, M. (ed.), *The Thistle and the Jade: A Celebration of 150 Years of Jardine, Matheson & Co.* (London: Octopus, 1982).

Kilbourne, R., Jr, *Slave Agriculture and Financial Markets in Antebellum America: The Bank of the United States in Mississippi, 1831–1852* (London: Pickering & Chatto, 2006).

Killick, J., 'Bolton Ogden & Co.: A Case Study of Anglo-American Trade, 1790–1850', *Business History Review*, 48:4 (Winter, 1974), pp. 501–19.

Kindleberger, C. P., *Manias, Panics, and Crashes: A History of Financial Crises*, rev. edn (New York: Basic Books, 1989).

—, *A Financial History of Western Europe*, 2nd edn (New York: Oxford University Press, 1993).

King, W. T. C., *History of the London Discount Market* (London: Frank Cass, 1936).

Knox, J. J., *A History of Banking in the United States* (1903; New York: Augustus M. Kelley, 1969).

Kynaston, D., *The City of London: A World of its Own, 1815–1890* (London: Chatto & Windus, 1994).

Landes, D. S., 'The Old Bank and the New: The Financial Revolution of the Nineteenth Century', in F. Crouzet, W. H. Chaloner and W. M. Stern (eds.), *Essays in European Economic History 1789–1914* (New York: St Martin's Press, 1969), pp. 112–28.

Lanier, H. W., *A Century of Banking in New York, 1822–1922* (New York: Gillis Press, 1922).

Lanier, J. F. D., *Sketch of the Life of J. F. D. Lanier* (1871), in J. C. Brown and J. F. D. Lanier, *Two Private Banking Partnerships* (New York: Arno Press, 1975).

Lewis, C., *America's Stake in International Investments* (Washington, DC: Brookings Institution, 1938).

Mallet, B., *Thomas George, Earl of Northbrook: A Memoir* (London: Longmans, Green and Co., 1908).

Martineau, H., *Society in America*, 3 vols (London: Saunders and Otley, 1837).

Matthews, R. C. O., *A Study in Trade-Cycle History: Economic Fluctuations in Great Britain 1833–42* (Cambridge: Cambridge University Press, 1954).

McCusker, J. J., *How Much is That in Real Money?: A Historical Price Index for Use as a Deflator of Money Values in the Economy of the United States*, 2nd edn (Worcester, MA: American Antiquarian Society, 2001).

McCusker, J. J., and R. R. Menard, *The Economy of British North America, 1607–1789* (Chapel Hill, NC: University of North Carolina Press, 1991).

McCulloch, J. R., *Dictionary of Commerce and Commercial Navigation*, 5th edn (London: Longman, Brown, Green, and Longmans, 1850).

[McCulloch, J. R.], 'Enquiry into the Circumstances that have Occasioned the Present Embarrassments in the Trade between Great Britain and the United States of America', *Edinburgh Review* (American edn), 65:132 (July 1837), pp. 263–73.

McGrane, R. C., *The Correspondence of Nicholas Biddle Dealing with National Affairs, 1807–1844* (Boston, MA: Houghton Mifflin Company 1919).

—, *The Panic of 1837: Some Financial Problems of the Jacksonian Era* (Chicago: University of Chicago Press, 1924).

—, *Foreign Bondholders and American State Debts* (New York: Macmillan, 1935).

Medbery, J. K., *Men and Mysteries of Wall Street* (New York: Fields, Osgood & Co., 1870).

Miller, D. L., *City of the Century: The Epic of Chicago and the Making of America* (New York: Simon & Schuster, 1996).

Miller, J. C., *Alexander Hamilton and the Growth of the New Nation* (New York: Harper & Row, 1959).

Minsky, H. P., 'The Financial Instability Hypothesis: Capitalist Processes and the Behavior of the Economy', in C. P. Kindleberger and J. P. Laffargue (eds), *Financial Crises: Theory, History, and Policy* (Cambridge: Cambridge University Press, 1982), pp. 13–47.

Mitchell, B. R., and P. Deane, *Abstract of British Historical Statistics* (Cambridge: Cambridge University Press, 1962).

Morison, S. E., *The Maritime History of Massachusetts, 1783–1860* (Cambridge, MA: Houghton Mifflin Company, 1921).

Myers, M. G., *The New York Money Market, I: Origins and Development* (New York: Columbia University Press, 1931).

—, *A Financial History of the United States* (New York: Columbia University Press, 1970).

Neu, I., 'Edmond Jean Forstall and Louisiana Banking', *Explorations in Economic History*, 7:4 (Summer 1970), pp. 383–98.

Nicolson, H., *The Congress of Vienna: A Study in Allied Unity* (London: Constable & Co. Ltd, 1946).

Nolte, V., *Fifty Years in Both Hemispheres, or Reminiscences of the Life of a Former Merchant* (New York: Redfield, 1854).

North, D. C., 'The United States Balance of Payments, 1790–1860', in *Trends in the American Economy in the Nineteenth Century*, Studies in Income and Wealth of the National Bureau of Economic Research, vol. 24 (Princeton, NJ: Princeton University Press, 1960), pp. 573–627.

—, *The Economic Growth of the United States, 1790–1860* (Englewood Cliffs, NJ: Prentice-Hall, 1961).

Orbell, J., *Baring Brothers & Co., Limited: A History to 1939* (London: Baring Brothers & Co., Ltd, 1985).

Perkins, E. J., *Financing Anglo-American Trade: The House of Brown, 1800–1880* (Cambridge, MA: Harvard University Press, 1975).

Platt, D. C. M., 'History of Barings', 2 vols (unpublished manuscript, ING Baring Archives, London).

— (ed), *Business Imperialism 1840–1930: An Inquiry Based on British Experience in Latin America* (Oxford: Clarendon Press, 1977).

Pressnell, L. S., *Country Banking in the Industrial Revolution* (Oxford: Clarendon Press, 1956).

Ratchford, B. U., *American State Debts* (Durham, NC: Duke University Press, 1941).

Redlich, F., *The Molding of American Banking: Men and Ideas* (New York: Hafner, 1951).

Remini, R. V., *Andrew Jackson*, 3 vols (New York, Harper & Row, 1977–84).

—, *Daniel Webster: The Man and his Time* (New York: W. W. Norton, 1997).

Ricardo, D., *The High Price of Bullion: A Proof of the Depreciation of Bank Notes* (London: John Murray, 1810).

Richardson, J. D. (ed.), *A Compilation of the Messages and Papers of the Presidents, 1789–1897*, 10 vols (Washington, DC: Government Printing Office, 1896–9).

Roberts, R., and D. Kynaston (eds.), *The Bank of England: Money, Power and Influence 1694–1994* (Oxford: Clarendon Press, 1995)

Rockoff, H., 'Money, Prices, and Banks in the Jacksonian Era', in R. W. Fogel and S. L. Engerman (eds), *The Reinterpretation of American Economic History* (New York: Harper & Row, 1971), pp. 448–58.

Rose, J. H., A. P. Newton and E. A. Benians (gen. eds), *Cambridge History of the British Empire*, 8 vols in 9 (Cambridge: Cambridge University Press, 1929–59).

Rostow, W. W., 'Business Cycles, Harvests, and Politics: 1790–1850', *Journal of Economic History*, 1 (1941), pp. 206–21.

—, *The World Economy: History and Prospect* (Austin, TX: University of Texas Press, 1978).

Rousseau, P. L., 'Jacksonian Monetary Policy, Specie Flows, and Panic of 1837', *Journal of Economic History*, 62:2 (2002), pp. 457–88.

Rousseau, P. L., and R. Sylla, 'Emerging Financial Markets and Early U.S. Growth' in *Explorations in Economic History*, 42:1 (2005), pp. 1–26.

Rubinstein, W. D., *Men of Property: The Very Wealthy in Britain since the Industrial Revolution* (London: Croom Helm, 1981).

Sayers, R. S., *Modern Banking*, 7th edn (Oxford: Clarendon Press, 1967).

Scammell, W. M., *The London Discount Market* (New York: St Martin's Press, 1968).

Scheiber, H. N., *Ohio Canal Era* (Athens, OH: Ohio University Press, 1969).

Schlesinger, A. M., Jr, *The Age of Jackson* (Boston, MA: Little Brown, 1945).

Schumpeter, J. A., *Business Cycles, I* (New York: McGraw-Hill, 1939).

Schweikart, L., *Banking in the American South from the Age of Jackson to the Reconstruction* (Baton Rouge, LA: Louisiana State University Press, 1987).

—, (ed), *Banking and Finance to 1913* (New York: Facts on File, 1990).

Sheppard, F., *London: A History* (Oxford: Oxford University Press, 1998).

Silberling, N. J., 'British Prices and Business Cycles 1779–1850', *The Review of Economic Statistics*, 5, Supplement 2 (October 1923), pp. 223–47.

Smart, W., *Economic Annals of the Nineteenth Century, 1801–1830*, 2 vols (London: Macmillan & Co., 1917).

Smith, A. *An Enquiry in the Nature and Causes of the Wealth of Nations* (1776), ed. E. Cannan (London: Methuen & Co., 1904).

Smith, W. B., *Economic Aspects of the Second Bank of the United States* (Cambridge, MA: Harvard University Press, 1953).

Smith, W. B., and A. H. Cole, *Fluctuations in American Business, 1790–1860* (Cambridge, MA: Harvard University Press, 1935).

Strouse, J., *Morgan: American Financier* (New York: Random House, 1999).

Studenski, P., and H. E. Kross, *Financial History of the United States*, 2nd edn (New York: McGraw-Hill, 1963).

Sturgis, J. (ed.), *From the Books and Papers of Russell Sturgis* (Oxford: privately printed, n.d.).

Sumner, W. G., *A History of American Currency* (New York: H. Holt and Company, 1876).

—, *A History of Banking in the United States* (New York: n.p., 1896).

Taylor, G. R., *The Transportation Revolution, 1815–1860* (New York: Rinehart, 1951).

Temin, P., 'The Causes of Cotton-Price Fluctuations in the 1830s', *Review of Economics and Statistics*, 49 (November 1967), pp. 463–70.

—, *The Jacksonian Economy* (New York: W. W. Norton, 1969).

Thornton, H., *An Inquiry Into the Nature and Effects of the Paper Credit of Great Britain* (London: J. Hatchard, 1802).

Thorp, W. L., *Business Annals* (New York: National Bureau of Economic Research, 1926).

Timberlake, R. H., *The Origins of Central Banking in the United States* (Cambridge, MA: Harvard University Press, 1978).

Tooke, T., and W. Newmarch, *A History of Prices and the State of the Currency*, 6 vols in 4 (1838; London: P. S. King & Son, 1928).

Trends in the American Economy in the Nineteenth Century, Studies in Income and Wealth of the National Bureau of Economic Research, vol. 24 (Princeton, NJ: Princeton University Press, 1960).

Trescott, P. B., *Financing American Enterprise: The Story of Commerical Banking* (New York: Harper & Row, 1963).

Trotter, A., *Observations on the Financial Position and Credit of Such of the States of the North American Union as have Contracted Public Debts* (1839; New York: A. M. Kelley, 1968).

United States Bureau of the Census, *The Statistical History of the United States from Colonial Times to the Present* (New York: Basic Books, 1976).

Wallis, J. J., 'What Caused the 1839 Depression?', *NBER Working Papers*, HO133 (April 2001).

—, 'The Depression of 1839–1843: States, Debts, and Banks', Working Paper, University of Maryland and NBER (n.d.).

Werner, W., and S. T. Smith, *Wall Street* (New York: Columbia University Press, 1991).

Wilkins, M., *The History of Foreign Investment in the United States to 1914* (Cambridge, MA: Harvard University Press, 1989).

Wright, R. E., *The Wealth of Nations Rediscovered: Integration and Expansion in American Financial Markets, 1780–1850* (Cambridge: Cambridge University Press, 2002).

Ziegler, P., *The Sixth Great Power* (New York: Knopf, 1988).

INDEX

For Product Safety Concerns and Information please contact our EU
representative GPSR@taylorandfrancis.com
Taylor & Francis Verlag GmbH, Kaufingerstraße 24, 80331 München, Germany

www.ingramcontent.com/pod-product-compliance
Ingram Content Group UK Ltd.
Pitfield, Milton Keynes, MK11 3LW, UK
UKHW021633240425
457818UK00018BA/382